1993

"BEYOND REASONABLE DOUBT"
AND
"PROBABLE CAUSE"

"BEYOND REASONABLE DOUBT"

AND

"PROBABLE CAUSE"

*Historical Perspectives on the
Anglo-American Law of Evidence*

BARBARA J. SHAPIRO

UNIVERSITY OF CALIFORNIA PRESS
BERKELEY   LOS ANGELES   OXFORD

University of California Press
Berkeley and Los Angeles, California

University of California Press, Ltd.
Oxford, England

Library of Congress Cataloging-in-
Publication Data

Shapiro, Barbara J.
  "Beyond reasonable doubt" and
"probable cause" : historical
perspectives on the Anglo-American law
of evidence / Barbara J. Shapiro.
        p.   cm.
  Includes bibliographical references
and index.
  ISBN 0-520-07286-3
  1. Evidence, Criminal—Great
Britain—History.   2. Evidence,
Criminal—United States—History.   I.
Title.
KD8371.S5   1991
345.41'06—dc20
[344.1056]   91-16753
                                        CIP

Printed in the United States of America
9 8 7 6 5 4 3 2 1

Chapter 1 is based on " 'To a Moral
Certainty': Theories of Knowledge and
Anglo-American Juries, 1600–1850," which
appeared in 38 *Hastings Law Journal*
(© 1986 Hastings College of the Law).

To Barbara Wolfinger and Reba Soffer

Contents

Acknowledgments

My interest in the history of law has been focused on the connections between law and other aspects of English intellectual life. My first efforts appeared as "Law and Science in Seventeenth-Century England" (*Stanford Law Review* [1969]) and were elaborated and extended in *Probability and Certainty in Seventeenth-Century England: A Study of the Relationships between Natural Science, Religion, History, Law and Literature* (Princeton, 1983). Some of the legal themes of that book were pursued further in "'To a Moral Certainty': Theories of Knowledge and Anglo-American Juries, 1600–1850" (*Hastings Law Journal* [1986]), which forms the basis of Chapter 1.

Chapter 2 on grand juries was aided by a research fellowship from the Huntington Library in San Marino. The research and writing of Chapters 3 and 4, which deal with the concept of probable cause and its migration through several pretrial procedures, the connections between Romano-canon and Anglo-American legal traditions, and the concept of circumstantial evidence, were assisted by generous grants from the Guggenheim Foundation, the University of California, Berkeley, Humanities Fellowship program, the University of California, Berkeley, Research Committee, and by sabbatical support from the University of California, Berkeley. A month's residence at the Rockefeller Foundation's Bellagio Conference Center provided idyllic writing conditions. I am grateful to all these institutions.

I would also like to thank the librarians of the Huntington Library, the Williams Andrews Clark Memorial Library, the Yale Law

Library, and Boalt Hall Law Library. The *Hastings Law Journal* has generously granted permission to use some previously published materials.

Martin Trow, Sheldon Rothblatt, and Janet Ruyle of the Center for Studies in Higher Education have been generous in providing library and word-processing assistance. Such assistance has also been provided by the Research Committee of the University of California, Berkeley, and by Kirsten Anderson, Rebecca Kidd, and Claudia Myers Pearce of the Department of Rhetoric. Norma Landau read the manuscript with great care and made many helpful suggestions.

My greatest debt is to Martin Shapiro who has read, edited, commented on, and suffered with the manuscript in all its forms. This book would never have been completed without his assistance and support.

Preface

Given the long and rich tradition of legal and historical scholarship, there has been surprisingly little work devoted to the history of the Anglo-American law of evidence. Although much recent scholarship in English legal history has focused on various aspects of the criminal justice system, relatively little attention has centered on the evidentiary aspects of that system. My study builds on the more general work of others, such as John Beattie, John Langbein, and Thomas Green, but seeks to look specifically at evidentiary elements in several phases of the criminal justice system.[1] My attention will be focused on the evidentiary doctrines which over time have been associated with arrest, pretrial examination, and grand jury indictment, as well as with the evidentiary doctrine associated with the trial jury.

The history of the Anglo-American law of evidence has for the most part centered on the jury largely because "evidence" as taught in law schools refers almost exclusively to the trial jury and because the foremost scholars of the history of the law of evidence were themselves leading law teachers of and treatise writers on evidence, for example, James Thayer and John Wigmore.[2] And precisely because law teaching and writing have so closely linked evidence to the jury, they have concentrated very heavily on admissibility. In this sense the jury is a black box. We cannot know what goes on inside it, and, indeed, it is often viewed as somewhat unseemly to inquire. Moreover, at least in criminal cases, what comes out of it is a general verdict of guilt or innocence, and it is altogether forbidden to inquire into the pieces and processes that went into that verdict. Lawyers thus concentrate on what can and cannot go into the box, for that is the sole realm in which the bench and bar legitimately may intervene in its workings. So the law of evidence becomes, willy-nilly, largely the law of admissibility. This book is not so much about what evidence may reach a jury, as it is about what juries and other criminal law deciders are supposed to do with evidence and how much of what kind of evidence is to trigger a decision against the accused.

What we can know about the history of this aspect of the law of evidence is very limited because the black box of the jury, and of the magistrate for that matter, is so impenetrable. Almost no historical or even contemporary record exists of what actually goes on in the minds of the actors in the criminal justice process. We must confine ourselves pretty much to the doctrinal instructions given to the actors by "outside" writers about evidence and by judges in the course of their opinions and charges to juries. Even judges officially say relatively little about this aspect of the law of evidence. What they do say typically reduces itself to such talismanic formulas as "beyond reasonable doubt" and "probable cause." This book is about the intellectual baggage that lies behind these talismans. It is about what educated persons, lay and professional, said to one another regarding the quantity and quality of evidence that was sufficient to justify imposing state processes and sanctions on accused persons. Thus it is about the written explanations and justifications that citizens gave to one another about the legal system under which they lived. Such explanations are not the be-all and end-all of legal systems or political regimes, but they are not an insignificant part of them. Of course it would be better if we could also know a great deal more about what magistrates, judges, and juries actually did. What they said they did and ought to do was an important aspect of how the English and American people made and came to terms with their law—even apart from the possible light that what was said may shed on what was done. And there is some reason to believe that the saying did have some impact on the doing.

So this book proceeds largely at the level of doctrine, not in the narrow sense of the legally authoritative, but in the broader sense of what was written about how the law was and should be. My primary focus is on early modern England, that is, from about 1500 to 1800, but I will frequently look backward into the medieval period and forward into nineteenth- and twentieth-century Britain and America. My study thus begins after the jury trial has been established, and the jury and grand juries are ceasing to be self-informing and have become fact evaluators. For most purposes I treat the Anglo-American legal system as a single one, though in certain areas the Americans and the English moved in somewhat different directions. I concentrate on felonies and will only rarely concern myself with misdemeanors or those acts which came under the jurisdiction of the ecclesiastical courts. The focus will be simultaneously procedural and doctrinal.

Three themes are explored. The first is the way in which religious and philosophical notions concerning the nature of truth and the appropriate methods of attaining it affect legal concepts of evidence and proof. I focus particularly on how changing conceptions of probability and certainty helped to shape legal formulations. I will not be arguing that philosophical doctrines determined legal goals, but rather that the formulations of some legal doctrine were shaped by developments in religion and epistemology. I will examine the way British empirical philosophy shaped the beyond reasonable doubt doctrine and the treatise tradition in the field of evidence. One theme, then, is the interaction between legal conceptualization and other intellectual traditions.

Another theme is the migration of evidentiary concepts from one institution or procedure to another within the Anglo-American legal system. We will observe how the concept of "probable cause" migrated from arrest, to issues of search and seizure, to the preliminary examination, and eventually to the American grand jury. In this context I will note the centuries-long difficulties of how to develop evidentiary concepts that, on the one hand, would not be so stringent as to virtually duplicate a trial and, on the other, would not be so vague as to permit citizens to become enmeshed in the criminal process without some screening standard. I also attempt to demonstrate that, unlike the doctrinal formulation for the trial jury, these formulations have constantly shifted and have never settled into legal pronouncements that have proved satisfying both to those interested in protecting the rights of individuals against the institutions of the state and to those eager to halt crime. The lack of a logical resting place between a full-scale trial before the trial and a purely discretionary preliminary decision about going forward is a perennial problem in all those processes that precede the trial.

A third theme is the relation of English law to the Romano-canon tradition. Although discussion of borrowing from the Romano-canon tradition has certainly not been absent from the study of English legal history, more often than not it has taken the form of attempting to answer the question of whether or not there was an attempt to "receive" the civil law. My concern is not with the general "reception" of the civil law and its institutions and procedures, but rather with whether Romano-canon ideas found their way into the English repertoire of evidentiary concepts. We will see that this influence can be traced in several stages of pretrial procedures and in the development of concepts of suspicion, presumption and circumstantial evidence. It will therefore be necessary at times to mention briefly the development of the Romano-canon system of investigation, trial, and doctrines of proof.

Basically, then, this is a study of the development and transmission, or migration, of a group of legal concepts such as suspicion, common fame, probable cause, *prima facie* case, presumption, circumstantial evidence, satisfied conscience, and beyond reasonable doubt. Some of these terms have become attached to a single procedure or institution, while others have been more migratory, so some of the chapters focus primarily on a single legal institution, while others deal with more than one institution or procedure. Inevitably, too, there is some overlapping and backing and filling in the chapters because of the way the law actually developed. For instance, although Chapter 2 focuses on the grand jury and Chapter 3 focuses on the preliminary hearing, it is necessary to deal with certain aspects of the preliminary hearing in Chapter 2 because the American grand jury "appropriated" the evidentiary standard of the preliminary hearing. Thus, too, Chapter 4, which centers on concepts of presumption and circumstantial evidence borrowed in large part from the Romano-canon tradition, returns to the theme of beyond reasonable doubt developed in Chapter 1.

Chapter 1 focuses on the institution of the trial jury and the evolution of the doctrine of proof "beyond reasonable doubt." Chapters 2 and 3 center on pretrial institutions and procedures, which required less certainty than the trial jury. Chapter 2 is about the grand jury and the evidentiary standard for indictment and its eventual competitor, the preliminary hearing. Chapter 3 is more disparate. It deals with the evidentiary elements in arrest, search and seizure, and pretrial examination. Emphasis is on the migration of concepts, particularly that of "probable cause," from procedure to procedure within the Anglo-American system of criminal justice and on the possible borrowing of concepts from the Romano-canon tradition. The chapter examines the concepts of suspicion, the *indicia*, and violent and probable presumption. We also explore the possibility that witchcraft materials indicate how some of the borrowing from civilian sources took place.

Chapter 4 returns to the jury trial in order to elaborate on two of our themes, the borrowing from the Romano-canon repertoire of evidentiary concepts, and the role played by philosophical writing, particularly those concerned with epistemology and logic. We examine issues relating to witnesses, the hearsay rule, and to the development of Anglo-American concepts of circumstantial evidence and presumption.

A brief concluding chapter summarizes the findings, which may be seen as being at the boundary between intellectual and institutional history and as making some contribution to a fuller description of Anglo-American legal culture.

Chapter One

The Trial Jury and the Evolution of the Doctrine of "Beyond Reasonable Doubt"

This chapter traces the development of the "beyond reasonable doubt" standard that has characterized the Anglo-American criminal justice system for more than two hundred years. That system has always depended heavily upon the jury so that any study of reasonable doubt necessarily must be linked to an examination of the jury. From the surviving records, it does not appear that judges initially concerned themselves much with the question of the jury's evidentiary duties. Early jurors reached decisions on the basis of a mixture of their own personal knowledge of events and the testimony of others. By the sixteenth century most of the personal knowledge had dropped away. Once jurors were clearly perceived to be reaching decisions on the basis of evidence presented in court, judicial charges to juries came to emphasize the duty of jurors to reach some sort of firm assurance of guilt based on the evidence. The formulations in these charges are of central concern to us here.

Sixteenth-, seventeenth-, and eighteenth-century judges faced a difficult task in telling juries what standards they should employ in reaching their decisions. The earlier common law offered no particular guidance. For reasons that we shall examine later, civil and ecclesiastical sources did not initially prove very useful. As a result, the judges had little choice but to borrow from the episte-mology that could be drawn from religious doctrine and philoso-phy. If judges felt they now had to instruct jurors on how to know about matters of fact and on how much to know, it was natural for them to turn to the ideas of their contemporaries who were prin-cipally concerned about knowing and who were attempting to con-vey their ideas about knowing to the lay population from which juries were drawn. This tendency was reenforced by the relative isolation of the judges from their normal source of professional sustenance, the bar, when dealing with jury matters. In normal circumstances, lawyers appeared for neither side in ordinary crim-inal cases.

In the course of the seventeenth century, English religious in-tellectuals engaged in many controversies that required them to develop intellectually and religiously satisfying grounds for deci-sion making. Their efforts were both shaped and complemented by the enormous upsurge in epistemological thinking that was a part of what is commonly called the "scientific revolution." Thus the judges confronted twin sources of epistemological guidance. One was the English religious tradition, particularly the casuis-tical tradition, which sought a rational method of decision making in everyday life. The other was the scientific movement of Ba-con, Boyle, and especially Locke and the empirical philosophers, who sought to establish scientific truth from the evidence they gathered. This chapter is about how judges created the beyond reasonable doubt standard for the jury, and so it is also about the religious and philosophical thinking from which that standard was derived.

There are two kinds of rules of evidence in common-law juris-dictions. The first, which deals with what kinds of evidence may get to the jury when and in what form, can be understood without much reference to nonjury developments. The second deals with the evaluation by the jury of the evidence, and how it is to decide whether there is sufficient probative evidence to justify a verdict. Such rules are drawn from the culture's general understanding of how we "know" things to be true. This chapter deals with this sec-ond variety and its relation to epistemological developments in seventeenth-century England.

Early Developments

The seventeenth-century intellectual crisis, however, was not the first to influence this body of rules. A much deeper crisis occurred during the twelfth century, when "irrational proofs," such as trial by ordeal, could no longer be seen as consistent with justice or with how truth determinations ought to be made. "Irrational proofs" were replaced on the Continent by the Romano-canon inquisition process, and in England by the jury trial.

The "rational" system of proof of the Romano-canon inquisition process provided a system of inquiry operated by professional judges. It was designed to obtain "full proof," defined by clearly established evidentiary standards which rigidly specified the quality and quantity of proof. A specified number of witnesses were required to prove facts, and once "full proof" had been achieved conviction was automatic. The judge in most criminal cases was essentially an accountant who totaled the proof fractions. Criminal cases, for example, required two good witnesses or confession. Because confession was of a particularly high evidentiary value, torture was used to assist in producing it. Complex rules determined whether there was sufficient evidence to justify judicial torture. Because the philosophical components in the Romano-canon system had been provided by late medieval scholastic philosophers, and because the system had become well entrenched on the Continent during that period, it seems to have been relatively uninfluenced by the epistemological issues that became acute in the early modern period—issues that would focus on the sources, nature, and limitations of human knowledge.

In England irrational proofs were replaced by the jury trial, which for several centuries required little in the way of rules of evidence or doctrinal standards for conviction. Despite a good deal of research, we still do not know a great deal about early trial juries. The abolition of the ordeal resulted in a dual system of presentment and trial juries. The accusing, or presentment, jury had developed before the abolition of ordeals in 1215. Originally it had sent those it considered appropriately accused to be tried by ordeal.[1] The verdicts of these early presenting, or "medial," juries were more statements about a defendant's character than about his factual guilt or innocence. The verdicts of the new convicting juries, which Roger Groot dates from c. 1219 to 1221, were "assertive" rather than evidentiary.[2] Although originally there was some overlap in the membership of the two juries, the separation of the presentment and the trial jury was well advanced by c. 1328.[3] Jurors, men of the neighborhood, were assumed to know the facts and to incorporate their own knowledge in their verdict. Juries thus arrived at findings of fact guided by common sense and common knowledge.

Recent research is modifying the traditional view that the medieval jury was entirely self-informing. It now appears that some jurors lived too far from the scene of the crime to have had firsthand knowledge of events. At least in private actions witnesses were examined occasionally. Verdicts were probably made on the basis of what was deemed to be personal knowledge of the facts, but that knowledge might be based on firsthand knowledge or derived from persons the jury believed. In the thirteenth and fourteenth centuries, trial jurors probably were both gatherers and weighers of evidence. Witnesses do not seem to have appeared as a regular part of criminal prosecutions.[4]

Sir John Fortescue's mid-fifteenth-century *De Laudibus Legum Anglie* clearly indicated that witnesses were already commonly employed in civil, if not criminal, cases.[5] J. B. Post has concluded that witnesses had probably become an acceptable feature of criminal trials by the end of the fourteenth century, but were not, as Fortescue makes clear, either a formal or essential part of the trial. We do not know, however, whether witnesses were speaking to the good repute of the accused or were providing evidence of events.[6]

Clearly by the early fifteenth century juries were no longer truly self-informing but were listening to and assessing evidence introduced by private accusers and government officials. If in many cases at least some members of the jury were drawn from the hundred, even many of these were no longer from the village where the offense occurred. Their selection was based as much on status and administrative experience as on geography. Nevertheless, it is still not clear whether the jury heard witnesses testify about the facts or only the reputation of defendants.[7]

Jurors did not have enough knowledge to arrive at verdicts without evidence. They gained information from a number of sources, including the defendant's replies to the charges and the judge's questioning. They evidently considered the plausibility of the denial and the demeanor of the accused. They also might consider statements of the victim, the victim's kin, and witnesses for the Crown, as well as the testimony of officials, such as the justice of the peace, the coroner, or the constable. Edward Powell has argued that Sir Thomas Smith's mid-sixteenth-century description of the criminal trial applies to the previous century as well and concludes that by 1400, jurors had already become passive viewers of fact.[8] John Langbein would place this movement toward passivity later, believing that it was a result of the 1554–1555 Marian bail and committal statutes, which he argues led to a substantial role for the justices of the peace in presenting trial evidence.[9]

By the sixteenth century, jurors were certainly hearing witnesses, although in the early part of the century they were still talking to them outside court. As early as 1523, however, Sir Thomas More was arguing that no one should give evidence to jurors except at bar.[10] Assize records for the second half of the sixteenth century clearly show witnesses at trial. Much of the evidence was produced by the justice of the peace or by witnesses who had been bound over by the justice to appear at trial. Although residential requirements were still important, trial jurors did not usually live in the immediate area where the offense occurred.[11]

Civil juries appear to have undergone similar changes. Indeed, it is likely that the introduction of witnesses occurred first in civil cases. Even in the thirteenth century, civil jurors were not expected to be eyewitnesses and seem to have informally consulted witnesses and other types of evidence. In the next century both jurors and witnesses were appearing in court. Gradually litigants in civil cases were permitted to call witnesses, and the distinction between witnesses and jurors became clear. Fortescue distinguishes witnesses from jurors in the late fifteenth century. Elizabethan legislation provided for the compulsory attendance of witnesses, and cross-examination by counsel is evidenced by Sir Thomas Smith's *De Republica Anglorum*. The early seventeenth-century civil juries were dependent on testimony heard and ex-

amined in court, and juries no longer investigated the facts of a
case out of court, though until the eighteenth century they were
permitted to consider personal knowledge.[12]

As society became more complex and mobility increased, both
civil and criminal juries became less familiar with the facts and
increasingly came to rely on the testimony of witnesses and documents that now had to be evaluated for truthfulness and accuracy.
Jurors became third parties who now had to evaluate and analyze
facts and events they had not personally witnessed or previously
known in order to reach conclusions and make decisions. A turning
point occurred in 1563, when legislation compelled the attendance
of witnesses and made perjury a crime. As witnesses became more
important, juries increasingly required standards for the evaluation
of testimony. Notions of credibility, borrowed in part from the civil
and the canon law, began to appear, although for a time there was
confusion between the concepts of legal and credible witnesses—
the former being legally competent to testify, the latter those
whose testimony is believable. Discussion of witness credibility
and the evaluation process thus enters the legal literature and the
cases as the character of the jury trial was modified. An early
seventeenth-century essay attributed to Sir Francis Bacon made it
clear that English law left "both supply of testimony and the discerning and credit of testimony wholly to the juries' conscience
and understanding, yea to their private knowledge."[13] The work of
Sir Matthew Hale indicates that by the late seventeenth century
the distinction between legal and credible witnesses was very
clear.[14]

The response to this new legal environment was slow, but when
the law of evidence emerged in the eighteenth century, it was
shaped not only by legal tradition but also by the intellectual environment. We must therefore turn to the intellectual currents that
would bear on how juries might reach rational conclusions based
on evaluations of fact.

By the sixteenth century humanist critiques had made the defects of scholasticism commonplace, though they did little to develop a substitute philosophy or theory of knowledge. The revival
of skepticism was philosophically more serious because it might
entail a repudiation not only of scholasticism but also of religious
doctrine, the validity of sense data, reports of events, and, indeed,

any claims to knowledge.[15] Philosophers, notably Descartes and Bacon, attempted to overcome the skeptical critique and the defects of scholasticism by refounding knowledge on a certain, but nonscholastic, basis. Cartesianism denied that certain knowledge might be provided by the senses and devalued disciplines dependent on experiment or testimony. It therefore had little impact on law. Bacon's new philosophy emphasized appropriately filtered and manipulated sense data and also sought absolutely certain axioms and universally valid generalizations.[16]

The dominant seventeenth-century English philosophic and scientific community, however, was neither Baconian nor Cartesian, for it did not claim that empirically derived facts would yield absolutely certain knowledge. It attempted to verify natural phenomena by experiment, direct observation, and testimony, and believed that these techniques, depending on the quality and the quantity of the evidence derived, might yield conclusions which were sufficiently true to serve as the basis for conduct of human affairs.

The attempt to build an intermediate level of knowledge, short of absolute certainty but above the level of mere opinion, was made by an overlapping group of theologians and naturalists. For the Protestant theologians, who rejected Roman Catholic assertions of infallibility, the central question was whether religious truths, such as the existence of God, miracles, the biblical narratives, and various doctrines and practices of the church, could survive skeptical attack, once they were stripped of claims to absolute truth and reduced to claims based on evidence. For the naturalists, the central problem was that of making truthful statements about natural phenomena which could be observed but could not be reduced to the kinds of logical, mathematical demonstrations that traditionally had been thought to yield unquestionable truths. Both groups concluded that reasonable men, employing their senses and rational faculties, could derive truths that they would have no reason to doubt.[17]

Although terminology varied, theologians and naturalists distinguished between "knowledge," or "science," on the one hand and "probability" on the other. There were three subcategories of knowledge, each possessing a different kind of certainty: physical, derived from immediate sense data; mathematical, established by logical demonstration such as the proofs in geometry; and moral, based on testimony and secondhand reports of sense data. This moral certainty was most relevant to law, history, and many kinds of natural science. Although moral certainties did not depend on evidence that compelled assent, they might be so clear that everyone "whose judgment is free from prejudice will consent to them. And though there be no natural necessity, that things be so, and they cannot possibly be otherwise . . . yet may they be so certain as not to admit of any *reasonable doubt* concerning them."[18] Moral certainty could thus "be styled" indubitable.[19] The "reasonable man" will not require demonstration or proofs that "exclude all Dubiosity, and compel assent," but will accept moral and physical proofs that are the best that may be gained. One could thus gain a "competent certitude where demonstration is impossible."[20]

"Probability" from the ancient world to the late seventeenth century traditionally had lumped together the noncertain, the seemingly true, and the merely likely. When evidence was unclear or unreasonable doubt existed, the result was probability or mere opinion, not knowledge. A late seventeenth-century development, however, suggested that probability consisted of a graduated scale that extended from the unlikely through the probable to a still higher category called "rational belief" or "moral certainty." This category, sometimes treated as "knowledge" and sometimes as the highest category of probability, would have a great impact on English law.[21]

We must take particular note of John Locke, both because his systematization of this approach in *An Essay Concerning Human Understanding* (1690) became so influential and because the first treatise writers on legal evidence attempted to build on Lockean foundations. What others called "moral certainty" was for Locke a species of probability, the very highest level of which commanded universal assent. It rose "so near to a certainty" that it governs "our thinking as absolutely as the most evident demonstration." Lower levels of probability produced "confidence," "confident belief," or "mere opinion." The level of assent was determined by the weight of the evidence.[22] For Locke, the

highest *degree of probability*, is, when the general consent of all men, in all ages, . . . concurs with a man's constant and never-failing experience in like cases, to confirm the truth of any particular matter of fact attested by fair witnesses: . . . These *probabilities* rise so near to *certainty*, that they govern our thoughts as absolutely . . . as the most evident demonstration. . . . We make little or no difference between them and certain knowledge. . . . The *next degree of probability* is, when I find by my own experience, and the agreement of all others that mention it, a thing to be for the most part so, and that the particular instance of it is attested by many and undoubted witnesses *v.g.* history giving us such an account of men in all ages, and my own experience, as far as I had an opportunity to observe confirming it. . . . And in this case our assent has a sufficient foundation to raise itself to a degree which we may call *confidence.*[23]

A still lower category existed "when any particular matter of fact is vouched by the concurrent testimony of unsuspected witnesses, there our assent is also *unavoidable.* . . . This though in the nature of things there be nothing for or against it, yet being related by historians of credit, and contradicted by no one writer, a man cannot avoid believing it, and can as little doubt of it as he does of the being and actions of his own acquaintance, where he himself is a witness."[24]

In all three of these categories

the matter goes easy enough. Probability upon such grounds carries so much evidence with it that it naturally determines the judgment, and leaves us as little liberty to believe or disbelieve, as a demonstration does. . . . The difficulty is, when testimonies contradict common experience, and the reports of history and witnesses clash with the ordinary course of nature, or with one another; there it is, where diligence, attention, and exactness are required, to form a right judgment, and to proportion the assent to the different evidence and probability of the thing; which rises and falls, according as those two foundations of credibility, viz. *common observation in like cases*, and *particular testimonies in that particular instance*, favour or contradict it. These, [however, were] liable to so great variety of contrary observations, circumstances, reports, different qualifications, tempers . . . of the reporters, that it is impossible to reduce to precise rules the various degrees wherein men give their assent. This only may be said in general, that as the arguments and proofs *pro* and *con*, upon due examination, nicely weighing every particular circumstance, shall to any one appear, upon the whole matter, in a greater or lesser degree to preponderate on either side; so they are fitted to produce in the mind such different entertainments, as we call *belief, conjecture, guess, doubt, wavering, distrust, disbelief, etc.*[25]

For the new scientists and philosophers, natural phenomena and processes were to be verified by experiment, observation, and the testimony of observers. Depending on the quality and quantity of the evidence produced by these methods, one might reach findings of fact and sometimes even conclusions that no reasonable person could doubt.[26] Historians, too, were attracted to this approach. Discussions of both historical events and Scripture frequently centered on the extent to which one might believe the testimony of witnesses reporting on past occurrences. References to eye- and earwitnesses, hearsay, and credible witnesses were common. This language, of course, suggests the courtroom. Indeed, naturalists, theologians, and historians often employed courtroom imagery. Historians were thus frequently admonished to act as unbiased and impartial judges rather than as partisan advocates.[27]

Seth Ward, a seventeenth-century scientist and theologian who became Bishop of Salisbury, in comparing sacred and secular history, for example, emphasized that where improbable events were related, it was particularly important to evaluate critically the relators and the manner of their relations. It was necessary to determine whether the event in question was knowable, whether the parties had sufficient means to obtain such knowledge, whether the relators were eye- or earwitnesses, and whether the occurrences "were publically acted and known." Historians might be believed if the relators had the opportunity to observe the events in question and no one had contradicted their accounts. Although fabrications were possible, there was little reason, given the lack of conflicting accounts, to doubt the events reported in secular history or the "History of Holy Scripture." Ward, in what became commonplace among historians and Anglican ecclesiastics in the late seventeenth century, thus argued that no impartial person could reasonably doubt the truthfulness of biblically reported events and matters of fact.[28] Virtually the same line of argument based on the absence of "reasonable doubt," rather than absolute certainty, was used by Edward Stillingfleet, another Anglican divine who wrote widely on theological and epistemological issues, to establish the moral certainty of scriptural history.[29]

By the early eighteenth century these views were commonplace among historians and required little defense or comment. Thus, Joseph Addison noted that secular historians were guided by the common rules of historical faith, that is, they examined the nature of the evidence which was to be met within common fame, tradition, and the writings of persons who related them, together with the number, concurrence, veracity and private characters of those persons; and being convinced, upon all accounts that they had the same reason to believe the history of our Savior as that of any other person to which they were not actually eyewitnesses, they were bound by all the rules of historical faith, and right reason, to give credit to this history.[30]

By 1690, when Locke's *Essay Concerning Human Understanding* appeared, ideas of witness credibility had become familiar to lawyers, naturalists, theologians, and historians. Locke's criteria for evaluating testimony—the number of witnesses, their integrity, their skill at presenting evidence and its agreement with the circumstances, and last, the presence or absence of contrary testimony—had obvious relevance to the law.[31] A considerable portion of the English intellectual community adopted this empirical approach to knowledge—which neither denied the possibility of gathering reliable and persuasive evidence nor made claims to absolute certitude. This approach also came to serve the needs of the English legal system.

As we have seen, initially there had been no need to construct a rationale for the truth-finding capacities of juries. As the role of witnesses increased, the problem of the credibility of secondhand reports of facts which had become central to theologians, naturalists, and historians became central to legal theorists who borrowed conceptual elements from the new empirical philosophy.

Concern for the credibility of witnesses in criminal trials can be traced from at least the early sixteenth century, although the distinction between legal and credible witnesses does not appear to be clear at that time. The jury's "conscience" was to evaluate the evidence. By the early seventeenth century, Francis Bacon, who we should recall was England's lord chancellor and a noted legal reformer as well as its preeminent natural philosopher, made clear that "the supply of testimony and the discerning and credit of testimony" were left wholly to the "juries consciences and understandings." Bacon's words were incorporated into a Royal Proclamation issued in October 1607.[32]

Sir Matthew Hale, the most distinguished judge of the mid- to late seventeenth century, emphasized the superiority of the jury trial as "the best method of searching and sifting out the truth," precisely because juries might "weigh the credibility of Witnesses, and the Force and Efficacy of their Testimonies."[33] Hale, however, not only emphasizes credibility but also makes the distinction between legal and credible witnesses very clear. Hale indicates if the jury has

just cause to disbelieve what a witness swears, they are not bound to give their verdict according to the evidence, or testimony of that witness. And they may sometimes give credit to one witness, though opposed by more than one. And indeed it is one of the excellencies of . . . [the jury trial] above the trial by witnesses, although the jury ought to give a great regard to witnesses and their testimony, yet they are not always bound by it; but may either upon reasonable circumstances, inducing a blemish upon their credibility, though otherwise in themselves in strictness of law they are to be heard, pronounce a verdict contrary to such testimonies; the truth whereof they have just cause to suspect, and may, and do often, pronounce their verdict upon one single testimony which the Civil Law admits not of.[34]

Hale's *Primitive Origination of Mankind* (1677) discussed evidence for matters of fact contained in Scripture in much the same way as in legal trials. It was necessary to weigh

the veracity of him that reports and relates. And hence it is, that which is reported by many Eye witnesses hath greater motives of credibility than that which is reported by light and inconsiderable witnesses; that which is reported by a person disinterested, than that which is reported by persons whose interest is to have the thing true or believed to be true . . . and finally, that which they receive by hear-say from those that report upon their own view.[35]

Evidence might be of such "high credibility" that "no reasonable man can without any just reason deny it." Belief, for Hale, rested on the direct experience of the senses and "upon the relation of another that we have no reasonable cause to suspect." "Evidence of Fact and Things remote from our Sense," though not infallible, yet might be of such "high credibility, and such as no reasonable Man can without any just reason deny his assent unto them."[36] While Hale did not use the words "moral certainty" or "beyond reasonable doubt," his terminology is consistent with those concepts.

The "Satisfied Conscience" Test
and Casuistry

Although it has been suggested that the medieval practice of granting equal weight to all evidence given under oath continued into
the eighteenth century,[37] the State Trials of the late seventeenth
century and beyond are larded with judicial insistence that juries
weigh the credibility of witnesses.[38] Issues of credibility, which became increasingly central to criminal trials, also helped to shape
the standard for the jury verdict. The "satisfied conscience" standard became the first vessel into which were poured the new criteria for evaluating facts and testimony. Satisfied conscience gradually became synonymous with rational belief, that is, belief
beyond reasonable doubt. The newer standards borrowed heavily
from religious and philosophical foundations, particularly from notions of moral certainty, or the highest degree of probability. This
is not to say that juries, particularly in capital cases, had not always
required convincing proof, but rather that legal formulations concerning that conviction were increasingly stated in terms that were
consistent with reigning epistemological formulations.[39]

The recorded cases after c. 1668 exhibit sufficient repetition to
suggest contemporary usage.[40] A number of phrases appear repeatedly in judicial charges. The first is "if you believe," the second, "if you are satisfied or not satisfied with the evidence." A third
was "satisfied conscience."[41] Verdicts were to be based on "belief,"
or "satisfied conscience," and were to be arrived at after evaluation
of the evidence. Edward Waterhouse's *Fortescue Illustratus* (1663)
employs similar language. He indicated that the jury's verdict was,
"as they think in their conscience the truth of the fact is," after
hearing the evidence. They were thus to "determine what their
conscience judge clearly proved concerning the Fact."[42]

In Bushel's case (1670), Judge Vaughan insisted testimony and
verdict were "very different things." A witness swears what he has
seen or heard, while a juror swears "to what he can infer and conclude from the testimony . . . by the act and force of his understanding."[43] By 1670, juries were expected to be careful and thorough fact evaluators.

The Popish Plot trials, many of which gained wide circulation in
pamphlet form, provide a substantial number of well-reported

cases. The most common judicial directives to the jury included phrases like "if you believe" or "if you believe on the evidence,"[44] "if you believe what the witness swore,"[45] and "if the evidence is sufficient to satisfy your conscience."[46] In some instances belief was linked to the satisfied conscience test.[47]

Several well-known and much-reprinted Whig political-legal writers employed the satisfied conscience test in 1680–1681, years when legal issues, grand jury indictments, and petty jury verdicts were much in the public eye. According to Sir John Hawles, a well-known Whig lawyer, a juror could not become "fully satisfied in their conscience" until he had carefully considered the matter, as well as the course of life of the testifier and the "credit of the Evidence."[48] A satisfied conscience was thus closely linked to the credibility of the testimony. Hawles also insisted that juries be "satisfied in their particular Understanding and Conscience" of the "Truth and Righteousness of . . . a verdict." Verdicts thus must be given "according to their Conscience and the best of their Judgement." Echoing Judge Vaughan, he noted that jurors must follow their own, not another's, "Understanding or Reasoning."[49]

Henry Care, another Whig writing in 1680 about the political trials of the day, also employed the fully satisfied conscience standard in much the same way.[50] There is no question that for Care, as well as for Hawles and Vaughan, jurors were expected to bring their own reasoning faculties to bear on the evidence and testimony before them, and that the term "satisfied conscience" was the one most often used to denote a proper verdict.

Seventeenth- and early eighteenth-century trials abound in references to "conscience," and writers on conscience often used the trope of "an inner tribunal." Satisfied conscience is central to the development of the beyond reasonable doubt standard. So we must look to what the English meant by "conscience," and that means looking to casuistry. Casuistry had a long tradition extending back through the High Middle Ages. It all but vanished in England by the end of the seventeenth century, perhaps because of increasing expectations that the need to make moral judgments was to be transferred from clergymen to individuals. But many concepts of the casuistical tradition, as represented by the works of William Perkins, Jeremy Taylor, Samuel Pufendorf, and others, were transposed to what became moral philosophy in the late seventeenth and eighteenth centuries.

English casuistry of the sixteenth and seventeenth centuries rejected the doctrine of "casuistical probabilism" associated with the Jesuits, a doctrine that required only a single authority to justify a course of conduct. It also rejected purely emotional or intuitive moral outcomes. Post-Reformation English discussions involved an analysis of rational moral choice or decision making based on a relatively comprehensive evaluation of the entire situation in which the decision maker found himself. What was being dealt with was "cases of conscience." It is easy to see how the terminology of conscience could be transferred from the realm of individual behavior to judgments of innocence and guilt in the legal arena.[51]

Perhaps the first thing to note is that English casuists insisted that the conscience involved an act of the intellect, not the will.[52] In English Protestant casuistry each person was to be his own strictest judge. The judgment of conscience thus could not involve deferring to the authority or the wishes of another person. The language of judgment and judging pervades the writing of cases of conscience. William Perkins's *Discourse of Conscience* (1596) and his later *Whole Treatise of the Cases of Conscience* were designed as practical guides in resolving moral dilemmas. According to Perkins, the conscience that was given by God to man "to declare or put in execution his just judgement against sinners" was "part of the Understanding in all reasonable creatures," and its function was to judge the goodness or badness of things or actions done and to "accuse or excuse."[53] Its duty was to give both testimony and judgment. The former was compared to a notary who recorded what was said and done, the latter to a judge who "holdeth the assize." Conscience functioned as "a little God sitting in the middle of men's hearts, arraigning them in this life as they shall be arraigned for the offenses" at the day of judgment. Perkins went beyond analogy: ". . . the courts of man and their authority are under conscience." For God had "erected a tribunal seat" in man, and "conscience itself" was therefore the "highest judge that is or can be under God."[54] If Perkins's legalistic view of conscience was widely shared, and there is every reason to think that it was, it should not be surprising to find the language of conscience associated with that

of jury verdicts. Although the recorded cases are not available for
the late sixteenth and early seventeenth centuries, it seems likely
that the satisfied conscience standard was commonplace prior to
the Restoration, when our evidence becomes better.

It is important for us to emphasize that the judgment of conscience was a rational decision. The conscience gave judgment, and
it proceeded by a kind of argumentation by means of a reasoning
process that Perkins called a "practical syllogism." If Perkins's conception of the rational process reflected the Ramist scholasticism
of his generation, later casuistical writers adopted the epistemological and methodological assumptions of their own generation.[55]

The Anglican Jeremy Taylor, whose lengthy casuistical treatise
Ductor Dubitantum went through numerous editions, explains the
role of the "satisfied" or "sure" conscience in moral theology. Taylor, like Perkins and Ames, repeatedly insisted that conscience is a
function of the understanding, not the passions. To go against conscience is to go against reason. "The conscience is the mind" and
is made primarily by the "Understanding."[56] The "Sure" or "Right"
conscience was characterized by "moral certainty," a concept
which, we have seen, was widely employed by natural theologians,
natural philosophers, and historians and would play an important
role in legal doctrine. Thus Taylor's discussion of conscience predictably asserts that if moral things were not capable of mathematical or demonstrative certainty, they might nevertheless be "very
highly probable." The "practical judgement of a right conscience"
was "always agreeable to the speculative determination of the understanding" and required "full persuasion." Thus, a "sure" or "satisfied" conscience, according to the most respected late
seventeenth-century English casuist, required the full persuasion
achieved by means of the rational faculties.[57] Like many casuists,
Taylor warns against the overscrupulous conscience. The overly
doubtful conscience which substituted excessive suspicion for care
would never find itself at rest. Conscience was to be concerned with
reasonable doubts, but it was not to become excessively doubtful.

The similarity between the casuistical and the legal conception
can also be seen in the formulations of Robert South, another Anglican cleric. South, like Taylor, insisted that the mathematical certainty of demonstration was not necessary in order to be assured of
the rightness of one's conscience. It was sufficient "if he know it

upon the grounds of a convincing probability, as shall exclude all rational ground of doubting it."[58] The language of rational or reasonable doubt was thus part of the language of the right and sure conscience in England before it entered the legal sphere.

The language of conscience and casuistry, however, also played a prominent role in the more epistemologically sophisticated thinking of John Locke and Samuel Pufendorf. And it is in the context of these turn-of-the-century philosophers that one can see how the language of conscience and casuistry came to pervade the discourse of eighteenth-century moral philosophy and natural law. Its original moorings in moral theology were gradually eroded and obscured as it reemerged in the discourse of philosophers and in the epistemologically oriented treatise writers of the law of evidence that developed from the mid-eighteenth century.

Locke, whose *Essay Concerning Human Understanding* would prove so important to that treatise tradition, wrote about conscience primarily in the context of natural law. Locke defined conscience as "nothing but an opinion of the truth of any practical position which may concern any actions as well moral as religious, civil as ecclesiastical." Indeed, the "law of conscience we call that fundamental judgement of the practical intellect concerning any possible truth of a moral proposition about things to be done in life. . . . Moral actions belong therefore to the jurisdiction of both the outward and the inward court, and are subjects to both dominations, of the civil as well as the domestic governor; I mean both of the magistrate and of conscience." Once convinced, conscience acted as "an legislature . . . constantly present in us whose edicts it should not be lawful for us to transgress even a nail's breadth."[59] Locke, like his casuistical predecessors, links conscience with the understanding, not the passions. "Indeed all obligations bind conscience, and lay a bond on the mind itself, so that not fear of punishment, but a rational apprehension of what is right, puts us under an obligation, and passes judgement on morals, and, if we are guilty of a crime, declares that we deserve punishment."[60]

Given the language of Perkins, Taylor, South, and Locke, it is not difficult to see how easily the doctrine of conscience, the inner tribunal, might be applied in the English courtroom. We must recall, however, that although English Protestant casuists of the sixteenth and seventeenth centuries may be distinguished from their

Roman Catholic counterparts, their basic principles were drawn from a common European tradition of casuistry and moral theology. The connection between the emerging "satisfied conscience" standard of the English courtroom and that of the individual Christian conscience may be more complex than we have been able to trace here.

The terminology of casuistry and moral theology also pervaded Samuel Pufendorf's *Of the Law of Nature and Nations*, which came to have a substantial following in England. This work too helps us chart the transition from casuistry to moral and legal philosophy. Pufendorf begins with a discussion of "moral entities" and the "certainty of moral science." He was anxious to refute both the common opinion that moral knowledge lacked the certainty of philosophy and especially of mathematics and the Hobbesian notion that ethics and politics were capable of demonstration.[61] What is interesting about Pufendorf for our purposes is the way in which "conscience," a concept so important in English legal terminology, is linked to the concepts of moral certainty and beyond reasonable doubt.

For Pufendorf the rightly informed conscience was of two sorts, persuasion built on certain principles or persuasion which is "true and certain; and sees no reason to doubt it." The latter he explicitly relates to the law. The concept of certainty beyond reasonable doubt is thus implicit in his argument from probabilities. Pufendorf argued for the "certainty of Moral sciences" and denied that they could "rise no higher than a probable Opinion." Moral knowledge (or at least portions of it) was not less certain than mathematics. Increasingly, discussions of conscience, casuistry, moral theology, and natural law were in terms of moral certainty. Moral discussions, like religious belief, scientific findings, and historical evaluation, required a reasoned assessment based on the most complete information and evidence available. The "satisfied conscience" of the juryman in the courtroom and of the individual in his closet required rational, unbiased, and unemotional acts of the understanding.[62]

The Cases

Before looking at the cases themselves, I must say something about the case materials and the conditions under which most of them were produced. Before the late seventeenth century very few criminal cases are well documented. Few trial records were preserved and even fewer printed. The decades of the Restoration mark a dramatic change at least insofar as criminal trials involving an important state interest are concerned. Beginning roughly with the spate of Popish Plot trials of 1678–1679, public interest arose in questions of the credibility of witnesses and of the standards for conviction. Many dramatic trials, mostly treason trials, were printed—typically in pamphlet form. And it was in this no doubt somewhat inaccurate form that they eventually found their way into the collection of state trials, which still forms a mainstay of our knowledge of late seventeenth- and early eighteenth-century criminal trials. The political controversies of the 1678–1690 era, with their intensely legal overtones, were particularly important in bringing evidentiary issues to a public forum. The believability of witnesses and the decision rule for jurors were not solely of interest to the legal profession and to those accused of crimes during these heady decades. These issues may have been of no more interest to the greater part of the legal profession than to the general public, given that lawyers during this era played little or no role in criminal trials.[63] In the absence of professional interest in jury verdicts in criminal cases, it is not at all surprising that judges would look to formulations by those who had seriously considered the basis on which ethical and rational decisions might be made. The standards of the satisfied conscience, moral certainty, and beyond reasonable doubt, which became characteristic of the late seventeenth- and eighteenth-century English criminal courts, were thus derived from disciplines or areas of thought which had already developed or were attempting to develop rules and standards in matters of fact and everyday life. Judges, in an era of intense concern with issues of credibility, probability, and certainty in many other fields, not surprisingly turned to religious and intellectual traditions where these were well developed or developing. As we have seen, such traditions were employed by theologians engaged in polemics with Roman Catholics about scriptural authority, proofs for the Creation, and the relation of such authority to the proofs of natural religion and the casuistical tradition. Similar discussions of proof occurred among historians and those seeking to establish the reality of various natural "facts," the validity of experiments, and the reliability of hypotheses and theories well supported by empirical data.

The cases between 1683 and 1700 employ language similar to the language of those between 1668 and 1683, although the number of judicial instructions which link believing the witnesses and reaching a satisfied conscience now outnumber other formulations.[64] In law, conscience was "satisfied" only when the reasoning faculties were exercised upon the evidence. The question of "doubt" in the mind of the jury was rarely raised explicitly by the late seventeenth-century judiciary.[65]

The language of the 1700–1750 cases does not differ substantially, although references to conscience become somewhat fewer. It was the "mind" or "judgment," rather than the "conscience," which was to reach conclusions on the evidence. The need to be "satisfied," however, did not decline.[66] The most common directives employed "belief" based on evidence.[67] Judges insisted that verdicts be based on evidence, and jurors were frequently admonished to take great care in weighing and examining it. In several cases the terms "belief" and "satisfaction" were used synonymously. A guilty verdict was appropriate if the jurors "believed," an acquittal if they were not "satisfied."[68] Notions of satisfaction and belief formed by evaluating evidence were the most common features of jury charges in this period.[69]

The second half of the century presents a somewhat more complex, but not fundamentally different, picture. Judges and legal counsel now began to concern themselves with doubts that legitimately might appear in the minds of jurors.[70] Most cases, however, still exhibited the familiar formulas emphasizing "belief."[71] The requirement that the jury be "fully satisfied" or "satisfied" on the basis of the evidence continues as a common feature.[72]

There is, however, a more secular terminology. The "if you believe the evidence" phraseology is often replaced by "if you think the evidence" terminology.[73] The term "judgment," or "understanding," also became more frequent. One judge advised a jury to "exercise your judgments" on the evidence.[74] The "understandings" of the jury must be "absolutely coerced to believe."[75] Another judge noted that they "were rational men and will determine according to your consciences, whether you believe those men guilty or not."[76] The understanding and the conscience were concerned with the same, not different, mental processes, and both involved rational deliberation. Although terms like "mind," "understanding," and "judgment" have an obviously more secular tone than "belief" and "conscience," and are sometimes substituted for them, it is important not to make sweeping statements about secularization, for the more secular terms often appear with the more traditional ones. Recall in this connection that Bacon, in the early part of the seventeenth century, already referred simultaneously to the jury's "understanding" as well as to its conscience, and that the High Court of Justice in 1649 indicated they were "fully satisfied in their judgement and conscience" of the king's guilt.

We can, however, trace a growing concern for situations in which juries might have doubts about evidence and thus about their verdicts. Their minds might be "suspended in such a degree of that doubt" that they could not be "satisfied."[77] In a 1752 case the prosecution suggested that the evidence was "so strong, so convincing, . . . that that Presumption that will rise to a Conviction; there will not remain the least Doubt of it."[78]

This period witnesses the first use of the beyond reasonable doubt standard that sounds so familiar to modern ears. Anthony Morano has suggested that the beyond reasonable doubt test was introduced by the prosecution, and that it actually was designed to provide less protection to the accused than the "any doubt" test, which did not require that doubts be reasonable.[79] My reading of the cases and the treatise literature is somewhat different. I do not think that the "any doubt" terminology ever meant that juries should acquit on the basis of frivolous doubt. The term "moral certainty" was taken to mean proof beyond reasonable doubt. If one had real doubts, moral certainty was not reached. The term "beyond reasonable doubt" was, I believe, not a replacement for the any doubt test but was added to clarify the notions of moral certainty and satisfied belief. Indeed, many of the cases that enunciate the beyond reasonable doubt test for acquittal employ the "if you believe," or "if your conscience is satisfied," or "if you are satisfied with the evidence" phraseology when stating what was required for conviction. Reasonable doubt was simply a better explanation of the satisfied conscience standard that resulted from increasing familiarity with the moral certainty concept.[80] The emphasis on doubt almost certainly owes something to the growing participation of defense counsel in criminal cases. It would obviously be in the interest of defendants to emphasize doubt.

Anthony Morano's research, however, has established that the beyond reasonable doubt standard was employed in the Boston Massacre trials of 1770, rather than first appearing in the turn-of-the-century Irish treason trials.[81] Interestingly, the Boston cases do not suggest that the standard was considered innovative, for both the prosecution and the bench emphasized that the accused were being tried according to traditional English usage. The prosecution, appealing to the jury's "Cool and Candid Reason," indicated that if the "Evidence is not sufficient to Convince beyond reasonable Doubt," then the jury must acquit. The prosecution, of course, asserted that the evidence was "sufficient to convince you of their guilt beyond reasonable doubt." The judges, however, employed the traditional "fully satisfied" and "satisfied belief" formulations, as well as "If upon the whole, ye are in any reasonable doubt of their guilt, we must then, agreeable to the rule of the law, declare them innocent."[82]

We should not be surprised, however, that its introduction appeared to be neither novel nor controversial in this case. Sir Geoffrey Gilbert's authoritative *Law of Evidence*, which employs similar language, had appeared in several editions before 1770.[83] The introduction of the beyond reasonable doubt language in the Boston cases caused no comment, precisely because it was consistent with the notions of "belief," "satisfied conscience," and "moral certainty" employed in and outside the courtroom.

Thus in 1777, in one of the rare cases fully recorded in shorthand tried at Old Bailey, Counsel Mansfield told the jury, "If the evidence be such as 'irresistibly proves' [the crime], . . . if you see any room upon the evidence to doubt of his being guilty, if you are not perfectly convinced you must find the accused not guilty."[84] The beyond reasonable doubt formulation appeared in a 1796 Canadian case as well. The jury was informed that if they had any reasonable doubt, then they must acquit, "for it is the invariable direction of our English Courts of Justice to lean on the side of mercy."[85]

We must look briefly at the language of the turn-of-the-century Irish trials, many of which employ the reasonable doubt standard in conjunction with the notions of satisfied conscience and belief.

In the *Trial of Weedon* (1795) one judge indicated a guilty verdict was appropriate if it "should appear" beyond all doubt "that the acts in question had been done by the Prisoner." Unless they were "perfectly satisfied," the jury must acquit. Another judge indicated that a guilty verdict should be forthcoming "if your understandings are absolutely coerced to believe" the testimony of the witness. Coerced assent was, as we have seen, equivalent to moral certainty and to Locke's highest degree of probability. If, however, the jury had "any rational doubt" in their "minds," they must acquit. A third judge combined the notions of conscience, belief, and rational doubt. The jury was "to determine upon the weight of . . . [their] observations, to consider the facts and circumstances" if they "believe it to be the truth." If, however, they felt "such a doubt as reasonable men entertain," they were bound to acquit.[86] The fact that several judges employed the same language should indicate that the terminology had gained widespread acceptance.

The same mixture appears in the *Trial of Leary* (1795). If the evidence "carries conviction to your minds . . . such a conviction as leaves no doubt that the prisoner is guilty they must declare him so. But if . . . you should have any doubt, such as reasonable men may entertain . . . ," acquittal was appropriate.[87] In the *Trial of Kennedy* (1796), the jury was told, "if you have no doubt such as rational men may entertain," a guilty verdict was called for. But if you should "entertain such a reasonable doubt," they must acquit.[88] Only reasonable doubts were acceptable. Jurors were expected to conform to the model of the rational man.

In the *Trial of Glennan* (1796), the judge said, "If you have a reasonable doubt, not such as the idle or fanciful may take upon remote probabilities, but such as cannot satisfy your judgement upon your oath," then the jury should acquit. "You are rational men and will determine according to your consciences, whether you believe those men guilty or not."[89] Here the languages of belief, the satisfied conscience, and beyond reasonable doubt are all linked together.

The beyond reasonable doubt standard was prominent in all the turn-of-the-century Irish treason trials. Yet there was no indication that a new standard was self-consciously enunciated. The new formula usually appeared with statements that conviction rests on a satisfied conscience or belief in the testimony of the witnesses. It was introduced most typically when judges added instructions about acquittal. I am not suggesting that juries had become more concerned with high levels of proof, for they seemed to have expected them, but rather that the judiciary, in its charges to the jury, were now articulating those high standards in language consistent with and influenced by the terminology of the established religious and philosophical communities.

The beyond reasonable doubt standard also appears in a number of U.S. trials around the turn of the century. The 1798 trial of Matthew Lyon for seditious libel in the Circuit Court for the Vermont District indicates that the standard was being applied early in the history of the new nation. The judge informed the jury, "you must be satisfied beyond all reasonable substantial doubt that hypothesis of innocence is unsustainable."[90]

Defense counsel in the *Trial of the Northampton Insurgents* before the U.S. Circuit Court, 1799–1800, advised the jury to "remember that it is enough for us in defense of the prisoner to raise a doubt; for if you doubt it (it is the principle of law, as well as of humanity) you must acquit."[91] A second defense counsel indicated that the presumption of innocence must be maintained "until the contrary is proved by the most incontrovertible evidence." The offense must be "proved in such a manner as to leave no possibility of doubt in the minds of the jury." Proof must "come from the purest sources, and be of that nature as to establish the crime beyond the possibility of a doubt." The jury was also reminded of the necessity of divesting itself of "opinion or bias, . . . otherwise there is not a fair scope for our reasonable faculties to act, nor can our consciences be acquitted of guilt." The prosecution in the case indicated the testimony offered had been "produced . . . to remove every doubt" from the jurors' "minds." The judge, like the prosecutor, invoked the beyond reasonable doubt standard.[92]

The beyond reasonable doubt standard, however, was not uniformly applied until well into the next century, when it was defined as follows:

It is not merely possible doubt; because everything relating to human affairs, and depending on moral evidence, is open to some possible or imaginary doubt. It is that state of the case, which, after the entire comparison and consideration of all the evidence, leaves the mind of the jurors in that condition that they cannot say they feel an abiding conviction of moral certainty, of the truth of the charge . . . the evidence must establish the truth of the fact to a reasonable and moral certainty; a certainty that convinces and directs the understanding, and satisfies the reason and judgement. . . . This we take to be proof beyond a reasonable doubt.[93]

By the late eighteenth century, the satisfied conscience and beyond reasonable doubt standards had become explicitly linked. The addition of the concept of moral certainty to legal language reflected the desire to make the language consistent with prevailing philosophical terminology. This terminology, however foreign sounding to modern ears, was part of the language and discourse of the educated classes in both England and America. Satisfied conscience, reasonable doubt, and moral certainty were widely used concepts, and these and related terms were found in moral, theological, historical, philosophical, and legal discourse.[94]

The Treatise Tradition

Even more than the cases, the new genre of the legal treatise on evidence that emerges in the early eighteenth century suggests that the evolution of the doctrine of proof beyond reasonable doubt was linked to the changing philosophical scene. One of the most interesting features of treatises on evidence and the more general discussions of law is that so many authors found it necessary to treat legal evidence in the context of current epistemological thought. It seemed to them essential to ground the rules of evidence, which were the bulk of the treatises, on what was considered to be a sound theory of knowledge. Legal rules, it was evidently felt, could not stand alone. Nor were they justified by tradition or a special sort of legal reasoning. The treatise writers attempted to demonstrate that the rules of evidence, some of them several centuries old, could and did rest on sound notions of what constituted appropriate evidence and good proofs—that is, on an intellectually satisfying theory of human knowledge. The rules, then, were not directly derived from philosophical principles, but were seen as conforming to sound epistemological and logical principles.

Several major Anglo-American writers attempted to integrate legal evidence with the reigning empirical English philosophies. The two earliest writers, Sir Geoffrey Gilbert and John Morgan, rely on Locke to provide the foundation for their treatises. James Wil-

son and David Hoffman, who prepared more general lectures, lean
heavily on the eighteenth-century Scottish Common Sense philosophers, and Thomas Starkie leans on a philosophical miscellany.
Thus, if the earliest treatises are liberally sprinkled with Locke,
the later ones include generous dashes of Hartley, Reid, Bentham,
Paley, Stewart, Kirwan, Whately, and others.[95]

The first real treatise on evidence, *The Law of Evidence*, was
written by Sir Geoffrey Gilbert, a respected judge and legal
scholar, knowledgeable about the mathematical and scientific work
of the day. He was also the author of *Abstract of Mr. Locke's Essay
on Human Understanding*. Not surprisingly, his posthumously
published treatise on evidence begins with a summary of Lockean
principles:

> There are several degrees from perfect Certainty and Demonstration,
> quite down to Improbability and Unlikeness . . . and there are several
> Acts of the Mind proportioned to these Degrees of Evidence . . . from
> full Assurance and Confidence, quite down to Conjecture, Doubt, Dis-
> trust and Disbelief.

> Now what is to be done in all Trials of Right, is to range all Matters in
> the Scale of Probability, so as to lay most Weight where the Cause ought
> to preponderate, and thereby to make the most exact Discernment that
> can be, in Relation to the Right.[96]

The law did not have access to certain knowledge because litigation
depended on transient events "retrieved by Memory and Recollec-
tion." The "Rights of Men" were therefore of necessity "determined by Probability," not by demonstration. Assessment of probability, however, required careful consideration of the degrees of
credibility of the witnesses. There was no more reason to doubt
the statements of credible witnesses than if "we ourselves had
heard and seen" what the witnesses reported. Verdicts, according
to Gilbert, would necessarily be devoid of absolute certainty or
demonstration, but trials, at least those with appropriately credible
witnesses, might proceed to verdicts which the jury had no reason
to doubt. Gilbert's Lockean formulation, as well as the evidence
from the state trials cited earlier, suggests that the beyond reasonable doubt rule first applied only to direct testimony and was not
initially applied to circumstantial evidence.

Although it is possible to argue that the Lockean epistemology,
which I have suggested provided the basis for Gilbert's treatise,

was more decoration than substance, it is noteworthy that the 1795 edition of Gilbert (edited by Capel Lofft) contains references not only to Locke but also to John Wilkins, mentioned earlier in connection with the development of the concept of moral certainty in the realms of natural religion and natural science. Richard Price, David Hartley, and Isaac Watts are also cited in later editions.[97]

John Morgan's *Essays Upon the Law of Evidence* (1789) similarly relies on a Lockean conception of knowledge.[98] He, like Gilbert, indicates that there are degrees of knowledge, ranging from perfect certainty and demonstration on the one hand to improbability and unlikeliness on the other, and that there are acts of the mind proportioned to the evidence. These ranged from "full assurance and confidence, to conjecture, doubt and disbelief." Although legal proceedings "must judge on probability . . . ," nothing less than the "highest degree of probability must govern" the courts.[99] When one had reached a judgment based on "the honesty and integrity of credible and disinterested witnesses," the mind had no choice but to "acquiesce therein as if [it had] a knowledge by demonstration." The mind "ought not any longer to doubt but, to be nearly if not as perfectly well-satisfied as if we of ourselves knew the fact."[100]

Morgan's "satisfaction" was also synonymous with judicial demands for jury "satisfaction" or "satisfied conscience." Jury verdicts must be based on the very highest knowledge available to humans in matters of fact. Morgan, like Gilbert, hoped to ground the law of evidence on a sound epistemological foundation.

James Wilson, professor of law at the College of Philadelphia and associate justice of the U.S. Supreme Court, in 1790 insisted that the law was and must be "comformable to the true theory of the human mind." Wilson's treatment centered on the concept of "belief," of which the most salient characteristic both within and without the legal context was that it admitted "of all possible degrees from absolute certitude down to doubt and suspicion."[101] Wilson, however, was critical of Cartesian and Lockean conceptions of knowledge and relied instead on the formulations of Thomas Reid and the Scottish commonsense school, which would dominate Anglo-American epistemological discussion and moral philosophy in the late eighteenth and early nineteenth centuries.

If Thomas Reid and his Common Sense school successors developed an inductive philosophy of mind which somewhat modified Locke on the nature of sensation, perception, and the formation of ideas, the most important feature of the Common Sense philosophers for our purposes is their emphatic rejection of the centuries-old philosophical tradition which insisted that demonstration alone yielded certainty and that everything else, including the best-attested matters of fact, yielded only probable opinion. Such a position, they insisted, might be taken by a logician but had no meaning in ordinary speech or everyday life. Thus a good deal of the evidence derived from testimony, which for the traditional philosopher was "merely probable," was properly classified as "certainty" by the rest of mankind. Thomas Reid thus insisted that the execution of Charles I was a certain fact—not a statement of probability. Human capacity for error, therefore, was irrelevant to consideration of whether one was correct or erroneous in particular cases. Common sense properly viewed well-attested facts as knowledge, not as mere opinion and probability.

The Common Sense school was especially anxious to counter the skepticism of Hume, which insisted that no amount of evidence could remove doubt. Thus Dugald Stewart, like Reid, insisted that while it was always logically possible that judgments in matters of fact might be mistaken, there were some instances in which they were as certain as any euclidean truth. It is, therefore, not surprising to find Hume absent from most writing on legal evidence.[102]

Like most of his predecessors of the late seventeenth and early eighteenth centuries, James Wilson, who had been educated in Scotland and was influenced by Reid and Scottish philosophy, identified two varieties of reasoning, the demonstrative and the moral. The former yielded abstract and necessary truths, or the unchangeable relations of ideas. The latter dealt with "real but contingent truths and connections which take place among things actually existing." Although Wilson rejected some of the Lockean terminology which he found in Gilbert and Blackstone, he noted that moral evidence arose by "insensible gradation, from possible to probable, and from probable to the highest degree of moral certainty."[103]

Testimony was, for Wilson, the most important of some fourteen sources of moral evidence. It provided both the "greatest part" of the jury's business and the most knowledge of "men and things."

Testimony provided the basis not only for "many parts of jurisprudence," but also for history, criticism, and "for all that acquaintance with nature and the works of nature, . . . founded on personal observation and experience." "The whole stupendous fabric of natural philosophy" thus had the same epistemological basis as the law.[104]

Wilson also enumerated and discussed the reasons for doubting or rejecting testimony: that the thing or event appeared improbable and that testimony might be given by someone incompetent to judge the matter, by someone who previously gave false testimony, or by someone with a temptation to deceive. The reputation of the witness and the manner in which testimony was delivered also entered into the jury's evaluation. All these elements considered jointly would render the force of the testimony believable or not. The concurrent testimony of many witnesses deprived of the opportunity for collusion thus would be "equal to that of strict demonstration." Testimony and concurrent circumstances might allow juries to gain a sense of moral certainty about facts and events. The jury's belief thus required a considered "act of the mind." In capital cases, Wilson thus insisted, the evidence must be so strong as to "force belief."[105]

Thus by the late eighteenth century the concepts of moral certainty and beyond reasonable doubt were tightly linked in philosophical literature, in legal treatises, and in legal discussions designed to reach the educated public. The language of moral certainty and beyond reasonable doubt and the provision of philosophically oriented statements concerning the nature of human knowledge were becoming commonplace in early nineteenth century evidence treatises, although not every text included both elements.

If Leonard McNally's much-used *Rules of Evidence on Pleas of the Crown* offers little in the way of philosophical underpinnings, McNally nevertheless played a crucial role in enunciating and publicizing the beyond reasonable doubt standard—both as defense counsel in several of the Irish treason trials and in his treatise on evidence. He insisted that it was a rule of law that if a jury "entertain[s] a reasonable doubt" as to the truth of the testimony of the witnesses, it must acquit. Reasonable doubt arose from testimony which the jury judged not to "deserve credit." Such doubt might arise from the "infamy" of the witness's character, his interest, or his manner of giving evidence. Showing resentment or partiality, for example, might "impress suspicion" or prevarication. If the witness's credibility was questionable, "unless his testimony be supported by clear and collateral proof, . . . doubt must arise in the minds of the jurors." It was the "indispensable duty" of the judges in charging the jury to ask "whether they are satisfied, beyond the probability of doubt, that he is guilty."[106]

In *The Philosophy of Evidence*, Daniel McKinnon, like Gilbert, Morgan, and Wilson, begins with a brief discussion of certainty, probability, and assent and refers to the epistemological theorists of the day—Locke, Reid, and Stewart. He thus makes the now commonplace distinction between intuitive, or demonstrative, knowledge and probable knowledge, under which he includes both presumption, or indirect proofs, as well as direct proofs. If demonstrative knowledge "exclude[s] all possible doubt," probable and presumptive knowledge did not. Degrees of certitude thus varied. For this reason, rules were needed "to restrain the latitude of individual opinion and conduct in the investigations of truth by a strict and methodical course of argument." The law of evidence was "framed with this intention." Although McKinnon does not use the language of moral certainty, he indicated that juries were to acquit if the evidence "is at all doubtful" and further indicated that this "very humane rule" was "fortified by the presumption that every man is innocent till his guilt appears."[107]

While Phillipps's *Theory of Presumptive Proof* does not use the term "beyond reasonable doubt," it does indicate that the "impression in the mind of a jury in a criminal case" not be "that the prisoner is probably guilty, but that he really and absolutely is so." If the jury had doubts, they were to acquit.[108]

In the late eighteenth and nineteenth centuries it was not unusual for a discussion of legal evidence to include or refer to treatises on logic or for general discussions of logic and modes of proof to devote considerable attention to matters relevant to the law. Because most Anglo-American philosophy and epistemology were empirical in their orientation, a great deal of attention was quite naturally devoted to questions relating to the probability and certainty of arguments and evidence which related to matters of fact.

While it is obviously not possible to undertake a detailed discussion of the relationship between concepts of legal evidence and the more philosophically oriented writings of moral philosophers, natural philosophers, and logicians, brief comments on a few such writers should indicate the overlap between the writing of members of the legal profession considering legal evidence and the writing on evidence in other areas. We have already noted the early dependence on Locke. The next generation of writers relied more heavily on David Hartley, Thomas Reid, and Isaac Watts, and still later ones on James MacIntosh, Richard Kirwan, Dugald Stewart, and John Stuart Mill.

David Hartley's *Observations on Man* (1749) was frequently cited by legal writers on issues of evidence and the nature of human knowledge. Topics of relevance to legal writers might include the nature of assent and dissent, the role of rational assent in mathematical and practical reasoning, and the differences among true, doubtful, and fictitious narrations of fact. Hartley noted that some facts were "practically certain," while others were "liable to doubts."[109]

Isaac Watts's *Logick, or the Right Use of Reason in the Inquiry after Truth* (1724), another frequently cited source, defined logic as the "art of using Reason in our Inquiries after Truth," and was a concept which he believed referred equally to the actions of life and to the natural sciences. Perhaps of most interest to lawyers was his discussion of the principles and rules of judgment in human testimony. He indicated that one must ask whether the event in question was possible, whether there were concurrent circumstances in addition to testimony, and whether the character and knowledge of the testifier made his testimony believable. If one theme dominated Watts's discussions of evidence, it was the need to exactly proportion assent to the degree of evidence. Where the evidence was insufficient, the mind was to suspend assent.[110] Most of the rules and principles were easily applicable to the courtroom, and it is not surprising that so many writers on legal evidence found his discussions useful.

George Campbell's *Philosophy of Rhetoric* also discussed evidence in ways relevant to legal writers. Discussion was largely limited to "moral evidence," because the sphere of demonstrable evidence was so small. He thus devoted a good deal of attention to experience and testimony. The latter, he insisted, was capable of providing certainty. One must give unlimited assent "when we have no positive reason of mistrust or doubt." Many beliefs are based on moral evidence which does not create doubts. All decisions of fact involved moral evidence, and these in turn involved degrees of certainty which ranged from possible, to probable, "to the summit of moral certainty."[111] Campbell, a common sense thinker, not only employs the language of reasonable doubt and moral certainty, but also allies this language and other issues relating to assent to philology and history, as well as to law. By the end of the eighteenth century the concepts of moral certainty and proof beyond reasonable doubt were widespread in the moral and philosophical literature. Their introduction into legal writing in the jury charges, which emerge late in the century, should thus not be surprising.

The same development continued in the nineteenth century. Kirwan's *Logick, or An Essay on the Elements, Principles and Different Modes of Reasoning* of 1807, a general treatment of the logic of proof, insists that the rules of evidence and the logic on which they were based must be "diligently attended to" in countries where "all men are liable to sit on juries."[112] Kirwan, in the manner of seventeenth- and eighteenth-century natural theologians, discriminates among metaphysical, physical, and moral certainty, as well as between demonstrative and other proofs. He not only discusses the bases for confident belief, "suspicion, doubt, or hesitation,"[113] but also devotes chapters to "indubitable proofs productive of certainty," "ambiguous or suspicious proofs," "fallacious proofs," and "probable proofs." Considerable attention is also given to direct and indirect proofs, the credibility of testimony, and presumptions. References to law, legal writers, and legal situations were thus not at all unusual in Kirwan's *Logick*.[114] Indeed Kirwan appears to have considered lawyers and prospective jurors as his primary audience.

It is thus not at all surprising that David Hoffman should recommend Kirwan's *Logick* and Reid's *Essays* to students of law or that other writers on legal evidence should recommend logical and epistemological oriented treatises such as those of Locke, Hartley, Reid, Abercrombie, Kirwan, and others. The list of recommended philosophical works, as one might expect, was modified over time, and later writers favored Kirwan, Whately, and John Stuart Mill over earlier works.

An example of this mutual borrowing or mutual reinforcement is found in James Gambier's *Guide to the Study of Moral Evidence, or of that Species of Reasoning which Relates to Matters of Fact and Practice.* The editor of this work, which deals with evidence in a wide variety of types of human knowledge, emphasizes the importance of such a work for jurors. He insisted that it is they and not counsel alone who "ought to be familiar with the rules of evidence."[115] He complained of the small portion of potential jurors who "have ever received one hour's direct instruction on the Science of Evidence," and recommended that "Every child who may hereafter stand in a jury-box to decide on a question of fact 'according to the evidence' ought to be instructed in the laws of evidence; so that he may *know for himself* when a fact is proven, and some of its details, to be imported even in the common school."[116] It was with that thought in mind that he introduced Gambier's treatise to the public.

Moral evidence was defined as that "species of proof, which is employed on subjects, directly or indirectly, connected with moral conduct." It was not, however, limited to those subjects, but was "extended to all those facts, and events, concerning which we do not obtain the evidence of sense, intuition or demonstration, and to all the general truths, which are deduced from observation."[117] Indeed, it dealt with all matters of fact.[118] Moral evidence was to be distinguished from demonstration, which led to absolute certainty, for the proofs involved in moral evidence were fallible. They, therefore, could not produce absolute certainty but only "probable judgment, or at most moral certainty." Probability, however, might "rise so high, as to exclude all reasonable doubt." Moral evidence involved degrees of assent ranging "from suspicion to moral certainty." The degree of assent depended on the degree of evidence: "Thus when the evidence on one side preponderates a very little, there is ground for suspicion, or conjecture. Presumption, persuasion, belief, conclusion, conviction, moral certainty, doubt, wavering, distrust, disbelief, are words which imply an increase or decrease of this preponderancy."[119] Lawyers and divines—and it is noteworthy that he pairs them—thus have their proofs, and

though they do not amount to demonstration, yet, if they be sufficient to exclude all reasonable doubt, they ought to be admitted to be proofs. In truth, wherever there is produced, in favour of any proposition, the highest kind of evidence of which it admits, and in a sufficient degree to outweigh all that can be urged against it, it may properly be said to be proved.[120]

Because the judgment required training in "estimating the relative worth of different kinds of evidence," the book was designed to describe the proper sort of reasoning about moral evidence.[121]

Although Gambier's *Guide* is not a legal treatise, its assumptions about the nature of knowledge and the way one should reach judgments in matters of fact were relevant to the legal community. The overlap between the legal and nonlegal work is often so great that it is difficult to know which should be labeled "legal" and which should not. What is clear, however, is that the growing treatise literature on the law of evidence participated in broader intellectual currents and shared rather widely held views on the nature of evidence and proof. The language of probability, certainty, moral certainty, and beyond reasonable doubt was part of the discourse of the educated classes. The works just cited were designed for the literate reader, not for the professional philosopher.

Similar attention to legally relevant epistemological issues was provided by John Abercrombie, whose *Inquiries Concerning the Intellectual Powers and the Investigation of Truth* was frequently cited in the evidence treatises. Not only does Abercrombie discuss probability, certainty, and the sources of certainty, but he was also interested in the role of testimony and doubts regarding testimony. He employed the notion of high moral probability and spelled out the grounds on which one can receive testimony with confidence. If his readers accepted his view that the "exercise of reason is precisely the same, and is guided by the same laws, whether it be applied to the investigation of truth or to the regulation of conduct," they must have found the interaction between the evidence treatises and the more philosophically oriented treatments of the nature of human knowledge both reasonable and normal.[122]

James Glassford's *Essay on the Principles of Evidence and Their Applications to the Subject of Judicial Inquiry* again suggests the overlap between the philosophical and legal writing of the early nineteenth century. Glassford's rather lengthy book was initially designed as an article for the supplement to the *Encyclopaedia Britannica* and was only published as a freestanding work because it had become so long. It was thus "not intended altogether as a professional book."[123] Glassford indicated that evidence might be treated generally as a part of logic or as part of particular sciences, and especially as part of law, a view that would probably have seemed commonplace to early nineteenth-century readers. Glassford therefore divided his treatise into two parts. The first dealt with "The Nature and Sources of Evidence in General," the second with "the several kinds of Legal Evidence, or the Evidence receivable in the courts of law."[124] As one might expect, Glassford, whose theory of evidence and proof was largely based on the then dominant Scottish Common Sense school of philosophy, deals with the whole range of evidentiary issues and concepts, including probability, certainty, gradations of certainty, moral certainty, testimony, and mental conviction beyond reasonable doubt. His work does not appear to have had any great impact on the legal profession, perhaps because it attempted to draw on both English and Scottish law; but like the works of Gambier and others, it does indicate the close relationship between legal and philosophical discussions of evidence and truth determination.

Thomas Starkie's immensely influential *Practical Treatise on the Law of Evidence*, which was designed for the legal practitioner, also reflects the epistemological traditions we have been examining. Indeed, the treatise is liberally sprinkled with references to epistemological issues. Juries, Starkie insists, must rely on the general principles of belief "on which any individual would act who was desirous of satisfying himself by inquiry as to the truth of any particular fact."[125] Legal facts were no different from others, although the law sometimes added special requirements, such as excluding certain kinds of testimony, to insure that the search for truth would in no way be contaminated.

Starkie, too, distinguished between absolute certainty and the moral certainty available in matters of fact.

Evidence which satisfied the minds of the jury of the truth of the fact in dispute, to the entire exclusion of every reasonable doubt, constitute full proof of the fact. . . . Even the most direct evidence can produce nothing more than such a high degree of probability as amounts to moral certainty. From the highest it may decline, by an infinite number of gradations, until it produces in the mind nothing more than a preponderance of assent in favour of the particular fact.[126]

The test for the jurors was the "sufficiency of the evidence to satisfy the understanding and conscience of the jury," and it was sufficient when the evidence and the proof "produce moral certainty to the

exclusion of every reasonable doubt." "To acquit upon light, trivial
or fanciful suppositions, and remote conjecture, is a virtual violation of the juror's oath, . . . on the other hand, a juror ought not
to condemn unless the evidence excludes from his mind all reasonable doubt as to the guilt of the accused."[127] Moral certainty was
equivalent to the highest degree of probability, and both were in-
dissolubly connected to the beyond reasonable doubt standard.
"Satisfied belief and satisfied conscience and understanding" gradually emerged as the familiar "beyond reasonable doubt." With
Starkie the modern standard was in place. The impact of his treatise
was profound and influenced Anglo-American writers for many
decades.

The influential early nineteenth-century American legal writer
David Hoffman also insisted that the science of evidence be
founded on the closest observation of man's moral and intellectual
nature. Although Hoffman especially admired the recent treatises
of Phillipps and Starkie, he still felt that the English law of evidence
tended to have "too little" recourse to the general principles of
human action and was impaired by "too strict adherence to the
analogies of the common law." He also criticized English writers
for their "almost total neglect" of Continental evidentiary jurists
such as Farinaccius, Menochius, and Domat. Hoffman also recommended that the philosophical and logical works of Kirwan, De
Moivre, Paley, Reid, Stewart, and, of course, Locke be considered
more seriously.[128] He further noted that "The effect to be allowed
to intrinsic evidence or that deduced from a combination of circumstances" had been "but little explored by the legal philosophers of
any country." This great work, if ever performed, could only be
accomplished by "some preeminent genius."[129]

As one might expect, the legal writings of Jeremy Bentham have
attracted more scholarly attention than those of most early treatise
writers and commentators I have mentioned. While it is not possible to discuss his enormously long and complex *Rationale of Judicial Evidence*, it is important to note that Bentham's intention
was to bring the law of evidence into conformity with the rules of
logic. Bentham's powerful work on evidence appears to have exerted relatively little direct impact on the legal profession, in part
because of its intense criticism of the profession and in part because
of his radical desire to eliminate all formal rules of evidence. Nevertheless, it is important for our purposes because it, too, bears wit-

ness to the powerful eighteenth- and nineteenth-century effort to ground the law of evidence on principles of sound reasoning. As noted earlier, Locke, Hartley, Reid, Paley, Abercrombie, Stewart, and others provided the basis, or at least the epistemological starting point, for many writers who concerned themselves with the problems of legal evidence. Bentham is no exception, although his approach was closer to that of Locke rather than to that of the Common Sense school. Lengthy portions of his massive treatise explore notions of probability, improbability, and impossibility, as well as the nature of testimony and circumstantial evidence, the hindrances to truthful testimony, and degrees of persuasion.[130]

As the nineteenth century progressed, the number of legal treatises increased in all fields. These included not only general treatises on evidence but also specialized works dealing with circumstantial and presumptive evidence, the latter in particular expressing considerable interest in epistemology and a receptiveness to civilian writers such as Domat and Pothier.[131] Many of these works, too, employed the language of probability, moral certainty, and degrees of assent, and attempted to ground their evidentiary standards on psychological and epistemological positions of the day. Chapter 3 examines the ways in which discussions of circumstantial evidence came to combine this English mode of analysis with that of the civil law tradition.

This pattern of philosophical discussion is to be found in Simon Greenleaf's famous *Treatise on the Law of Evidence*, which was indebted to both Starkie and Phillipps. This famous nineteenth-century American legal treatise followed the conventional pattern of beginning with a brief discussion of epistemology. In addition to incorporating the epistemological authorities cited by Starkie and Phillipps, Greenleaf uses Whately's *Logic*, Gambier's *Guide to the Study of Moral Evidence*, Abercrombie's *Inquiries Concerning the Intellectual Powers*, McKinnon's *Philosophy of Evidence*, and Reid's *Inquiry into the Human Mind* to support his distinction between mathematical and moral evidence in his discussion of the "grounds of Belief."

Matters of fact are proved by *moral evidence* alone; by which is meant, not only that kind of evidence, which is employed on subjects connected with moral conduct, but all the evidence, which is not obtained either from intuition, or from demonstration. In the ordinary affairs of life, we do not require demonstrative evidence, . . . and to insist upon it would be unreasonable and absurd. The most, that can be affirmed of such things, is, that there is no reasonable doubt concerning them. The *true question* therefore, in trials of fact, is not, whether it is possible that the testimony may be false, but whether there is a *sufficient probability* of its truth, that is whether the facts are shown by competent and satisfactory evidence. . . . By *satisfactory evidence* . . . is intended that amount of proof, which ordinarily satisfies an unprejudiced mind beyond reasonable doubt. The circumstances, which will amount to this degree of proof, can never be previously defined; the only legal test of which they are susceptible, is their sufficiency to satisfy the mind and conscience of a common man, and so to convince them, that he would venture to act upon that conviction, in the matters of the highest concern and importance to his own interest.[132]

What is interesting historically about Greenleaf's formulation is that "satisfied mind" and "satisfied conscience," the formulas most common in seventeenth- and early eighteenth-century charges to the jury, are explicitly equated with the concept of "beyond reasonable doubt." Greenleaf, like most of his predecessors, also insisted that the courtroom shared its principles of evidence with the historian, the naturalist, the traveler, and the astronomer. Thus, one of the bases of evidence, the connection between "collateral facts or circumstances, satisfactorily proved, and the fact in controversy," was viewed simply as the legal application "of a process familiar in natural philosophy, showing the truth of an hypothesis by its coincidence with existing phenomena." The force of the connections and coincidences, which may be either physical or moral, thus "depends on their sufficiency to exclude every other hypothesis but the one under consideration." Greenleaf also indicated that the doctrines of presumptive evidence, which were so important to law, were "shared . . . in common with other departments of science."[133]

Although most early and mid-nineteenth-century treatises emphasize the similarity between legal reasoning and evidence and ordinary reasoning and evidence, it must be admitted that James Thayer's influential *Preliminary Treatise on Evidence at the Common Law* represents a departure from this position. Because Thayer distinguished the evidentiary method of the law from that of the natural sciences and history, it is not surprising that he does not attempt to ground his treatise on the epistemological treatises of the day. Thayer appears to be of several minds whether, or to what degree, legal evidence and reasoning differ from evidence and reasoning in other fields of inquiry. At one point he differentiates between legal evidence and historical and religious evidence and insists that legal evidence is concerned with what is admissible, not what is logically probative. Yet he also admits that the rules of legal argument are "mainly an affair of logic and general experience, not legal precept," and they do not call "into play any different faculties or involve any new principles or methods." Legal reasoning does not differ "in any fundamental respect from any other reasoning," and lawyers possess no "peculiar organs or methods for tracking and apprehending the truth. What is called the 'legal mind' is still the human mind, and it must reason according to the laws of its constitution." But for Thayer, if legal reasoning was "at bottom, . . . like all other reasoning," there were nevertheless "a thousand practical considerations" which shaped it. It was thus both the same and different, and he tended to emphasize the differences more than the similarities. Thayer thus represents something of a departure from previous thinkers. On the one hand he differentiates legal from mathematical reasoning on the traditional ground that the law does not deal with demonstration; it "deals with probabilities [but] not with certainties." On the other hand, unlike most of his predecessors, he distinguishes legal reasoning from other types of evidence that deal with probabilities.[134]

If Thayer represents something of a departure from earlier tradition, John Wigmore's monumental *Principles of Judicial Proof as Given by Legal, Psychological and General Experience* is more typical of the earlier treatise writers with its emphasis on the close connections between legal evidence and ordinary reasoning. Wigmore insists that the principles of proof—the ratiocinative process of persuasion—were of far greater importance than the rules of admissibility. For Wigmore, the principles of proof were "the natural processes of the mind in dealing with evidential facts after they are admitted to the jury; while the rules of admissibility represent artificial legal rules."[135] Wigmore believed that there had been very little interest in the principles of proof and thought himself to be the first scholar since Bentham to emphasize the principles of proof and to distinguish them from those of admissibility. It was the former that "bring into play those reasoning processes which are al-

ready the possession of intelligent and educated persons."[136] As his
most recent analyst has suggested, "Wigmore's epistemology . . .
adopted without fuss or argument, a common sense empiricism in
the tradition of Locke, Bentham, and John Stuart Mill."[137] Wigmore was especially eager to introduce rationality into the field of
evidence and to ground the principles of evidence and proof in the
context of the best current knowledge about logic and psychology.

Conclusion

From the late seventeenth to the early twentieth century and beyond, most, if not all, legal scholars were devoted to showing that
the standards of evidence and proof in the law conformed to those
in other forms of inquiry. The beyond reasonable doubt and moral
certainty standards that have been so central to Anglo-American
courts for well over a century were the result of this effort.

The beyond reasonable doubt standard articulated in both the
cases   and   the   evidence   treatises   stemmed   from   the   late
seventeenth-century cluster of ideas associated with the concept of
moral certainty and with, to use Lockean terminology, the highest
degree of probability. Once it became evident that trial by jury
required the critical evaluation of witnesses, legal thinkers began
to adopt the then current religious and philosophical ideas about
dealing with matters of fact. The writings of Wilkins, Tillotson,
Boyle, and Locke, and later Paley, Hartley, Reid, Stewart,
Whately, and Mill thus played a significant role in the evolution of
Anglo-American concepts of evidence. Although one might wish to
go behind these thinkers and investigate the contributions of scholastic philosophy and medieval and early modern canon and civil
law, there can be little doubt that eighteenth- and early nineteenth-
century legal practitioners and writers attempted to bring English
law into conformity with the most advanced philosophical thought.
Early in the seventeenth century the concern for evaluating evidence was encapsulated in "satisfied conscience," or "satisfied belief," formulas that resonated both to the cases of consciences of
the casuistical traditions and to the moral and religious obligations
of jurors serving under oath. During the seventeenth and eighteenth centuries, the concepts of probability, degrees of certainty,
and moral certainty were poured into the old formulas so that they

emerged at the end of the eighteenth century as the secular moral standard of beyond reasonable doubt. Despite the many changes in terminology we have traced over the centuries, the goal has remained essentially the same. The earliest standards we have identified were "satisfied belief" and "satisfied conscience." They were succeeded by "satisfied mind," or "satisfied understanding," or something closely approximating them. Gradually this language, too, was dropped and replaced by the concept of moral certainty and beyond reasonable doubt.[138]

Throughout this development two ideas to be conveyed to the jury have been central. The first idea is that there are two realms of human knowledge. In one it is possible to obtain the absolute certainty of mathematical demonstration, as when we say that the square of the hypotenuse is equal to the sum of the squares of the other two sides of a right triangle. In the other, which is the empirical realm of events, absolute certainty of this kind is not possible. The second idea is that, in this realm of events, just because absolute certainty is not possible, we ought not to treat everything as merely a guess or a matter of opinion. Instead, in this realm there are levels of certainty, and we reach higher levels of certainty as the quantity and quality of the evidence available to us increase. The highest level of certainty in this empirical realm in which no absolute certainty is possible is what traditionally was called "moral certainty," a certainty which there was no reason to doubt.

I am not suggesting that most technical rules of evidence flowed from philosophical principles, but rather that such rules, some of them old and venerable, could be modernized and defended through an alliance with contemporary philosophy. Thus allied, they might be viewed as both rational and in harmony with the best understanding of the human mind. In this way, selective use of religious and philosophical formulations helped to provide continued legitimacy for the jury trial and the Anglo-American legal system.

Chapter Two

The Grand Jury and the
Instability of Legal Doctrine

For long periods of English history, attitudes toward the grand jury
and the petit jury marched together because both represented popular and local elements in the system of justice. Nevertheless, the
evolutions of standards of proof for the two types of juries were
quite different. Because there was fundamental and continuous
agreement after the mid-thirteenth century that the petit jury was
to be the instrument for the final determination of guilt in felony
trials, it was in everyone's interest that the petit, or trial jury, be
accurate. Thus as we saw in Chapter 1, thinking about jury decision
making reflected long-term developments in epistemology, or,
more precisely, in conceptions of certainty and probability as they
developed in religious and philosophical discourse. The history of
grand jury standards, on the other hand, is marked by frequent,
and essentially political, conflicts over the proper role of the institution itself. The evolution of standards of proof for the grand jury
is more a reflection of these political tensions than of changes in
English epistemology.

This political conflict surfaces most dramatically in late
seventeenth-century England as one facet of the debate over royal
and judicial authority. By the seventeenth century the grand jury
was well established as the crucial screen used to sort those under
some suspicion of crime into two groups, one against whom there
was insufficient evidence to warrant trial and the other to be sent
on to trial by petit jury. The grand jury had initially been an im-

position of central government, but it actually represented a certain compromise or balance between royal centralization on the one hand and popular and local governance on the other. Although they served the interests of the central government in royal justice, grand jury members were drawn from the local populace. That particular balance was one of many that were of special concern to the English in the midst of modifying royal authority and to Americans in constructing a new central government.

This concern reflected itself in two basic positions toward the grand jury. One was associated with communitarian and quasi-democratic sentiments and, even more strongly, with support for localism. It confronted overweening central authority with honest, local men. It lauded the independent grand jury as crucial to the liberties of Englishmen, one of the key institutions distinguishing England from the centralized, bureaucratic, and oppressive states across the channel. This identification of the grand jury with individual rights is seen not only in English polemic but also in the American Bill of Rights. The other position viewed with alarm the partisanship, bias, and corruption alleged to be endemic to the grand jury. Judges, rather than biased and possibly turbulent juries, were the guarantors of English justice.

From these two positions, which were obviously part and parcel of the tension over royal authority, two differing grand jury standards of proof were derived, which for the moment we can simply call the high and the low. One required a great deal more convincing evidence than the other. Those who favored the low, or "probability" standard, wished to increase the number of indictments whether for political, religious, or more conventional crimes. The high evidentiary standard was espoused by those interested in protecting individuals, particularly those with unpopular political or religious ideas, from unwarranted prosecution. The history of grand jury evidentiary standards in this period is composed of dramatic incidents, partisan clashes, and devious maneuvers.

Before proceeding on a tour through the sometimes fugitive and incomplete—and always maddeningly imprecise—materials on the history of grand jury standards, a brief road map may be in order. Readers can best gain control over these materials if they bear in mind two distinct, but closely interacting, vectors along which ideas about the grand jury arrange themselves, the major tension or conflict internal to each vector, and the major tension or conflict between the two.

The first vector is the epistemological one that we have already examined in connection with the beyond reasonable doubt/moral certainty standard. Like trial juries, grand juries soon arrived at a point at which they no longer could determine guilt or innocence by their own personal direct experience and had to rely on testimony. They, too, found the intermediate realm of probability—lying between mere opinion, which in this context is called "suspicion," and logically demonstrable truth—to be an important tool in their new task of empirical investigation. Much of the debate on grand jury standards is an epistemological one over the level of probability the grand jury must attain before rendering a true bill of indictment.

The internal tension, or instability, of this epistemological vector is obvious. The realm of probability is a clearly intermediate one between absolute certainty and mere opinion or rumor, but it contains no clear steps, degrees, or levels of probability in the scale of just above opinion to just below certainty, and it has no agreed upon measure of quantities of probability. We have seen the difficult struggle to achieve just one such step that was finally labeled "moral certainty" or "beyond a reasonable doubt." In the range below moral certainty, lawyers and judges simply have not been able to construct steps. So if a grand jury asks simply, "How probable must guilt be before we act?" no one can answer, "You need step 3 probability or six BTUs of probability." Purely epistemological discussion of grand jury standards is inherently unstable. It constantly moves up the scale toward "satisfied conscience," "moral certainty," and "beyond reasonable doubt," or down the scale toward "suspicion" or "opinion" because there is no fixed intermediate spot at which to rest.

The second vector is one of institutions or procedures. As an institutional link in a process of prosecution, the grand jury lies somewhere between accusation and final decision on guilt or innocence. Before the trial jury replaced trial by combat, ordeal, and oath, the institutional place of the grand jury was fairly clear. It was the point at which a decision was made as to who should be put to a trial. The grand jury, or presentment jury as it is more appropriately labeled at this point, made a preliminary human judgment as to whether or not to query God. God made the final judgment. Subsequently, with both the petit jury and the grand jury as separate human groups hearing evidence to determine the probability of guilt, the problem of institutionally differentiating the grand from the petit jury became insoluble. The debate veers between a two-trial position, in which both grand and petit jury do virtually the same thing, and an accusation position, in which the grand jury is a mere formal device for registering an accusation that triggers a trial. One side accuses the other of reducing a traditionally sanctioned bulwark of liberties to a rubber stamp and the other side dwells on the absurdity of conducting two trials.

The way in which the two vectors interact to cause problems for one another is also obvious. If there were a defined probability step somewhere considerably above suspicion and considerably below beyond a reasonable doubt, then the grand jury could be clearly anchored institutionally at an intermediate point between accusation and trial. The grand jury could be the institution that determined whether the evidence was sufficient to attain this defined intermediate level of probability, and it could thus trigger the next step of determining by jury trial whether the evidence justified the higher level of beyond reasonable doubt. As long as the epistemological vector could not provide such a fixed step, the institutional problem appeared insoluble.

If one believed in teleology, it would be possible to order the long historical development which we are about to trace in the following way. For many centuries those debating grand jury standards pursued the two vectors independently. When rigorously confining themselves to the epistemological vector, they could not solve the problem of finding an intermediate probability step. As a result, their debate consisted of repeated indeterminate, fluctuating answers to the question, "How probable is probable enough to justify a trial?" When rigorously confining themselves to the institutional vector, a similar debate would ensue over rubber-stamp accusation versus double trial. Then, in the nineteenth century, the debaters rather miraculously discovered a solution if they combined the two vectors. If one fixed institutional or procedural step, hearing only the prosecution's case, was combined with one fixed epistemological step (beyond a reasonable doubt or to a moral certainty), then the epistemological problem of finding an intermediate probability step below moral certainty and above suspicion could be solved. That step would be moral certainty of guilt after hearing only one side of the case, which is roughly what lawyers mean by a *prima facie* case. Once the epistemological problem is solved, the institutional problem is solved. The grand jury is clearly placed at an intermediate point between the stage of accusation and the stage of petty jury trial.

Whether one does or does not believe in teleology or progress, it may help to understand the following discussion by visualizing the two vectors, epistemological and institutional, each of which contains an insoluble contradiction, intersecting in the nineteenth century to provide a common solution, the *prima facie* case standard, which for a brief time settled the debate over grand jury standards. Then it becomes clear that if a *prima facie* case standard avoids the absurdity of holding the whole trial twice, it still involves the major cost of holding half the trial twice. For the prosecution will have to parade its case to the grand jury and then, if successful with the grand jury, parade it again to the trial jury. As a result, the last part of this chapter is about the substitution of preliminary hearings for the grand jury *prima facie* case proceeding, and the subsequent reintroduction of all the old themes that had characterized the debate before its *prima facie* case resolution.

The Early Period

The origins of the grand jury, like those of the petty jury, are murky and will not be a major concern to us here. Its emergence generally has been tied to the Assize of Clarendon (1166), and conventional wisdom suggested that prior to that time criminal charges were usually brought by the victim. The accused then submitted to trial by ordeal, a procedure proscribed in 1215, or presented oathtakers who swore his innocence. This conventional view has been increasingly eroded, and the presentment jury is now thought to have come into existence prior to 1166, alongside private accusation by victims.[1] It may well be that early presentment juries, which were the ancestors of grand juries, based their responses on some kind of rational consideration of the evidence, or even that they sent on to the ordeal only those they thought truly accused.[2] The concept of "suspicion," which we will explore more fully in Chapter 3, appears to be significant very early in the history of criminal justice.[3] Studies now suggest that even before the Assize of Clarendon, the abolition of the ordeal, and the introduction of the petty, or trial, jury, early presentment juries were in practice stating whether or not they felt there existed a credible basis for suspicion. In this sense the accused were not sent to the ordeal until after a jury "verdict" determined probable guilt.[4] Thus, mechanisms to evaluate communal accusations seem to have been in place even before the Assize of Clarendon and the introduction of the trial jury.[5] According to Glanvill, writing not long after the Assize of Clarendon, those accused by "fama . . . publica" were sent to the ordeal, but only after "multas et varias inquisitiones et interrogationes."[6] Bracton, too, indicated that presentment jurors were questioned concerning the accuracy of accusations. It would appear, then, that while presentment juries may have had a duty to report all crimes and suspects, they announced at least some initial evaluation of community accusations.[7] Their verdict was as much a statement about character as about factual guilt or innocence. By c. 1221–1222, presentment juries functioned primarily to report persons about whom there was "suspicion." Before 1215 an adverse verdict sent the accused to the ordeal, to what afterward would become the trial jury.[8] Thus when the trial jury replaced the ordeal, a reasonably well-articulated system of accusation was already in place. There was no need to invoke the Continental inquisitorial system, whose preliminary phase depended so heavily on confession and torture.

Although it is not altogether clear how rapidly the two-tiered system came into widespread use, the Assize of Clarendon clarified and emphasized the role of the presentment jury, composed of local men who were required to accuse all those suspected of having committed crimes. The presentment jury, sometimes called the "grand inquest," typically contained twenty-three persons selected from the county. Essentially an accusing body, proceedings were initiated either by the jurors on their own knowledge (presentment), or by the victim, or by a representative of the Crown, who provided the witnesses to support the accusation (indictment). The grand inquest presented those commonly suspected. It employed the concept of "public," or "common," fame, a concept probably borrowed from ecclesiastical courts and thus from the Romano-canon tradition.[9] Public or common fame was not a capricious concept, however much it sounds so to modern ears. It excluded rumor that originated from a single source or malevolence of enemies. Public fame, in effect a requirement of consensus among a considerable number of respected persons, appears to have been a workable juristic requirement. Grand jurors found the evidence either sufficient, and returned a *billa vera*, or insufficient, and returned a finding of *ignoramus*.

Although the two-tiered system was in place soon after 1215, changes—many of which remain to be investigated—continued to take place. By the mid-fourteenth century, if not earlier, members of the presentment juries were no longer permitted to serve on trial juries in the same case. By the fifteenth century, indictment seems to have largely replaced presentment for cases of felony.[10]

Like petty juries, grand juries originally required no clearly articulated evidentiary standards, for it was assumed that they would have personal knowledge of the events and persons involved. After hearing accusations and witnesses in indictment proceedings, or on the basis of its own evaluation of community sentiment in presentment proceedings, the grand jury reached a decision. We know little more than this because little attention appears to have been paid to instructing grand juries in the early period. In addition, little subsequent research has been done on the thirteenth- to sixteenth-century period in which the two-tiered grand and petty jury system developed into that paragon so praised by Sir John Fortescue as the bulwark of English liberties against the secret, centralist, torture-ridden inquisitorial system of the Continent.

There is considerable debate among historians about how active and independent early modern grand juries were. Both John Langbein and Thomas Green see a growing passivity in the face of increased activity by justices of the peace. A substantial number of detailed studies however suggest that the grand jury remained active.[11]

While further investigations of early modern grand juries are obviously necessary, it does not appear that grand juries performed a merely ceremonial function. However, we are concerned here with the basis on which grand juries were advised or were expected to make their decisions. William Lambarde's late sixteenth-century speeches, delivered prior to the formal charge, contain little more than the usual exhortations concerning bias, vengeance, and impartiality. Such commonplace general admonitions could provide little guidance for the sixteenth- or seventeenth-century grand juryman. Lambarde, at one point, however, warned grand jurors against usurping the judicial office, suggesting tension between judges and grand jurors. Some grand jurors were going beyond their prescribed duties by hearing the "offenders that are to be charged," as well as those who "upon oath do offer their bills for the Queen."[12] Lambarde's admonitions suggest that grand juries took their investigative charge seriously, perhaps more seriously than the law demanded. The practice of hearing the defendant as well as the prosecution was evidently not unknown. The few surviving grand jury charges, although often lengthy, provide little guidance on evidentiary standards. Typically they consist of descriptions of indictable crimes, discussion of pressing legal or political problems, and conventional admonitions about impartiality.

Writing in a much earlier era, Bracton attempted a standard. Using language reminiscent of ecclesiastical courts, he wrote,

From rumour suspicion arises and from rumour and suspicion a strong presumption, which must stand until the man indicted has purged himself of such suspicion, since it admits of proof to the contrary, that is, purgation. . . . It is clear that the rumour which begets suspicion ought to arise among worthy and responsible men, not among those who wish and speak evil but wise and trustworthy persons, and it must be not once but repeatedly that complaint arises and ill-repute is made manifest. For uproar and public outcry are at times made of many things which in truth have no foundation, and thus the idle talk of the people is not to be heeded.[13]

The concepts of common fame and suspicion are overlapping, if not precisely identical, and were still associated with early seventeenth-century indictments.

Cynthia Herrup's detailed studies of East Sussex grand juries shed light on suspicion standards during this period. These grand juries concentrated on serious crimes of theft and felony and followed an informal, yet fairly consistent, set of evidentiary guidelines. The "essential ingredient for indictment was a cohesive accusation that interlocked crime, alleged criminal and, if relevant, stolen property. . . . The concern for tightly investigated accusa-

tions is the predominant pattern that emerges from examining specific cases accepted and rejected."[14]

Where the death penalty was required, grand jurors proved un-
sympathetic to accusations based "too heavily upon circumstances
and mere suspicion." Suspicions unsupported by substantial proof
were thus regularly turned away. General suspicion might constitute sufficient ground for questioning or accusation, but grand juries were wary about returning indictments based upon supposition. We should note here that information collected by the justice
of the peace was itself not introduced in court, except under special
circumstances, and that witnesses thus appeared directly before
grand and petty juries. "Ill fame" and a previous criminal record
alone were not enough to insure indictment if "cohesive evidence"
linking the accused and the crime was inadequate.[15]

Herrup's study suggests that earlier notions of "common fame"
and "suspicion" continued to provide the common formulation.
The concept of "suspicion," to be found in the justice of the peace
manuals in connection with arrest, was employed by grand juries
as well, despite the fact that the manuals do not mention it in connection with indictment or presentment and provide almost no instruction on grand jury evidentiary standards.[16] The concept of
common fame was a familiar one from the medieval period onward
and was employed routinely by, but not limited to, the ecclesiastical courts. A 1626 speech in the House of Commons outlined the
distinction used in the ecclesiastical courts between fame, which
was a majority suspicion, and rumor, which was only a minority
suspicion. Later the same year the House of Commons debated
whether common fame provided sufficient grounds to accuse the
duke of Buckingham.[17] William Fulbecke defined fame as "a common report proceeding from suspicion, and published by the voices
of men." Following Bracton, he distinguishes it from rumor, "because that is adverse whispering of men, which is not as effective
as fame. Fame constans is that which is dispersed abroad neyther
by men unknown, nor of light credit."[18]

The lack of concern with evidentiary standards in grand jury
charges and in the magistrate handbooks suggests either that there
was no problem perceived or that the oath, "To present the Truth,
the whole Truth, and nothing but the Truth," on the basis of diligent inquiry, was deemed self-explanatory. Dalton's famous *Coun-*

try Justice, an extremely popular work read by many generations of English and Americans, describes grand jury proceedings *as a trial*, rather than as an accusation, noting that, in matters of crime, the English "passed a double jury." For Dalton, indictment was "as much found to be true" by grand juries as by petty juries.[19]

The greatest legal authority of this period, Sir Edward Coke, had relatively little to say about indictments, although what he did say was to be widely quoted in the 1680s, when the issue of evidentiary standards had become controversial. In a comment concerning the reign of Edward I, Coke noted that "in those days (as yet it ought to be) indictments, taken in the absence of the party, were formed upon plain and direct proof, and not upon probabilities or inferences."[20] This reference to cases in which the accused were absent attracted little notice or comment for several decades. Indeed, there is little to suggest that Coke or his contemporaries considered grand juries to be a problem.

The Crime of Witchcraft

What little late sixteenth- and early seventeenth-century discussion of grand jury evidentiary standards exists is largely found in connection with the relatively new felony of witchcraft. It is always difficult to know whether practices connected with this crime were peculiar to it or were common to other felony proceedings, most of which were less well documented than the witchcraft cases. This problem arises particularly in relation to the intrusion of Romano-canon concepts into English law, a topic discussed subsequently in greater detail. Although it is reasonable to argue that the introduction of Romano-canon language of proof into English sources was peculiar to this crime, it is also possible that there was some spill-over into the discussion of criminal procedure more generally, or that Romano-canon concepts were more familiar in discussions of crime than we have traditionally believed. As we shall see, such concepts, particularly in connection with arrest, seem to have entered legal literature rather early, perhaps via Bracton or through the ecclesiastical courts. They also seem to have increased in the mid-sixteenth century, when justices of the peace were given statutory authority to examine criminal suspects. Romano-canon concepts clearly made an impact on discussion of grand jury evaluation, at least in connection with the crime of witchcraft.

John Cotta's *Trial of Witchcraft* (1616) makes it clear that the grand jurors must evaluate the credit of the witnesses to the "manifest magical and supernaturall act," and should consider whether they were "substantiall, sufficient, able to judge, free from exception of malice, partialitie, distraction [and] folly." They were to have "conference and counsell" with those learned and experienced in "those affairs," in order to insure that there was "no deception of sense" or "mistaking of reason or imagination."[21]

Cotta also made use of the distinction between probability and certainty: "in things that carry only probability, diligence doth beget and produce verity and truth of opinion." He who could "discerne the validitie, nature, difference and right use of probabilities, doth most seldom in his opinions mistake or erre." Although "circumstances and presumption," which carried only probability, were not sufficient for a jury to condemn a witch, they did provide "sufficient warrant" to bring the matter to trial.[22] Clearly then, in Cotta's view, grand juries were to actively evaluate the case against the accused witch, rather than engaging in *pro forma* confirmation of accusations, and were to bring indictments on a lesser standard of proof than would be required for conviction. The witchcraft literature of the early seventeenth century thus seems the first occasion on which the differing standards for indictment and conviction are explicitly discussed, but we cannot tell whether Cotta conceived of this difference as applying only to witchcraft cases or as a general rule for all felony indictments.

Richard Bernard's *Guide to Grand Jurors in Cases of Witchcraft* (1627), a more widely known work, insisted that unless the "Witchcraft be very cleere," it was better "to write an *Ignoramus* than upon oath to set down *Billa Vera* and so thrust an intricate case upon a Jury of simple men," who too often proceeded "upon relations of meere presumptions, and these sometimes very weake ones too, to take away men's lives."[23] Grand jurors, being men of higher status, were expected to have a greater capacity to distinguish between truth and falsehood.

"So as not to be deceived," grand jurors were not to be credulous "in receiving reports as true and over confidently averring them to be." They were not to passively accept the testimony offered them, but were to diligently inquire into "the wisdom and discretion of the witnesses, whether they can discern well between reall and counterfeit acts, . . . what sufficient triall has been made of the supposed bewitched, as also by whome and how long." In addition to determining whether the testifiers were "indifferent neighbors" or "fearful, superstitious, . . . children or old silly persons . . . not easily credited," grand juries were to consider whether "trickery or fraud" were possible and whether illnesses might be explained by natural causes. Bernard, like Cotta, advised grand jurors to consult expert witnesses. If a physician were unavailable, they were to consult other learned persons and medical books. Parties were to be examined separately and attempts made to distinguish the partial testimony of friends and relations from that of "indifferent relators." He pointed out that "there may concurre many seeming probabilities which commonly mislead . . . for want of judgment and for want of thoroughly weighing the weight of them . . . taking such presumptions for sufficient proofe."[24] Strong presumptions were required for indictment. Even "if the suspicion upon great probabilities, and very strong presumptions, yet unless they doe leade to prove" the diabolic compact required by the statute, the suspects should be released.[25] Bernard clearly assumes and requires a grand jury that is actively engaged in investigation and evaluation, which he urges to be especially careful in analyzing testimony and evidence in witchcraft cases.

Bernard's book, which was reprinted in 1629, 1630, and again in 1680 and 1686, proved even more influential than its publication history suggests. Portions were included in Dalton's handbook for justices of the peace, perhaps the most influential seventeenth- and early eighteenth-century legal compendium in both England and the American colonies. Like Cotta, Bernard employs the Continental legal language of presumption. In Roman law jurisdictions, however, such presumptions would have come into play in making the decision as to whether the accused would be examined under torture. Various evidentiary concepts seem to have migrated from Roman to English common law, and it may well be that cases of witchcraft, a crime of European-wide significance, where Continental scholarly discussion was widely read in England, were an important link in that transmission.

Although the Civil War and interregnum era witnessed an outpouring of criticism of the English legal system, and considerable attention was given to various aspects of criminal procedure and punishment, no issues relating to the grand jury were raised by the reformers.[26]

Prior to the late seventeenth century, grand jury proceedings in general, and evidentiary standards in particular, aroused little comment. Only in the relatively new and troublesome crime of witchcraft did evidentiary matters relating to the grand jury appear to merit discussion. A good deal of Romano-canon terminology of presumptions, probabilities, and full and half proofs entered the literature concerning witchcraft. Despite the enhanced role of the justice of the peace in the criminal process, grand juries appear to have actively evaluated evidence of crimes brought to their attention, although they did so without very specific evidentiary standards to guide them. Notions of common fame and suspicion, however, appear to have been commonly employed. This situation appears to have continued until the Restoration era, when the nature of grand jury indictments and appropriate standards of evidence became a hotly debated issue in both professional and lay circles.

The Late Seventeenth Century

As we have seen in Chapter 1, the late seventeenth century was a period in which epistemological and evidentiary issues were gaining the attention of a very diverse group of philosophers, naturalists, theologians, and historians. It was during this period that questions of the nature of probability and degrees of certainty available in matters of fact were being explored by English intellectuals.[27] Some of the terminology being used by intellectuals in these fields was also found in legal discussions, although usually with some time delay. Discussion of grand jury standards of evidence thus was not taking place in an intellectual vacuum. More important, it took shape in the context of evolving concepts of trial jury verdicts and in the context of heated political debate.[28]

The Restoration era, and particularly the years 1681 and 1682, brought evidentiary issues into public discussion of the competing claims of the judiciary and the grand juries. At times this tension was described as one between the people and the judges; on other occasions it took the form of a party issue between Whig and Tory. As the debate became more politicized, issues were more likely to be aired in poem or pamphlet than in legal treatises or judicial pronouncements. Indeed, there was no standard place where judicial pronouncements or instructions might be expected to appear because grand jury proceedings were not recorded.

The first skirmish, which occurred in 1667, involved a conflict between Chief Justice John Kelyng and a Somersetshire grand jury over a bill of indictment for murder. According to an unfriendly critic, Kelyng "would have usurped a lordly dictatorial power" and had "commanded" the grand jurors to find the bill "for which they saw no evidence." Upon their refusal, Kelyng threatened them and "assumed an arbitrary power to fine them." Had he been successful, the grand jury would have become "the basest Vassals of the judge."[29] The foreman of the jury, himself a member of Parliament, took his complaint to the House of Commons, and impeachment proceedings were initiated against Kelyng for illegally fining and imprisoning a number of grand and petty juries. A parliamentary committee was appointed to inquire and report on how judges "at their own wills and pleasure impose fines and imprisoning grand and petty juries for adhering to their verdicts." In the course of defending himself, Kelyng said that in charging grand juries he generally advised that "if they find the proofs be slight or not material, then to find it *Ignoramus* and if sufficiently proved . . . to bring it in *billa vera*."[30] Kelyng further claimed he had consulted his fellow judges on this point, and they with "one consent" held his position to be a "just and lawful" one.[31]

Sir Matthew Hale, writing his *History of the Pleas of the Crown* about this time, felt not only that fining of jurors was "an arbitrary practice," but also that the practice was of recent origin and was increasing.[32] Although the House of Commons eventually dropped its proceedings against Kelyng, it resolved after a four-hour debate that he "hath used an Arbitrary and Illegal Power . . . dangerous to English Lives and Liberties" which "tends to the introducing of an Arbitrary Government."[33] A bill was introduced forbidding justices and judges from menacing, fining, and punishing juries. John Vaughan, soon to become chief justice of common pleas, appears to have been the sole speaker on the bill's second reading.[34]

Although the bill did not become law, Chief Justice Vaughan's

landmark decision in Bushel's case (1670) ended the practice of fining jurors. The principles enumerated in Vaughan's opinion, which
resulted from consultation with all the king's judges, were quickly
adopted for grand juries and passed into the law and lore of both
grand and petty juries. Bushel's case had an enormous impact on
the evolution of the jury. Its significance becomes clear only in the
light of late seventeenth-century politics.[35]

Evidentiary criteria for grand jury decisions were first critically
examined in Zachary Babington's *Advice to Grand Jurors in Cases
of Blood*.[36] The *Advice*, which appeared in 1677 and was reprinted
in 1680 and 1692, circulated fairly widely during the period in
which grand jury issues were most hotly debated. The fact that
Babington's *Advice* had the approval of Francis North, a prominent
Tory judge, may have given his volume semiofficial status, at least
temporarily. If Babington's pamphlet did not have a party flavor at
the time it was initially published, it acquired a Tory identification
by the time it was reprinted. The *Advice* was motivated by Babington's concern that grand jurors were failing to find indictments in
cases of murder and were frequently reducing charges of murder
to lesser offenses. Babington's *Advice* is important for our purpose
because it initiates public exploration of grand jury fact evaluation,
and indicates that the Restoration era was one of considerable ambiguity, confusion, and lack of consensus on the nature and function
of grand juries.

Babington himself, who had served as the assize clerk on the
Oxford circuit for twenty years, was troubled by the standard practice in which grand jurors heard only the prosecution, and wished
"to be instructed how any Grand Juror (that hears one side) can
satisfie his Conscience." He might well be puzzled, for a "satisfied
conscience," as we have seen, could only be obtained after full and
rational consideration of all the relevant evidence. Babington man-
ages to turn on its head the fact that the grand jury heard only the
prosecution's case. He argues that because it did not hear both
sides, the grand jury might enlarge, but not reduce, charges and
ought not to dismiss an indictment simply because it concluded the
party was innocent. He also acknowledged that the grand jury was
bound by oath to present the truth. He argued, however, that the
truth referred to in oath was not to be understood "in a plain literal
and Grammatical sense," but only in a "legal sense, and according

to" what he called the "common practice of legal proceedings in these cases." Grand juries were not sworn to say the whole truth of the offense, for that would mean "there would be no need of another trial." Their duty to tell the truth meant only that they must neither suppress nor falsify the truth.[37]

For Babington, an indictment was simply an accusation, and the evidentiary standard for an accusation was not the "satisfied conscience" test of the petty jury. Grand jury proceedings were thus by definition incomplete and might be cursory. Though grand juries might examine all the prosecution witnesses, a single one would suffice if it "induced a strong and pregnant Presumption." If the grand jurors found "only probable matter contained," they were nonetheless to introduce it to the court as their presentment or accusation: "if they have sense or Smell of Blood in the Indictment, it is enough for them to leave it to a further quest of what shall come after." Like Fulbecke before him, Babington compared the indictment to a citation to the ecclesiastical court for a public fame, suggesting that "A strong Suspicion, and the Fame of the Country may (in many cases) be sufficient for a Grand Jury to find a Bill."[38]

Babington referred favorably to an allegedly ancient form of indictment, which "is as much as if the Grand Jury should say, We judge it fit that it be further enquired of, whether it be truly so indeed, as it here supposed." An indictment, thus, was "no more [than] an offense supposed and laid to one's charge to answer." Indeed "Supposal . . . is all that can be inferr'd from the Indictment." It was merely a "Declaration upon Oath, and must, therefore, (for the satisfaction of those that are sworn) contain that which for substance seem to them (*prima facie*) to be a probable truth, and a transgression of a Law."[39]

A *billa vera* was the endorsement of any indictment or presentment "which they find to be probably True (mark these words) probably true." The adjective, *vera*, thus did not "signifie Truth," but only "meet, reason or fit . . . for the further enquiry of another Jury." The *billa vera*, therefore, should not be called a "verdict," because verdicts "ought to be as true as the Gospel the Jurors swear upon."[40]

Employing Coke's civil law derived terminology of presumption, Babington insisted that a "great and violent Presumption" was "sufficient for a Grand Jury to find an Indictment."[41] Any "strongly suspected" person should therefore be brought to trial. Babington, however, failed to note that "great and violent presumption," as defined by Coke and the civilians, implied far better evidence than that which would engender mere "supposal." "Great and violent presumption," as used by Coke, was exemplified by being found holding a bloody knife at the scene of a murder, something far closer to certitude than Babington's "smell of blood." If at one point Babington suggests that a "great and violent presumption" was not only sufficient but also necessary, and at another that the party must be "strongly suspected," the position that mere "supposal" was sufficient dominates the *Advice*.

Evidently, at the time Babington wrote there was no authoritative statement on grand jury decisions or "verdicts." Coke, as we have seen, was vague about grand juries. Although Sir Matthew Hale was the most respected and admired judge of the era, the results of his immense legal erudition would not be published until many years after his death in 1676. His *History of the Pleas of the Crown*, which became so influential in the eighteenth and nineteenth centuries, was thus unknown to his contemporaries, and could not figure in the debates of the Restoration era. His comments on grand jury standards, however, may be taken as a fairly accurate description of the state of law of the 1660s and 1670s. Hale took the position that grand juries "in a case [where] there be probable evidence, . . . ought to find the bill, because it is but an accusation, and the party is to be put on his trial afterward." If on hearing the king's witnesses or "upon their own knowledge of the credibility of the witnesses they are dissatisfied," grand jurors might return the bill *ignoramus*. Like Babington, Hale criticized grand juries for anticipating the evidence of the petty jury. Hale and Babington thus were not far apart. Hale did not define the "probable" in "probable evidence," and associated it neither with the low standard of "supposal" nor with the far higher one of "violent presumption," and, like Babington, Hale is firm about hearing only the prosecution. He does allow assessment of witness credibility, a point which would be hotly debated in the 1680s.[42]

Such other scattered evidence as exists for the 1660s and 1670s indicates considerable confusion and potential for later conflict and also indicates that the Babington-Hale probability standard was rather widely employed, although not to the total exclusion of a far higher "satisfied conscience" standard.[43]

If lack of clarity characterized the 1660s and 1670s, that ambiguity was not viewed as having momentous consequences for the political and legal fabric. From about 1680 on, however, we can usefully speak of Whig and Tory positions, though it is necessary to be cautious about attributing modern notions of party to these groupings. Whigs became identified with the rights of grand juries to remain independent of the judiciary. They also became increasingly hostile to the probabilistic standard, which they felt put citizens at risk whenever the government or others might wish. Tories, on the other hand, tended to perceive the grand jury as an accusing body that required relatively little in the way of evidence to support an indictment. Politics shaped criminal trials and the evolution of legal doctrine to an enormous degree between 1678 and the end of the century. Indeed, the party-laden formulations of the 1680s shaped the discussion of grand jury standards for well over a century in both England and the United States.

The new political entanglements with legal proceedings began with the Popish Plot trials, which were a part of the Whig effort to divert the succession from the Roman Catholic James, duke of York. The political conflict then shifted temporarily to the efforts of the Whig controlled Parliament to exclude James from the throne by legislative means. During this period, the Whigs firmly controlled the London City government. Elected Whig sheriffs thus controlled the selection of the London and Middlesex grand juries, insuring that political cases coming before them would be decided in "appropriate" ways. The political implications became increasingly clear when, after the dissolution of Parliament, Charles II launched a number of counterattacks against the Whigs. The first of these consisted of a series of treason charges laid against Whigs, such as Stephen Colledge and Lord Shaftesbury, for participating in an alleged Protestant plot against the Crown. The second involved a struggle for control of the City government through *quo warranto* proceedings to deprive city corporations of their privileges, particularly that of electing sheriffs. The king's purpose was to insure the selection of Tory sheriffs, who would in turn provide panels of Tory grand jurors.

In the process the grand jury evidentiary issue became deeply imbedded in politics, particularly the politics of the City of London. Whig sheriffs selected political sympathizers who would willingly provide *ignoramus* verdicts in cases involving violations of the Conventicle Act and other legislation unfavorable to their dissenting allies. Tory authors of this repressive legislation were angry at grand jury outcomes that appeared to effectively nullify the statutes. Given their more unreserved support for the monarchy and their greater inclination to be favorable to the king's government, they could hardly be expected to favor theoretical apologies for Whig *ignoramus* verdicts.

The 1680 case of the well-known radical bookseller Francis Smith, who had been the official Parliamentary printer during the period of Whig control, suggests how politicized the issue had become even before the Shaftesbury case brought the grand jury issue to the national stage. Smith's case also shows how antagonism to the king's judges was enmeshed in the controversy over grand juries. Smith, whose case had been thrown out by the grand jury, defended himself in an apologia addressed to Shaftesbury. In it he described how Jeffreys, then recorder of London, had perverted the legal process by "subtle Suggestions, wheedling Speaches" and "lowd and often repeated Reproaches and Threats," which were designed to draw the grand jurors from the "true Judgement" of their conscience. Although they "could not in their conscience bring it in any otherwise than *Ignoramus*" and thew out the bill, their verdict had been "scraped out" and the bill brought in again. When grand jurors returned it *ignoramus* as well, Jeffreys reportedly became enraged and returned the bill of indictment to them for a third time, with the predictable result. Not only had Jeffreys "villified" and "reproached" the grand jurors in open court, but had treated them as if "void of Honesty and Conscience." After polling the grand jurors individually and separately with the same result, Jeffreys accused them of perjury and attempted to get Smith, to accuse himself.[44] Whatever the merits of the case, the grand juries and judges in cases of this kind were likely to view one another with hostility and imputations of party malice.

It is in this highly charged atmosphere that we must take note of the 1680 tract *The Grand Jury-man's Oath*. The first of several pamphlets of the 1680s dealing with grand juries, this tract takes the form of a dialogue in which a barrister, who obviously speaks for the author, instructs a naive grand juryman. Grand jurors should take pains that they are "proceeding on a mature and strict examination" resulting in a verdict based on both testimony and their own knowledge. The barrister's analysis of the "truth, the whole truth and nothing but the truth," like Babington's, required stretching common usage. The truth required was that "Truth sufficient to make a just Accusation against a nocent Person." The "whole truth" meant only that no portion be concealed. "Nothing but the truth" meant that no known falsity of accusation be presented.[45]

The barrister acknowledged that not all those indicted were convicted. Yet both outcomes "may be true in their several proper respects. . . . I may (for certain weighty Reasons and Proofs that I have considered) *verily believe*, that the accused is guilty. . . . I may *swear* that I believe so, and judge it my Duty to Present him."[46] Yet he may be innocent. "And perhaps" when the defense is heard, "I may think so too." Grand jurors thus "Present offenses which they find *fit for a Trial*," after hearing the witnesses against the accused. They

do not, nay cannot, hear anything of his *defense*, Nor to Confront or weaken the Evidence brought against him, and so cannot be intended to give in more than a *verisimilary* or *probable* Charge; which by what they have heard, they do aver upon their Oaths, does seem to them to be *Just* and *true* and fit for Justice to take Cognizance of.[47]

The oath requirement that jurors decide, "According to their best skill and knowledge," thus denoted "not an absolute Certainty, but as things appear." A *billa vera* was thus only an "Accusation on Just and Reasonable Grounds." It was "only a laying on, or probable Charging of a Crime, and speaks of it but as a supposition so that by *Billa Vera* can only be understood a Bill that appears to have Truth in it, . . . fit for the Enquiry of another Jury: the adjective *Vera* in this place not so strictly signifying *True* as *meet*, fit, or reasonable."[48] An *ignoramus* meant they "find *no Cause* either from what they have heard from the Witnesses, or know of their own knowledge to Commend it to a further Inquiry." "They must . . . have some knowledge or good probable proof on Oath on which they verily believe the matter deserving Tryal, and the Party

guilty." The difficulty with this formulation was that the standard
of "meet, fit, and reasonable" did not mean "true," but at the same
time did require *belief* in guilt. These were separate and not altogether compatible standards. While the barrister sticks to the
rather permissive Hale-Babington probability standard, his sym-
pathies are obviously Whig. He defends the secrecy of grand jury
proceedings and denounces judicial attacks on their independence.[49]

The primary thrust of *The Grand Jury-man's Oath* is to confirm
the probability standard of Babington and Hale. Nevertheless it
also insisted that the jury must "verily believe" the party to be
guilty. Pushed by the events of the next several years, the Whigs
soon dropped or qualified the probability doctrine and put far
greater emphasis on belief of guilt. It is noteworthy that while many
Whig tracts on juries and grand juries were reprinted, this tract
had only the 1680 printing.

The Cases of Stephen Colledge and the
Earl of Shaftesbury

In 1681 the appropriate standard for grand jurors became a major
political issue. The first case to attract nationwide attention was that
of Stephen Colledge, "the Protestant joiner," accused of treason in
July 1681 for participation in an alleged Protestant plot against the
Crown. After the Whig-dominated London grand jury considered
the matter and returned the indictment *ignoramus*, Colledge was
indicted by an equally partisan Tory Oxford panel. The testimony
of one Crown witness favored Colledge and that of six others did
not. Argument centered on whether the grand jury necessarily
must believe the six or might weigh their credibility, or whether
the grand jury had merely expressed its political preferences.
These issues were widely discussed in London and were explored
in pamphlet and broadside.

A *Modest Vindication*, for example, asserted that the grand jury
must judge the "Credit and Validity of the Evidence" and give more
credit to one Protestant than to half a dozen "Church Papists, or
Masquerading Protestants," who might well have been hired by the
Pope, the Devil, or their agents, the Jesuits.[50] The *Letter of the*

Grand Jury of Oxford to the Grand Jury of London in turn criticized the London grand jury for its eagerness to indict in the Popish
Plot trials, and insisted that "we do really believe in our Consciences," that treasonable words were spoken, and that there were
Protestant as well as Popish traitors.[51]

In a companion case against John Rouse, the court did not wish
to allow the London grand jurors to consult privately. There followed a long debate on the customs and privileges of grand jurors
and, most particularly, on whether the practice of the day required
secret or public examination of witnesses.[52] The jurors eventually
agreed to hear the witnesses in open court, but insisted on a "long
and tedious Examination," and then spent three hours in private
conference. When questioned about their *ignoramus* finding, they
insisted "that they were satisfied in their consciences of what they
had done, and further added, that they could not believe what the
witness had Sworn."[53]

In these skirmishes, preliminary to the Shaftesbury case, the
high "satisfied conscience" standard had been invoked, indeed invoked by both sides, and there had been considerable agreement
on the duty of the grand jury to evaluate the credibility of
witnesses.

Soon afterward, Anthony Ashley Cooper, first Earl of Shaftesbury, the most prominent Whig opponent of royal policy, was
charged with treason. Recently removed from the seat of power,
Shaftesbury had spent some weeks in the Tower of London before
being brought before the grand jury of Middlesex, a body expected
to be favorable to the Whig leader. Lord Chief Justice Pemberton,
who was anything but sympathetic to Shaftesbury and the Whigs,
and must have anticipated a stubborn partiality, took a good deal
of time and effort to acquaint the grand jury with "the nature of
these bills." Indeed, Pemberton's partisan comments were virtually
the sole judicial analysis of the grand jury for well over a century.
Grand jurymen were to consider "upon what evidence you shall
have given to you, there be any reason or ground for the King to
call these persons to an account, if there be probable ground, it is
as much as you are to enquire into: you are not to judge the persons."[54] While they were not to indict where there is "no colour
nor ground of it: where there is no kind of suspicion of a crime,
nor reason to believe that the things can be proved," yet "any rea-

son or ground" was enough. They were to "enquire, whether that what you hear be any cause or reason for the King to put the party to answer it." They were obviously not to inquire as strictly as the trial jury. "A probable cause or some ground . . . is enough, for you to find a bill."[55] Indictment thus required relatively little evidence and little mental conviction or belief on the part of those listening to the evidence—and certainly not the full satisfaction of conscience claimed necessary by some in the wake of the Colledge trial.

Acting in an extremely partisan fashion, Pemberton supported the request of the King's Counsel that evidence be given publicly. The equally partisan grand jury, four members of which had been Whig members of the Exclusion Parliament, insisted, albeit unsuccessfully, that it be permitted to follow the traditional mode of private and secret examination. Pemberton also informed the grand jury that it was not to concern itself with the credibility of the witnesses. Witnesses were *"prima facie* credible, unless you of your own knowledge know the contrary." Credibility, he argued, could not be questioned because the king was not present to defend the credit of his witnesses, and because "all men are intended credible till there are objections against them, and till their credits come to be examined." Mr. Papillon, a sophisticated Whig grand juror, did not accept this view, and asked whether the judge "doth not think that we are within the compass of our own understanding and conscience to give our judgement?" Papillon insisted that if the jurors could not consider the credibility of the witnesses, they could "not satisfy their conscience."[56]

Papillon thus invoked the standard of "satisfied conscience," which by the later seventeenth century had become the accepted standard for petty juries. Pemberton, nevertheless, insisted that the grand jury was to hear "only evidence against the prisoner; therefore, for you to enter into proofs, or expect any here, concerning the credit of the witness, it is impossible for you to do justice at that rate."[57] The grand jury, however, returned an *ignoramus*, to the pleasure and shouting of the London crowd.

We must not assume that the Whig position was completely unrepresented on the bench. Lord Commissioner Keble, if only in passing, noted that no life was taken under the English system of justice unless two separate juries were satisfied that the accused was guilty.[58] He assumes that the degree of mental satisfaction was the same for both grand and petty juries.

Despite the Whig victory in the Shaftesbury case, the legal issue was far from settled. It remained unclear how the grand jury, which heard only evidence for the prosecution, might arrive at a "satisfied conscience" or present the "truth" required by the oath. This was particularly perplexing if grand juries were not permitted to assess the credibility of the witnesses' testimony and were to reach decisions merely on the basis of "any reason or ground" and/or "probable cause."

If the *ignoramus* in the Shaftesbury case halted the judicial attack on the Whigs, it also brought the question of evidentiary elements in grand jury proceedings directly before the public. Several influential tracts appeared that argued against the probability standard propounded by Babington, Hale, and Pemberton and that emphasized instead the "truth" requirements of the juryman's oath and the need for a "satisfied conscience."

One of the tracts, *Ignoramus Vindicated*, consists of a dialogue in which "Indifference" explains to "Prejudice" the error of his ways. Prejudice complains of "the Ignoramus men, that refuse sometimes to find Bills, though there be Positive Oaths before them." He is soon taught, however, that "*Positive Oaths* are not always *true Evidence*" and that the grand jurymen in question were neither dishonest nor such "Ignoramus fellows as you take them for," but rather "Persons that have . . . due regard" for their duty and office. Positive proof or testimony itself was not necessarily good evidence, for the jurors themselves were "Judges of the Evidence." If they were not judges of the evidence, then they were "just nothing" and had no function at all. Grand jurors must be fact evaluators. If they have "good and sufficient Grounds, not to believe" those who testify, they must record an *ignoramus*, "because there comes no credible proof to satisfy them."[59]

The author invoked the distinction between legal and credible witnesses. He emphasized the role of grand jury inquiry. If the grand jury determined that prosecution originated in malice, then it was obliged to find an *ignoramus* verdict. Malice, of course, could not be determined unless those who testified were "strictly" examined. Referring directly to the Shaftesbury and Rouse cases, the author noted that grand jurymen were "being forced (as of late), for I know no ancient precedents for it to hear and Examine Evidence in Court" rather than in private. He objected vehemently to this departure from tradition because secrecy was essential to prevent exposure of individuals before a proper trial.[60]

Jurymen were "upon their Oaths, and ought to follow the Dictates of their own belief and Understanding." It thus went without saying that the "court should not meddle or interrupt" because it was "bound by Verdict, not by the Evidence."[61] It was impossible for the Court even to know whether or not "a Jury goes contrary to Evidence." The pamphlet made good use of Bushel's case, which determined that juries could not be punished for their verdict. Vaughan had carefully distinguished between the evidence of witnesses and the jury's verdict: "A Witness swears but to what he hath heard or seen, generally or more largely, to what hath fallen under his sense: But a Juryman swears to what he can infer and conclude from the Testimony of such Witnesses, by the Act and Force of his Understanding."[62] The reasoning faculties must, therefore, be applied to the evidence put before it. The "Act and Force" of the jurors' understanding must evaluate, "infer and conclude." Their intellectual processes must be employed in order to reach a verdict in which they could believe.

The question was then raised as to whether the judge, who after hearing all the same evidence as the jury, should be permitted to direct the verdict or punish the jury for a wrong verdict. Following Chief Justice Vaughan in Bushel's case, the author states that judge and jury might honestly differ about the evidence, much in the same way that two judges might differ.[63] It was clear that "a man cannot see by another's Eye, nor hear by another's Ear; no more can a Man conclude or infer the things to be resolved, by another's Understanding or Reasoning: And though the Verdict be right that the Jury give, yet they being not assured that it is so from their own Understanding, are forsworne, at least in *Foro Conscientiae*."[64]

Vaughan's argument in Bushel's case was thus applied to grand juries, which, it was asserted, must both inquire diligently and assess the credibility of testimony before reaching their verdicts. This attempt to enlist Vaughan's prescriptions for petty juries in support of the grand jury is the most powerful argument of the pamphlet. When the pamphleteer insists that the grand jurors evaluate credibility on the basis of their own knowledge and understanding, and mixes this insistence with invocation of the words "satisfy" and "conscience," all in the context of former discussions of the trial jury, the message is pretty clear. Although it may hear only Crown witnesses and should operate secretly, the grand jury should indict only if it is as persuaded of the guilt of the accused as a trial jury must be to convict.

The most famous and most frequently reprinted pamphlet on grand juries was Sir John Somers's *Security of English-Men's Lives*. Reprinted six times in England between 1681 and 1771 and printed in the American colonies in 1720 and 1773, this Whig response to the Shaftesbury trial transcended its immediate political origins and became a classic Whig statement of political freedom. Somers works his way through a number of themes that will be frequently repeated by others: Recent judicial action threatens to render grand jurors "the basest vassals to the judges." The independent grand jury is the linchpin of the entire criminal justice system. It brings offenders to justice *and* protects the innocent from false accusation, guaranteeing the traditional rights of Englishmen, particularly their political rights in relation to the Crown. And then the partisan note: the grand jury protects honest men from the "Forgeries, Perjuries, [and] Subordinations" of "our Popish faction." The grand jury joins Parliament as a Whig counterweight to the arbitrary power of the monarch and his judges. Its true functions must not be eroded by Crown lawyers and judges who seek to dominate it.[65]

Integral to this stance is a fully articulated standard of proof for indictment. Basing himself on their oath, and rejecting attempts to interpret away the oath's "known and understood" and "genuine common meaning," Somers insists that the grand jurors "enquire diligently after the Truth of everything." He notes that "many have of late" claimed that "the grand jury is neither to make so strict enquiry . . . nor to look for so clear Evidence of the Crime as the Petty Jury." The notion that they might indict "Upon a Superficial Enquiry, and bare Probabilities" was extremely dangerous because it would "be equal to the total laying aside of Grand Juries." The probability standard would obliterate any difference between arraignment without presentment and presenting on "slight grounds." Somers explained that "probable" was a logical term, meaning the "appearance but no certainty of truth." "Probability" might be appropriate to rhetoric which "worketh up the passions,"

but it had no place where the "Object is Truth." It was thus wrong
to admit of propositions "as may be false as well as true." The rules
to be followed were those which were "least liable to Deception."
Probabilities must be "banished from uncorrupted Tribunals as a
hindrance to the discovery of Truth."[66] Rhetoric, ever since its inception in ancient Greece, has been associated with probability and
contrasted with the truth sought by philosophers. Somers's statements suggest not only something about late seventeenth-century
attitudes toward rhetoric but also something about the erosion of
traditional concepts of probability and certainty, the latter of which
was associated with truth.

One of the chief dangers of the probability standard was "the
degree of probability" required to find a bill of indictment. Because
it was impossible to fix that degree, decisions would inevitably depend on the "Fancies" of men. The innocent would thus be
"brought into danger." If the term "probability" was taken according to common usage rather than its meaning in traditional logic,
that is, "no more likely, or rather likely than unlikely," then the
situation was just as bad. For this situation, Somers insisted, was
like a wager, and wagers were obviously inappropriate to a court of
justice. He therefore explicitly rejected the view presented in the
Grand Jury-man's Oath of the previous year that "only a Verisimilar or probable charge" would do or that far less evidence was
required by grand jurors than petty jurors.[67] Thus Somers and the
Whig author of *Ignoramus Vindicated* had moved beyond the position taken in the *Grand Jury-man's Oath*.

Following the language and categories of the philosophers of the
day, Somers noted that if grand juries could not expect "infallible
mathematical demonstration," the highest standard of certainty,
then conscientious grand juries "often find that which in their consciences doth fully persuade them, that the accused Person is
guilty." Full persuasion, he assured his reader, did not mean that
the bill they swore to was necessarily true, but "that they believe
that it is so." They must be "fully convinced." "Full persuasion,"
"belief," "fully convinced," and the "satisfied conscience" were the
standards which, for Somers, must replace the pernicious "probability." "Suspicion and probable Causes" must not be permitted to
"bring any men's life and estate into danger."[68] These presumably
laxer standards for arrest and search warrants were inappropriate
for grand juries.

It should be noted that Somers, although conversant with the philosophical terminology of his day, was still writing in the pre-Lockean era. John Locke's *Essay Concerning Human Understanding*, published several years later in 1690, gave a new clarity to the concept of probability. According to Locke, an extremely close associate of Shaftesbury, no statement or conclusion based on human testimony could ever reach any higher than probability. Locke and his followers saw that courts could only deal in probabilities, so issues of degree of probability were crucial. According to a Lockean perspective, "satisfied conscience," "moral certainty," and "beyond reasonable doubt" remained in the realm of the probable. Their probability, however, was much higher than those engendered by notions of "probable cause," "suspicion," or general statements of probability. Somers uses the term in the more traditional pre-Lockean sense, meaning verisimilar, likely, or possible, and associates it with "suspicion and probable cause."

In a sense then, the debaters of the late seventeenth century are talking past one another. Somers attacks a traditional "probability" standard defined as mere opinion unsubjected to critical examination, while those who espouse the probability standard are beginning to define it as that level of truth arrived at in the empirical realm through critical inquiry. At a purely epistemological level, and leaving aside the real partisan conflict over institutional processes and powers, a late seventeenth-century "seer" might have propounded for the grand jury a standard based on the "new probability" on which Somers, and those he perceived as his opponents, could have agreed. Such a standard would have specified that a grand jury ought to indict on the basis of a critical examination of the evidence, which would produce a level of probable knowledge that could be distinguished from mere opinion—but not a level of probable knowledge so high as to produce a satisfied conscience or moral certainty of the guilt of the accused. Both out of ignorance and partisan convenience, Somers constructs an epistemological world with only two choices: opinion, which he labels probability, and truth. Faced with such a choice, truth must be the grand jury standard, and the grand jury must be pushed all the way over to the functional role of the trial jury.

Thus when Somers comes to specify the very kinds of critical inquiries that the new probability men would have required to establish any degree of probability as distinguished from mere opinion, he necessarily ends up with a mode of inquiry that is nearly identical to that prescribed for the trial jury. "Diligent enquiry" was essential to reach "full persuasion" and "belief." That diligent inquiry included consideration of all the circumstances surrounding the crime, the motives of accusers, the credibility of statements and confessions, and the character of witnesses. Grand jurors must not permit witnesses to make "probable arguments, and from thence infer" guilt. Testimony must be "positive, plain, direct, and full" and "free from all blemish." Indeed, "absolute certainty" was required of their depositions for that was the "one principal ground of the Juries most rational assurance of the Truth of their Verdict." For Somers, "rational assurance" was the proper basis of a grand jury verdict.[69]

The grand jury, he argued, "ought to be ignorant of nothing whereof they enquire, or to be informed, that may in their Understandings enable them to make true Presentment or Indictment." Indeed, in treason cases, they must listen to *anyone* who could present truth. Although Somers does not explicitly say that grand jurors hear the accused or his witnesses, his position seems to suggest dissatisfaction with the long-standing procedure that only the prosecution and prosecution witnesses be heard at this stage.[70]

Given all this, it is natural that Somers sees himself as combating twin "vulgar errors," which, if not corrected, would "in time destroy all benefit" from the "Constitution." The first error is the probability standard. The second is the idea that grand juries were to inquire less strictly and might be satisfied with a lower standard of evidence than trial juries. As devices for achieving certain truth, grand juries even had some substantial advantages over petty juries. Not only had they a "larger field" of inquiry and were they "better capacitated" to a more strict inquiry, presumably because of their better education and higher social status, but also they were "obliged to search into the whole matter" that in any way concerns the case. Unlike a petty jury, they could "send for persons, or Papers." If petty juries were limited to hearing the witnesses presented in court, grand juries could "use all the means they can" to understand the truth. The function of the trial juries was thus not to hear "fuller proofs," but to provide the accused an opportunity to make his defense.[71]

Somers's themes—hostility to judges, rejection of the probability standard, and insistence on active and critical grand jury inquiry—

are also found in Henry Care's immensely popular *English Liberties, or The Free-Born Subject's Inheritance*.[72] As its title suggests,
it marshalls these themes in a great hymn to the grand jury as
defender of rights, particularly of men's reputations, against "Malice, subordination or wicked Designs" practiced by whom the
reader easily could guess. Like Somers, Care ends up with a grand
jury whose standards of proof and style of inquiry are difficult to
differentiate from those of the trial jury.

While no one would dispute the Whig bias of Somers and Care,
it has not been recognized that several late seventeenth- and early
eighteenth-century grand jury guides were also party documents,
not impartial or semiofficial descriptions of current practice. The
first of these, the anonymous *Guide to English Juries, Setting forth
Their Power and Antiquity by a Person of Quality*, was perhaps the
most influential.[73] It was first published in 1682 in the wake of the
Colledge and Shaftesbury proceedings and was reprinted in 1689,
1699, and 1702. Large portions of it were reprinted again in a late
eighteenth-century American edition of Somers's *Security of English-Men's Lives*. Its association with Somers and its recommen-
dations of Care's *English Liberties* are clues to its partisan
character.

The *Guide to English Juries* concentrated on three themes. The
first was an instruction to the grand jurors to be extremely critical
of the particulars contained in the bill of indictment, because clerks
of the court and prosecutors, while purporting to present merely a
formal accusation, often loaded it against the accused.[74] The second
was a vigorous rejection of the probability standard in favor of a
"truth" or satisfied conscience or "beyond all doubt" standard that
included assessments of witness credibility.[75]

The third was a two-trial theme. Although a grand jury proceeding was "no determinate tryal," the author bitterly attacks those
who say that "this is no Tryal" but simply a means of bringing an
individual to trial, an action in which "the Party is at no prejudice
if the Bill be found." He refutes those like Babington and Pemberton who imply that "*vera*" means "probable or fit for enquiry." Like
Somers, the author asserts that criminal cases required "two
Tryals." A citation to Dalton that "no less care or concern" lay with
"the Grand Jury than does the Petty Jury," suggests the centrality
of both institutions.[76]

While the author of the *Guide to English Juries* recognized that it was current practice, backed by precedent, to hear only the prosecution, he suggests that the consequence of this practice resulted in violations of truth and justice. Grand jurors "ought to hear both Parties, if present, or easily, conveniently to be heard." After all, he argued, the juror's oath required them to present the "whole truth." How could they be satisfied that they had done so unless they "hear both Parties"?[77]

Thus the *Guide to English Juries* illustrates dramatically the interplay of epistemology and institutional practice. Once an epistemology of truth is championed for the grand jury, irresistible tension arises between the grand jury's epistemology and its institutional practices, such as hearing only one side of the case. This tension necessarily pushes, and is exploited to push, the institutional role of the grand jury over to a position nearly identical to that of the trial jury.

The Whig position engendered the response that might have been expected. Roger North, the staunchly Tory brother of Francis North, Lord Guilford, a Tory judge, and Dudley North, soon to be Tory sheriff of London, attacked both Whig pamphleteers and the Whig grand jury standard. According to Roger North, the Shaftesbury grand jury had misrepresented the proceedings by willfully refusing to recognize that they were to accuse, not try. An *ignoramus* might have been an appropriate response had they heard only one witness rather than the two required by law, had the testimony been unrelated to the matter charged, or had they felt the accusations to be "frivolous or Nonsense." If, however, "the Testimony be lawful and full," as North thought it had been, the proper result "could only be a *Billa Vera*." For the grand jury "to grow up, as they pretended, from . . . Informer, to Triers of the Fact, is contrary to Law, . . . they are not to return to the Court, their private Opinion, as the Triers do that when they say not Guilty; but they return . . . their Information only, which being legal, is, to all the Intents of Inquest, *vera*."[78]

Another hostile Tory critic also denounced the position of the Middlesex grand jury and the Whig standard in *Billa Vera: or the Arraignment of Ignoramus*. He began by turning the satisfied conscience standard on its head. If Shaftesbury's jury were not satisfied having before them sufficient and more than probable grounds for an Accusation, why did they not submit the whole business to "a stricter Examination and the Prisoner to a Legal Trial?" He was prepared to follow the Whig writers, who insisted that under their oath grand jurors "follow Truth and Justice as far as the best of their Understandings can carry them," but he took a quite different position on how those understandings might be directed. They were to be directed: "(1) either by Public Fame; or (2) by the Notoriety of the Fact; (3) or by ocular inspection and personal knowledge; or else (4) by the Information of credible Witnesses."[79]

The author of *Billa Vera* readily admitted that individuals of integrity might be accused unjustifiably by the malicious and that such indictments were "deservedly disowned and thrown out." He announces the Tory standard for indictment in the form of a rhetorical question about the Shaftesbury bill. "Was there no *Colour*, no probable ground, no sufficient matter for an Accusation?" The grand jury should bring in a *billa vera* "where they find a probable ground for Accusation."[80]

The author at one point appears to set the standard even lower than "probable ground." Where the king was personally concerned in an indictment, "severer Examination" was required. In such cases inquiry into the accused's "manners, . . . the tenour of his Conversation; what Principles he has own'd; . . . what *Party* he has espoused, what Speeches he has utter'd, . . . Upon such Inquisition it will be easie to resolve, and with *moral certainty*, whether the *Party* is to be suspected liable to such an Accusation brought against him."[81]

The grand jury must investigate the character and reputation of the accused and the circumstances of his life to determine whether suspicion was legitimate. The author thus employed something like the Romano-canon *indicia* as a means of determining whether "suspicion" was appropriate. These criteria had been included in Dalton's handbook for the justice of the peace in examining accused persons and frequently had appearanced in late seventeenth- and eighteenth-century justice of the peace handbooks in a special category labeled "suspicion."

This pamphlet departed from Judge Pemberton's earlier position and did condone grand jury consideration of witness credibility, but only grudgingly, because such matters "were more properly done upon the Trial." Grand jurors, moreover, were "obliged to weigh and ponder" and exercise "a Judgment of Discretion." Set against this acknowledgment that grand juries must be guided by their conscience, which had a "judicature set up in it," is the conclusion that "No loyal stomach" could digest the accused's escape without trial, especially in those cases which concerned the king.[82]

There is no question, of course, about who suffered from a disloyal stomach. If the pattern of the Shaftesbury proceedings were continued, no one would ever be accused "that be of such a Faction, tho never so guilty: None will be *safe* that are against it, though never so Innocent. And then what will become of our English Libertye." Whigs were not to be permitted a monopoly on proclaiming the rights of Englishmen. Indeed, should grand juries continue to move "out of their own proper sphear" and engage in "fawning Popularity" and "execrable Partiality," as had the Shaftesbury jury, they not only risked the same impeachment as would a corrupt judge, but also the lives, property, and privileges of Magna Carta would be lost by the loyal and become the "Monopoly of Traitors and Dissenters."[83]

This tract, then, was far more sensitive to the needs of the government than those of the Whigs, but did not take the extreme position of Pemberton. If the author did not wish to make indictment difficult, particularly in cases involving the Crown, he does not deny that grand jurors might weigh the credibility of the witnesses. It is nevertheless evident that his position on the criteria for grand jury verdicts was to a large extent a product of the intense political conflict of the last years of the reign of Charles II.[84]

The intensity of the political conflict over the Shaftesbury case insured that the debate over grand jury standards would move beyond legal circles into more general public discourse. Writing not long after the trial, the Whig historian Gilbert Burnet admitted that grand juries had generally found bills "upon a slight and probable evidence," but went on to state the Whig case that the grand jury's oath and the "reason of law seemed to oblige them to make no presentments but such they believe to be true."[85] An age increasingly committed to precise standards of inquiry was not likely to find indictments based on "slight and probable" evidence to be satisfactory, regardless of prevailing practice.

The controversy over the appropriate criteria for grand jury decisions also became the subject of political verse and satire. John Dryden's famous vilification of Shaftesbury was part of the government's propaganda campaign, *Absalom and Achitophel* being timed to appear shortly before the Shaftesbury grand jury met. *The Medal*, another Dryden attack on Shaftesbury, for whom a medal was struck upon his release, was in turn answered by Thomas Shadwell's *Medal of John Bayes*.[86] Shadwell's dedicatory letter suggests just how well known the new Whig standards for grand juries had become: "If you look upon the oath . . . ye will find that the meaning of these two words *Billa Vera* is [that] they do believe the matter of the bill in their consciences to be true. . . . The law provides that in capital cases a man shall not be wrongfull accused, and therefore appoints two juries, both [of] which are bound to find according to their beliefs."[87] The evidentiary standard of satisfied belief, or satisfied conscience, which had emerged out of bitter partisan struggle, directly challenged the probability standard, which was increasingly associated with a "Tory," or at least a governmental, position.

The defense of grand jury independence and the satisfied conscience standard thus had political implications from the outset. It was widely argued that grand jury proceedings and the jury trial were special institutions that had historically protected the English from the arbitrary and "illegal" actions of government. Although the English legal system and trial by jury were praised in comparison with their Continental neighbors from at least the time of Fortescue, it was felt in certain circles that judges were part of the authority of the Crown and might not always provide sufficient protection for individual rights and liberties. Throughout the seventeenth century, the judiciary, appointed by the king and removable at his pleasure, was expected to support government policy. There should be no surprise, then, that the attack on Charles I and the civil war which followed were accompanied by virulent attacks on the judiciary.[88]

Although the judiciary of Charles II and James II was not as subservient as sometimes supposed,[89] it was expected that judges would support the Crown against allegedly treasonous activities. Those who felt most strongly that the Crown was prosecuting innocent victims or infringing on the rights and privileges of individuals thus tended to criticize the judiciary and to emphasize the importance of juries and grand juries as bulwarks of liberty against arbitrary or potentially arbitrary governments[90] and as one of the few independent, local, popular institutions. That late seventeenth-century grand juries were increasingly filled with justices of the peace made that claim even more plausible to an essentially aristocratic society. Moreover, justices of the peace had become more and more engaged in party politics,[91] and so the grand jury increasingly was seen as a bulwark not only of individual liberties but also of opposition politics. As a result, the grand jury waxed and waned in public attention with changes in party fortunes.

The grand jury issue lapsed into quiescence after the collapse of the Whigs, and relatively little was heard about it from 1683 to 1689.[92] The revolutionary events of 1688–1689 led to a minor renewal in interest. The post-revolutionary decades were significant more for reprinting the 1681–1682 pamphlets than for the production of new works or new formulations. There were, however, a few important exceptions. Earlier I noted the 1682 Whig *Guide to English Juries*, which was reprinted in 1689, 1699, and 1702. This guide was challenged in 1703 by Sir James Astry's *A General Charge to all Grand Juries*, prepared both for justices of the peace and for freeholders who might be called to jury service. Astry's guide rejects the Whig position and explicitly supports that of Babington.[93] Astry insists that a *billa vera* was required "in case they find upon the Evidence any probability," and that grand jurors were simply inquisitors for the Crown, not triers of the offense. He reiterates Babington's discussion of the meaning of the grand jurymen's oath. If the oath were to be understood in the ordinary, "plain, Literal and Grammatical Sense," rather than in the "legal sense, and according to the Common Practice of the legal proceedings in these Cases, . . . I must confess I am to be instructed how any Grand Juror (that hears but one side) can satisfy his Conscience" that what emerged from the grand jury proceedings contained, "the Truth, the whole truth and nothing but the truth." This tension between a satisfied conscience standard and the admittedly lower standard of probability that seemed to follow inevitably from hearing only one side of the case was as troubling to Astry as it had been to Babington. Both solved the problem by a nonliteral, "legal" interpretation of the words of the oath and by reference to past practice. Astry, however, does employ the satisfied conscience standard, which he tries unsuccessfully to reconcile with the probability standard. Astry is very clear, however, that proceedings must be secret, suggesting that later Tory spokesmen did not follow the lead of the judges in the Shaftesbury and Rouse cases.[94]

A juxtaposition of the two grand jury handbooks illustrates rather neatly how Whig and Tory views marched on in opposition to one another after the Revolution of 1688. The most influential statement of the post-revolutionary decade, however, was a very brief one contained in Sir John Hawles's vindication of various Whig martyrs. His *Remarks upon the Trial of Fitzharris*,[95] which attempted to set the legal record of the 1680s in proper Whig perspective, borrowed heavily from Somers's *Security of English-Men's Lives*. The prominence of Hawles's statements was assured because they were included in the published *State Trials*, a series of volumes that was frequently cited and studied on both sides of the Atlantic. Hawles, rather than Somers, became the most frequently cited proponent of the satisfied belief standard and enemy of the probability standard.

Hawles, like Somers and Burnet, suggested that "Of late days," it was being said that the duty of the grand jury was to find "Whether the Accusation is Probable." "That saying," he insisted, was warranted neither by "positive Law, or ancient authority." No one should even be questioned by the king on a capital matter unless a grand jury swears "that they believe the matter of the accusation to be true." They must, on the basis of their own knowledge or the evidence given them "verily believe the accusation is true." "Probabilities" could not "satisfy the Jury."[96]

As one might expect, Hawles emphasized the literal meaning of the grand juryman's oath to tell the truth and used the language of two trials. Like Somers, he outlined the grand jury's advantage over the petty jury, noting it would make no sense to have the "more substantial and Understanding Men" of the grand jury serve if their business were a "mere formality."[97] Hawles's brief, unoriginal comments might well have slipped into oblivion had they not been included in the published *State Trials* and then been rendered authoritative by incorporation into the remarks of the editor of Sir Matthew Hale's *History of the Pleas of the Crown* (1736), which I shall examine shortly.

Hawles's, however, was not the sole 1689 critique of the Shaftesbury proceedings. The revolutionary decade witnessed a number of works which referred back to the treason trials of the previous decade.[98] In comparing the late seventeenth-century discussion with that of the earlier period, what is striking is the change in the terms of discourse. Not only has the political element been enormously heightened but so has the evidentiary terminology. Concepts of "probability" have largely replaced those of "common fame" and "suspicion."

The Eighteenth Century

By the end of the seventeenth century, evidentiary issues receded from public debate. Whig governments were firmly in control and judges became less susceptible to government pressure when their tenure was changed from at the pleasure of the Crown to a term of good behavior. Yet the less polemic treatments of the eighteenth century did remarkably little to clarify evidentiary standards. If anything, we should probably speak of two rival standards, the probability standard and the satisfied belief standard which were both employed for nearly 150 years. Treatise writers tended either to be vague or to present, but not to resolve, the debates of previous generations. The most striking features of eighteenth-century and early nineteenth-century discussion are confusion and lack of resolution.

It is, therefore, necessary to understand why consensus was so difficult to reach and how it was possible for the law to remain in such an ambiguous state for such a long time. The problem stemmed in large part from the dual institutional and epistemological tensions noted at the beginning of this chapter. If grand juries required precisely the same mental satisfaction of judgment based on the same evidence and the same modes of evaluation as did the petty jury, there seemed little reason to proceed with two nearly identical procedures. The notion of two identical or near-identical trials seems to loom up as an institutional paradox whenever the same or similar standards of certainty were enunciated for both grand and petty juries. The introduction of an epistemology of probabilities aggravated rather than resolved this paradox. It might appear relatively easy to assign the trial jury a position at one end of the sliding scale of probabilities, that of moral certainty, but precisely where was the grand jury to go? The scale of probabilities had no precise steps nor any agreed unit of measure. As we shall see in Chapter 3, for a time it had appeared that Continental thought, with its signs and *indicia*, might provide a system of measurement, but by the eighteenth century Continental reformers themselves were looking longingly at the English jury with its system of "free proof." Without a distinct series of steps, the probabilistic judgment expected of grand juries was so conceptually unstable that it kept sliding either toward the "satisfied conscience," or "moral certainty," required of petty juries or toward a level of probability so low that the grand jury would become a mere conveyer belt for any and all accusations. The eighteenth- and early nineteenth-century discussion continuously juggled these institutional and epistemological instabilities without arriving at a successful formula. Neither the language of the law nor the language of philosophy provided an adequate solution. The Anglo-American legal system developed a psychologically and politically satisfactory standard, "satisfied belief," in the late seventeenth century and its cognate, "beyond reasonable doubt," in the late eighteenth century for the trial jury, but no psychologically or philosophically satisfying standard emerged for the grand jury. The literature of the eighteenth and early nineteenth centuries most typically reveals the simultaneous enunciation of both high and low probability standards for grand juries or an uneasiness with one or the other.

Thomas Wood's popular *Institute of the Laws of England*, a work eventually replaced by Blackstone's *Commentaries*, simply noted that charges must be "sufficiently Grounded" and that an *ignoramus* was a "Groundless Accusation."[99] Such a statement could have been of little direct assistance to grand jurors. I have already noted Sir Matthew Hale's great work, *The History of the Pleas of the Crown*, which finally appeared in 1736, and which popularized the views that Hale had formulated over six decades earlier. Hale viewed the indictment as an accusation and had invoked the probability, rather than the satisfied belief, standard. Grand jurors were expected to assess the credibility of the prosecution witnesses, but were not to anticipate the evidence to be presented to the petty jury. Hale's position certainly could not be identified with what I called the Whig position, however much the earlier Whigs liked to contrast Hale to the arbitrary Scroggs and Jeffreys. Hale's state-

ments, written prior to the Shaftesbury proceedings, gave cre-
dence to Babington's 1677 claim that the probability standard was
then the authoritative one. However, by 1736, the debate had raged
unresolved for several generations. Indeed, Hale's editor disagreed
with him on a number of points, and these disagreements were
invariably cited in subsequent discussions of the grand jury. The
editor notes that Hale's probable evidence standard was employed
by Chief Justice Pemberton in Shaftesbury's case. However, he
goes on to argue that Sir John Hawles's comment on the Shaftesbury case "unanswerably shows" that a grand jury ought to have
the same persuasion of the truth of the indictment as is required
of a trial jury to convict.[100]

The editor also disagrees with Hale's criticism of grand juries for
anticipating the evidence to be given to the petty jury. Although
Hale had indicated that "all hands agree" on this point, his
eighteenth-century editor noted that it was impossible for the
grand jury to avoid anticipating the evidence because they were
bound by oath to present the whole truth and nothing but the
truth. These editorial disagreements with Hale had an enormous
influence on late eighteenth-century discussion on grand juries and
were reported in most, if not all, subsequent discussion. Hale's
probability standard and his critics' satisfied conscience standard
thus appeared side by side.[101]

Henry Fielding, the novelist and an extremely active and well-
known mid-eighteenth-century London magistrate, held a position
largely based on Hale. Fielding perceptively noted that the origins
of the grand jury were difficult to trace and that both Coke and
Hale had avoided detailed discussion of the institution. Citing
Hale, he noted that the business of the grand jury was only "to
attend to Evidence of the King; and if on that Evidence there shall
appear a probable Cause for the Accusation, they are to find the
bill true, without listening to any Circumstance of Defense, or any
matter of Law." "Probable cause" was sufficient to indict: "for wherever you shall find probable Cause, upon the oaths of the King's
Witnesses, you will not discharge your office without finding the
bill to be true, showing no regard to the Nature of the Crime, or
the degree of Guilt, which are Matters for the cognizance and determination of the Court only."[102]

The *only* basis for a finding of *ignoramus* was dissatisfaction on hearing the king's evidence and the grand jurors' "personal knowledge of the Incredibility of the witnesses." Grand jurors were obviously not to make a concerted effort to evaluate the testimony of witnesses, and there is no suggestion of Hawles's investigative body, no emphasis on the truth demanded by the oath, and no discussion of the grand juries' right to discuss law as well as fact. Because grand jurors in the metropolis were unlikely to know much, if anything, about witnesses who testified, their role would certainly be a perfunctory one. Fielding thus not only approved of Hale's views, but also wished to extend them from capital cases "to any Indictment whatsoever."[103]

Fielding, it should be noted, was unconcerned with the political and constitutional issues of an earlier generation. He was alarmed by the rates of theft, robbery, and murder in the metropolis. Fielding illustrates Herbert Packer's point that those concerned primarily with crime control are inclined to advocate or support doctrines designed to maximize indictments, while those concerned primarily with preventing governmental invasion of individual rights or protecting those accused of crimes with political implications are more likely to search for doctrinal formulas that might protect those individuals.[104] Fielding's work, like that of Babington much earlier, was inspired by the belief that not enough ordinary criminals were being punished for their crimes. On the whole, eighteenth-century English critics of the criminal justice system were more concerned with the problems of crime control than with the protection of individual liberties.

On the grand jury question, as on so many others, Sir William Blackstone's famed *Commentaries on the Laws of England* is more a compendium than an analysis. Like Hale he insists that the grand jury was "only to hear evidence on behalf of the prosecution: for the finding of an indictment is only in the nature of an inquiry or accusation, which is afterward to be tried and determined." And like most of those who saw the body as primarily accusatory, he minimized the similarity between petty and grand jury. Grand juries were only to inquire "whether there be a sufficient cause to call upon the party to answer it." Hale's "probable evidence" and Blackstone's "sufficient cause" were thus quite similar in effect. For Blackstone, an *ignoramus* signaled a "groundless accusation," indicating that "though the facts might possibly be true, that truth did not appear in them." Yet like earlier Whig writers, Blackstone had become disturbed that indictments might be made on slight grounds. He therefore insisted that the grand jury "ought to be thoroughly persuaded of the truth of the indictment, so far as their evidence goes: and not to rest satisfied with remote possibilities: a doctrine that might be applied to very oppressive purposes."[105] Here, then, we get the notion of something like probable cause accompanied by thorough persuasion or satisfied belief on the basis of the prosecution's presentation. Blackstone's views suggest a possible, though still undeveloped, compromise to the evidentiary dilemma of grand jurors. Despite the possibility of oppression, Blackstone was concerned that prosecutions go forward. He offers a combination of what, for lack of better terms, I have called the Tory and the Whig positions. He represents an uneasy effort to somehow combine the notion that indictment is not a full trial based on complete evidence with a standard of full persuasion on the part of the grand jurors.

Employing his usual method of combining everything, Blackstone has actually stumbled upon the *prima facie* case standard that subsequently resolved the institutional and epistemological tensions surrounding the grand jury. We shall examine that resolution later in this chapter. The institutional element of hearing solely the prosecution case plus the epistemological element of thorough persuasion does yield *prima facie* case. Even though Blackstone made this fruitful combination of institutions and epistemology, he also continued to combine the seemingly opposed epistemological standards of Tory probability and Whig thorough persuasion. As a result, neither he nor others viewed the *Commentaries* as providing a resolution. Subsequent commentators continued to pursue the epistemological vector independently, and thus continued the old Tory-Whig debate about probability or full persuasion, reading Blackstone as being on either one side or the other of that debate.

There are suggestions that the balance was shifting away from the probability standard. We have seen Blackstone's uneasy combination of the two standards. Richard Woodeson's Vinerian lectures for 1777, published as *A Systematic View of the Laws of England*, noted that Hale and Pemberton favored the probable evidence standard because an indictment was only an accusation. Woodeson also noted, however, that others, chiefly Hale's editor and Blackstone, on "humanely ponderating the anxiety excited by criminal trials, the dangers of perjury, and the calamities and ignominy of a dungeon, have maintained that a grand jury ought to have a firm persuasion of the justice of the charge, for they are sworn to present nothing but the truth."[106] Woodeson clearly read Blackstone as having rejected the probability standard. Woodeson and the authors of most eighteenth-century handbooks for the justices of the peace also cited Coke, noting that what Coke had laid down with respect to treason might be "applied to prosecutions for other crimes, . . . seeing the indictment is the foundation of all, and is commonly preferred in the absence of the party suspected, there ought to be substantial proof." Woodeson was at one with Blackstone, however, in insisting that grand juries were only to hear the prosecution's side and seek to determine whether "there be reasonable cause to put the accused on his trial."[107] What is confusing in both Blackstone and Woodeson is the use of "reasonable" or "probable cause" in speaking of whether the accused should be put on trial, combined with explicit reservations about the probability standard as enunciated by Hale and Pemberton.

Grand jury charges for the eighteenth century are somewhat more numerous than their seventeenth-century counterparts and occasionally provide glimpses of doctrinal issues and practical problems. Only a handful remain of the hundreds delivered, and it is difficult to assess their representativeness especially because most of those extant were considered sufficiently important to be worthy of publication. They should be read in the context of the reprinting of *Guide to English Juries, Setting forth Their Power and Antiquity* in 1702, its rejection in Astry's *General Charge to all Grand Juries* the following year (reprinted in 1725), and the varying commentaries of Hale, Woodeson, and Blackstone. Most charges simply offer a brief outline of the criminal code and provide conventional statements concerning bias, impartiality, and corruption. A few are more interesting. One 1714 charge, which emphasized that "much weaker Circumstances" were required for grand juries, nevertheless favored grand juries altering theft charges to petty theft.[108] Advocacy of a low standard, therefore, did not necessarily go hand in hand with a desire for harsh application and might be accompanied by a position that allowed grand jurors to deal with questions of law as well as fact. Other charges indicate that differences

of opinion about the standard of evidence continued, as did conflicting views on the nature and role of grand juries. Thus the
charge of William Cowper explicitly rejects the idea that indictment requires the same degree of evidence as conviction by petty
juries. All those "fit to be Accused" should be brought to trial by
the grand jury. If the grand jurors had "a probable suspicion," they
should find the bill. "Just Cause of Suspicion given upon Oath is
your Rule," while "Direct and Certain Evidence" was that of the
trial Jury.[109] The charge of Sir Daniel Dolbins, however, explicitly
rejects the idea that indictments might be made on the basis of
"Surmise and Probable Evidence."[110] Grand jurors were to use "ut-
most Caution and Circumspections" both to prevent unnecessary
and ill-disposed persons from accusing out of malice and to insure
legitimate prosecutions. An "honest and impartial Search and Examination" was required by their oath.[111] Another early eighteenth-
century charge noted the need to protect juries and grand juries
against judges, and referred his auditors to the usurped authority
of Justice Kelyng.[112]

Contrasting and ambiguous pronouncements appear in charges
of the middle decades as well. Although the evidence is thin, it
suggests that the probability standard was still the more common.[113] Even the older language of suspicion continued to be aired.

A charge delivered by Richard Burke in 1793 may well summarize the developments of the century. It emphasizes the duty of the
grand jury to engage in "deliberate examination" of the evidence
and argues that, far from performing a mere ceremonial function,
the grand jury is an essential, time-honored barrier against malicious or oppressive prosecution.[114] At the same time it confesses:

But on what kind of Evidence; under what degree of approach to certainty, a Grand-Jury should deliver the Prisoner over to further . . . Trial,
is another consideration, and is, as I think, incapable of definition, and
not subject to any known Rule, or admitting of any direction from your
Government, from the Court. Were I to risque anything by way of rec-
ommendation . . . I should first draw your attention to the circumstance
of the accused not being permitted to make any defense before You, and
then I should say, you ought to see that the Commission of the Crime
itself, was fully established by the Evidence, and then that such a presumption is raised by Evidence of the Crime so established, being com-

mitted by the party accused, as to satisfy your judicial understanding, that he is reasonably called on for a defense, and that the whole matter is worthy of further, and more detailed examination. In the application of these principles . . . your own informed Understandings and enlightened Conscience must be your Guides.[115]

A few examples taken from the scattering of printed grand jury charges cannot adequately inform us of eighteenth-century doctrine or practice. What is clear, however, is that few printed charges addressed the question at all. Of those few that did, the probability standard seems more common. However, the charges do not suggest that the grand jury be a ceremonial rubber stamp for the prosecutor. An active, inquiring, and judging grand jury that carefully considered the evidence before it was viewed as having an important political function and serving as protection of individuals against malicious neighbors and possibly arbitrary ministers.

John Beattie's monumental study of crime in Surrey from 1660 to 1800 provides some evidence of the actual conduct of English grand juries. About 25 percent of the bills of indictment for assault and about 15 percent of the bills of indictment for property offenses were rejected. Approximately 13 percent of males and 35 percent of female homicide indictments were rejected. The figures were much higher for accessories to murder, with about 28 percent of male and 67 percent of female indictments found *ignoramus*.[116] Beattie's figures of *ignoramus* verdicts for various crimes suggest that grand juries from the Restoration to the beginning of the nineteenth century exercised considerable discretion. While judges were in positions to overawe and control many petty juries, the socially prominent and politically powerful members of the county who manned grand juries were less controllable. Many of these prestigious and powerful men were experienced, having served on numerous occasions.[117] We should not assume, however, that they were hostile to the magistrates, who were responsible for gathering crucial pretrial depositions, given that many were magistrates themselves.[118] Beattie's study of grand jury behavior, combined with the known social position of grand jurors, suggest neither passivity nor a willingness to perform a merely ceremonial function.

While it appears as if the focus of attention shifted from politics and protection of the individual from oppressive judges to a greater focus on apprehending and punishing crime, we should not make that distinction too sharp. Babington had been interested primarily in homicide, and the eighteenth-century justices who manned many grand juries were self-consciously political.[119]

The American Experience

With the eighteenth century, we must begin to incorporate American experience into our discussion. The American scene for many decades was much like the English. The first grand jury appeared in Massachusetts in 1635. By 1683, some form of the grand jury was found in all the American colonies. By the end of the colonial era, the grand jury had become an "indispensible part" of the government of each colony,[120] although colonial administrators were not always familiar with English practice.[121] The grand jury was retained in all states after the American Revolution and was included in the federal Constitution.

Richard Burn's justicing manual, whose nineteen editions between 1755 and 1800 made it one of the most consulted lawbooks on both sides of the Atlantic, cited both Hale and Pemberton in prescribing that grand jurors "ought only to hear the evidence for the King, and in case there be probable evidence they ought to find the bill, because it is only an accusation." Then he notes that Hale's "learned editor observes upon this, that Sir John Hawles in his remarks on the [Shaftesbury] case, unanswerably shows that a grand jury ought to have the same persuasion of the truth of the indictment as a petty jury, or a coroner's inquest; for they all swear to present the truth, and nothing but the truth."[122] He also cited Coke to the effect that indictment required "substantial proof."

American readers of Burn's and of other similar manuals must have been somewhat puzzled. Hale's and Pemberton's probability views were clear enough, but the questions of how much authority was to be given "Hale's learned editor" and how to combine the two positions were left unresolved. Both views were evidently to be considered authoritative in some sense. The invocation of Coke may even have seemed to offer a third alternative, although he was being quoted out of context. Whatever conclusions can be culled from these coexisting eighteenth-century standards, it is clear that Shaftesbury's case, and the discussion that surrounded it, continued to be the center of discussion of grand jury evidentiary standards for well over a century in both England and America.

Burn's ambiguities were transmitted to the colonists not only by its own American editions but also by a number of handbooks modeled on his that were written and published in America. Richard Starke's *Office and Authority of the Justice of the Peace*, William Hening's *New Virginia Justice*, and a 1773 American abridgment of Burn all reproduce the same confusing combination of quotations. Hale's editor's contrary remarks that incorporated Hawles's commentary on the Shaftesbury case which had appeared in the published *State Trials* and the out-of-context quotation from Coke are offered again without explanatory comment. Thus probable evidence, satisfied belief, and the two-trial approach are all jumbled together.[123]

American grand juries also went through a highly politicized stage. It came in the late eighteenth century, as tensions with Great Britain grew. Grand juries provided a means of frustrating the policies of imperial authorities. They sometimes refused to indict political offenders and prevented the enforcement of unpopular laws. Perhaps the most famous instance was the refusal of the Boston grand jury in 1765 to indict the leaders of the Stamp Act Riots.[124]

The late seventeenth-century Whig texts of Somers, Hawles, Care, and *A Guide to English Juries* were frequently reprinted in the course of the colonial conflict as weapons against the English authorities, especially in cases of political import.[125] Other works extracted relevant portions. The anonymous author/editor of a colonial compendium of Whig writers rejected the probable evidence standard, and he suggested that Hale may have been led to that "uncertain way of speaking, from some charges which were given to Grand Juries in the reign in which he lived, and which have met with universal disapprobation in all after times." He supported his view with the familiar editorial comments contained in Hale's *History of the Pleas of the Crown*. He went on to stress the similarity between grand and petty juries, and added that the treason statutes of Edward VI, Charles II, and William III, among others, required that the identical proof be brought to both juries. A minimum of two lawful witnesses and creditable circumstances were required for both accusation and conviction. Circumstances "which might create a Suspicion against the Party to be indicted" were not enough; an overt act was necessary, and probabilities, inferences, and conjectural evidence were insufficient. The oaths of both juries also required the "Indictment to be True." The law thus "has established a double Fence for Security, . . . in all such Trials." The evidence, therefore, seemed conclusive to him "that a Grand Jury ought to be satisfied with no less Evidence" that would convince them "than if they were on the Petty Jury." Every subject was, therefore, entitled to "two Juries," who with equal care were to "weigh the Evidence and certify that the charge is true."[126]

Yet one must recall that the seventeenth-century Whig texts, with their emphasis on a high evidentiary standard, circulated simultaneously with the confusions of Burn's manual and other justice of the peace manuals, Hale's *History of the Pleas of the Crown*, and Blackstone's *Commentaries*. If the grand jury in colonial America was depicted as an institution that protected colonial subjects against arbitrary prosecutions, its evidentiary standard nevertheless remained uncertain. As in England a century earlier, positions, at least to some extent, reflected partisan concerns. The writings of Hawles, Somers, and Care, who themselves had been politically motivated, were used again for political purposes under a different set of circumstances. Hawles's tract for juries was published in America on the very day that the trial of John Peter Zenger for seditious libel opened. By the time the United States became an independent nation, the English debate over grand jury standards was well known and already shaped by American political controversy.[127]

Separation from England, however, did not end the possibility of a partisan role for grand juries. There was a certain amount of conflict between grand juries and federal judges in the early history of the nation.[128] Perhaps for this reason, debate over the probability standard continued to be linked to suspicion of the judiciary. The seventeenth-century Whig vision of grand juries as bulwarks against the agents of arbitrary government appears yet again. And the Babington-Hale-Pemberton and Somers-Hawles lines of a century earlier are repeated.

One such replay of the old debate occurred in Pennsylvania in 1783. After a printer was "ordered indicted" for criticism of the Pennsylvania Supreme Court, a grand jury inquiry resulted in an *ignoramus*. The judges allegedly attempted to overcome the jury by verbal reproofs. After being instructed to reconsider, the jury not only refused to alter its finding, but also justified itself publicly. This action in turn led to the publication of several essays, believed to be the work of Chief Justice McKean and Justice Bryan, under the names of "Jurisperitus" and "Adrian," which in turn led to counteressays by Francis Hopkinson in *The Pennsylvania Packet*.[129]

Hopkinson particularly emphasized the independence of the grand jurors from the judiciary. He insisted on the jurors' "right to make a strict inquiry" and to consider "all manner of legal testimony of what nature soever, that may in anywise tend to the discovery of the whole truth," and he pointed out the dangers of judicial interference. If the grand jury were permitted to hear only what the judge and the attorney general brought to court, it would be contrary to its oath, and there would be no point to the proceedings. "Adrian's article," thought to have been penned by one of the judges in the case, asked, "Was there not . . . the usual probable evidence?" If so, "why stifle the cause" in the grand jury? Hopkinson found the phrases "probable evidence" and "stifle a cause" to be "horrible language" and was outraged that the lives, fortunes, and reputations of citizens might be "hung upon the tenderhooks of logical possibilities." As Hopkinson himself indicated, much of his rejoinder consists of lengthy passages from Somers's *Security of English-Men's Lives*.[130]

In another essay, Hopkinson points to the conflict between the rights and duties of the grand jury and the "Prerogatives of the bench." Given that the struggle for liberty was not yet over, it was impossible to know what sort of judges Americans might have after the war. In Hopkinson's view, "Jurisperitus," with the help of Blackstone, had interpreted incorrectly the words of the oath "diligently inquire." Although "Jurisperitus" had suggested that only an accusation alleging a "sufficient cause" is necessary, the law as embodied by the oath itself required the presentation of the truth. Even Blackstone had said that a grand jury must be thoroughly persuaded of the truth of an indictment. For Hopkinson, "slight grounds and probable testimony" were not enough: "Now some have said, that sufficient cause means probable cause: and probable means likely, and everything that is likely is at least possible: and so, by an irrefragable chain of reasoning, we may be hung in chains, according to the good pleasure of the judges and learned expound-

ers of the law."[131] The problem of a lack of a readily available terminology to clearly indicate gradations of probability thus reap-
peared. Probability retained too many meanings to be satisfactory
in this context.

On visiting England the following year, Hopkinson described the
English legal system. While generally favorable, he noted the del-
eterious effect of partial sheriffs and party rage on grand juries. His
comments confirm that the role of party had not abated in the late
eighteenth century. He describes the charge to the grand jury as
merely a "general delineation of their duty" and a definition of
indictable crimes. Grand jury charges obviously had not changed
much over several centuries. But English judges, he reported,

> often take the opportunity of going farther: he insinuates to them, that
> they may indict on mere probable testimony, that they should attend only
> to the testimonies on behalf of the prosecution, and have nothing to do
> with any witnesses but those whom the King's Attorney shall send to
> them; and that if they find the bill it will amount to nothing more than a
> kind of legal accusation, which if wrong, will afterwards be set right by
> the petit-jury.[132]

Hopkinson's description, if in fact based on widespread observation, would confirm that the probability standard was widely employed in late eighteenth-century England. Hopkinson, however,
found such judicial direction to be "a deviation from the original
constitution" which "placed the grand jury at the first entrance of
the law to screen the innocent from malicious prosecution." With
the probability standard as practiced in England, he thought, "A
man may be effectually ruined by the grand jury finding a bill
against him, although he may be afterwards fully acquitted by the
petit jury." A *billa vera* should be recorded when the grand jury
"find sufficient cause to believe that the party is guilty." As one
might expect, Hopkinson again emphasized the potential conflict
between judge and jurors and noted the harmful judicial influence
over both grand jury and petty jurors.[133] Here again, rejection of
the probability standard was associated with distrust of the
judiciary.

In 1788, Chief Justice McKean of Pennsylvania, perhaps the author of one of the essays so much deplored by Hopkinson, informed
a grand jury,

The bills or presentments found by a grand jury amount to nothing more than an official accusation, . . . till the bill is returned, there is, therefore, no charge from which he can be required to exculpate himself. . . . Here then is the just line of discrimination. It is the duty of the grand jury to inquire into the nature and probable grounds of the charge, . . . you will therefore readily perceive that if you examine the witnesses on both sides, you do not confine your consideration to the probable grounds of the charge, but engage completely in the trial of the cause; and your return must consequently be tantamount to a verdict of acquittal or condemnation. But this would involve us in another difficulty; for, by the law, it is declared that no man shall be twice put in jeopardy for the same offense; and yet it is certain that the inquiry, now proposed by the grand jury, would necessarily introduce the oppression of a double trial. . . . Considering the bill as an accusation grounded entirely on the testimony in support of the prosecution, the petit jury receive no bias from the sanction which the endorsement of the grand jury has conferred upon it . . . the court is of the opinion, that it would be improper and illegal to examine the witnesses on behalf of the defendant. [134]

One of the grand jurors, after hearing Chief Justice McKean's charge, requested an explanation of those troubling words of the oath, "diligently inquire." As in the past, a literal interpretation was associated with a rejection of the probability standard. McKean replied that

the expression meant, diligently to inquire into the circumstances of the charge, the credibility of the witnesses who support it, and from the whole, to judge whether the person accused ought to put upon his trial. For though it would be improper to determine the merits of the cause, it is incumbent upon the grand jury to satisfy their minds, by a diligent inquiry, that there is a probable ground for the accusation. [135]

His position, as Hopkinson had noted, was that of Blackstone.

A grand jury guarantee appears in virtually every early state constitution. We know little about the particulars of its inclusion in the federal Bill of Rights. There does not appear to have been any significant debate between Federalists and anti-Federalists on the nature of grand jury proceedings. The framers of our early state and federal constitutions neither explicitly identified nor resolved earlier grand jury issues. [136]

Hopkinson's Somers-like position was advanced again in 1790–1792 by James Wilson, one of the earliest justices of the U.S. Supreme Court and a professor of law at the College of Philadelphia. Wilson's published public lectures on jurisprudence and government devoted considerable time to the grand juries, the "peculiar boast of the common law." "The Trust," which "reposed in grand juries is of great and general concernment. To them is committed the custody of the portals of the law. . . . They make, in the first instance, the important discrimination between the innocent and the guilty."[137]

Wilson noted with disfavor the view that grand juries were only to inquire "whether what they hear be any reason to put the party to answer . . . that a probable cause to call him to answer, is as much as is required by law." Such a view was "consonant" neither with their oath nor with ancient practice. Following Somers and Hopkinson, he asked: "Now, is it consistent with reason or sound sense, that a verdict found upon oath—upon an oath to make diligent inquiry—should be vague, perhaps the visionary result merely of probability?"[138] The notion that jurors might be satisfied merely with probability was "dangerous as well as unfounded: it is a doctrine which may be applied to countenance and promote the vilest and most oppressive purposes: it may be used, in pernicious rotation, as a snare in which the innocent may be entrapped, and as a screen, under the cover of which the guilty may escape."[139]

Wilson also rejected the view that grand juries must follow the lead of the prosecution. They must declare innocent those they felt to be so, whether or not the charges were drawn in proper form or "marshalled in legal array." And like most other rejecters of the probability standard, Wilson linked his position to the "contest between judges and juries" and to the jurors' claims to deal with law as well as fact.[140] For Wilson, it was "moral certainty" not probability, which must be "the necessary basis" for the verdict. The standard of moral certainty, the highest available in matters of fact, is here explicitly made the basis of grand jury indictments. As I have argued in Chapter 1, the concept of moral certainty provided the basis of the beyond reasonable doubt standard which was becoming the required standard for petty jurors. The beyond reasonable doubt standard was itself an elaboration of the satisfied conscience standard which had for many decades been required for conviction. What is significant here is that Wilson, like the Shaftesbury supporters of a century earlier, insists that the same standard of certainty in the mind of fact evaluators was required for both petty and grand juries.

Despite the constitutional provision and the ringing statements of Wilson, no commonly accepted evidentiary standard emerged in the early years of the Republic. Nor can we offer anything very concrete for England in the same period. The English tended to take the institution for granted.[141] Case materials do not usually preserve judicial directions to grand jurors, and such judicial charges as were published rarely refer to evidentiary elements. Most legal treatises and legal dictionaries of the period say little that is new.

The *Prima Facie* Case Standard

The legal climate, however, was clearly changing. The balance which had once tipped on the side of the probability standard seems to have been moving in the opposite direction in both England and the United States. Joseph Chitty's well-respected and much-used *Practical Treatise on the Criminal Law*, first issued in 1816, indicates that it was "formerly held" that grand juries ought to find a true bill "if probable evidence were adduced to support it" because it was only an accusation. But he noted "great authorities have taken a more merciful view" and have argued, "as far as the evidence before them goes," that they must be "convinced of the guilt of the defendants." Indictments "ought to be supported by substantial testimonies," and jurors must be provided with the "best legal proofs of which the case admits." He cites Hale as the principal authority for the earlier, now rejected, probable evidence standard and cites Coke, Hawles, Blackstone, Woodeson, and Hale as authorities for the current revised standard.[142] For Chitty, the new standard appears to have been created out of an amalgam of older works: The arguments of the defenders of Shaftesbury were now becoming victorious.

At the same time that the law appeared to be turning its back on the probability standard, a new formulation, the *prima facie* case standard, came to replace the language of the Shaftesbury defenders. The appearance of the new standard was rather sudden and remains somewhat mysterious.

Thomas Starkie's immensely influential *Practical Treatise of the*

Law of Evidence provided the first lengthy treatment of the *prima facie* evidence standard that found its way into late nineteenth-century case law, legal treatises, and law dictionaries. According to Starkie, who would soon be cited with great regularity and authority, *prima facie* evidence was "That which, not being inconsistent with the falsity of the hypothesis, nevertheless raises such a degree of probability in its favor that it must prevail if it be credited by the jury, unless it be rebutted or the contrary proved."[143] It differed from conclusive evidence which "excludes, or at least tends to exclude, the possibility of the truth of any other hypothesis than the one attempted to be established."[144]

Starkie's distinction between *prima facie* evidence and conclusive evidence was easily applied to the respective standards of grand and petty juries. By Starkie's time, the conclusive evidence required by the trial jury had already been formulated as sufficient evidence to prove guilt beyond a reasonable doubt. It would prove simple to apply the *prima facie* evidence or case standard in grand jury proceedings. On the basis of the unrebutted prosecution case did the grand jury believe in the guilt of the accused? The hypothesis presented by the prosecution might be rebutted when the petty jury heard the defense. When hearing only the prosecution side of the case is combined with "confident belief," suddenly the problem of specifying a level of probability lower than beyond reasonable doubt and higher than "suspicion" is solved. As a result, a stable institutional niche could be assigned the grand jury, clearly distinct from initial accusation on the one hand and final determination of guilt by the trial jury on the other.

This new, distinct level of probability was not achieved by a breakthrough in the epistemology of probability; rather, it was achieved by bringing together an institutional element and an epistemological element—which by hindsight we can see had almost perversely been kept apart in the past. The epistemology of beyond reasonable doubt had been settled for some time. The institutional practice of hearing only the prosecution was long settled, if occasionally challenged. No one previously, however, seems to have perceived that the two could be brought together with startling results. If the grand jury heard only the prosecution, it could use the well-established beyond reasonable doubt standard, and by doing so it could actually resolve the long-standing conflict between the Tory "probability" and the Whig "satisfied conscience" positions. From the internal perspective of the grand jurors themselves, the grand jury brought a true bill only if its conscience was satisfied as to the guilt of the accused on the basis of the evidence it had heard. From an external perspective, the grand jury acted on the basis of a far lower probability of guilt than did the petty jury, because it heard only part of the evidence. These two perspectives not only provided a rationale that institutionally distinguished grand juries, but also provided a balance between crime control and individual liberties.

Formulations similar to Starkie's began to appear in the courts from about 1830. The ambiguity of previous generations seems to have vanished, and judges from that time until quite recently have enunciated with considerable uniformity the rule cited in Chief Justice Shaw's 1832 charge to a Massachusetts grand jury.

As to the nature and amount of evidence which is sufficient to warrant a Grand Jury in finding an indictment, the rule is this, that it must be legal, *prima facie* evidence of guilt; that is, it must be of such a nature, that if it stood alone, uncontradicted and uncontrolled by any defensive matter, it would be sufficient to justify a conviction on trial.[145]

A similar position was enunciated by Justice Taney in charging the Circuit Court for the District of Maryland in 1836.

You will, . . . carefully weigh the testimony, and present no one, unless in your deliberate judgment, the evidence before you is sufficient, in the absence of any other proof to justify the conviction of the party accused. And this rule is the more proper because he is not permitted to summon witnesses or adduce testimony to the grand jury.[146]

Both Shaw and Taney refer confidently to a rule. They see no reason to indicate the source of the rule nor feel a need to refer to the confusion, perplexity, and divided opinion that had puzzled and angered jurists and pamphleteers for so many generations. It is almost as if the probability standard had never existed. In reality, of course, what was being enunciated was a probability standard more precisely operationalized than the old Tory standard had been.

Despite the confident rulings of Shaw and Taney and the treatise of Starkie, some uncertainty remained. Francis Wharton's influential treatise of 1841 runs through the old debate as if it were still unsettled, placing Hawles, Blackstone, Wilson, and Chitty on one side and Hale and McKean on the other, with no mention of Shaw or Taney.[147] An opinion of federal Judge Leavitt in 1861 associated the grand jury standard with both that of the trial jury and something approximating the probability standard. He found it "inexpedient" to indict for crime in cases where "it is certain the evidence required by law cannot be produced before a traverse jury, and where consequently there can be no conviction." He also indicated that, given the fact the grand jury only heard the case for the prosecution, "They ought therefore, to be able to say under the solemnity of their oath, that there is a reasonable ground for the inference of guilt."[148] The phrase "reasonable ground" and the notion of "inference" suggest something less than the beyond reasonable doubt standard then being routinely required by trial judges or the *prima facie* case standard. At the same time, it was clear that cases should not be submitted to the grand jury if there were not sufficient evidence for conviction by a petty jury.

Although the standard was not absolutely clear in Leavitt's opinion, it is obvious there was a growing precision about the relationship between the standards of the two juries. In 1869, Judge Shipman told a federal grand jury that "the proof should be such as, in your judgment, would warrant a petty jury in pronouncing the accused guilty."[149]

It was not until 1872 that a controlling authority emerged. Justice Field, in a lengthy and much-cited opinion, discussed not only the appropriate standard of truth but also the history and functions of the grand jury. Its duty was to charge "upon just grounds" and to insure that citizens were not subject to accusations "having no better foundation than public clamour or private malice." Grand jurors were to receive only legal evidence and, like petty juries, must exclude "mere reports, suspicions, and hearsay evidence." Subject to these considerations, they will receive "all the evidence presented which may throw light upon the matter under consideration, whether it tends to establish the innocence or the guilt of the accused." If in the course of inquiry the grand jury had "reason to believe" that there existed other evidence not presented which "would qualify or explain away the charge," it must order "such evidence be produced."[150]

Unlike Shaw, Taney, Leavitt, and Shipman, Field noted the divided opinion of the past on the nature of the required standards of proof.

Formerly it was held that an indictment might be found if evidence were produced sufficient to render the truth of the charge probable. But a different, more just and merciful rule now prevails. To justify the finding of an indictment, you must be convinced, so far as the evidence before you goes, that the accused is guilty—in other words, you ought not to find an indictment unless, in your judgment, the evidence before you, unexplained and uncontradicted, would warrant a conviction by a petit jury. [151]

George Edward's 1904 study of the grand jury indicates that Field's opinion had become authoritative in the federal courts as well as in the states of Pennsylvania, New York, Massachusetts, Virginia, and California. He also reported that the probability standard was no longer used in England. [152] In 1883, Stephen's *Digest of the Law of Criminal Procedure in Indictable Offenses* had also enunciated the *prima facie* standard. [153] Edwards stated the then current American position.

The duty of the grand jury is to determine whether or not the evidence presented by the state raises a *prima facie* presumption of guilt of the defendant, in other words, is the evidence for the prosecution sufficient to sustain a conviction. [154]

Grand juries were to be governed by the "ordinary rules of evidence and no indictment should be found upon evidence, which before the petit jury and uncontroverted would not support a conviction." This meant not only that the "best evidence" was required, but also that grand juries must ignore suspicion, hearsay and rumor—the very basis for indictment in the time of Bracton. [155]

By the end of the nineteenth century, it appeared that the probability standard was only of historical interest, and that the inconsistencies and doubts of earlier generations had finally been resolved. Companion standards were now in place: beyond reasonable doubt for the trial jury and *prima facie* case for the grand jury. The *prima facie* case standard began to appear in both American and English law dictionaries from about 1850. [156]

Prima facie case standard permitted a balance between the societal and governmental needs of prosecution and the protection of individual rights from both governmental arbitrariness and private vexatious suits. It provided certainty on the part of grand jurors but avoided the repetition of two nearly identical trials. One of the major doctrinal problems of Anglo-American law had been solved.

Adequate doctrine alone, however, was not enough to make the grand jury a viable institution. Although the grand jury was now provided with an intellectually satisfying and workable evidentiary standard, the institution itself was eroding. As the institution eroded, so did the doctrinal stability of the *prima facie* case standard. By mid-twentieth century, Americans seem to have reverted to something that resembled the old Whig and Tory positions.

Criticism of the Grand Jury

When Chitty published his classic text on criminal law in 1816 he could say with confidence that grand jury indictment provided "the most constitutional, regular, safe, as well as by far the most usual mode of proceeding upon criminal charges."[157] A decade or two later, however, there would be far less unanimity on the political value and the efficacy of the institution. Because the fate of the grand jury proved to be quite different in Great Britain than in the United States, we will treat them separately, although much of the dissatisfaction in both countries derived from similar sources. Critics on both sides of the Atlantic, and this includes Canada as well, came to feel that the grand jury had outlived its usefulness.[158]

Jeremy Bentham, who offered the first important critique, denounced the grand jury as "an engine of corruption." His opposition was based on its upper-class composition and its inefficiency. He proposed substituting professional prosecutors, who would prove far less costly and far more efficient. The subject was discussed in and outside Parliament for several decades beginning about 1830. Parliamentary resolutions of 1834 and 1836, designed to curtail the use of grand juries, aroused considerable national interest but did not succeed. During the next two decades many judges and lawyers joined the movement for reform or abolition.[159] Some defenders still insisted on grand jury protection against arbitrary government, but that argument did not seem as important as it once had. Grand juries, it was argued, were excessively expensive in time and money and at times obstructed, rather than contributed to, justice. The growing size of the London metropolitan area and its high crime rate meant that hundreds of people were needed to operate the criminal justice system. In London the development of the police and the police court magistrates, who engaged in a judicialized preliminary hearing, increasingly made the grand jury appear redundant.

We still know relatively little about how pretrial examination of the seventeenth and early eighteenth centuries evolved into the judicialized preliminary hearing of the nineteenth century. It was, however, fully institutionalized by parliamentary legislation of 1848. The development of this procedure increasingly made the grand jury redundant. The justice of the peace was transformed from a fact gatherer with modest prosecutorial overtones, whose activity level varied enormously and who might or might not be present during grand jury and jury proceedings, into a judge who evaluated evidence according to a legislatively prescribed standard. If the magistrate acted as an impartial judge rather than as fact gatherer or prosecutor, there seemed to be little need for a grand jury to review his disposition of the case. The problems of the grand jury became clear first in the metropolitan areas. Thus William Forsyth, writing in 1852, distinguished between London, where there were active vigilant magistrates, and the countryside, where the magistracy was still dominated by the traditional landed gentry. Forsyth felt that the old system of grand jury and justice of the peace still functioned satisfactorily in the English countryside. It was 1872, however, before Parliament eliminated grand juries even in the London metropolitan area. By the 1880s, if not earlier, grand juries rarely were rejecting indictments. Most accusations brought on insufficient evidence had already been rejected at the preliminary hearing.[160]

Pressure for complete abolition continued. In 1913 a parliamentary commission again emphasized useless expenditure of money and time and found the grand jury to be "little more than an historically interesting survival" that had outlived its usefulness.[161] For all practical purposes, the English grand jury ceased to exist in 1917 when the labor shortages of the war caused its operation to be suspended. When suspension was lifted in 1921, a large part of the legal profession and magistracy supported permanent abolition. Given the economic pressures of the Depression and the continuing advocacy for abolition, the grand jury, which had been virtually nonoperative since the war, was abolished in 1933. From the middle of the nineteenth century, when the preliminary hearing took on a judicialized format, the grand jury's screening function was increasingly performed elsewhere.

Although the history of the grand jury in the United States exhibited many parallels, the outcome has been somewhat different. Complete abolition would have required successful campaigns in all the states and a federal constitutional amendment. Americans have had less faith than the English in the government officials who operate the criminal justice system. The investigative functions of American grand juries have made them less redundant than their English counterparts. And the role of the public prosecutor in America meant that both the grand jury and the preliminary hearing would function somewhat differently.

The reform and abolition campaign in England nevertheless had its reverberations in America. Several of the earliest American reformers, for example, Edward Livingston, a Benthamite, and Chancellor James Kent, were concerned with depoliticizing the grand jury. Debate over the wide-ranging investigative powers of the grand jury played a prominent role in American controversies. Discussion took place in several forums—law journals, law textbooks, legislatures, and state constitutional conventions. American discussion did not emphasize redundancy with the examining magistrate or public prosecutor, although that factor played some role and abolition would have been inconceivable without an institutional alternative for commencing criminal proceedings. The reform movement was played out in many states and in the territories approaching statehood. Political arguments emphasizing the grand jury as the citizen's protection against the bureaucratic state were voiced, as was the abolitionist view that while grand juries once provided needed safeguards against governmental tyranny, the protection of individuals was now insured by other means. By the time America entered World War I, many state jurisdictions had abandoned or limited the institution.[162]

Twentieth-century evidentiary grand jury standards developed in tandem with the developing standards for the preliminary hearing, which in so many jurisdictions was entirely or partially replacing the grand jury. They also developed in the context of the rise of professional public prosecutors, whose decisive roles in many jurisdictions made it appear as if grand juries were becoming rubber stamps.

The constitutionality of the shift from indictment to information, which began with Michigan's 1859 decision to allow felony cases to be brought by a prosecutor's information, was confirmed in 1884, when the Supreme Court ruled that the grand jury requirement of the Fifth Amendment did not apply to the states.[163] California law upheld by the Court specified a prosecutor's information followed by a judicialized preliminary hearing. After hearing the witnesses for the prosecution and their cross-examination by defense counsel, a magistrate was to determine whether there was probable cause to believe the defendant guilty. If so, the defendant was bound over for trial.[164] In "information states" prosecutors typically are given the option of employing indictment or information—a choice that usually results in the latter. By the 1890s, only twenty states and the federal government maintained a right to grand jury proceedings for felony prosecutions. Even in those jurisdictions where the grand jury continued to play a role, it fell increasingly under prosecutorial domination.[165]

Although the evidentiary standard of the judicialized preliminary hearing varied slightly from jurisdiction to jurisdiction, that institution on the whole adopted a standard of "probable cause," a concept derived from arrest and search and seizure standards.[166] The preliminary hearing was often, though not always, accompanied by a variety of defendant safeguards, such as a right to cross-examine government witnesses. It thus came somewhat closer to approximating the two-party adversarial character of the jury trial than did the grand jury proceeding, which did not hear the defendant, his witnesses, or his counsel.

Although the meaning of "probable cause" as employed in the preliminary hearing was not articulated as clearly as some might wish, it soon appeared as if those defendants who came to trial *via* the preliminary hearing route rather than the grand jury route, were being exposed to rather different evidentiary requirements and differing degrees of participation. To many, the *prima facie* case of the grand jury appeared to impose considerably higher standards of proof on the prosecution. The notion that there were alternative routes to trial, one with a "higher" and one with a "lower" standard, did not appear reasonable or fair, particularly where the

prosecutor was free to choose one or the other.[167] The courts and
the legal profession have attempted to bring the standards of the
grand jury and the preliminary hearing closer together. Thus probable cause increasingly replaced *prima facie* case as the standard
for grand juries, including federal grand juries.

Although probable cause has generally triumphed, *prima facie*
case has not entirely disappeared. As late as 1981, Alaska required
that a grand jury indict only "when all the evidence taken together,
if unexplained or uncontradicted, would warrant a conviction of the
defendant."[168] This may be contrasted with a 1967 California case
in which the judge ruled that evidence to justify prosecution by
information need not be sufficient to support a conviction. In the
court's view there was probable cause for prosecution, "if a man of
ordinary caution or prudence would be led to believe and consci-
entiously entertain a strong suspicion of the accused."[169] In some
jurisdictions, probable cause is roughly the same as that required
for arrest. In others, such probable cause is thought to require
more than probable cause for arrest but less than beyond a reasonable doubt of guilt.

The shift of the grand jury to probable cause has resulted in
ambiguity and confusion, although the confusion has been reduced
somewhat in the last decade. Probable cause is now the prevailing
grand jury evidentiary standard. The 1969 edition of Wright's *Federal Practice and Procedure* noted both the *prima facie* case and
the probable cause standards as appropriate for the grand jury and
puzzled about the relationship between them as well as their respective meanings. The 1981 edition, however, entirely dropped
the mention of *prima facie* case standard.[170] A leading textbook,
Modern Criminal Procedure, also reflects this confusion wrought
by the change. It indicates that *prime facie* case and probable cause
are both employed, and notes that *prima facie* case and probable
cause are generally regarded as quite different standards, each of
which suggests different degrees of probability. The authors believe
the difference can be explained as merely reflecting two ways of
expressing the same degree of probability adjusted to the non-
adversarial procedures of the grand jury and the adversarial preliminary hearing.[171] That, of course, might be true if probable cause
were never used for grand jury proceedings and *prima facie* case
never used for preliminary hearings. As we shall see, however,

some jurisdictions do use probable cause for grand jury proceedings, and a few even come close to *prima facie* case for preliminary hearings.[172]

Many courts have attempted to combine probable cause with *prima facie* case or to label a definition of *prima facie* case with the words "probable cause." Thus a federal judge instructs that the function of the grand jury

is to decide whether or not sufficient evidence has been produced to indicate that a crime probably has been committed by the person accused. Or stated another way: if upon the credible evidence which you have heard absent an explanation by the defendant, you would be willing to convict, you should indict.[173]

Another federal grand jury was instructed "conviction would be warranted if the evidence were presented to a trial [jury] where there is no evidence to rebut."[174] Yet the previous year another federal judge had instructed,

You're not a Trial Jury. That is, it is not your responsibility to determine the innocence or guilt of an accused defendant, but solely to determine whether or not sufficient evidence has been produced to indicate that a federal crime has been committed by the person accused.[175]

By "sufficient evidence" the judge appears to have meant enough evidence to satisfy the probable cause requirement for arrest.[176] Yet in 1978, another federal judge indicated,

Probable cause exists only where there is evidence, direct or circumstantial, which leads the grand jurors to believe that the proposed offender is guilty of the offense charged. [The grand jury] should be satisfied from the evidence which is submitted to it that a conviction would be warranted if the evidence were presented to a trial jury where there was no evidence to rebut it. This is what we call in the law *prima facie* evidence of probable cause.[177]

This *prima facie* formulation of probable cause is also used in a number of states for preliminary hearings. Yet if "probably has been committed" and "probable cause" as used in grand jury and preliminary hearing settings bear any relation to the "probable cause" we hear about in the context of arrest and search standards, then "*prima facie* case" most certainly is not probable cause "stated another way." Whatever its precise meaning, many jurisdictions employ probable cause as a far less demanding standard than *prima facie* case. Reflecting this fact, Moore's *Federal Practice* (1979) asserted that prosecutors "usually go further than the required probable cause and set forth what amounts to a *prima facie* case against the defendant."[178]

The confusion about *prima facie* case and probable cause of the last few decades is the product of a number of tensions and conflicts that arise in the course of partially, but not entirely, eliminating the grand jury from the American judicial system. It might be supposed that if those favoring the elimination were only trying to reduce the cumbersomeness of the criminal justice process, they might simply have substituted a single judge for the grand jurors and retained the *prima facie* case standard. Instead not only was a single judge substituted for the grand jury, but also probable cause was often substituted for *prima facie* case. In a number of jurisdictions that have retained the grand jury, the indictment standard nevertheless falls to probable cause. One begins to suspect that what is really going on is not simply a streamlining of the system but a shifting from individual liberties to crime control. Perhaps Americans want to ease the prosecutor's job of getting the accused to trial.

This explanation, however, is clearly an oversimplification. The situation was not one in which people were shopping around for something to replace the grand jury and so might most naturally have arrived at a judge, but with retention of *prima facie* case. Instead, as our English story has already shown, movements to eliminate the grand jury did not gain momentum until something else was in place to forward the accused to trial. At that point the issue is not seen so much as one of finding a replacement for the grand jury because it is cumbersome, but of simply eliminating the grand jury because it has become redundant. Grand juries disappear only after preliminary hearing procedures have been established. Such a simple elimination means that no one thinks much about what evidence standard should be introduced. Whatever evidence standard preliminary hearings were using at the time they rendered the grand jury redundant will almost automatically or by default become *the* standard for commitment to trial. The preliminary hearing is closely tied in time to the arrest and is intended in large part to provide judicial supervision of arrest. A probable cause

standard is employed for arrest. The preliminary hearing was originally preliminary to a grand jury proceeding, which would safe-
guard the defendant by employing a high or *prima facie* case standard. So it made sense for preliminary hearings to employ a
probable cause standard. Such a standard provided an adequate
check on police arrest decisions without creating a situation in
which examining magistrate and grand jury decided exactly the
same question. When grand juries are swept away as redundant,
probable cause replaces *prima facie* case without anyone giving it
serious thought simply because it is the standard in place for preliminary hearings.

At this point a number of new dynamics come into play. In those
states in which preliminary hearings and grand juries come to co-
exist as alternatives for prosecutors, it seems unfair to allow them
to have their pick of evidentiary standards by choosing one or the
other. So there is pressure toward moving both to either probable
cause or *prima facie* case standards. In federal jurisdictions and
states that retain the grand jury as the primary pretrial screen,
crime-control enthusiasts, casting jealous eyes on preliminary hearing states, seek to move the grand jury standard down to probable
cause. At the same time, those who see the removal of grand juries
as the removal of an important civil liberties protection will seek
to find various substitute protections, including moving the probable cause standard for preliminary hearings up to *prima facie* case.
And in the time-honored tradition of common-law judges and academic lawyers, considerable ingenuity and verbal slight of hand
will be employed to make it appear that there is no problem, that
somehow probable cause and *prima facie* case are the same or
nearly the same.

The central arena for much of the current American controversy
about the grand jury lies in an area that I have promised *not* to
consider in this book—rules governing the admissibility of evidence as opposed to rules defining the quantum of evidence necessary to justify finding against the accused. This controversy is so
closely tied to the *prima facie* case versus probable cause problem,
and so neatly reenacts in contemporary garb the seventeenth- and
eighteenth-century experience we have been examining, that it
seems appropriate to make some room for it here. The controversy
concerns what sorts of evidence ought to be admissible at grand

jury and/or preliminary hearings, and raises again the two-trial theme that keeps appearing in this chapter. Whether or not the grand jury proceeding is a trial is a question already being raised in Lambarde's sixteenth-century charges. As we have seen, it was central to the Shaftesbury case. Whig advocates, emphasizing safeguards for defendants, wished to move the grand jury in the direction of the trial jury. They thus spoke of "verdicts," not accusations, and insisted that the same level of certainty accompany both trial and grand jury decisions. Their opponents wished to view grand jury proceedings as accusatorial and prosecutorial rather than as a form of trial. Eighteenth-century discussion, for the most part, repeated that of the seventeenth.

The issue of how trial-like the grand jury should be was raised in its modern form with the introduction of the *prima facie* case standard. If grand juries were to be as convinced as the petty jury, albeit after hearing only the prosecution, must they hear only legally admissible and competent evidence, that is, evidence which could be introduced in a court of law? Indeed one could argue that the *prima facie* case standard implied the legal evidence standard. Thus as early as 1832, Chief Justice Shaw, who stated the *prima facie* case standard, insisted on the necessity of legal evidence,[179] and in 1852, Justice Nelson stated "evidence before a grand jury must be competent legal evidence, such as is legitimate and proper before a petit jury."[180] In 1861, a supporter of the *prima facie* case standard, Judge Leavitt, found it "inexpedient" to indict if evidence required for the trial jury was unavailable.[181] Justice Field's authoritative opinion of 1872, which clearly stated the *prima facie* standard, explicitly excluded "reports, suspicions, and hearsay" and insisted legal evidence alone was permissible—legal evidence being that which could be heard by a trial jury.[182]

Once we observe the connection between the *prima facie* case standard and the demand that grand juries hear only trial-admissible evidence, we can expect that, as a movement occurs away from *prima facie* case and toward probable cause, new questions will arise about what a grand jury may hear. More generally, as we move away from grand juries toward preliminary hearings, and as we shift preliminary screening away from the trial end and toward the accusation end of the process, such questions will arise. Once the questions are asked in a situation in which the stability of the *prima facie* case solution has been eroded, the same old dialectic reappears that marks the evolution of the grand jury itself. If only trial-admissible evidence is permitted, then the grand jury proceeding, or even the preliminary hearing, may not be a whole trial before the trial, but it comes close to being half a trial before the trial. Why make the prosecution prove its case twice? On the other hand, if standards of admissibility that have been developed for trial are not used at the preliminary stages, how do such stages rise above mere suspicion and prosecutorial allegation? How can they possibly protect the accused's substantial interest in not being arbitrarily or maliciously accused? And if the function of the preliminary stage is to make some sort of rough prediction about the chances of conviction by a trial jury, then is that predictive function compromised by hearing material that will not serve as any basis for the trial court's decision? All these questions become even more pressing in the context of plea bargaining practices, which often result in the preliminary stage being the only trial-like procedure that a defendant will receive.[183]

While Shaw, Nelson, Leavitt, and Field felt only legally admissible evidence was appropriate, a position in line with the *prima facie* case standard that they asserted, the Supreme Court slowly moved in the opposite direction from the beginning of the twentieth century. As early as 1910, in a unanimous opinion written by Justice Holmes, the Court held that indictments were not invalid simply because the grand jury considered some incompetent evidence along with some competent evidence.[184] The issue of how much and what kind of evidence might invalidate grand jury proceedings was explored in several cases in 1927 and 1928. Although for several decades the courts did not permit indictments where all the evidence was considered incompetent,[185] it was not entirely clear where the line was to be drawn.

In several important decisions, which have been followed in many, but by no means all, state jurisdictions, the U.S. Supreme Court decided that hearsay, under certain circumstances, was permissible in grand jury proceedings, even if it was the sole evidence presented.[186] The leading case, *United States v. Costello*, again shifted the grand jury away from a trial-like proceeding toward an accusatorial body. The judicial opinions expressed at both circuit court and Supreme Court levels illustrate the swing of the pendulum and the arguments for the change. Judge Learned Hand, who wrote the opinion upholding Costello's conviction, sharply distinguished jury trials from other proceedings. All proceedings except jury trials were to be "decided under the ordinary postulates of reasoning." "[T]he exclusory rules [of the trial] are an exception, for they apply to evidence that is relevant, rationally." Such evidence is excluded at trial "not because it does not prove, but it is thought unjust to . . . use it, . . . or because it is within some privilege to suppress the truth." A grand jury was entitled to proceed unless "no evidence" had been provided to "rationally" establish the facts.[187]

Costello involved an indictment for income tax evasion based on testimony that technically was hearsay because the proper foundation for it had not been laid. Judge Hand argued that hearsay evidence was rationally relevant to a determination of guilt and was excluded from the ultimate trial basically because it was not subject to cross-examination. That kind of adversarial, fairness consideration was inapplicable to grand jury proceedings, which were not adversarial in character (as were trials) and permitted no cross-examination.

Judge Frank, although concurring, expressed some leanings toward the late nineteenth-century, more trial-like position, indicating he had serious misgivings about the conclusion that a grand jury may indict solely on the basis of evidence that would not support a trial verdict.[188] Judge Frank was obviously disturbed at how far this decision took the grand jury from the model of the jury trial.

When the case reached the Supreme Court, Costello's indictment was again upheld. Justice Black, writing for the Court, argued that, traditionally, English grand juries could act "on such information they deemed satisfactory" in order to provide freedom "from control by the Crown on the judges." Grand juries had in the past, he argued, not been "hampered by rigid procedural or evidential rules." He thus appears to have harkened back to the pre-mid-nineteenth-century English grand jury discussion and practice. The grand jury was to screen factual guilt, not to determine legal guilt in adversarial proceedings. He was also concerned that a more trial-like procedure would lead to long delays and would involve "a kind of preliminary trial to determine the competency and adequacy of the evidence" to be presented to the grand jury. The spectre of two trials was raised again.[189]

Costello is one of those hard cases that make bad, or at least new, law. At trial the government had to call 144 witnesses to testify as to their firsthand knowledge of particular transactions. This testimony was necessary to lay the groundwork that would allow three agents to testify about Costello's records to pass over the hearsay barrier. Confronted with evidence that *was* ultimately admissible at trial and *was in fact* seen by the trial jury, judges balked at putting the prosecutor to the Hobson's choice of either keeping this crucial evidence from the grand jury or having to parade his 144 witnesses twice.[190] Neither Hand nor Black took the opportunities available to them to write a narrow opinion that would stress the particular facts or the particular kind of hearsay involved, or that would differentiate between the grand jury admissibility of hearsay and the grand jury admissibility of other kinds of evidence excluded from trial jury consideration. Indeed, they took the opposite tack, resting on a broad Tory vision of the grand jury as an accusatory body and laying the groundwork for grand jury admissibility of nearly anything the prosecutor wished to bring in.

Quite predictably, given Hand's lumping of hearsay with other "exclusory" evidence, later cases held that illegally seized evidence and evidence that was the product of unconstitutionally obtained self-incrimination were not barred from grand jury consideration.[191] Thus, in 1974, the Supreme Court ruled that the "validity of an indictment is not affected by the character of the evidence considered" and is "not subject to challenge on the basis of inadequate or incompetent evidence; or even on the basis of information obtained in violation of a defendant's Fifth Amendment privilege against self-incrimination."[192] The application of trial rules to the grand jury would hamper its accusing function. The grand jury "does not finally adjudicate guilt or innocence." "Traditionally" it has "been allowed to pursue its investigation and accusatorial functions unimpeded by the evidentiary and procedural restrictions applicable to a criminal trial."[193]

The last two or three decades thus have virtually reversed the position of late nineteenth-century judges. The balance has shifted away from the two-trial orientation toward one emphasizing accusation and prosecutorial needs and the distinction between accusation and trial. The Supreme Court and the federal courts thus currently assume that the grand jury will "screen out cases where there are no reasonable grounds for believing that the accused committed the crime."[194] This line of cases assumes that the *ex parte* proceeding is not designed to determine questions of guilt or innocence. That is assumed to be the function of the trial jury, which is conceived as a very different institution with different evidentiary standards. Yet, if the evidence, legal and illegal, is controlled by the prosecutor, the grand jury cannot be in a position to make an independent judgment. It must become virtually a rubber stamp of the prosecutor.

Perhaps one can fruitfully compare the position of Field and other late nineteenth-century judges cited earlier with the Shaftesbury-derived Whig view and *Costello* and its progeny with the Tory view that sharply distinguishes accusation from trial. The history of evidentiary issues in pretrial screening suggests that the current situation too will be unstable and that Whigs and Tories will continue their conflict.

That instability is clearest if we pose the following questions: Should a grand jury indict if there is a good chance that the accused is guilty in fact or only if there is a good chance that the trial jury will find the accused guilty? If the grand jury ultimately is part of a legal judicial process, rather than a process of strictly empirical inquiry, then the latter position may well be the proper one. Put another way, should we inflict upon an accused the damage that an indictment surely causes if we are not fairly sure whether he or she will ultimately be convicted?

The advantage of *prima facie* case standard is that it tells the grand jury not to inflict harm on the accused unless it can fairly predict that the accused would be found guilty by the trial jury. The advantage of the admissibility standard implied by the *prima facie* case rule is that it puts the grand jury in the best position to predict what the petty jury will do—a position in which it hears only the kind of evidence the trial jury will hear.

Given the fact that most pretrial screening is done in connection with the preliminary hearing, it is not surprising that the issue of how trial-like that institution should be has also become important. In that connection, perhaps one of the most salient issues has been whether the preliminary hearing must only employ evidence admissible at trial, or whether it may employ some "lower" standard.

The introduction of a probable cause standard to replace *prima facie* case almost inevitably has led to instability in this area, not only because "probable cause" is an inherently slippery standard, but because its employment necessarily imports resonances of arrest and search and seizure probable cause. It would, of course, be unrealistic to the point of absurdity to demand that police rely only on trial-admissible evidence to build up the probable cause for a search warrant that will render what they seize admissible at trial.

There is an enormous variety among the various U.S. jurisdictions concerning the preliminary hearing, with the California model being perhaps most trial-like, requiring only legally admissible evidence to establish probable cause, which is interpreted as if it were the *prima facie* case standard. Federal standards currently are far "lower" because the federal prosecutor need only find probable cause to believe the person has committed a federal offense. In making that judgment, prosecutors may consider much information that goes to the issue of factual guilt, for example, the statements of informers, illegally obtained evidence, and hearsay, which cannot be used at trial.[195] Justice Department guidelines, however, indicate that the prosecutor should especially consider "the weight of the evidence that will be available and admissible at trial. . . . [He] should have reason to believe that he will have sufficient admissible evidence at trial to sustain a conviction."[196] These standards need not be met, however, before the trial itself. That is, they do not need to be met before the preliminary hearing or even before the grand jury indicts.[197] Other American jurisdictions array themselves at every possible point in the spectrum between the California and the federal positions.[198]

Conclusion

This chapter has delved into current controversy because of the almost irresistible conclusion that certain fundamental dynamics are a historical constant whenever Anglo-American jurisdictions seek to devise some proceeding between accusation and trial. In Chapter 1 we saw the development of a legal doctrine that drew much of its inspiration and formulation from philosophy and religion. The driving forces behind grand jury developments are political conflict and tensions in the institutional structure of law itself. The perennial institutional problem is, of course, finding a securely anchored place for the grand jury somewhere between first accusation and final conviction or acquittal. The political conflict involves striking a balance between the power to prosecute and the protection of the individual against government power and malicious prosecution. In its earlier version, the political conflict was Whig versus Tory over the Crown's power either to inflict damage on its partisan opponents or to protect society against treason, depending upon which side was speaking. Whigs sought to push grand jury proceedings as far as possible in the direction of trials; Tories sought to render them a mere channel for formalizing accusation. In its contemporary version, the conflict is still over governmental power versus individual liberties and is easily described in terms of the Packer model or any of its variants.[199] Those concerned with facilitating criminal prosecution push the grand jury toward accusation either directly or by transformation into preliminary hearing. Those concerned with individual rights push both the grand jury and the preliminary hearing toward trial.

We have seen that while political stance and legal institutional concerns are central, epistemological problems are also relevant to grand jury developments. For it is impossible to anchor the grand jury securely between accusation and trial unless we can discover some standard for grand jury action that is securely anchored between "suspicion" and "beyond a reasonable doubt," or "moral certainty," of guilt. The epistemology of probabilities does not present the distinct intermediate steps or units of measure that would provide such a stable resting place. In the absence of such distinct intermediate degrees of probability, political pressure and institutional ambiguity will keep the grand jury, and its successor, the preliminary hearing, oscillating between the poles of accusation and trial.

In Chapter 2 we have encountered one of the genuine inventions of legal technology. By bringing together the well-established beyond a reasonable doubt standard rooted in the epistemological developments traced in Chapter 1 with the well-established legal institutional practice of allowing the grand jury to hear only the prosecution's case, judges invented the *prima facie* case. That concept provides a distinct, intermediate probability step, not by adding adjectives or measures to the word "probability," but by specifying a legal procedure for arriving at an intermediate probability. A grand jury that decides on guilt beyond a reasonable doubt on the basis of hearing only one side of the case clearly has employed a probability standard far higher than mere opinion, common fame, or suspicion and far lower than beyond reasonable doubt after hearing both sides of the case. The epistemological problem and the institutional problem are solved simultaneously. A stable place is found for the grand jury.

This stable place, however, proves in its turn to be subject to the same institutional and political tensions that it briefly appeared to have resolved. We are soon back to the two-trial problem. For if a *prima facie* case standard does not require two trials, it does logically entail two half-trials. The prosecution must present its case twice, once to the grand jury and once to the trial jury. Once the invention of *prima facie* case grand jury indictment is attacked, however, we return to the inherent instability that it was designed to correct. Whether we debate today over grand juries or preliminary hearings or both, the question again becomes how probable is probable enough to provide an institutionally distinct, politically justifiable and economically practical screening point between what the police and prosecutor do and what the trial court does. There is no reason to expect anything other than more instability and more Whigs and Tories until a new invention emerges that is as clear as *prima facie* case.

Chapter Three

Species of Probability and Institutional Migration

The law of evidence in criminal cases necessarily has two goals, that only appropriate persons be tried and that only guilty persons be convicted. Chapter 1 examined how, in pursuit of the second goal, the English came to formulate the doctrine of beyond reasonable doubt. Chapter 2 traced how indictment by grand jury and later the preliminary hearing have struggled to find an evidentiary standard somewhere between no evidence and the evidence required by the trial jury for conviction. The dilemma has been to find a level of probability that was neither so low that individuals would not be damaged and resources entailed in trying the innocent would not be wasted nor so high that pretrial itself became a trial.

Chapter 3 continues the discussion of pretrial procedure and the varieties of probability employed in bringing suspected persons to trial. A number of institutions and procedures wrestled with the problem of formulating standards of proof less certain than those required for conviction but high enough to serve a satisfactory screening function. We will focus on arrest, its offshoot search and seizure, and the pre-twentieth-century preliminary hearing.

An examination of these institutions and procedures will reveal a family of concepts that includes common fame, suspicion, probable cause, presumption, and circumstantial evidence—concepts that exhibited a tendency to migrate from one procedure to another. We have already seen one such migration, that of probable cause from the preliminary hearing to the grand jury in many mid-twentieth-century American jurisdictions.

Our efforts to understand the evidentiary requirements of pretrial procedures in the Anglo-American tradition requires a brief discussion of the European context and England's relation to it because we can understand the English developments far better if we understand both what they did and did not share with the Continental tradition. Thus a brief description of Romano-canon procedure and English and American attitudes toward it will serve as a necessary introduction to both this chapter and Chapter 4.

The Romano-Canon Tradition

Both common lawyers and civilians developed methods of assigning legal guilt only on the basis of the highest degree of certainty attainable in human affairs. The Romano-canon tradition hoped to achieve that goal with its method of legal proof—the testimony of two unimpeachable witnesses or confession of the accused. The Anglo-American tradition developed, albeit somewhat later, the jury verdict based on the concepts of satisfied conscience and moral certainty and their cognate, conviction beyond reasonable doubt. Both legal systems experienced greater difficulty in defining levels of probability to be met at earlier stages of criminal procedure. The Romano-canon law constructed concepts such as common fame, as distinguished from mere rumor or report, to serve as standards for arrest. The threshold for judicial torture aimed at eliciting confession was defined by a rather elaborate system of *indicia* and presumptions. And the Romano-canon system developed, albeit hesitantly and for use only in exceptional situations, methods of reaching decisions based on circumstantial evidence. The English system was similar in that it, too, attempted to develop criteria for moving from one pretrial stage to the next while screening out capricious accusations. The English sometimes borrowed concepts employed at one stage for use at another, and sometimes, either consciously or unconsciously, borrowed from the civilians as well.

The Romano-canon system of proofs had begun to develop even before the ecclesiastical prohibition of the ordeal of 1215.[1] Indeed the ordeal could not have been effectively abolished had there been no institutional and procedural alternative available. The Romano-canon system also had antecedents, and we must at least briefly note the heritage of the classical tradition of rhetoric, which had developed methods for treating the evidence and arguments of the everyday world.

The categories and concepts of probability and certainty were first explored in ancient Greece and Rome. Philosophers concentrated on developing methods that would yield certain or demonstrative knowledge, while rhetoricians focused on those areas of thought and life in which only probability was possible. Probability was thus a central concept for everyday decision making of which the law courts were part. The rhetorical tradition was concerned with argument rather than evidence, but eventually the categories established for one were transferred to the other. The rhetorical tradition was transmitted to and further developed in Rome, where rhetorical training became part of a gentleman's education and was necessary for participation in the forum and the law courts.

While many of these concepts were explored by Aristotle and Cicero, those most relevant to this study appear to have been transmitted most directly to later generations in Cicero's *De inventione* and Quintilian's *Institutes of the Orator*. A number of these concepts were developed further by canonists and civilians and then adopted and adapted by common lawyers. Quintilian's discussion was directed at the judicial oration and was not a part of the ancient Roman law of evidence, which was largely undeveloped.

Quintilian differentiated between inartificial and artificial proofs, a distinction already to be found in Aristotle's *Rhetoric*.[2] The first were proofs that were not the result of the art of the orator. In this category were witnesses, deeds, tortures, reports, and precedents. Although not created by the orator, they might be reenforced or countered by the powers of eloquence. Quintilian emphasized the oratorical uses of rumor and fame and noted how they might either be credited or discredited as idle stories. Torture similarly could be used positively by the orator as a necessary means of obtaining truth or denounced as yielding false testimony given only to avoid pain. Witnesses also could be used pro and con, and hearsay could be denounced as relying on the testimony of those not sworn to tell the truth.[3]

Artificial proofs—those constructed by the orator—were described and analyzed. The "things proper to enforce credibility and conviction" in the oration included signs, arguments, and examples. Quintilian's treatment of arguments is important because he discussed a variety of types which later found their way into canon and civil law and then into English law, particularly into the English "causes of suspicion" which provided the conceptual basis for both arrest and pretrial examination.[4] The rhetorician's distinction between inartificial and artificial proofs also had a long life—after these concepts had been translated, albeit somewhat incorrectly, into direct and indirect, or circumstantial, evidence. The rhetorical concept of artificial proofs would have an extremely long life, playing an important role in both canon and civil law and in the Anglo-American tradition.

For Quintilian, "arguments" of the judicial orator dealt with the probable. One kind of probabilistic argument might be drawn from "persons." Because it was widely believed that children were similar to their parents and ancestors, arguments from family might be employed in establishing honesty or scandalous life-style. Arguments based on nationality, sex, age, education, bodily habits, and personal fortune or condition might be significant. Men were more likely to be robbers and women poisoners. Eminent men, magistrates, and freemen were more likely to be innocent than those who followed mean occupations or who were private men or slaves. An individual's "passion or inclination" toward avarice, cruelty, or luxury provided strong arguments against him.[5] It would not be difficult for medieval and early modern legal thinkers to adapt these rhetorical categories to the examination of suspects and witnesses.

For Quintilian and the ancient rhetoricians, arguments might also be drawn from the causes of things done or that may be done. Questions of time, place, and the powers or abilities thus could be used, as could antecedents of the affair, collateral circumstances, consequences, opportunity, instrument, and method.[6] Here, again, what were categories and types of argument for Quintilian and the ancient oratorical tradition were translated into evidentiary categories in later legal traditions. Other varieties of argument, such as those from similarity and definition, did not find their way into the evidentiary tradition, though they remained a mainstay for speakers and writers both in and outside the courtroom.

That portion of the rhetorical tradition dealing with public issues was largely eclipsed in the late imperial period. The law under

Justinian had not found a stable theory of evidence in any event.[7] And much of rhetoric's legal application was lost in the early Middle Ages as the legal institutions of Germanic groups overlay and succeeded Roman institutions and practices. The era of irrational proofs, ordeals, compurgation, oaths, and oath helping did not require much of what we would call evidence or even argument.

Scholasticism, however, did concern itself profoundly with questions of evidence, proof, and appropriate modes of argumentation in a wide range of subject matters from theology to physics. Scholasticism was, of course, primarily an ecclesiastical development, and so naturally it looked first at its own institutions and priorities, including the procedures of the ecclesiastical courts. This intersection of scholasticism and courts reintroduced elements of the rhetorical tradition into legal practices. The decades both preceding and following the abolition of the ordeals developed rational approaches to a large variety of intellectual and legal issues.

The ecclesiastical courts spread over all of Christendom, including England, and administered an ecclesiastically developed canon law. Central to that law was the Romano-canon inquisition process, which left significant residues in English law, particularly in the evidentiary aspects of pretrial criminal procedure. One of the reasons that this indebtedness has not been sufficiently recognized is that the history of the Anglo-American law of evidence has focused almost exclusively on the trial and has largely ignored pretrial procedures.

The Romano-canon inquisition process was developed early in northern Italy. From there it spread to France and other northern European countries, where to varying degrees it combined with and replaced not only the ordeal but also other Germanic and feudal modes of trial. Canonists and the northern Italian civilian jurists developed an elaborate and systematic jurisprudence, which contained rational methods of proof, techniques for examining witnesses, methods of discovering and verifying facts, and rules to prevent the introduction of superficial and impertinent evidence.

All legal systems require methods of bringing accused persons to the attention of the court as well as rules for establishing guilt or innocence. Ecclesiastics were the first to develop techniques, or criteria, for bringing accused persons, frequently ecclesiastics, before an appropriate tribunal. Concepts of suspicion and common fame were introduced as elements in the screening process. By the thirteenth century there was already considerable discussion of *fama* and its procedural role. Fame, which arose from people who had reason to be knowledgeable, was to be believed but was not held to be certain or true. Common fame was sufficient to detain a suspect and initiate criminal proceedings but alone was insufficient to convict or even to torture.[8] Chapter 2 described how Bracton employed the Romano-canon distinction between common fame and rumor.

Either confession or the testimony of two unimpeachable witnesses was required for "full" or legal proof in serious criminal offenses.[9] Circumstantial evidence was considered inferior and did not constitute legal proof. Nor did the testimony of a single witness, even if consistent with other evidence.

Full or complete proof in serious criminal matters was not always readily available. Two good witnesses were not always conveniently present at the commission of a crime, and confessions often were not forthcoming. The Romano-canon inquisition process thus developed judicial torture as a means of eliciting confession. Judges, both ecclesiastic and civil, could not act capriciously. Only if signs, or *indicia*, were available in sufficient quality and quantity could torture be applied to the accused. A learned literature dealing with the *indicia*, which were drawn from the rhetoricians' categories (for example, time, place, and the power and ability to do the act), came into existence to provide the necessary guidance and uniformity. Unlike the area of legal proof, in the areas of *indicia*, circumstantial evidence, and presumption, the subjective persuasion of the judge played a substantial role.

The Romano-canon inquisition process required a legally trained bureaucracy and was not characterized by the combination of lay jurors and professional judges so typical of the Anglo-American system. A hierarchical arrangement allowed for appeal, which was lacking in the nonhierarchical English legal system. Professionalization permitted the development of a sophisticated and complex approach to matters of evidence and proof. A highly sophisticated and technical treatise and procedural tradition developed to insure uniformity and the exploration of difficult evidentiary issues. It resulted in a learned Latin literature of European scope. That literature, continuously enriched by canonists and civilian jurists, became even better and more widely diffused with the advent of the printed book. This body of writing dealt not only with witnesses and formal legal proof but also with circumstantial evidence, the *indicia*, and presumptions. The names of Tancred, Durantis, Bartolus, Baldus, Menochius, Mascardus, Alciatus, Clarus, Matthaeus, Farinaccius, and Carpzov suggest the richness and longevity of this tradition.

The system of legal proof proved difficult to operate, and over time alternatives were developed which permitted a role for circumstantial evidence and less than full proof. The first modification was the introduction of the category "manifest," or "notorious" crime, a crime so well and widely known that it would not even require an accuser. Another circumvention that had developed by the thirteenth century allowed conviction on the basis of undoubted *indicia*, the *indicia* being that circumstantial evidence or those signs which were the criteria for torture. Thus undoubted *indicia*, or "violent presumption," might sometimes allow conviction. In addition, there was a special category of secret or difficult to prove crimes, the *crimen exceptum*, which permitted proof by undoubted *indicia* or violent presumption.

Another modification that blurred the distinction between legal and lesser proofs was the development of the *poena extraordinaria*, which permitted an enhanced role for circumstantial evidence and conviction on less than full legal proof. Partial punishments were permitted for partial proof. The *poena extraordinaria* thus permitted punishment, albeit not the death penalty, with less than full or legal proof. Two half proofs might lead to judgment. The proof of a single witness and grave *indicia* also made a decision possible. This device, developed by Italian jurists, spread to France and other Continental nations.[10] Still another device was to withhold judgment when less than full proof was available. Although judgment theoretically might be given at a later date, presumably when more or better evidence became available, this device effectively functioned as a kind of probation because, at least in France, defendants typically did not return to court.[11] There were thus a number of developments and procedures which blurred the line between full proof and lesser proofs.[12]

As we shall see shortly, many of the conceptions of the Romano-canon inquisition process, for example, common fame, the *indicia*, presumption, circumstantial evidence, and exceptional crimes, were eventually found in the Anglo-American legal tradition, albeit with their Continental sources unacknowledged. They were adapted to a quite different set of institutions and procedures and were largely administered by laymen rather than legal professionals. Both this and the following chapter trace the migration of conceptual elements of the Romano-canon evidence system to the English. Some of that transmission has already been referred to in connection with grand juries.

If the English legal community faced many of the same problems as the Continental, then it is important to ask why it did not openly borrow, or at least openly discuss, Continental alternatives. The answer to this question is rather complex. The English did selectively borrow from the canon and civil law, but they were reluctant to admit it for a number of reasons. One was the national chauvinism so clearly expressed in Sir John Fortescue's late fifteenth-century *De Laudibus Legum Anglie*, which contrasted Continental and English legal and political systems. England's superior system was defined by a monarchy limited by law and trial by jury, while the French monarchy was unlimited by law and employed a legal system characterized by inquisitorial procedure and torture. Civil law was associated both with the absence of local and lay participation and an absolutist form of monarchy.[13] This association was for many generations a potent element in English political ideology.

Rivalry between ecclesiastical and common-law jurisdictions also militated against explicit borrowing. When borrowing did occur, it was safely anglicized through citations to Bracton or Coke. Star Chamber and Chancery procedure exhibited some Romano-canon features, such as the absence of juries and the use of written depositions. Admiralty was run largely by civilians employing civilian procedure. Romano-canon conceptions of proof were thus well known, continuing virtually unchanged in the post-Reformation ecclesiastical courts. The very fact, however, that these conceptions of proof were employed by the rivals of the common-law courts provided a strong incentive for common lawyers to associate them with the evils of Continental despotism. The many sixteenth- and seventeenth-century editions of *De Laudibus Legum Anglie* thus had the effect of reinforcing the contrast between the nefarious inquisition process and the trial by jury, the former associated with Continental despotism, the latter with English constitutional monarchy.

There were, of course, civilians in England, and civil law was taught at the universities by the Regius Professors. The civilians added a comparative perspective on English law that generally was lacking among the common lawyers.[14] But even that academic perspective was translated into political controversy. Thus, the civilian John Cowell, like William Fulbecke before him, wished to explain the differences and similarities between the English and civil law. Cowell's *Institutes* and the *Interpreter* appeared during the heyday of adulation of the common law. Coke's approach was thus to accuse Cowell of being foreign and disloyal.[15] The ideologically based rejection of Cowell's work thus obscured many of the common elements in English and Continental law. Cowell also hoped a side-by-side comparison of civilian and common-law cases would show "that they both be raised of one foundation, and differ more in language and terms" than substance.[16] Cowell noted that citations to Bracton and other medieval English legal sources typically failed to note that these sources were themselves frequently citing Roman law "in disguise." But it was dangerous, in Coke's opinion, for canonists and civilians "to write either of the common laws of England which they profess not, or against them which they know not."[17] Coke's influential posthumously published *Institutes* continued the attack. The hostility of the common lawyers was thus an important factor in obscuring the comparativist approach of sixteenth- and seventeenth-century civilians. The similarities among the various European legal traditions were thus obscured.

Nevertheless, leading legal thinkers and reformers such as Sir Francis Bacon and Sir Matthew Hale were well read in the civil law tradition. Indeed, it has been suggested that Bacon's empirical philosophy owes something to methods of Chancery interrogation. Bacon's correspondence too suggests his admiration for the civilians as well as his commitment to the common law.[18] Mid-century civilians Arthur Duck and Sir Robert Wise also emphasized the importance of the civil law for the common law. Duck suggested that common lawyers "were excellently well-versed in the Civil Law, from whence they have borrowed a great deal, both to explicate and to illustrate the law of England" and denied that the civil law was "foreign."[19] Sir Matthew Hale, the most prominent jurist in the decades following Coke's preeminence, exhibited an increasingly open but still circumspect attitude toward the civil law. Hale "set himself to the study of the Roman Law" because the "true grounds and reason of the Law" were so developed there that "a man could never understand law as a science so well as by seeking it there," and he "lamented much that it was so little studied in England."[20] Yet Hale's writings rarely indicated openly a dependence on the civil law. National hostility had not yet sufficiently abated to allow Hale to indicate that he occasionally was merely translating civilian doctrine into English law.[21] Those who relied on Hale were thus unaware of the ways in which English law made use of Roman legal concepts.

By the beginning of the eighteenth century, however, attitudes toward the Roman law were changing. Not only was the comparative perspective becoming more respectable, and the books of earlier civilians like Cowell reissued, but works like Thomas Wood's *New Institute of the Imperial or Civil Law* became quite popular. Wood was anxious to show the gentlemen of the realm how the Roman law had influenced England as well as other European nations. He insisted that the English had borrowed many rules and modes of reasoning from the civil law, although English lawyers were "apt to think that it was all their own from the Beginning because they have Possession and find it as present in their Books."[22]

Perhaps more important than Wood's project was the revived interest in natural law. From a natural law perspective the English common law and the civil law might have been seen as cousins within a universal natural law family. A natural law perspective thus was important in overcoming the almost automatic dismissal of non-English law. If borrowings from the civil law are most obvious and had their greatest impact on commercial law, the erosion of fear and hostility also made it easier to incorporate concepts relating to evidentiary matters. The development of treatise literature in the eighteenth and nineteenth centuries also was important, for many treatise writers hoped to base their work on a general or universal foundation.[23]

Many of the eighteenth-century natural lawyers were Continental civilians who incorporated large portions of the civil law tradition into their work. The absorption of civilian principles into natural law formats made them more palatable to the English. Domat's much-praised late seventeenth-century *Civil Law in Its Natural Order* (1694), which was widely read in England, contained a lengthy section on proofs and presumptions.[24] Though many of Domat's statements on these matters were civilian in character, proofs and presumptions were explained in general terms rather than as the law of a specific place and time. Similarly Pothier's *Treatise on the Law of Obligations or Contracts* (1761) provided a short section on the law of proof, which is a "general view of the law of evidence," in a form that did not obviously smack of foreign influence.[25] The translations of Domat and Pothier mark a new openness to Roman law, as well as to the spirit of systematization and the efforts to establish a general science of jurisprudence. The development of the treatise tradition also is linked to these developments.

A second major eighteenth-century development that influenced English writers on evidence was the self-conscious absorption of philosophical principles into the law. We have already seen the philosophical and epistemological bases of the concepts of moral certainty and beyond reasonable doubt. We shall see in Chapter 4 how treatments of circumstantial evidence and presumption were similarly affected by efforts to place them in the context of epistemology and logic. We should note here the importance of the Scottish Common Sense school of philosophers upon which so many English and American writers would draw. This school was not only associated with a kind of natural law approach but also informed by the evidentiary concepts of the civilians who played an important part in the law of Scotland. English writing on evidence drew heavily on Scottish philosophy.

The combined impact of the Continental natural law tradition and the philosophical developments of the eighteenth and nineteenth centuries thus created an attitude far different from that of earlier times. As we shall see in Chapter 4, the work of the treatise writers grafted these principles onto the traditional practice and lore of English evidentiary rules and principles and expanded them enormously in the process.

The experience of the United States ran along similar lines. Indeed it was heightened by the temporary post-revolutionary desire to lessen dependency on English law. The advantages of the civil law were thus paraded in most of the former colonies.[26] Even before the Revolution, however, Americans were making use of the natural law tradition. In America that tradition was often facilitated or mediated through the Scottish Common Sense school. The Scottish philosophy carried not only a natural law but also a Scottish civil law approach to evidence. As Americans absorbed one from the Scots, they were bound to absorb some of the other as well.

During the eighteenth and early nineteenth centuries the civil law in America was associated with order, clarity, and coherence and provided, if only briefly, a counterweight to the somewhat suspect British tradition. The civil law, often filtered through the natural lawyers, thus made a considerable impact on early American legal thought. Joseph Story (1770–1845), associate justice of the Supreme Court, typifies the new attitude. Not only did Continental jurisprudence rest on the foundations of ancient Roman law, but also the English common law "condescended silently to borrow many of its best principles" from it as well.[27] Chancellor James Kent's Columbia law lectures exhibit a similar attraction to the civilians. He, like Story, notes the long-term prejudice of the English lawyers against the civil law and the new appreciation of the "intrinsic merit of the Roman system."[28]

The silent borrowing observed by Story and others is often difficult to trace in the English texts. Open borrowing, however, became easier and more acceptable for the Americans when it was derived from or placed in the context of natural jurisprudence, which appeared less foreign. Pufendorf, Heineccius, Burlamaqui, Domat, and Pothier were thus far easier to absorb than the civilians of earlier centuries.[29] Americans of this generation were relatively free of the ideological need to dissociate themselves from the Continental legal tradition.[30]

American legal educators also hoped to make better use of civil law principles. David Hoffman's *Course of Legal Study* emphasized the current importance of the civil law and, like Story and Kent, the degree to which the common law had silently borrowed from it.[31] Hoffman recommends the writings of several early modern civilians, and praised the recent philosophically oriented evidentiary treatises of Starkie and Phillips.[32] Evidence for Hoffman was "without doubt the most important branch of a student's course" and "should be founded on the clearest observations, of man's moral and intellectual nature." Proper education in evidence required not only the study of the English treatises, but also "such works as manifest the great and pervading truths of the science— evince the general philosophy—and teach the experience of other ages and other nations." "The philosophy of the English law of evidence has been much impaired by a . . . neglect of the civilians" and of the Continental evidence tradition. In addition to works by civilians, he recommends the logical and epistemological writings of Bacon, Locke, Watts, Reid, Butler, Paley, and Stewart.[33]

Hoffman is particularly important for our purposes because he suggests not only the new willingness to incorporate the evidentiary tradition of the European civilians but also the concern to bring to bear the philosophical traditions of epistemology on legal evidence. Like so many treatise writers on evidence, Hoffman insisted on the need for law to be placed in the context of contemporary theories of knowledge. The willingness to use the civilians and the philosophical work of the epistemologists and logicians was already bearing fruit in Anglo-American writings on evidence. We have already seen how philosophical works resonated in the development of the concepts of moral certainty and beyond reasonable doubt. In Chapter 4 we will see how they provide the intellectual underpinnings for works dealing with presumption and circumstantial evidence.

America's brief but important enthusiasm for the civil law reached its height in the 1820s and 1830s and ceased to be a major intellectual force by 1850, largely because the enthusiasm never made substantial inroads on most practitioners and because intellectuals were becoming more attracted to Benthamism and the historical school.[34] The period of increased openness of the upper echelons of the English and American legal community, however, coincided with the flourishing of the legal treatise. And it was the treatises employed by law teachers and practitioners which conveyed philosophical and civilian influences into the mainstream of Anglo-American legal culture. Practitioners were thus often unaware that portions of the law of evidence which treated such matters as circumstantial evidence and presumptions were at least partially derived from philosophical and foreign legal sources.

It has been necessary to present this general background material on Roman law influences because developments in the law of arrest, preliminary examination, and grand jury indictment that are discussed here and the discussion of presumption and circumstantial evidence reviewed in Chapter 4 reveal a complex pattern in which the standards of evidence for each are compounded out of borrowings from the others, from earlier stages of their own development, and from the Romano-canon legal tradition.

Arrest

Explicit evidentiary elements appear much earlier in connection with arrest than with other stages of the pretrial criminal process. Arrest is a very old procedure. It is the stopping and holding of one individual who is suspected by another of having committed a felony. Pollock and Maitland have suggested that arrests in the thirteenth century were quite rare except in cases of hot pursuit,[35] and it has also been suggested that by the fourteenth century there had developed a notion of adequate and inadequate grounds for arrest and a procedure for suits for false arrest.[36] Initially arrest was conceived of as an act of the individual rather than that of some official, but constables were probably also given such authority. In 1360 the justices of the peace were given statutory authority "to take and arrest all those that they may find by indictment, or by suspicion."[37] Many arrests thus followed, rather than preceded, indictment by a presentment jury. The justices of the peace only gradually acquired the authority to issue arrest warrants. Because arrest procedures had initially been formulated for private persons and only later extended to officials, the conditions under which the justices of the peace could issue warrants for arrest were vague and disputed for several centuries. Post-indictment arrests did not, of course, raise independent problems of levels of evidence and so do not concern us here.

The most important concept in connection with arrest of an alleged wrongdoer for felony was "suspicion," a concept that appears to have owed a good deal to the formulations of Cicero and Quintilian. The concept was well developed by the medieval canon law, and the English probably borrowed from that usage in connection with arrest. The concept of "light suspicion" appears in a 1275 English statute, suggesting that it was already playing a role in English criminal law, albeit not always in connection with arrest.[38]

The concept of suspicion was well developed by Bracton, although he employs it in the context of indictment rather than arrest. Nevertheless, when later writers discuss the causes of suspicion justifying arrest, they frequently cite Bracton. Such citation provides an excellent example of the way in which a concept first used in one procedural context becomes detached from it and employed in another. Evidentiary concepts often have a legal life that continues long after the original procedure to which they were attached has altered or even ceased to exist.

Bracton was greatly indebted to the canon and civilian traditions. For Bracton, rumor, a lesser category, "begets suspicion," but only rumor that arises "among worthy and responsible men, not among those who wish and speak evil but wise and trustworthy persons, and it must not be once but repeatedly that complaint arises and ill-repute is made manifest."[39] Suspicion might also arise from "a precedent act." And from rumor and suspicion a "strong presumption" may arise. As I have noted, Bracton's language suggested the influence of the Romano-canon process where notions of common fame, rumor, and suspicion were employed. Once encapsulated in Bracton, however, the "foreign" origins of these concepts could be conveniently forgotten, and they could assume the status of English principles. Later writers, particularly the compilers of the handbooks for the justice of the peace citing Bracton's authority, dealt with suspicion in connection with both arrest and preliminary examination. Suspicion thus became the focus of the appropriate criteria for arrest.

We do not have much information as to how the process of arrest developed in England. Arrest originally was closely connected to the hue and cry, but, as Pollock and Maitland have suggested, often the hue and cry did not occur when it should have.[40] The Statute of Winchester (1285) permitted arrest of those behaving suspiciously at night, and the Statute of Northampton (1332) permitted arrest at any hour of armed persons or those suspected of evil doing who pass through townships. Only a moderate degree of suspicion appeared to have been required in those instances. John Bellamy has suggested that by the late fifteenth century individuals were being required to make arrests if they knew felonies had been committed or if trespasses might lead to felony. If, however, they only suspected a person of having committed a felony, they might but were not required to make arrests. Such suspicions required good evidence, but how good was not spelled out. Citizen arrests were contemplated, but the criteria for them remained poorly defined. There was, however, a substantial distinction between the criteria for constables and that for private citizens. The constable's grounds of suspicion might be less certain than those of the private citizen.[41]

The advent of printed handbooks for the justice of the peace in the sixteenth century makes the state of the formal law concerning arrest and the evidentiary requirements for arrest much clearer, although the authors of the handbooks do not tell us a great deal about actual practice. These handbooks, from their inception, included a list of the "causes of suspicion." Typically a list included the age, sex, education, parentage, character, associates, and habitual behavior of the suspect, as well as his ability to commit the crime, his whereabouts at the time of the crime, the presence of witnesses and/or signs (for example, blood) that engender suspicion. Parallel elements in the Romano-canon inquisition process are obvious as are its origins in classical rhetoric. The causes of suspicion justifying arrest in England are virtually the same as the *indicia* that on the Continent served to determine if a suspect should be examined under torture.

These parallels are seen most clearly by an examination of the imperial criminal code of 1539, the *Carolina*, which required "legally sufficient signs, suspicion, and presumption" before legal torture might occur. While noting that not all "circumstances of suspicion" could be "set forth," it does set forth five deemed basic for regulating examination under torture.

First: When the accused is an insolent and wanton person of bad repute and regard, so that the crime could be credibly ascribed to him, or when the same person shall have dared to perform a similar crime previously or shall have been accused of having done so. However this bad repute shall not be adduced from enemies or wanton people, [but] rather from impartial and upright people.

Second: When the suspected person has been caught or found at a place suspicious in the context of the deed.

Third: When a culprit has been seen in the deed or while on the way to or from it: in the case [where the culprit has been seen but not recognized], attention should be paid to whether the suspect has such a figure, such clothes, weapon, horses . . . [as the observed culprit].

Fourth: When the suspected person lives with or associates with such people as commit similar crimes.

Fifth: In cases of damage to property or persons, attention shall be paid to [possible] . . . envy, enmity, formal threat, or the expectation of some advantage.[42]

The evidentiary elements in the *Carolina* had been incorporated into the ecclesiastical court proceedings familiar to the English and into the procedure of most other civil law systems.

This fairly obvious English borrowing of the causes of suspicion does not mean English law was moving in the direction of the Continental inquisition process, but only that these particular evidentiary formulations proved useful to the English for their own purposes. Guidelines were needed that would insure accusations had some rational basis but that would not require citizens who suspected others of having committed a felony to fully prove their suspicions. The Romano-canon doctrine of signs, or *indicia*, was reasonably well adopted to this purpose. Indeed, it proved to be so handy in the context of arrest that when the justices of the peace became involved in examining accused felons, they too were expected to employ the causes of suspicion. The repetition of the causes of suspicion in several centuries of handbooks gave them the status of law.

What must be carefully noted, however, are the shifts in institutional context of the machinery of causes of suspicion. In civil and canon law, the *indicia* of suspicion were tools used by professional officials distanced from the events. When suspicion is inserted in the early English context, it necessarily must take on far more subjective overtones because it becomes a standard for judging the conduct of lay persons immediately involved in the events and the social context in which they make the decision to arrest. As police arrest and arrest warrants issued by magistrates come to replace citizen's arrest, causes of suspicion again become a more objective tool of officials—but now with an overlay of several centuries of English experience with citizen's arrest.

The Handbook Tradition

William Lambarde's handbook *Eirenarcha, or Of the Office of the Justice of the Peace* identifies arrest as a Norman creation, derived from the "execution of the commandment of some Court or of some Officer in Justice" which involved "restraint of a man's person, . . . and becoming obedient to the will of the Law."[43] Lambarde, who cites Bracton on the subject of suspicion, generally assumes that arrest will be instigated by a private party. Lambarde does not discuss the role of the justice in evaluation of the facts supporting an arrest. He does, however, mention such a role in another context which may provide a clue to the ways in which the justices of the peace came to have an evaluative role in the arrest process. For Lambarde, the justices clearly had such a role in reference to bonds of "good abearing" for keeping the peace. The justices had the authority to demand such bonds on their own initiatives or on the complaint of others. Lambarde noted, in words which suggest some hesitancy about his position, "yet I would wish rather, that they do not command it but only upon sufficient cause seen to themselves, or upon the suit of complaint of others, and the same very honest and credible persons." In addition he noted that whether "the cause of suspicion be good" would be determined by a judge in an action of false imprisonment or upon a *habeas corpus*.[44] In requiring bonds, the justices were to determine the adequacies of the charges and take into account the fame or lack of good fame of the person involved. Reputation and lifestyle were explicitly a primary feature of that evaluation. The printed marginal notations in Lambarde indicate that any of a list of items was a "sufficient cause" to require sureties for good behavior. The constant involvement of the justices in such evaluation may have eased the transition to a more evaluative role in the process of arrest.

Michael Dalton's *Country Justice* was the most influential and widely distributed handbook of the seventeenth century in both England and the American colonies. It conveyed the law and practice of the English criminal process to lawyers and nonlawyers alike for several generations. Although originally a nonofficial handbook for the justices, it became virtually an official legal document which

later authorities such as Sir Matthew Hale would cite as legal authority. For the most part Dalton repeats traditional notions. Arrest
by private individual without benefit of a warrant was the model
whatever the legal practice might have been. When one individual
arrested another "there must be some just cause, or some lawful
and just suspicion at the least." The private individual can also
make an arrest "when he knoweth or seeth [another] to have committed a . . . felony, and may deliver him to the Constable." After
a felony has been committed, anyone can arrest "suspicious persons that be of evil fame." Dalton emphasized, however, that the
arrest of suspicious persons required the actual commission of the
felony and that the party making the arrest must have the suspicion
himself. The person making the arrest must allege some special
matter to prove that he did actually suspect. Otherwise anyone
could arrest another. This suspicion might involve evil fame or the
fact that the person was a vagrant. Dalton's language, and that of
his successors, thus clearly emphasizes the role of the private citizen, although it appears as if that role had in practice severely
contracted and was actually being replaced by the intervention of
the justice of the peace who issued warrants for arrest on the request of some complainant or informant. Nevertheless the 1635 and
later editions of *The Country Justice* added materials concerning
the suspicions of the arresting private citizen.[45]

Dalton also discussed arrest by sheriffs, bailiffs, constables, and
justices of the peace. His main point is to insist that these officers
may make arrests without warrants in all cases where a private
person might—but only upon suspicion.[46] The conditions under
which a justice of the peace might grant a warrant for a felony
arrest, either on his own discretion or upon complaint, were obviously becoming more important. Traditionally the justice might
arrest those who broke the peace or those that he "shall suspect to
be inclined to break the peace." Such warrants, however, did not
involve felonies.

Dalton noted that "it [was] much controverted" whether the justice could grant warrants to arrest those suspected of felony, or
against offenders upon a penal statute," unless they were first indicted, a practice which appears already to have disappeared. Dalton argued that because the justice of the peace was a judge of
record, he must have "a Record whereupon he doth award his pro-

cess or precept."[47] Dalton indicates that the conditions under which the justice might grant a felony arrest warrant were confused. He did little to sort out this confusion which had developed as the justices increasingly became involved in granting warrants for arrest.

The large literature on legal reform during the English Civil War and interregnum did not touch on the question of pretrial procedures.[48] Thus William Sheppard, perhaps the most prolific mid-century reformist author, repeated the statements of his handbook predecessors. Any citizen could make an arrest without a warrant if he had seen the felony done or "suspected" a felony. In connection with suspicion he mentions the hue and cry, common voice and fame that the individual did the act, was the companion of thieves, hid, or fled. An abbreviated list of what might appropriately result in suspicion was included. He noted that whether or not "the cause of suspicion be good" would be determined by a judge in the action of false imprisonment or upon a *habeus corpus*. After a felony had been committed, anyone, including a constable or officer, "that suspects another" may arrest and bring the suspect to the justice of the peace. The accuser must have "some cause and reason to suspect that party that he doth arrest." Sheppard, however, indicated that if an individual were to "suspect and complain" to the constable, then the officer may not arrest him "on my suspicion."[49] "If I arrest him the constable may keep him."[50] Sheppard's citation to a recent decision also suggests that there was difficulty in distinguishing between what was appropriate for individual citizens and what was permissible for officers.[51]

The language of the handbooks frequently did not change as practice changed but retained residues of former practice or legislation which had never been updated. The medieval practice of arrest following indictment was thus retained in the handbooks, although after the passage of the mid-sixteenth-century Marian bail and committal statutes arrests typically occurred before examination, which itself took place prior to indictment. And although Sheppard and other writers refer to the hue and cry, the practice of community pursuit of suspected criminals appears largely to have ceased several centuries earlier.[52] The terms nevertheless remained in use, typically in connection with granting warrants for arrest.[53] Sheppard noted that any citizen or constable who had "some cause and reason to suspect that party that he doth arrest" might lawfully bring a man to a justice, "yet the contrary is practiced, and seems necessary at this day: for the constables were ignorant and fearful of doing anything without the justice's warrant."[54] "Besides when the justice of the peace hath information upon oath, he hath good cause to suspect, and so may proceed on his own suspicion."[55] Here Sheppard is desperately clinging to the old rule of personal suspicion even for the justice, but obviously somewhere during the course of the sixteenth and seventeenth centuries the justice had begun to be an evaluator of informants' suspicions. The practice of arrest by citizens was being replaced by informants' bringing their suspicions to the justice, who in turn made some estimate of their validity or reasonableness.

We cannot exactly date the transition from arrest by an individual who suspects to arrest on the basis of a warrant issued by a justice of the peace. The latter process was certainly well in place by the seventeenth century and had probably been so for several centuries. The change caused problems for legal thinkers because the suspicion was no longer directly engendered in the mind of someone who had personally observed a crime or by other more or less immediate circumstances. The criteria for suspicion thus had somehow to be transferred to the official who issued the warrant.

Coke vigorously resisted such a transfer. He argued that it was not appropriate for the justice of the peace to issue an arrest warrant merely because private citizen A suspected B "and shewed his cause." He should not do so because an arrest must be based on the suspicion of A himself. And if A had such a suspicion, then he was entitled to arrest B on the basis of his own suspicion without warrant issued by the justice.[56]

The eighteenth century witnessed two important scholarly works in criminal law, Sir Matthew Hale's *History of the Pleas of the Crown* and William Hawkins's *Treatise of the Pleas of the Crown*. The results of Hale's vast legal erudition were not published until many years after his death, though, of course, they reflect his experience of the mid-seventeenth century.

Hale explicitly takes a very different position than Coke on the question of whether the justice of the peace must himself "suspect" the accused in order to issue an arrest warrant. The question had become important because it was no longer common for individuals to become actively engaged in apprehension of suspected wrongdoers. The transition from the views of Coke to those of Hale was thus important in providing a doctrinal base for this long-term transfer from private persons to public officials.

Hale does not differ from his predecessors with respect to arrest by private persons or by constables.[57] Hale found Coke's position that the justices of the peace could not issue arrest warrants except upon personal suspicion "too straight laced in this cause" and suggested that Coke had grounded his opinion on a "sudden and extrajudicial opinion," which would have the effect of obstructing "the peace and good order of the kingdom." Citing Dalton, Hale writes, "The law is not so, and the constant practice in all places hath obtained against it, and it would be pernicious to the kingdom if it should be as he delivers it, for malefactors would escape unexamined and undiscovered, for a man may have a probable and strong presumption of the guilt of a person, whom yet he cannot positive swear to be guilty."[58] According to Hale, if A swore that a felony had been committed and that he suspected B and "shows probable causes of suspicion, the justice may grant his warrant to apprehend B" for examination.[59] Justices, he insisted, could "issue a warrant, to apprehend a person suspected of felony though the original suspicion be not in himself, but in the party that prays his warrant." He reasoned that the magistrate was "a competent judge of the probabilities offered to him of such suspicion."[60]

Here then the justice of the peace became a second-level fact evaluator. Instead of making the arrest himself, which he was unlikely to do, an individual came to the justice with his suspicions. The justice then was required to consider them and make an estimate of the "probabilities offered" to him. He thus had to come to a preliminary estimate of the probability of the party's guilt before issuing his warrant. He could evaluate the causes of the complainant's suspicion, because he was "in this case a competent judge of" the circumstances which justified granting an arrest warrant. Hale's prescription seems to have already become a well-established practice at least by the early seventeenth century when Dalton wrote. Even prior to conducting a preliminary examination, the justice of the peace was already involved officially in an assessment of the evidence or at least the suspicions of an accuser.

Hale's statement was an extremely important one for two reasons. First, it provided the justice of the peace a clearer standard on which to justify his issuance of arrest warrants. Second, it gave prominence to the concept of "probable cause," which became attached to the notion of suspicion. For later generations the notions of probable cause and reasonable cause would become more salient than that of suspicion. Hale was emphatic that if A had "probable cause of suspicion," he could justify the arrest in an action of false imprisonment.[61] He does not provide a list of the appropriate causes of suspicion. He simply indicates they are "many, as common fame, finding goods upon him," and refers the reader to Dalton's familiar treatment.[62] The list, initially based on rhetorical sources and Romano-canon formulation, presumably was familiar enough not to have to be repeated for Hale's reader. Hale repeats the old argument that the suspicion that arises from these causes "may become his [the justice's] suspicion as well as the suspicion of A and so justify the issuance of a warrant," but that argument was transformed into something quite different by Hale's insistence that the justice is "a competent judge of the probabilities."[63] The justice is no longer simply adopting someone else's personal suspicions as his own, but instead is exercising an independent judgment on the merits of another's suspicions. Even if Hale was not the author of the concept of probable cause, his formulation was often cited as the appropriate authority on the necessary conditions for arrest.[64]

Hale's formulation of the probable cause standard was not known to his contemporaries. We thus need to determine if the handbooks or other evidence of the Restoration era can be used to establish any change in opinion or practice in the seventeenth century. The 1667 edition of *The Complete Justice* offers no modifications of the traditional treatment.[65] An arrest warrant issued by a Westmoreland justice, however, included the phrase "for as much as we are informed by credible persons" that the accused was "a person of ill name and fame, and a companion of thieves." It suggests that the justice took into account both the reputation of the accuser and the accused, that is, he assessed the credibility of the informant, before issuing the warrant.[66]

Richard Chamberlain's *Complete Justice*, drawn mostly from Lambarde, Dalton, Crompton, and the statutes, remained traditional. He repeated the outdated notion that a suspect ought not to be arrested by a warrant issued by the justice of the peace unless he had been previously indicted. Otherwise the suspicion must be that of someone who actually suspects. Without a suspicion, the justice's warrant was not a warrant at all. The party causing the arrest thus must suspect and also show "some cause of suspicion." A warrant, however, was unnecessary in such a case.[67] Bolton's *Justice of the Peace in Ireland* and Kilburn's *Choice Presedents . . . Relating to the Office and Duty of the Justice of the Peace* contain sections on suspicion which related both to arrest and to pretrial examination.[68] They, too, contain the traditional statement that common voice and fame are sufficient for suspicion. They also note that "probable presumptions" are sufficient for suspicion but relate suspicion to committal, not arrest. Suspicion was clearly playing a role in both arrest and pretrial examination. And William Nelson's handbook of 1707, which treats suspicion in the same way, indicates the appropriateness of the concept for both arrest by individuals and pretrial examination by the justice of the peace.[69]

In a case of 1709, Chief Justice Holt ruled that the suspicion of the arresting officer must not be a "mere causeless suspicion."[70] By 1751, Henry Fielding had become well aware of Hale's view that arrest warrants should indicate that the suspecting individual should go to the magistrate, who would issue a warrant which would be served by the constable. But Fielding also continues to emphasize the role of the individual's suspicion and indicates that he did not have to be an eyewitness to the felony. If it turned out that an innocent party had been arrested, and a felony had in fact been committed, there was no problem if he had "reasonable Cause of Suspicion."[71]

We have noted that the causes of suspicion are for the most part included in the early handbooks in connection with examination. Some of these treatments also included a brief treatment of presumption largely derived from Coke. It is interesting, therefore, that Hawkins, whose work became definitive, also uses the notion of presumption in connection with arrest. He indicates that "presumptions and suspicions in Criminal cases are Causes of Arrests."[72] As a result of the presentations in the handbooks and in Hawkins's work, the concepts of suspicion and presumption had become intertwined and together were being applied to both arrest and examination.

Hawkins's authoritative *Treatise of the Pleas of the Crown* (1716) is particularly important in facilitating and formalizing the transfer of the causes of suspicion from examination to arrest. Unlike the sixteenth- and seventeenth-century authors of the justicing handbooks, Hawkins places a list of the causes of suspicion in the arrest portion of his treatise, and from that point onward it became a standard part of the arrest canon of the English and the American handbook tradition. Hawkins's treatise illustrates how concepts and criteria might migrate from one procedure to another. Hawkins's treatment of the causes of suspicion that justified arrest included the familiar "common fame" and life-style. The former ought to have "some probable ground," and the latter might be gained from the suspect's living a vagrant and idle life with no visible means of support. Keeping company with known offenders at the time of the offense, and more generally associating with those of scandalous reputation, was also an appropriate cause of suspicion. Social and economic status thus had an important role in determining the legitimacy of an arrest. Circumstantial evidence that indicated "a strong presumption of guilt" was another cause of suspicion. Here Hawkins employed the famous presumptions that arose from being found with a bloody sword in hand, leaving the house of a murdered person, and being in possession of stolen property. Behavior which "betrays a consciousness of guilt," for example, flight, was also numbered among the causes of suspicion.[73] These passages were garnered from materials from Crompton, Lambarde, Dalton, Coke, and Hale, with their sources duly noted. When these passages of Hawkins were retransferred to the justicing handbooks and placed in chapters dealing with arrest, the citations were dropped. They thus floated free from their more distant Romano-canon and rhetorical origins and their proximate pretrial examination associations. The most influential justicing handbook of the eighteenth century was that of Richard Burn. Burn, and most of the English and American handbooks modeled on Burn's work, followed the Hawkins treatment and provided a list of appropriate causes of suspicion which might engender arrest.[74]

Hawkins, like Coke and Hale before him, remained concerned with the question of what parties in the arrest process must possess the "suspicions," and he indicated rather cautiously that "it seems probable" that the established practice of the justices of granting warrants before indictment "is now become a law."[75] The justices claimed this power "rather by connivance" rather than by express warrant of law. The practice, as we have seen, had been in effect for well over a century. Warrants, Hawkins indicated, must not be granted "groundlessly and maliciously, without such a probable Cause, as might induce a candid and impartial person to suspect the Party to be Guilty."[76] In Hawkins, then, we have both probable cause associated with enumerated causes of suspicion and the notion of evaluation of those causes by a candid and impartial evaluator. Hawkins, however, remained troubled by the direction he had taken, because he notes that the "old books" disallowed arrests for suspicion except by the person who actually had the suspicion. The "safe way" was therefore for the person who had the suspicion to make the arrest *and* to obtain a warrant from the magistrate.[77] In this instance the handbooks tended to follow Hale. Thus William Hening's *New Virginia Justice* (1795), based on Burn's text, noted that warrants for felony arrests were to be granted by the justices "on probable grounds of suspicion." The justices did not have to personally suspect, but should "be well satisfied of the reasonableness of the accusation."[78]

Blackstone, writing slightly later than Hawkins, indicated that both private persons and the constable might arrest on probable suspicion. Following Hale, he indicated that the justice may issue an arrest warrant, though the suspicion originated in the person who prays the warrant because the justice was competent to judge the probability of the suspicion.[79]

We must recall, however, that many crimes, especially crimes against property, were ignored entirely and never resulted in arrest. The decision of a victim to pursue criminal process entailed a considerable loss of time. Simply arresting or having the justice arrest the accused would only be the beginning. Even if the time and energy spent in obtaining a pretrial examination were relatively little, the accuser would have to anticipate traveling a considerable distance for the trial. In small communities where the parties were often well known to one another and where hanging for relatively small offenses was always a possibility, the victims frequently did not vigorously pursue the perpetrators. If the justice did not receive information from a victim, he was unlikely to know anything of the matter. Much crime thus was unreported. While private

arrangements between victim and perpetrator technically constituted the crime of compounding a felony, it is likely that many such
arrangements were made, especially because arbitration in nonfelonious crimes was commonplace.

This situation must have changed as urbanization increased and
as crimes more often involved strangers rather than neighbors. It
must also have altered considerably in the course of the nineteenth
century with the introduction of the police. These altered circumstances probably increased concern about the criteria for arrest and
concern about whether these new officials also had to personally
suspect.

The Nineteenth Century

By the nineteenth century treatises on criminal law or pleas of the
Crown had replaced justice of the peace manuals as authoritative
texts. The content of some of these works, however, remains reminiscent of the older mode. In spite of the movement toward arrest
warrants that we have traced, most of the new treatises still concentrated on arrests without warrants. Thus Joel Bishop's treatise
on criminal law continues the notion that either an individual or an
officer must personally have "reasonable cause to suspect" to justify
making an arrest.[80] Bishop notes the difficulty of defining "a reasonable and proper cause to suspect" and says little more than that
it is "a mixture of law and fact."[81] He does not, however, include
the list of suspicions contained in Hawkins and in the post-Hawkins
justicing handbooks. He notes that Foster inclines toward a "bare
suspicion" standard, while East seems to assert that the actual guilt
of the suspect is the ultimate standard for arrest.[82] Bishop's omis-
sion of the typical eighteenth-century list and his citations of other
authorities who themselves offer contradictory standards of suspicion suggest the continuing uncertainty of the law. Something between mere suspicion and conclusive proof of actual guilt was required, but even Bishop could not state exactly what that
something was. If this difficulty existed even for those who must
have personal, direct suspicion, it must have been greatly compounded for those who issued arrest warrants on the basis of suspicion engendered by what they heard from citizens or officers.[83]

In 1839 the standard for the Birmingham police was "just cause to suspect." The appropriate causes of suspicion were presumably known. One wonders if those very loose notions of common fame, being in bad company, and mere vagrancy were still sufficient. It seems likely that the "causes of suspicion" listed in Hawkins's and other handbooks were gradually being replaced with a more general notion of suspicion. The police officer must arrest anyone positively charged by another with felony "if the suspicion appears to the Constable to be well founded" and providing that the charger accompany the constable. The constable should arrest suspects "if he has reasonable grounds for his suspicion," even if he as yet had no evidence that a felony had actually been committed. He was advised, however, that he "must be cautious" when acting on his own suspicions.[84]

Even Stephen's *Digest of the Law of Criminal Procedure*, published late in the nineteenth century, continues the sixteenth-century focus on arrests by either private individuals or police officers without warrants, even though police officers increasingly made the bulk of the arrests. An officer may arrest "any person whom he suspects upon reasonable grounds of having committed a felony, whether a felony has in fact been committed or not."[85] With the development of police forces, justices of the peace were no longer likely to be much involved in the arrest of most suspects. The magistrate's supervision would come into play largely when there was need for authorization to search. The focus then would be on the search, not the arrest warrant.

Yet if we move beyond treatises to actual practice, there are strong suggestions that Hale's writings on arrest warrants are reflected in nineteenth-century practice. In several American cases from the 1880s echoing Hale and Chitty, justices of the peace were held to have legitimately issued arrest warrants on the basis of the suspicion of those praying the warrant because the justice was competent to judge of the probability of the suspicion.[86]

For several centuries the legal literature had listed causes of suspicion. The notion of probable or reasonable cause for suspicion eventually enters the literature either to summarize or supplement the lists, but it enters without much concern for the precise meaning of probable and reasonable. The concept was thus well entrenched in connection with arrest before there were any attempts to define the meaning of those terms. As noted, the specific causes

of suspicion, which so closely parallel the *indicia* of the *Carolina*
and other Continental codes, gradually were replaced by a more
generalized notion of suspicion which might be evaluated for reasonableness and probability. Hale's probable cause of suspicion was
becoming the rule—but a rule lacking the substance that had been
provided by the now vanished lists of causes of suspicion. The
origins of probable cause in ancient rhetoric and the *indicia* of the
civil law had passed out of English legal memory.

The original causes which were thought to render suspicion
probable eroded gradually. The notion disappeared that one's life-
style, common fame, or the frequenting of ale houses was alone
sufficient to render one liable for arrest for a felony. No alternate
list was created, but the idea of an adequate basis for arrest remained. Most of the nineteenth-century American decisions which
involve discussion of probable cause do not really deal with arrest
but instead consider what is needed to justify a prosecuting attorney's decision to go forward.

Thus what began as a list of oratorical strategies and then became a concrete list of *indicia* of suspicion gradually becomes probable or reasonable cause to suspect and then simply probable
cause. Suspicion, moreover, moves from the personal and subjective state of mind of an arrester who is typically involved directly
in the events to the state of mind of an officer. At first, the law
analogizes the officer as closely as possible to the private person
directly involved, but eventually it comes to recognize his more
distant role and, therefore, the degree to which he acts on the
subjective suspicions of another. Then the introduction of the arrest warrant issued by the justice of the peace further attenuates
the subjective suspicion element and places the arrest decision far
along the temporal chain that runs from victim complaint through
police intervention, arrest, and trial. The same language of probable cause becomes linked to the prosecutor's decisions and so focuses attention even further along the chain. The net effect of these
developments is an intellectual evolution that runs as follows:
causes or signs *to suspect*, probable cause *to suspect*, *probable
cause* to suspect, probable cause. Gradually probable cause floats
free of subjective suspicion and moves toward objective guilt. Our
attention focuses less on the tentative decisions that take place at
the very beginning of the criminal process and more on the final

judgment that eventually will be rendered. The question becomes not "why do you suspect him?" but "what reasons do you have to believe that he eventually will be convicted?" Probable cause to suspect has quite a different connotation than probable cause to believe that a conviction is warranted. Once we understand the migration of probable cause away from personal suspicion and toward impersonal judgment of guilt by an official, the current uncertainties about probable cause to arrest become more comprehensible. For the migration has not yet been, and in the nature of things cannot be, completed. In the context of arrest, probable cause must live somewhere between suspicion and prediction of ultimate trial outcome. It has moved quite far toward the latter. As it does so, however, it encounters the problem of having the trial before the trial that we encounter in all pretrial determinations. And when it encounters that problem, it draws back a little toward suspicion.

This dynamic is central to understanding twentieth-century American developments. In the United States, the constitutional requirement of probable cause in the warrant provisions of the Fourth Amendment insured that probable cause would become a central concept for both search and arrest. The English, in the course of the nineteenth century, relinquished the language of suspicion and substituted that of reasonable cause which had once been connected to that of suspicion.[87] The Americans instead used the language of probable cause which also floated free of suspicion.

In 1878, the U.S. Supreme Court indicated that probable cause did not concern itself with the subjective belief of the arresting officer. The law was concerned with whether "the facts and circumstances before the officer are such to warrant a man of prudence and caution in believing that the offense had been committed."[88] Shortly after, in *Carroll v. United States*, the Supreme Court declared that probable cause existed where "the facts and circumstances within their knowledge and of which they have reasonably trustworthy information were sufficient in themselves to warrant a man of reasonable caution in the belief" that an offense had been committed. The Carroll decision became the classic definition of probable cause in the United States.[89]

Wayne LaFave's work on arrest, written in 1965, suggests that the terms "reasonable grounds to believe" and "probable cause" have had a long history of interchangeable usage. LaFave notes that probable cause was also employed for evidence necessary to charge a suspect and that current practice required more evidence to hold that suspect for trial than for arrest. The rule for arrest for felony in 1959 was "if there are reasonable grounds for believing a crime has been or is being committed."[90] LaFave indicates that the probable cause for a warrant has been held to be comparable to the reasonable grounds, or reasonable cause of belief, test for felony arrests without warrant.[91] In most jurisdictions an arrest without a warrant was proper if the officer "has reasonable grounds to believe" that a felony had been committed and that the arrested person participated in it.[92] Another similar formulation—probable cause to believe or suspect—retains the element of suspicion. Other formulations are "probable cause to believe" and "has reasonable probable grounds to suspect."[93] Neither LaFave nor the authorities and jurisdictions he cites are interested in a distinction between "believe" and "suspect," and, indeed, it makes no difference at all what words, or even whether any words, follow the term "probable cause." Probable cause can mean many different things. Often, however, even when we cannot define a standard precisely, or even specify measurable gradations within a spectrumlike standard, we can discern from historical context and movement whether it is becoming more or less demanding. When we see "believe" overtaking and then largely replacing "suspect," and then see even "believe" falling away, we are alerted to a shift from the low end of the spectrum, where a mere good-faith subjective suspicion of guilt would be enough, toward the high end, where some definite, objective probability of guilt must be established.

Yet as LaFave indicates, lawyers and scholars have had difficulty specifying what constitutes reasonable or probable cause. Justice Waite, writing in 1930, noted that "reasonable cause" was "not an objectively appreciable proposition, and is not a question of law, in the sense that there are no standards or guide for its determination."[94] Yet it was clear that probable cause for arrest was not the same as probable cause for a charge.[95] Reasonable cause, though undefined, was often characterized by the courts as a balance between the needs of effective law enforcement and the interests of individual freedom, a tension noted earlier with respect to indictments. "The rule of probable cause is a practical nontechnical conception affording the best compromise that has been found for accommodating these often opposition interests."[96]

The American probable cause standard represents the latest stage in a long historical evolution in which the justification for arrest moves from the personalized suspicion of a directly involved party, through the generalized suspicions of a more distanced party based as much on the suspect's life-style as on particular events, to the rough estimate of a very distanced official of the chances that a suspect will be convicted if tried.

Search Warrants and Probable Cause

The concept of probable cause appeared quite early in connection with warrants to search premises incidental to arrest. The development began in the prepolice era when victims might be involved both in arrest and search, usually for stolen goods. The issue of search warrants did not seem to have been of much interest during the sixteenth century. The reigns of James I and Charles I, however, witnessed a good deal of arbitrary use of power in connection with Star Chamber. Sir Edward Coke suggests that there was interest in distinguishing appropriate from inappropriate searches, although Dalton not much earlier had indicated that constables might search "all suspected places as he and the party complaining shall think fit."[97] Coke's still-rudimentary standard indicated that "bare surmise" was an insufficient basis to search for individuals or goods, arguing that the justices of the peace had been created by Parliament, and it would be "full of inconvenience" if the justices, who were judges of record, possessed the power "upon a bare suggestion to break the house of any person, of what state of quality, or degree soever, either in the day or night upon such surmises."[98] If "bare surmise" was not sufficient, Coke does not indicate how strong the suspicion must be or what it must be based upon. Some years later, William Sheppard, in his 1659 manual for the justices, mentions only that search warrants "must be warily and tenderly used."[99]

The formulations of Sir Matthew Hale are significantly different and suggest a new attention to evidentiary concerns which we have noted in connection with the evolution of the beyond reasonable doubt standard, the attention to evaluating witness credibility, and the debate over the appropriate standard for indictment. Hale's formulations are especially important, for they are linked to the best philosophy of the day and provide the basis for the concept of probable cause that has continued to be the dominant formulation.

Like Coke, Hale emphasized that search warrants were judicial acts and therefore must be "granted upon the examination of the facts."[100] The place to be searched must be specifically designated by the complaining party, who must inform the justice of the peace of "his suspicions" and the "probable cause thereof." The well-developed concept of suspicion, which appears in so many contexts, is thus joined to a standard of probable cause, which is to assist in determining how much suspicion is necessary. We thus have an attempt to become more precise than Coke's rejection of "bare surmise." A still higher standard was required for nighttime searches. If "probable suspicions" were sufficient for daylight searches, "positive proof" was required for warrants executed at night. The formulations of Hale, and later of Hawkins, which were similar, became the basis for subsequent law. We should recall, however, that the concept of probable cause, which would eventually extend far beyond the granting of search warrants, was based on the idea that an appropriate but undefinable quantum of well-grounded suspicion was required for what was considered a judicial act. Later generations, however, would ignore many of the sixteenth- and seventeenth-century causes of suspicion such as ill fame, social and economic status, and the nature of one's associates.

The language contained in eighteenth-century search warrants, which varied slightly depending on whether the search was requested by the victim or being granted by the justice of the peace, reflect the evidentiary doctrines enunciated by Hale. The complainant swore on oath that the items had been stolen from him and that "there is just cause to suspect" that they were concealed in some specified location.[101] A similar warrant form contained in a 1773 abridgment of Burn's handbook uses the "probable cause to suspect" language.[102] The warrant form for the justices reads "it appears to me" by information on oath of a complainant that specified goods were "feloniously taken, stolen, and carried away," and that the complainant "hath probable cause to suspect" that the goods are concealed in a particular location.[103]

Hale's position had become the standard one, and it provided the basis for the Fourth Amendment of the U.S. Constitution, which states that no search warrant might be issued "but upon probable cause."[104] The constitutional status of probable cause with respect to search warrants insured the longevity of the concept in America.

Recent efforts with respect to probable cause have provided relatively little conceptual clarification. Indeed, they have insisted that probable cause is incapable of definition. Thus, in 1983 the Supreme Court indicated that "the central teaching of our decisions bearing on the probable cause standard is a 'practical, nontechnical conception.' . . . [P]robable cause is a fluid concept—turning on the assessment of probabilities in particular factual contexts—not readily or even usefully reduced to a set of legal rules."[105] It appears as if search warrants required the "detached scrutiny of a neutral magistrate," but that "great deference" is to be given to that magistrate's determination.[106] It has thus been suggested that recent cases are concerned with how the probable decision is made rather than the content of the decision.[107]

When imposed as an "appropriate level of suspicion," it "requires more than a bare suspicion but less than that needed to support a conviction."[108] This, of course, suggests the same problem of vacillation from one end of the probability spectrum to the other that I observed with respect to grand juries. This problem has led courts to try to find some method of tying probable cause to various factual elements. Thus in 1986, probable cause to search has been said to be satisfied when there are "reasonably trustworthy facts and circumstances that are sufficient to lead a reasonable person [to believe] that there is a fair probability that the items sought constitute fruits, instrumentalities, or evidence of crime and will be present at the time and place of search."[109] The courts, however, have not drawn distinctions between probable cause for arrest and for searches, and they cite the same authorities for both.[110] We may be a long way from an involved individual's subjective suspicions, but we are little closer to defining a place somewhere between mere surmise and beyond reasonable doubt—no doubt because we have no conceptual or linguistic stages between nothing and moral certainty. Indeed, the Supreme Court recently has dealt with the problem by resolutely refusing to review the probable cause findings of the magistrates who issue warrants.[111]

Preliminary Examination

Arrest, grand and petty juries, and the justices of the peace were institutionalized long before the development of the preliminary examination, which was formally established with the Marian bail and committal statutes of 1554 and 1555. From an evidentiary standpoint the history of the preliminary examination is shrouded in mystery. It is not until the mid-nineteenth century that standards began to be enunciated that governed when an English preliminary examiner should send a matter forward to a grand or a petty jury.

The office of the justice of the peace developed in the late medieval period. His miscellany of administrative and judicial duties was gradually expanded to include the examination of those suspected and accused of serious crimes. For some justices, at least, that expansion may have resulted in a modest prosecutorial role. But justices did not always perform their duties energetically or impartially, and the Marian statutes appear to have been government sponsored measures designed to prevent collusion in the bailing process between the suspects and the justices. The legislation regularized certain aspects of that procedure and obliged the justices to examine suspects and witnesses, to record that part of their testimony which was relevant, and to certify that record to the court, which would in turn prepare the necessary indictment and conduct the trial.

This examination process, which in some respects exhibits similarities to the examination of the Romano-canon examining magistrates, does not appear to have been inspired by the Continental practices which were being codified in France with the Edict of Villers-Cotterets (1539), itself a restatement of French criminal procedure, and the *Constitutio Criminalis Carolina* (1532) of the Holy Roman Empire. In explaining and contrasting the differences between the English and the Continental developments, John Langbein has cast the justice of the peace more as a detective and prosecutor than as a Continental examining magistrate.[112]

Langbein is quite right to conclude that the English justices did not perform the same kind of preliminary examination as did their Continental counterparts and that there was no danger of a major reception of Roman law. Certainly the English did not consider adopting the Romano-canon system of legal proof. Nor did they formally accept the set of rules, or procedures, or *indicia* by which Continental examining magistrates determined, in the absence of the testimony of two unimpeachable witnesses or confession, that the accused should be subject to torture in order to gain the requisite standard of full proof.[113] That does not mean, however, that the *indicia*, or signs, which by the sixteenth century had already had a considerable history in canon law, did not play a role in the English examination process. We have already noted their role in determining whether or not arrests were appropriate. The causes of suspicion were an only slightly modified version of the *indicia*, and suspicion initially played a large part in the preliminary hearing. In one form or another the *indicia*, or something very similar to them, would play a significant role in the development of evidentiary standards for preliminary hearings.

Given the state of the remaining documentation, the law and lore of the pretrial examination must be drawn largely from the handbooks published to assist the justices of the peace. These handbooks consist of collections of rather undigested materials compiled by editors of considerable legal learning for the use of a not very legally sophisticated group of English magistrates, typically respected members of the landed gentry.[114]

As seen from the discussion of arrest, the handbooks, which began publication in the sixteenth century, did not differ a great deal from one another. To a large extent new ones copied the material of their predecessors. The requirements of the Marian statutes are repeated in each, together with other comments and materials relating to the justices' examination. The genre is thus conservative in nature and often does not record the changes in legal practice which are sometimes reflected in other sources. Although we must rely heavily on these manuals, we must not assume that they provide an accurate measure of the then contemporary practice. When conflicting materials appeared in the manuals, they were rarely commented upon. Manuals tended to repeat conflicting material from generation to generation without attempting to resolve them. Several of these contradictions are central to the development of the preliminary examination. We will also be alert to concepts like common fame, the causes of suspicion, half and full proofs, and presumption, which had their roots in the Romano-canon tradition.

The most important question for our purposes is whether or not the English magistrates, who beginning in 1553–1554 were required to conduct an examination of the accused and witnesses in felony cases, dismissed cases where the evidence was insufficient. There is no question that the justices disposed of various kinds of misdemeanors by summary procedures. In those cases they not only conducted examinations but also decided cases. Some misdemeanors, however, had to be decided at quarter sessions by a jury. Individual justices thus were accustomed to making some decisions about which cases to send on and which to decide themselves. No established rules or evidentiary standards seem to have guided the justices in their summary misdemeanor deliberations. Presumably they used some kind of commonsense standard to reach their decisions.

The Marian statutes governed felony. They required that the justice take the examination and record, certify, and transmit the testimony gathered to the court. These depositions were used by the clerks of the court to assist in drawing the indictment and to provide lists of individuals required to appear at trial. The depositions were not to be used as part of the trial itself, except in cases where the witness had died or was too ill to travel. The orality of the court proceedings were thus unaffected by the preservation of the depositions, though the judges evidently familiarized themselves with them. These depositions were not required to be a verbatim record of a witness's testimony. The testimony forwarded to the court thus played a far more modest role than it did in the ecclesiastical or the civil law courts. In those courts the materials developed by the examining judge formed the very basis for the trial, and determinations included in civil and in ecclesiastical court dossiers were treated as fully established facts on which a final decision would be made. Although Langbein has suggested that the justices of the peace used the deposition to assist in the prosecution, the justices of the peace do not seem to have attended the assizes or the quarter sessions with enough regularity to have performed this function.[115]

These examinations, unlike those which were created by legislation in the mid-nineteenth century, were usually informal and private and often took place in the justice's home. The accused, unlike the witnesses, was not interrogated on oath. He was not represented by counsel nor was he entitled to discover the evidence against him. After the examination the justice was to commit or bail. The handbooks reasoned that he had only these two options because it would be inappropriate for anyone arrested and charged with felony or suspicion of felony to be "delivered upon any man's discretion, without farther trial."[116] This statement appears in Lambarde and thereafter in virtually all the practice manuals.[117] The fear was not that the justices would bring weak cases to trial, but rather that they might drop cases out of bias or favoritism. The Marian legislation was designed to prevent lethargy and biased dropping of charges.[118] Magistrates were not to circumvent the jury trial.

Perhaps there was some reluctance to take Lambarde's position categorically. The handbook of Giles Jacob indicates that "it is said" that a magistrate should not discharge a defendant even if he believes him not to be guilty.[119] Yet the justice was to take and certify "information, proof, and evidence as goeth to the acquittal or clearing of the prisoner, as much as make for the King and against the prisoner." Exculpatory material was included because the examination procedure was "only to inform" the king and his judges "of the truth of the matter," not to present the prosecution case.[120] And indeed we know that at least in some instances the justices did write to the clerks of the court concerning their opinions of the prosecuting parties or the defendants.[121]

Given our interest in civil law comparisons, we should note that similar admonitions to include evidence indicating the innocence of the accused were to be found in the Edict of Villers-Cotterets and in the *Carolina*. The *Carolina* required not only that suspicions be noted but also that evidence favoring the suspected person or that which could exculpate him of the crime be noted. Indeed if the "ground of exculpation" appeared stronger than the "weight of the suspicion," examination under torture was not permitted.[122]

The English examining magistrate certainly did not have full authority to balance the evidence *pro* and *con*. Even Dalton, however, indicates that if the person accusing someone suspected of a felony "cannot declare anything material to prove the felony, nor any other person then present, it seemeth" that the justice should not commit.[123] The "it seemeth" indicates some uncertainty. Still employing tentative and uncertain language, Dalton says that if "any just cause of suspicion" occurs, or if the man is of "evil fame," the justice would do well "not to let him go, but at least to bind him over to the next gaol delivery, and in the mean time to take further information against him."[124] If there was "any probability" that the prisoner "was guilty," he was to commit or to bail. [125] Thus the handbooks seem to leave an escape hatch through which the magistrates could release a few of the most unjustifiably arrested.

There are sections of the handbooks of Lambarde, Fitzherbert, Dalton, and others that indicate that justices of the peace were to do more than simply record and certify relevant testimony. Many, though not all, contain particular elements or a list of circumstances to be considered as causes of suspicion. In some instances the causes of suspicion, which as we have noted closely resemble the Romano-canon *indicia*, are to be used in connection with arrest. In others, however, they appear in connection with a justice's examination of a previously arrested accused person. We do not have any evidence as to when they were first employed in connection with examination. It is certainly possible that they were used by fifteenth- and sixteenth-century magistrates examining for misdemeanors, though the handbooks mention them only in connection with felony. But it is more likely that they were brought into the context of examination with the passage of the Marian bail and committal statutes of 1554–1555. Even if they were in use prior to the development of the published handbooks, knowledge of them could not have been widespread, because it is unlikely that most justices of the peace were literate before the sixteenth century.[126]

William Lambarde's *Eirenarcha* included an elaborate Ramist-style diagram providing in compact form the causes of suspicion to be employed in examining a suspect. Like most handbook compilers, Lambarde was reluctant to point out the Romano-canon source or even the similarities, noting only that "the causes of suspicion" were "collected out of Cicero and others."[127] It is of course true that many of the Romano-canon *indicia* could be traced to Cicero, Quintilian, and other ancient rhetorical texts, which were significant elements in the Renaissance rhetorical tradition. In the legal context, however, they were systematically employed by the civilians on the Continent and in ecclesiastical jurisdictions in England and elsewhere. It seems unlikely that Lambarde's sole exposure to them occurred in his reading of the classics.

Lambarde, perhaps reflecting the rhetorical tradition, notes that the examination of an offense is a "conjectural state of a cause" and must be "weighed by matter," which he categorizes as "precedent," "present," or "subsequent."[128] The notion that suspicions and presumptive proofs can be viewed as falling into three periods—those preceding, contemporaneous with, and following the crime—is found in Cicero's *De inventione* and the *Rhetorica ad Herennium*, which was often attributed to Cicero.[129] Each category is subdivided in the Ramist manner. The precedent category is divided into the "will to do the fact" and the "power to commit the act," both of which must be considered carefully by the magistrate. "The will to do the fact" is further divided so as to consider the disposition of the person (which includes the character and behavior of his parents), sex (some offenses being more commonly committed by one sex than another), and education (from childhood to adulthood). Education also involves consideration of whether or not the accused has an idle or honest occupation, whether he is riotous in diet or apparel, whether he was "brawlingly, quarrelsome, lightfingered," and so on. The second division, "the causes inducing him to undertake" the act, might be "forcible or impulsive" (for example, motivated by revenge or "upon sudden offense"), or it could be "persuasive" (that is, in hope of gain or out of fear). The "power to commit the act," the second subdivision of the precedent category, calls for an evaluation of the suspect's intelligence, physical capacity, and his "country," which includes consideration of whether the accused's kindred, wealth, friends, or office might "cover" him.[130]

Considerations of present category involve questioning the accused's presence at the fact, taking into account the time of day, space (sufficient to do the act), and location. The "occasion," too, must be analyzed, which, if absent, "the fact could not follow." The justice is to engage in the mental operation of "comparison," which required consideration "as none but he, or not so commodiously as he, could commit the fact."[131]

Considerations of the subsequent category, which follow the commission of the felony, include "common voice and fame that he did the offense. Witnesses that prove it, either probably or necessarily. Signs which discover him; as by having blood, or the goods about him; his flying away: his blushing, or change of countenance:

his being in the company of other offenders: his offer of composition: the measure of his foot: the bleeding of the dead body, . . . Confession, as his doubtfully or inconstance speaking."[132]

It is difficult to believe that Lambarde's elaborate schematic treatment of considerations in the examination of an offense would not encourage the justice of the peace to reach some mental judgment concerning the innocence or guilt of the party. Lambarde's scheme, or something very similar to it, also appears in other handbooks. We will examine these in some detail, because I believe they provided a counterweight to the explicit statements that magistrates were not to drop charges they felt to be without adequate foundation.

Instead of Lambarde's complex late scholastic formulations, *L'office et auctoritie de justices de peace*, traditionally cited as Crompton, contains a six-page list which the justice was to use in examining those who appear before him. Crompton's treatment, like Lambarde's, avoids mention of foreign sources or authorities, although he does refer to Cicero's Cataline orations in connection with the testimony of conspirators. He indicates, however, that most of the causes of suspicion he cites are to be found in civilian Thomas Wilson's popular Ciceronian *Art of Rhetorique* (1553).[133] Here again we have a tantalizing suggestion of the relationship between rhetoric and civil law. Given the English national hostility to things Continental in the political and the legal spheres, it is not surprising that both Lambarde and Crompton prefer to cite either Cicero or Wilson's *Art of Rhetorique* as the source of the causes of suspicion, rather than the Romano-canon *indicia*. As noted earlier, Cicero, Quintilian, and the ancient rhetorical tradition supplied the Romano-canon tradition with many of the *indicia*. With Dalton and his successors, however, references to Wilson and Cicero disappear, and the "rules" to assist the magistrate in evaluating testimony simply stand on their own authority. Such is the creation of legal authority.

Crompton notes the importance of the Marian bail statutes as well as those statutes that date from the reign of Henry VII, which required taking information of the accused's good or bad fame.[134] Although offered without Lambarde's organizational structure and diagrammatic forms, Crompton's treatment is a near duplication. Sudden anger, hope of gain, temperament, upbringing, occupation, and trade are to be considered, along with whether the suspect was a haunter of alehouses or a gamester. These and other items could easily have fit into Lambarde's precedent category, though the terms are not used in Fitzherbert or Crompton. Our earlier brief discussion of Quintilian suggests their distant rhetorical origins.

Considerations of time and place—for example, whether the suspect was seen near the location of the crime—could similarly fit into Lambarde's present category, and indeed at one point Crompton cites Lambarde. Some items, such as those dealing with common fame, however, rely on the authority of Bracton.[135] The suspect's behavior while being questioned must carefully be observed. Trembling and staggering clearly were significant. Biblical references are rare. However, the rule stating that if two persons inform in a matter of felony and vary their tales, then neither one is to be credited, is supported by citation to the story of Susanna and the elders, and this biblical reference continues throughout the seventeenth century in later handbooks.[136] It was also found in the civil and the canon law.

Crompton's *L'office*, like Fitzherbert's manual on which it was based, was written in law French and printed in difficult-to-read Gothic typeface. It was quickly replaced in common use by Michael Dalton's *Country Justice*, whose numerous seventeenth- and early eighteenth-century editions provided the basis for competitors and successors.[137] Dalton's text remained the standard authority until it was gradually replaced in the mid-eighteenth century.

Although Dalton soon acquired the status of a legal authority, we should note that *The Country Justice* had the modest goal of assisting those who "have not been much conversant in the studies of the law of this realm."[138] The materials "containing the practice of the justice of the peace" had been "gathered" for their convenience. The same eclectic principle of "collection" and compilation of relevant materials that characterized Fitzherbert's and Lambarde's work is found in Dalton's. Despite some rudimentary organization, its material is often undigested, unreconciled, repetitive, and sometimes even contradictory. It, too, presented the Marian bail statute as imposing a duty to send all cases forward, even when the magistrate believed the prisoner not to be guilty, because it was "not fit" that he "be delivered upon any man's discretion, without further trial."[139] It is not clear, however, whether Dalton's use of the phrase "not fit" constituted a complete prohibition. As we have seen, there were directives and maxims that could only be used to sift the evidence and accusations which came before the justice of the peace. If he did not have the discretion to drop extremely weak cases, all these materials would have no function. The examination would not be an examination but only the compilation of a written record of statements. For instance, in a section devoted to taking the examination of accused felons, the magistrate is advised by Dalton, on the authority of Crompton, not to credit the remainder of an individual's testimony if part of the testimony is proved to be false.[140] If such testimony was discredited, how could it be used? What was he to do with the information provided by witnesses who were not to be believed? Dalton himself seems puzzled by the contradictions of his own materials. He concluded "it seemeth safest" to commit the suspect and then inform the assize court concerning the credit of those witnesses. Dalton's post-1618 editions include additional evaluative material, which too was passed on to later manuals. Among these are "two old verses" that derived from Romano-canon tradition.

Conditio, sexus, aetas, discretio, fama,
Et fortuna, fides: in testibus esta requires.[141]

We must also note that Dalton's language is frequently tentative rather than absolute. He uses the phrases "it seemeth," "it seemeth safest," or "it seemeth right and just" to indicate uncertainty, or when contradictory materials are being placed side by side. Thus it "seemeth just and right" that the magistrate certify "information, proof, and evidence, as goes to the acquittal or clearing of the prisoner," because his task is to inform of "the truth of the matter." Dalton indicates that the magistrate is not simply to preserve just those materials and evidence for the prosecution but must include all "information, proof, and evidence," including that favorable to the accused.[142] Dalton is obviously uncertain as to how far and in what way that duty should go. The statement concerning evidence on behalf of the accused does not appear in legislation, but reflects Dalton's own sense of justice. It is also found in the Romano-canon tradition.

Dalton's most obvious contradiction concerning the magistrate's role came (as it did in Lambarde's and Crompton's works) in those *indicia*, criteria, or "circumstances . . . to be considered" in examining accused felons. The treatment of the "circumstances" varies in detail from that in earlier handbooks, but it is essentially the same and need not be described in detail here. There is the same concern for the parentage, background, life-style, and character of the accused; his reputation in the community; his demeanor, motives, opportunity, and capacity to commit the crime; and any direct or circumstantial evidence that bore on the crime's commission, including alibis and supernatural indications of guilt, such as the bleeding of the body in the murderer's presence. Many of Dalton's "circumstances" are also found in the civil law texts and in Cicero and Quintilian. It has been recently suggested that the justices might have used the causes of suspicion to construct a portrait of the criminal stereotype.[143]

Dalton, like Crompton, follows this discussion with Bractonian materials on suspicion and common fame, materials also used in connection with arrest and indictment. By 1635, Coke's brief definitions of the three varieties of presumption were also added to Dalton's manual with no indication of how these might be employed by the justice of the peace in his capacity of examiner of accused felons.

Coke said that violent presumption (itself a Romano-canon concept) was *plena probatio*, or full proof, that probable presumptions "moveth a little," and that light presumption "moveth not at all."[144] How could a magistrate possibly take such an analysis to mean anything other than that if he reached only light presumption which "moveth not at all," he should not send the case on?[145]

A chapbook of 1624 also employed the language of presumption in connection with committal. The author noted that various presumptions led to the questioning and examination for murder, and, there "being great presumptions of his guiltiness," the accused was committed. The language of presumption in connection with examination thus must have been familiar prior to Coke's formulation. Indeed, we shall see it employed in connection with witchcraft trials at an even earlier date. The hierarchy of presumptions, which were highly developed in the sophisticated treatise tradition of civil and ecclesiastical law, appear in Coke and in the handbooks in extremely truncated versions that cite the authority of Coke rather than the Romano-canon source.

Dalton also includes brief comments on the status of confessions made during the examination process. Such confessions would not independently support a subsequent conviction and had to be repeated at arraignment or trial. Interestingly there was a similar civil law rule.[146] The Dalton materials described here appear in some later handbooks in connection with examination and in other handbooks in connection with witnesses or arrest.

These later manuals followed roughly the same pattern, though they sometimes introduced additional contradictions or expressed the need to perform actions that did not seem entirely reasonable. Joseph Keble's *Assistance to Justices of the Peace*, which repeats much of the Dalton and the Crompton materials, provides an example. Keble indicates that if the accused felon confessed during the examination, he was to be committed. If, however, "upon his examination there shall appear any just cause of suspicion; or if the Prisoner be a Man of evil Fame" and felony had in fact been committed, he advised "the Justices shall do well not to let him go."[147] He does not say what the justices could or should do if the accused was of good fame, if there were less than "just cause for suspicion," or if the magistrate discovered that in fact no felony had been committed. It is not inconceivable that someone reading Keble might interpret him to mean that he might dismiss such an accusation.

There are some other puzzles as well. Examination of accused or suspected felons was by a single justice, while the decision to bail required two. That suggests two quite separate decisions in presumably two different times and places. The bail-granting decision was, of course, one in which the magistrates did exercise discretion. But the handbook materials often conflate decisions about bail and committal with those concerning examination, thus blurring any distinction between discretionary and nondiscretionary decisions. And Keble, in providing information for the justices taking the examination, himself demonstrates uncertainty by using phrases such as "yet it seemeth," "yet it seemeth safest," and "not much to be credited" in connection with various kinds of less than credible testimony.[148] Such tentative phrases, though quite traditional, suggest that the justices were being asked to certify evidence or commit individuals whom it did not make much sense to commit.

The handbook tradition continued to be of immense importance in the eighteenth century. Additional statutory materials were added, and older treatments were supplemented by excerpts from Coke, Hale, and Hawkins. The addition of material from Hale and Hawkins brought further confusion. We have already noted that Hale's pronouncements on the grand jury evidentiary standard were simply placed alongside others which contradicted them. We have also noted that such unreconciled texts might stand side by side for many generations. Hale, writing in the late seventeenth century, and thus after Dalton's initial composition of the handbook that continued to bear his name, moved slightly beyond him. Hale's position was that if there was "no cause to commit found by the justice on examination of the fact, he may discharge him." The magistrate would, however, be the judge of what constituted "no cause." Perhaps no cause was to be considered an equivalent to Coke's "light" presumption, which "moveth not at all." Hale, as we saw earlier, refers to the causes of suspicion, but in connection with arrest rather than examination.[149] Hawkins did not discuss examination, but his discussion of bail indicates a serious element of discretion, consideration of the circumstances "of the whole matter," and "the Probabilities of both sides." If the justice found it "reasonable strongly to presume them to be guilty," he ought to commit rather than to bail.[150]

Unfortunately we have very little evidence as to how the justices actually employed the contradictory materials. The form in which depositions were certified reveals little of the opinion or evaluation of the justices, although on some accusations they seem to have sent additional evaluative comments to the clerks of the court. Of course if the justices were in fact dismissing unfounded charges and/or persuading accusers in weak cases to accept informal arbitration or to convert felony into misdemeanor charges, no evidence of such activity would appear in the records. We do, however, have a few bits of evidence in addition to the handbooks. Sir Thomas Smith's *De Republica Anglorum* may be the sole sixteenth-century nonhandbook source which refers to the question of the magistrate's involvement with evidence in connection with pretrial examination. Smith's book, designed to describe the English government and legal system, was written in the 1560s and published in 1583, some thirty years after the passage of the Marian statutes. It was the work of a legally sophisticated Elizabethan civil servant and diplomat. His description of the pretrial examination clearly indicates that the justice did have to make evidentiary evaluations, and that he was required to commit if he "does find cause."[151] Although Smith discusses the process in connection with committal for gaol delivery and quarter sessions, Langbein, who has insisted on the justices' absence of discretion, has argued that Smith mistakenly conflated the procedures for felony with those for petty crime.[152] Smith, however, was an extremely knowledgeable person, and there is no reason to assume that he would make such an error. If Langbein is correct that Smith was confused, then confusion was also imbedded in the handbook tradition that the magistrates relied on for instruction and guidance. If someone as learned and experienced as Smith might have conflated the procedures for misdemeanors and for felony, we should not be surprised if less sophisticated justices of the peace did so as well.

Some magistrates kept notebooks of their activities, but very few of these are extant. Lambarde's *Ephemeris* of 1580–1588 suggests little more than passive recording and certifying of the required documents.[153] A few seventeenth-century justice of the peace notebooks that have come to light, however, are more revealing than Lambarde's. One early seventeenth-century notebook indicates that the justice, after one party had accused another "upon very slight suspicion of felony of stealing a horse," examined "both Sydes" and decided that the charge "hath no probability." The accuser was therefore persuaded to relinquish his accusation. In another case a drover was brought before him on suspicion of sheep stealing. He was discharged on the evidence of some letters. This justice also arbitrated a great many nonfelonious assault cases, noting "I agreed them."[154] Another late seventeenth-century justice indicated that his role in the examination process was to "sift out . . . the truth" of the matter at hand.[155]

Joel Samaha's study of Elizabethan Essex finds that Elizabethan justices often played the roles of both prosecutor and judge and exercised discretion in examining accused felons, setting "the suspect free if [they] did not think there was 'reasonable cause' to believe the accused had committed the crime." One justice ordered a prisoner who had been committed set free because there was no evidence other than the "bare information of him that charges him."[156]

The research of several other scholars suggests that the justices often engaged in considerable informal coercion and arbitration instead of prosecution. The few available tidbits from the justices' notebooks that we have just examined support this view. Significant numbers of cases of both serious and nonserious crimes were settled without formal legal action, though arbitration was most commonly employed in settling minor criminal disputes.[157] Over half the cases heard by William Hunt between 1744 and 1749 were settled informally. Although most of these involved petty theft and assault, they included felonious thefts and attempted rape. Hunt dismissed cases for lack of evidence as well as for frivolity. In matters of theft, even felonious theft, his objective was preservation of the peace, even though it might involve ignoring the letter of the law. On one occasion a person was brought before him on suspicion of stealing a silver watch. "But on hearing his defense, I adjudged the grounds of it to be so very little, that at the request of the heads of the parish I excused" the accused shepherd. In another instance of substantial theft he noted, "The complaint upon hearing, proved so frivolous that I excused the defendant." Many small thefts, which were not felonies, were "agreed." An accusation for illegal entry and stealing household goods was "dismissed for want of proof, the charge being false against the parties."[158]

J. A. Sharpe's study suggests that discretionary discharge, arbitration, and informal coercion were alternatives to prosecution. It is difficult, however, to determine the extent to which such practices spilled over from misdemeanor to felony. One justice, on the occasion of a rather serious game offense, advised the offenders that if they would reform, the offense would be "passed by." Relatively small thefts, even when technically felonious, seem to have been treated with considerable latitude. Known thieves were often not prosecuted until they were implicated in the theft of a large or valuable item. Catching and prosecuting all offenders was not characteristic of most seventeenth- and eighteenth-century communities. Prosecution, which remained largely in the hands of the victim, required very considerable costs in terms of time, money, and effort of the victim. The absence of public prosecution meant that a great many crimes of property were likely to be ignored, "agreed," or arbitrated by some trusted individual, usually the local justice of the peace, who technically was responsible for turning over all the acquired testimony to the court. Sharpe, unlike Langbein, did not find that the magistrates played an active prosecutorial role, but that they instead only took an interest in crimes where accusations reached them.[159] One needs to be reminded constantly that the law books and the statutes did not always reflect current practice. If we were to take the statute book at face value, we would have to conclude that there were huge numbers of executions on the gallows in the early modern era. Current research, however, reveals not only that many crimes were not prosecuted, but also that relatively few convicted felons reached the gallows.

When all is said and done, what we have is the lists of circumstances, or "causes of suspicion," offered in connection with examination. It is not clear how these lists were used. On the Continent, similar criteria were used to determine whether or not prisoners should be tortured. In England the causes of suspicion were used in determining whether or not to issue an arrest warrant. Thus, such lists were usually associated with a discretionary authority vested in the magistrate to decide whether or not to go forward. The Marian statutes do not specifically grant or deny such authority. Of course the very manuals that provide the causes of suspicion to be used in the course of examination explicitly deny that the magistrate has such discretion, but they then suggest that, at least in extreme cases, he does. The manuals do not say how the causes of suspicion are to be used, although they appear in connection with both arrest and preliminary examination. As we have seen these manuals had a certain anthology quality, wherein materials were collected rather than systematized. It is quite possible that the early compilers, who knew about the signs, or causes of suspicion, in connection with English arrest, and perhaps because they had secondhand knowledge of civil law practices, simply piled them into the preliminary hearing sections without really considering how and if they fit. Later compilers simply copied earlier ones. It is also possible that they really did not fit at first but came to fit later as magistrates in practice exercised more discretion.

Ultimately it is difficult to believe that a justice who had dutifully worked his way through the manuals' causes of suspicion and found none for a particular accused person would then commit the obvious injustice of sending that accused person on to trial. Why all the concern about the quantity and quality of suspicion if every accused person was to be sent to the grand jury even if no valid causes of suspicion could be found?

It is a truism of comparative law that in all societies local judges carry out their duties far away from the formal doctrines and close to the practical necessities of conflict resolution. English justices of the peace were hardly the kind of disciplined, professional judges who would follow the doctrine from on high. Knowing what we do of justices, it is simply implausible that they would have dutifully passed cases onward once they had heard all the evidence and were very, very sure of the innocence of the accused. It is even more implausible if the accused were a friend, a reputable citizen, a dutiful client, a dependent of themselves, or one of their high-status friends.

Indeed the Marian statute seems to have been aimed at breaking up the protective practices of the justices of the peace toward their friends and dependents. It is hardly likely that the words of the statute would have so utterly succeeded as to prevent the examining magistrates from quashing a case when the evidence against the accused was preposterously thin and the accused was a "worthy" person. The equivocal passages in the handbooks hint of this. Above all, it is impossible to believe that persons with as much self-esteem as the justices of the peace could go through the complete mental examination suggested by the handbooks and then act as automata, sending the suspect on to trial even when to do so would have been completely unjustified by the evidence presented.

Imperial China gives us an interesting comparative control. The Chinese magistrate was a captive and controlled bureaucrat, imbedded in a fiercely disciplined hierarchy and subject to dismissal (and worse) for any infraction of the detailed laws governing his behavior. He lived under a strict legal mandate that any criminal complaint brought to him must be prosecuted by him. Every serious case brought to a verdict had to be passed on to a higher court. The magistrate was also a figure of great social and moral authority who could be a powerful mediator in a society that highly valued mediation. It is quite clear that in spite of the command to prosecute all criminal complaints, the magistrates treated many such complaints as if they were requests for mediation and treated some requests for mediation as if they were criminal complaints. Indeed, they could, and did, shift easily between mediation and prosecution modes in the course of handling a given conflict. That capacity itself greatly enhanced their powers as mediators. Of course in many instances the person coming to the magistrate for help did not know or care whether he was requesting mediation or filing a criminal complaint.[160]

The justice of the peace was in a comparable position, except that he was far less constrained to proceed by the letter of the procedural rules than was the Chinese magistrate. There is evidence that he mixed prosecutorial, judgmental, and mediatory roles at least in lesser offenses. There was a large category of offenses that were in fact lesser but were technically felonies. It is improbable that the magistrate who handled nonfelonies by a mixture of mediation, final legal judgment, and prosecutorial sending on to higher courts would suddenly shift to an absolutely nondiscretionary mode just because the word "felony" was uttered. The most common felony by far was theft, and we know that accusers, the justices of the peace, grand jurors, and jurors often felt free to devalue stolen goods so as to avoid felony charges. In many instances, no one in the community, including the accuser, would have wanted anything more than a local resolution. Even an adamant accuser who wanted the suspect sent to trial would rarely have been in a position to insist that a justice, who was convinced of the innocence of the accused, do his duty. Everything we know about the nature of seventeenth- and eighteenth-century English society suggests that probable cause, sometimes in the form of causes of suspicion and sometimes in a more general way, must have served as an important screen that determined when even felony complaints did and did not go forward.

Witchcraft Cases

As noted in connection with the grand jury, the crime of witchcraft, which was made a felony at common law in the mid-sixteenth century, provides one of the few instances where discussion of early modern evidence is to be found. The witchcraft materials present special problems, not only because witchcraft appears to modern minds as a nonexistent crime, but also because it fell into a special category of crime, the *crimen exceptum*. This category, known to both the common and the civil law, was composed of secret crimes unlikely to produce the usual kinds of evidence or witnesses. The *Carolina*, for example, treats clandestine murder, infanticide, secret poisoning, and sorcery separately from other crimes.[161] It is, therefore, unclear whether or not English commentary on witchcraft procedure offers us a window into the normal operations of the criminal law. Nevertheless, the evidence of the magistrate handbooks with respect to the justices' evidentiary role in witchcraft cases is suggestive. It does indicate an active prosecutorial role. It also suggests an evaluative one when it comes to the evidence presented at the pretrial examination. In addition, it raises, if it does not resolve, the question of Romano-canon borrowing. The English witchcraft materials are replete with the Romano-canon language of half and full proofs and frequently employ the language of violent, probable, and light presumption.

Published just a year before the first edition of Dalton, Thomas Cooper's *Mysterie of Witchcraft* emphasized not only the need for the magistrate to prosecute but also the necessity for him to proceed carefully, "not upon every corrupt passion, or sleight occasion, but upon weighty presumptions." The signs, or presumptions, which were to be taken into consideration by the justice of the peace were "notorious defamation, accusation of a fellow witch, if mischief follows after quarrelling or threatening." These and other indications all contributed to a presumption of guilt. Cooper, however, carefully distinguishes the higher proof required for conviction from the presumptions and probable conjectures needed for the magistrate to take cognizance of the situation. Cooper does not indicate that the magistrate was simply to record and forward the relevant depositions. He was an active, inquiring, and evaluating agent. Cooper's language is also laden with civil law concepts, indicating that two witnesses were necessary for conviction. Two witnesses were not, in fact, required by English law.[162]

The same approach and the same civil law terminology appears in the many editions of Dalton's *Country Justice*. Dalton dealt with witchcraft as a *crimen exceptum*, a type of crime "where open and evident proofs are seldom to be had" and which therefore was thought to require exceptional treatment. In cases of witchcraft, that "most cruel, revengefull, and bloody of all felonies," the justices were "not always to expect direct evidence, seeing all their works are the works of darkness, and no witnesses present with them to accuse them."[163] To assist the justices in their "better discovery," he inserted a number of observations taken from the 1612 *Wonderful Discovery of Witchcraft* in the first (1618) edition of *The Country Justice* and then added additional "signs" taken from Richard Bernard's *Guide to Grand Jurymen in Cases of Witchcraft* (1627) in the fourth (1630) edition. Dalton's lengthy list included having familiars, the familiar's having a teat for sucking by the witch, witchmarks, possession of clay or wax figures, excessive inquiry after a sick party, common report, and the testimony of other witches. These signs are designated by the term "presumption." Magistrates are instructed to become active investigators searching the suspect's house for evidence. Dalton also provides "signs" (civilians and clerics would have used the term *indicia*) to assist the magistrate, for example, in determining whether the sick party was in fact bewitched. Examination followed the initial investigation, and it required "good care." In cases of witchcraft and other secret crimes, "half proofs, or probable presumptions" were both good causes of suspicion and sufficient for the magistrates to commit the suspected party.[164]

The language of half proofs and presumption is interesting for several reasons. The first is the obvious reference to the system of legal proofs of the civil law. This reference could have been, but was not, corrected or commented upon in many of the editions of Dalton's handbook and was adopted in other handbooks as well. There was evidently no need to eliminate the references to the notion of half proofs and full proofs which had no basis in English law. Indeed the absence of set decision rules based on a specific number of witnesses or on confession was the hallmark of the English jury trial.

The evidence of the manuals suggests that with witchcraft it was widely accepted that the justices might commit if there were half proofs or probable presumptions. Half proofs in the Romano-canon system consisted of such things as the testimony of a single reliable witness—actually enough to convict in an English court—or a certain number of *indicia*. The Romano-canon tradition had a complex treatise literature on the theory of legal presumption. Dalton indicates that where "probable presumption" exists, the justice is to commit.[165] Thus if there was insufficient proof to reach "probable presumption" or, as Cooper had put it, "mighty presumptions," and only "light presumptions" existed, the justice seemingly would discharge the accused. In the witchcraft cases, Dalton implies that the justices were dismissing cases and deciding when there was sufficient evidence to require committal. They had to evaluate the evidence before them in order to determine whether light or probable presumption existed. Despite the Marian legislation, at least in certain kinds of cases, the magistrates had some decision rules to guide them in dismissing or forwarding cases, the decision rule being the distinction between probable and light presumption. As I have just noted, there was ample opportunity to modify these materials. They were not removed from Dalton and indeed were repeated in other manuals. Dalton's 1635 edition even added Bernard's materials for the "better riddance" of witches.

We must recall that despite the retention of these lengthy materials to be used in detecting and examining witches, extremely few cases of witchcraft came to trial in England after 1620, with the exception of a brief flurry in the 1640s. Yet the materials remain in the handbooks until repeal of the statute in 1736. Recent studies indicate that witch belief lasted much longer in the countryside among the peasantry than among the more educated.[166] Given the fact that witchcraft remained a crime punishable by death until 1736, but that few cases ever reached the indictment stage, we must conclude that magistrates not only had ceased pursuing witches themselves but also were deflecting and dismissing accusations of a crime they no longer believed it was possible to commit.[167] The manual materials gave them a legitimate basis for refusing to commit after examination, even though they were under a statutory duty to commit. The experience relating to the crime of witchcraft thus suggests that justices were making evaluations and were deflecting and dismissing cases which did not meet a high enough standard.

Although witchcraft eventually disappeared, the category of *crimen exceptum* did not. The French added infanticide to the list in 1556, and the English followed suit. Hale placed rape in a similar category. Only gradually, as we shall see in our later discussion of presumption and circumstantial evidence, did the notion of distinct evidentiary criteria for different kinds of crime erode. A 1683 handbook for the justices thus repeated that in secret murders, poisoning, and witchcraft, where "open and evident" proofs are seldom to be had, "there seemeth half proofs are to be allowed and are good causes of suspicion."[168] If the magistrates exercised discretion over committal for these secret crimes, why would they not exercise a similar discretion over committal for open offenses in which, precisely because they were open, it was often possible for them to discover that the accused could not have done the deed?

Discretion

As early as the fourteenth century, justices were empowered to make the decision whether to commit the accused or to bail him. Here discretion is clearly vested in the justices. The Statute of Westminster of 1276 employs "light presumption" as a criterion for bail, so we know that even before bailing authority was shifted from the sheriffs to the justices in 1360, evidentiary standards had been introduced and Romano-canon borrowings had begun.[169] The Marian legislation which introduced examination was actually a reform of the bail system but did not eliminate judicial discretion to bail or to commit. Even though bail decisions formally required two justices and examination required only one, the handbooks often conflated the two procedures and offered the same evidentiary standards for both. And even when they were kept separate, the standards for bail were stated in terms of light, probable, and strong presumption, causes of suspicion, ill fame, and the whole repertoire we have already reviewed in the area of arrest and examination. The language of presumption continued to be associated with bail during the eighteenth century. Hawkins's authoritative *Treatise of the Pleas of the Crown* indicates that those under "violent presumption of Guilt," that is, those taken with stolen goods or known to be notorious thieves, might not be bailed for any "fresh felony" where there be "probable evidence against them." Hawkins's general test for when bail should be denied is whether the magistrate may "reasonably strongly . . . presume [the accused] to be guilty."[170] The statute of 1848 finally recognized that one justice, rather than two, had been making both bail and examining decisions, using the same evidentiary standards in both, and exercising discretion in both. The statute provided that the justice should choose between bail and committal if a "strong probable presumption of guilt" existed, and otherwise he should dismiss the charges.[171]

The handbook authors had difficulty distinguishing decision rules for bail-committal proceedings from those for examination. Both were governed by the same evidentiary rules, and the former clearly granted discretion to the justices. It hardly seems probable that an initially semiliterate magistracy, prone to discretion in all things, could have rigorously debarred itself from the exercise of discretion in the latter. We would have to imagine the following steps. A justice sitting alone would conduct a rigorous examination, checking to see whether or not a whole host of causes of suspicion had been met. Even if he were absolutely persuaded that none had been met and were personally certain of the innocence of the accused, who was a worthy person, a lifelong acquaintance, and the loyal tenant of one of his fellow justices of the peace, he would loyally prepare to send the case forward to trial. Then he would summon another justice. The two justices would then hold a bail proceeding in which they would again review the same material. Then they would say to themselves, we have the discretion to bail or to commit to prison, but not the discretion to discharge. If this were a misdemeanor, we would individually have discretion to discharge, but technically this is a felony even though it only involves an argument over some farm tools. Even if we are both clear that the defendant is a worthy person and could not possibly have committed the offense charged, all we can do is bail him rather than commit him. We must send the case forward for trial.

Clearly what must have really happened in many instances, and indeed what the nineteenth-century statutes finally recognize and legitimate, is that a single justice did examination and bail commitment all at once. He decided either to quash, bail, or commit on the basis of how strong his suspicions of the accused were, more or less employing the accumulated paraphernalia of the causes of suspicion, presumptions, and probable cause to calibrate his suspicions.

Was the elaborate set of probable cause categories used in examination merely a set of pigeonholes into which the justices sorted the evidence for the reports accompanying the felony complaints, which they dutifully sent forward for trial? Or were they also guides to the justices of the peace in exercising a discretion to send or to not send forward such complaints?

There is no reason to assume that the justices followed to the letter their duties as outlined in Dalton and the other handbooks. The justices have never been uniformly conscientious in carrying out any of their other duties. Though many of these duties required their attendance at quarter sessions, it remained spotty, and legislative efforts to remedy this situation altered their attendance records very little. Royal proclamations might require the justices to spend nine months a year in the county or else lose their commissions, but they were often not to be found.[172]

The justices held positions of influence and authority in their respective communities and performed a wide range of judicial and nonjudicial duties in addition to their roles in connection with serious crime. Given the practice of arbitrating and settling a variety of disputes, it would not be surprising to find the justices behaving similarly when certain serious misdemeanor complaints, or even some kinds of felony complaints, reached them. From the few remaining justices' notebooks, we know that justices sometimes settled various disputes, violent assaults, and small thefts. Such action meant that there would have been no trial. While it is unlikely that a justice would behave in such a manner in a case of murder or substantial theft and robbery, it is reasonable to assume that he would not push on to trial every theft over twelve pence. Such a theft was a felony, conviction for which entailed capital punishment. We know that grand jurors and judges frequently undervalued stolen goods so as to avoid felony convictions. It seems likely that the magistrates acted similarly to reduce the charge or to assist in its being dropped. It is not likely that such behavior would have been viewed as a serious dereliction of duty in an era in which relatively few thefts were prosecuted at all. Thus, despite the weight of legal opinion recorded in the handbooks, it is difficult to believe that during the seventeenth and much of the eighteenth centuries English magistrates never short-circuited the Marian procedures. It is also difficult to believe that they did not take account of malicious accusations, especially in situations where they were aware of the enmities of the parties. Thus certain kinds of accusations would surely be forwarded, while others might be "agreed" or compounded. The law forbade compounding between victim and criminal, but the practice continued.

The law also required capital punishment for the crime of witchcraft until 1736. Although belief in witchcraft continued throughout the second half of the seventeenth century and into the early eighteenth century, particularly in the countryside, magistrates appear to have deflected most accusations from the legal process. Although we cannot date this precisely, the number of witchcraft prosecutions declined sharply from about the 1620s. The justices exercised discretion in this type of case and no doubt frequently did so in others where the accusations seemed weak.

Perhaps we can glean something of the general intellectual qualities that were thought desirable for the magistrates from a few of the manuals. William Sheppard (1652) indicated that a justice must be a man of "understanding and judgment" who could "distinguish the weight and Justice of the complaint and malice of the plaintiff" and "who counts it his duty and dignity to sift [the Truth] out of all things." Edmund Bohun's *Justice of the Peace* (1684) also emphasized the need for intellectual abilities which could assist in the difficult task of finding "the Truth of Things." Language used by those the justice examined was often confused and uncertain, and the justice must "not expect that either Party will at first frankly or ingeniously represent the truth of things to him." He must with industry and patience "search out" the truth and recognize that people will lie even under oath. He was therefore to cross-examine carefully, for "the Truth will sometimes appear through all their disguises." He should evaluate all he hears "according to the Quality, and the Number of the Witnesses of the thing, more or less to be believed." He was reminded that "matters of fact" and things that are past require testimony, "and According to the Credibility of the Person that relates it, is the belief Stronger or Weaker." Bohun also provides advice on how to distinguish true from false stories.[173]

The justice of the peace had a number of duties in which these qualities might be required. It seems very likely that the decision rules designed for one or more of these spilled over into others. The justice had to make decisions about arrest warrants and search warrants, in the process considering the causes of suspicion and the requirement of probable cause. He was required to deal with misdemeanors as well as felonies. Some cases he encountered would be tried at quarter sessions, others at assize, and still others would be disposed of by himself or with a colleague by summary procedures without jury. He was required to make many decisions which turned on assessments of character and credibility. Examination of those accused of felony and misdemeanor were only two. Decisions also were to be made about bail or committal. He also made decisions about granting sureties of the peace, either when requested to do so by others or at his own discretion. Here again he was to evaluate the fame or reputation of the party, which included whether the party was often found in suspicious company or was of honest conversation. He had to determine whether he had "sufficient cause" to insist on such sureties, and, if he was relying on the discretion of others, he had to consider whether the complaint issued from "honest or credible persons."[174] One could no doubt multiply the activities, quasi-judicial, judicial, and administrative, in which magistrates were required to evaluate character and evidence in order to determine whether the evidence or circumstances were sufficient to undertake this or that action or procedure.

In many instances there might be little need for the justice to act in a discretionary role during examination, not because he was forbidden by law to do so, but because he had already done so at an earlier stage of the case. If he had been requested to issue an arrest or search warrant and had followed the appropriate guidelines in granting it, he would presumably already have evaluated much of the evidence and character of the parties. He would have considered the "causes for suspicion" before granting an arrest warrant and presumably would not feel the need to do so again explicitly, especially if he knew the parties and the crime in question. The easiest time for the justice to exercise discretion was thus just prior to the arrest. At this point he was in the best *legal* position to dissuade an angry victim or one who made an accusation on slender evidence. If the same justice who was asked to issue an arrest warrant was the one to whom the accused was brought, and this was likely to be the case, arrest and examination might easily occur within the same day or even hour. If a justice wished to dissuade, or arbitrate a theft rather than prosecute it, he might do so before the arrest. It is thus possible that arrest often provided the more important screening institution. If, however, the victim personally arrested the accused and brought him to the magistrate, the magistrate was in a somewhat different position than if he had been involved in issuing the arrest warrant. In this instance he proceeded directly to examination in a relatively formal setting. In such circumstances he would probably be inclined to consider the evidence, using Lambarde's, Crompton's, and Dalton's notions of probable and light presumption and the causes of suspicion.

Probable Cause and
Preliminary Hearings

In the discussion of the grand jury in Chapter 2, I noted the centuries-long dilemma of finding a level of probability that was neither too high nor too low, that turned the indictment process neither into a trial nor into a rubber stamp. A similar dilemma seems to have confronted the preliminary hearing. On the one hand, it did not seem right that the magistrate could simply dismiss cases of felony on his own discretion, because to do so would short-circuit the most sacrosanct element in the English legal system— trial by jury. On the other hand, malicious or unfounded accusations could impose the costs of trial on an obviously innocent person. The dilemma was not solved in the early modern era because there did not appear to be a safe and logical decision rule. The causes of suspicion borrowed from Romano-canon law and other elements of the English process which are gradually boiled down to "probable cause" are attempts to construct such a rule.

The process by which the early modern preliminary hearing was transformed into a judicial hearing is still murky. We must nevertheless chart what we can of that transition and the evidentiary standards which have come to mark the modern English and American preliminary examination. However, it is necessary to backtrack a little to incorporate the pre-mid-nineteenth-century American materials. Here too we enter largely unknown territory where evidence is substantially limited to the handbooks prepared for the justices. Initially, English handbooks were imported, often by the colonial authorities. Most "American" handbooks were modeled on, if not simply copied from, their English counterparts.[175] Yet copies of such volumes were originally rare and expensive, and many justices must have lacked any written guide. It is not even clear how soon justices of the peace were established in some of the colonies. We know even less about seventeenth- and eighteenth-century practice in the colonies than we know about in England. If the evidence of the handbooks can be considered evidence of actual behavior, we must assume that American practice was on the whole similar to that of the English.

There are, however, a few known exceptions to English procedure. In Massachusetts the examination procedures seem to have permitted witnesses to be questioned in the presence of the accused.[176] The early New Haven colony departed further from the English model than most colonies. Here the justice, or more often the justices, were formally permitted to dismiss charges when they became convinced of the accused's innocence.[177] In Virginia County, courts initially appear to have examined arrested suspects to determine whether the accused should be tried before the general court. In 1705, a new institution, the examining court, was introduced. After a preliminary hearing before a justice of the peace, the case was sent to a special examining court where the accused was again questioned by several justices of the peace. Here the accused was entitled to require the sheriff to summon witnesses on his behalf. Either the accused was released or the case went to the grand jury and eventually to a trial jury. Starke's handbook indicated that this new institution enlarged the means of "coming at the Truth of a supposed Fact" and gave the accused "a third opportunity of Acquittal." Such protections, designed for the "Liberty and Quiet of the Subject," were "not to be boasted in any other Part of the British Dominions."[178]

Some discretion must have crept into other American practices, especially in instances of obvious vexations or malicious accusations. Discretion would be used in granting bail. In 1736, the Webb handbook, in connection with bail, indicated on Dalton's authority that persons taken on suspicion of burglary, robbery, theft, or other felonies may be bailed if they were not of "evil fame" or if there were "no strong presumption" against them.[179] This is bail, however, and not examination. Webb indicates that in cases of witchcraft the justice should refuse information "without strong and apparent Cause, proved by sufficient witnesses upon oath."[180] Whether dismissals were considered appropriate in other kinds of crimes is not clear. The phrase "without strong and apparent Cause" perhaps presaged the more modern and familiar "probable cause," which eventually came to be the American decision rule for discharging or forwarding cases.

The American colonial handbook tradition, consisting as it did largely of reprints or abridgments of Nelson or Burn, provided nearly identical statements concerning discretion. Little appears to have changed by the late eighteenth century. James Wilson, a severe critic of English grand jury evidentiary standards, appears to accept the traditional position as stated by Hale and Hawkins. After taking the examination of those arrested, the magistrate might discharge, bail, or commit, but the first was permissible only if no crime had been committed or if the suspicion conceived against the prisoner was "entirely unfounded."[181] We cannot, of course, be sure how that threshold was interpreted. It seems to be compatible with the idea that if only "light presumption" could be established, dismissal was appropriate. The justice thus would send on most cases and discharge those for which the evidence was extremely slight or nonexistent.

As in England, the transition process by which the justice of the peace came to forward only cases where probable cause existed is invisible. It is not unlikely, however, that statements like Wilson's, based on Hale and Hawkins, provided one of the concepts which were expanded in practice. In some respects the emergence of the probable cause standard in America is even more mysterious than that in England. Legislation established it in England in 1848, but there is no similar American legislation. Nor were the scattered and often ill-educated American magistrates likely to be as sensitive to reformist sentiment as were their mid-eighteenth-century English counterparts. And the early development of the public prosecutor in America is doubtless a complicating factor.

With the early American background in mind we can now turn to nineteenth- and twentieth-century developments on both sides of the Atlantic. The Marian legislation formalized the adoption of misdemeanor examination to felony. The 1848 Jervis Act, which formally judicialized the preliminary hearing, adopted what was considered the "best practice" of the mid–nineteenth-century justices of the peace.[182] That practice had gradually come to permit the magistrate a larger discretionary and evaluative role and at the same time increased protections for the defendants. I have already suggested that the confusions and discrepancies in the handbook tradition allowed some leeway for discretion, which was gradually extended over time. John Beattie, whose *Crime and the Courts in England, 1660–1800*, represents the most thorough and thoughtful treatment of crime in the eighteenth century, argues that Restoration magistrates were probably not dismissing cases where insufficient evidence existed to justify an individual's being held, but that such discretion was already being exercised by the second quarter of the eighteenth century.[183] The magistrate's role in summary cases was no doubt important in that transition. Langbein has shown that pretrial examination was not created by the Marian statutes but rather had developed out of examination procedures for less serious crime. Similarly, it seems likely that the justices' discretionary role in dropping minor cases spread to major ones. The belated statutory authorization of defense counsel at examination too probably derived from existing practice in lesser crimes, whose procedures increasingly may have seemed fairer than traditional felony procedure. It was, after all, the same men who engaged in summary proceedings for minor matters who on other occasions had to take part in examination, bail, and commitment hearings. Beattie has attributed the judicialization of the preliminary examination to the activity of lawyers rather than to the justices. He associates the change with the introduction of defense counsel into criminal proceedings about 1730. When lawyers became involved in criminal trials, it seems reasonable to suppose that they would have sought to push their defense of their clients back to pretrial proceedings as well and would have pressed for discretionary discharge.[184] Yet it seems unlikely that such pressure from lawyers would suddenly move magistrates to begin exercising a discretion which they had previously rigorously eschewed. It is more likely that lawyer intervention accelerated previous discretionary practice than created it.

The institution of the magistracy also changed with the development of the early eighteenth-century trading justices. These urban justices became more professionalized than their country counterparts, who saw far fewer cases of serious crime.[185] By 1752, John Fielding, a London magistrate, was openly ridiculing the position of Dalton and Hale on delivering the accused when little or no evidence existed. He did not hesitate to discharge prisoners despite the weight of traditional legal opinion. Fielding commented on the absurdity of the inability to discharge when an accusation of a trifling theft was backed only by slight suspicion.[186] Even earlier, in 1745, magistrates were dismissing cases because they "found nothing material to prove the fact" or because they "adjudged the grounds . . . to be so very little." Another magistrate of the 1760s dismissed cases for "insufficient evidence."[187] Blackstone, in his *Commentaries* (1769), however, was somewhat more conservative. He indicated that the justices are free to discharge only when the "suspicion entertained of the prisoner was wholly groundless."[188]

A substantial official break in the traditional pattern began in 1792, when Parliament created a paid professional magistracy in metropolitan London which was given many of the roles previously assigned to justices of the peace. The new magistrates had the authority to dismiss insufficiently substantiated charges of serious crime. Sitting alone, a justice could dismiss serious criminal charges or send the accused to trial at quarter sessions or Old Bailey. By 1792 there was thus a national consensus that it was appropriate for an urban magistrate to examine the evidence before him and assess whether there was sufficient evidence to proceed with the case. If, at this point, we do not know what standard, if any, he was instructed to employ, such assessment and discharge was deemed both desirable and legal. Change in the practice of rural justices must have followed quickly, if indeed it had not preceded it.[189]

Before the 1848 Jervis Act, foreign observers commented on the judicial character and discretionary role of the justices. One reported that when a case came before the committing magistrate, he became a patron of the accused, and if any case of doubt arose, he did not hesitate to discharge the prisoner.[190] Charles Cottu, writing in the 1820s, noted that the justice, whom he compared to the French judge d'instruction, could dismiss charges which seemed too light.[191] The pace of change which now permitted justices to drop cases on insufficient evidence was no doubt stimulated by urbanization. The number of felony cases enormously increased. If every accusation, no matter how feeble, had to be tried by grand jury and petty jury, the system would have become too clogged to operate. The discharging function thus was necessary if the criminal justice system, initially developed for small aggregations of people, many of whom knew one another, was to continue to operate successfully in cities.

The introduction of the police, itself a response to urbanization, also had profound effects, first in London and then elsewhere. In 1829 a metropolitan police force was created with the duties of arresting, collecting statements from prosecution witnesses, and operating under quasi-judicial rules.[192] The magistrates were thus relieved of any prosecutional function they might have been performing. The shift to a more openly judicialized role was thus a natural one. The metropolitan police courts to which the police now brought their accusations had been dropping unfounded charges for some thirty years, when the Jervis Act signaled the national legitimization of the change. The institution of the police soon became generalized, and they were to be found everywhere in England by 1856. If the police became *de facto* public prosecutors, legally they remained private citizens.

The transition also was hastened by the growing concern for the rights of the accused. In 1826, legislation permitted accused felons to examine depositions. Counsel was increasingly found at felony examinations, and misdemeanor trials had become more trial-like. The presumption of innocence in its modern form was being expressed from the 1780s.[193]

Magistrates were now regularly discharging cases for insufficient evidence. We do not know how strong cases had to be before they went to trial. Chitty's widely respected *Practical Treatise on the Criminal Law* (1816) prescribed not only discretionary practice but also an extraordinarily high evidentiary standard, one even higher than that included in the 1848 legislation. Chitty anticipates later events in writing that the magistrate exercises discretion, though he was "clearly bound in the exercise of sound discretion, not to commit anyone unless a *prima facie* case is made out against him by witnesses entitled to a reasonable degree of credit."[194]

The Jervis Act of 1848 confirmed and consolidated the practices I have been describing.[195] The examination process now permitted legal counsel who were free to cross-examine prosecution witnesses. All known prosecution evidence had to be presented at this time. The defense was permitted to make a statement and answer the charges. For the first time the "caution" was introduced, which warned the accused that anything he said would be written down and might be used in evidence against him. The justices shed whatever residues remained of the prosecutorial role and settled into a judicial mode. A clear evidentiary rule was provided for the justices, which eliminated the contradictory set of instructions that had existed for several centuries. They were given the discretion, indeed the duty, to discharge if the evidence did not "raise a strong or probable presumption" of guilt of the accused. When that threshold was reached, they were required to bail or to commit. "Strong and probable presumption" language was repeated in legislation of 1867 and continued throughout the nineteenth century.[196] This strong and probable presumption standard would remain until 1937, when the higher *prima facie* case standard was introduced by judicial decision a few years after the final abolition of the grand jury. The English standard then became that "such evidence, that if it be uncontroverted at the trial, a reasonable minded jury may convict upon it."[197]

The nineteenth- and twentieth-century American developments were somewhat different. The American cases that deal with the examination phase tend to focus neither on probable cause for arrest nor on the decision of the magistrate, but rather on the prosecutor. While private prosecution may have been the original model, the growth of the office of the public prosecutor seems to have triggered a major judicial response in the United States.

Although we typically speak of the Anglo-American legal system, students of Great Britain and the United States are aware that the criminal justice systems of the two countries are not identical. One of the areas in which they have diverged is in their adoption of a system of public prosecution. Although the movement for a system of public prosecution gained considerable momentum in the third quarter of the nineteenth century and again in the early decades of the twentieth century, the English were reluctant to adopt it in any of the forms it was taking in the United States, Scotland, Ireland, or on the Continent.[198] The Jervis Act does not regularize prosecution, and frequently it was left to the committing magistrate to determine who the prosecutor should be. It might be the injured party, the magistrate's clerk, or the police. The domination of private prosecution in England meant that many crimes went unprosecuted. In the early eighteenth century, voluntary prosecution associations and newspaper advertising, promising financial rewards for the apprehension of criminals, attempted to fill the gap. These associations, which were at their height between 1750 and 1840, attempted to overcome the high costs of prosecution, for example, transporting prisoners and witnesses, employing lawyers, and paying the fees due to the clerks of the peace and the assize. Such associations, and there were probably about one thousand of them, typically forbade members from dropping prosecution and assessed penalties for compounding. The police became the *de facto* prosecutors in the late nineteenth century, although their legal status remained that of private citizen.[199]

There were proposals for a public prosecutor from the late eighteenth century on, and Bentham, William Fielding, Lord Brougham, and others suggested a variety of reforms of this type, though none came to fruition. In the end a rather truncated Director of Public Prosecution came into being, but prosecution remained largely in private and police hands.

In the United States public prosecution began early.[200] This institution, which had come into existence by the time of the Revolution, albeit not in its fully developed form, was not part of the common-law heritage. It was thus far easier for the English to ignore crime or to charge on weak cases at least until the police began to take over some of the prosecutorial functions. Although the American justicing manuals took no notice of divergence from English practice, most private prosecution for crime had disappeared in the American colonies by the end of the eighteenth century. Here again, the justicing manuals ignored practice. The power and status of federal, state, and local prosecuting attorneys increased rapidly from about 1820. Jacksonian democracy produced not only popularly elected judges but also elected prosecuting attorneys.[201]

What is important about this development is that prosecuting attorneys exercised discretion to initiate and terminate criminal cases, and thus were engaged in eliminating cases with inappropriate or insufficient evidence. Although we cannot easily trace the evidentiary basis on which the public prosecutor's information was based, probable cause became the appropriate standard. The appropriateness of his bill's "probable cause" would typically be ruled on by a judge at a preliminary hearing or by a grand jury. As noted earlier, the grand jury lost ground in America as more cases were prosecuted by information and as the prosecutor came to dominate grand jury proceedings.[202] The public prosecutor thus initiated the prosecutions he chose and could terminate them. He decided what crimes to investigate, whether to prosecute, and the level to be charged. His decision to prosecute was thus enmeshed with that of the police, an institution which developed somewhat later than that of the public prosecutor, as well as with the magistrate and the grand jury. It is not hard to see how difficulties and confusions might arise as the same verbal formula of probable cause came to serve the needs of institutions that dealt in different, yet overlapping, ways with pretrial procedures. Most jurisdictions have ruled that the concept of probable cause for arrest is less demanding than the concept used by prosecutors and magistrates because the former deals with rapidly changing street conditions rather than the calmer and slower conditions of the office and courtroom. The relationship between the varieties of probability and the varieties of probable cause is, and is likely to remain, somewhat unstable.

It was thus the public prosecutor who stood as accuser at the preliminary examination or hearing. It was natural, therefore, that the question of probable cause became not a question of whom the victim might justifiably suspect, but one of whether the prosecutor was justified in requesting that the case move forward. Prosecutors are state officials. That is important in two respects. First, they are distanced from the events, so the standards they employ ought to be, and indeed must be, less subjective than those of the victims. Second, prosecutors are armed with the power of the state, so their discretion must be carefully founded if citizens are to be adequately protected against overweening state authority. The case of *Munn v. Dupont* indicated that probable cause was "a reasonable cause of suspicion, supported by circumstances sufficiently strong in themselves to warrant a cautious man in the belief that the person accused is guilty of the offense with which he is charged."[203] An 1849 case indicates that probable cause is "Such a state of facts in the mind of the prosecutor as would lead a man of ordinary caution or prudence to believe, or entertain an honest and strong suspicion that the person arrested is guilty."[204] These opinions echo the language of the causes of suspicion of the magistrates' handbooks. Another case indicated "probable cause consists in that degree of evidence, which would induce a reasonable man to believe the accused party guilty; such as would convince or satisfy men of the usual and ordinary caution and judgment when not governed by malice."[205] A Maine case, *Humphries v. Parker*, indicated that probable cause was

A belief honestly entertained, and derived from facts and evidence which in themselves are sufficient to justify a man who is calm, and not governed by passion, prejudice, or want of ordinary caution and care, in believing the party guilty. Belief and reasonable grounds for that belief are undoubtedly both essential elements in the justification of probable cause.[206]

Still another indicated that "probable cause does not, therefore, depend on the actual state of the case in point of fact, but upon the honest and reasonable belief of the party prosecuting."[207] Contemporary discussions of probable cause in the preliminary hearing almost invariably boil down to just how much a preliminary hearing must be a trial before the trial or a prediction of the trial outcome.

The contrasting British and American developments show very clearly the movement of the evidentiary standard from one focusing retrospectively on the conditions at the time of the crime to one focusing prospectively on the outcome of the trial. The causes of suspicion essentially directed the attention of their appliers to the facts surrounding the crime and the characteristics of the accused. On the basis of what *had* happened and what the accused was like at the time it happened, is whatever we are now doing to the accused justified? The probable cause standards of the American courts and the *prima facie* case standard directs the attention of the applier forward. Does our best guess as to what will happen at a future trial justify what we are now doing to the accused? We know from its ancient rhetorical and Romano-canon ancestry and its initial English context that the language of light and strong presumption is initially about suspicion. The language of probable cause grows out of the presumption language, as is still clear in the nineteenth-century English "strong and probable presumption" standard. Probably in the seventeenth, and clearly in the eighteenth and nineteenth centuries, the causes of suspicion, presumption, and probable cause were employed retrospectively by magistrates to supervise accusation and arrest decisions. The essential question was whether the accuser or arrester had been justified in doing what he had done. In the nineteenth-century American cases we can watch attention shifting from the earliest point in the criminal justice process, the decision of the victim or other lay person to accuse, to a midpoint in the process, the decision of the professional prosecutor to prosecute. And then, adumbrated by Chitty and enacted in England in the late nineteenth century, the *prima facie* case standard completes the shift by centering attention on what will happen at the trial, which concludes the process. The American probable cause standard is not so openly prospective, but its frequent invocation of the reasonable person surely suggests that the prosecutor's job is to anticipate the response of that set of ultimate reasonable persons, the jurors.

We can watch probable cause float free of suspicion and then in certain circumstances turn into *prima facie* case, or something close to probable trial outcome, at precisely the historical period when the number of arrests and potential prosecutions are rising and the need to set priorities for or ration trial opportunities jumps into prominence. At precisely this point the preliminary hearing evidence standard shifts from a device for appraising and rationing initial accusation and arrest conduct to a device for assessing the chance of ultimate conviction and screening out cases that do not have a justifiable claim to precious trial time. Its adoption also must have contributed to the growing belief in the redundancy of the indicting grand jury.

Of course in the real world things are never as neat as they are in academic analysis. In actual application, probable cause, stripped of its older context and hovering short of *prima facie* case, remains a Janus-faced standard, looking both backward at what happened and forward at what the trial outcome is likely to be. Ultimately that is the reason that the content of the standard becomes more generalized and more unclear rather than less so.

Conclusion

In *Our Man in Havana*, Captain Segura assures Mr. Wormold that someone will not be tortured because "he doesn't belong to the torturable class."[208] In choosing those words, Graham Greene dug deeper into his Roman Catholic heritage than perhaps even he was aware. The *indicia* that the medieval and early modern canonists and civilians used were standards to be employed by professional judges to decide when torture to extract a confession was justified. As such, they may be seen as an attempt to establish objective standards to limit the discretion of officials and to legitimate official violence. Beyond that, however, the substantive content of the standards of ill fame, bad company, and so on did go a long way toward defining a torturable class.

As adapted to England, however, the functions of the causes of suspicion were somewhat different. They did indeed endow the respectable with a tool to protect themselves against the under-classes. They made it much easier to justify the arrest of a poor vagabond than of someone well settled in the web of ordinary status relationships. More generally they served less to control the discretion of officials than to insure that the system of justice would not be used by accusers to unjustifiably harass personal enemies. The central issue was really the good or bad faith of the private person making the arrest. As arrest moves from private persons to magistrates and police, the standard moves from causes of suspicion to probable cause to suspect, to probable cause to believe, to just plain probable cause. The central issue is no longer the good faith of an involved, private complainant. When probable cause to arrest becomes a matter of judicial weighing of evidence presented by police officers and public prosecutors, it becomes a tool for predicting the ultimate outcome of a public trial. To some degree the police officer is still analogized to the interested private complainant, and the question of his or her good faith continues to be put. Given the contemporary context, however, the judge applying the standard is far more likely to frame the question another way: "Is the evidence presented to me now a sufficient portion of the total evidence needed to convict at a subsequent trial to justify the arrest that will initiate the trial sequence?" Moreover, as we come to reject the notion of a torturable or arrestable class, we move from generalized or class-associated signs, or causes of suspicion, to particularized consideration of a preliminarily gathered body of concrete facts that bear upon the probability of guilt in the particular case. Such a movement also leads to a probable cause standard far less concerned with the individual motives of the accuser and far more concerned with screening out cases that cannot be tried to conviction. Such screening is, of course, partly designed to husband the society's scarce judicial resources. In part, however, we have come full circle and are demanding that officials justify the pain they inflict—but this time the pain of arrest and trial and this time justification on an individual, not a class, basis.

Chapter Four

Species of Probability and Doctrinal Borrowing

Now that we have completed our tour of pretrial procedures, we come full circle back to jury trial. This time we are concerned particularly with borrowings from the Romano-canon tradition and from epistemological writings and more generally with those sources and varieties of evidence on the basis of which juries arrived at their beyond reasonable doubt verdicts. Most of the evidence the jury hears comes from witnesses, and so Chapter 4 begins with witnesses. Witness testimony naturally brings up the question of hearsay, so the second segment of the chapter is devoted to hearsay. Far more significant than hearsay, however, is the problem of circumstantial evidence and presumption. Chapter 3 examined the ways in which presumption and circumstantial evidence, or signs, were employed in connection with pretrial examination of accused felons and migrated from one to another pretrial institution and practice. The third segment of this chapter traces the lengthy and still murky process by which these doctrines came together with "beyond a reasonable doubt" and "to a moral certainty" in the jury trial.

Witnesses

The discussion of witness testimony will be relatively brief because I have already explored the development of the concept of witness credibility in connection with jury verdicts. Witnesses were unlikely to emerge as a salient doctrinal issue as long as they were not viewed as a central feature of the jury trial. The traditional view, represented by both Fortescue and Coke, which emphasized the distinction between the great freedom guaranteeing English right of trial by jury and the oppressive Continental trial by witnesses, obscured the fact that, from the fifteenth century and perhaps even earlier, witnesses played an increasingly important role in jury trials. By the sixteenth century the change could not be ignored. Marian legislation provided a mechanism to insure that justices of the peace examined and bound over those who would appear in court as witnesses in criminal cases, and Elizabethan legislation required witnesses in civil cases to appear in court. Clearly witnesses were being recognized as an extremely important, if not legally necessary, part of the jury trial.

Once that importance was recognized, a number of questions would immediately emerge. How many witnesses are necessary to reach a decision: none, one, two, or more? What is the relationship between jurors and witnesses when jurors are still, in some sense, knowers of the fact? How could jurors decide whether or not witnesses should be believed and their testimony credited? On what basis, if any, might witnesses be excluded from testifying? Convicted criminals, convicted but pardoned criminals, accessories, those convicted of minor offenses, interested parties, family members, children, the mentally incompetent, and perjurers were all candidates for exclusion. How would jurors treat sworn, as opposed to unsworn, testimony? What were the relative weights of testimonial evidence and documentary evidence? What were the relative weights of testimonial evidence and indirect, that is, circumstantial, evidence? How were juries to deal with conflicting and concurring testimony? What, if any, was the role of the expert witness? All of these questions had to be faced as jurors confronted witnesses.

Not all of them were answered during the sixteenth, seventeenth, or even the eighteenth centuries, and where answers were produced they were sometimes confused and contradictory. The attempt to construct answers was marked by considerable borrowing from the Romano-canon tradition, which was familiar to the English legal profession from the ecclesiastical and other English non-common-law courts. Those borrowings were not only partial and sporadic but also often disguised because of hostility to the

188   *Probability and Doctrinal Borrowing*

Continental legal and constitutional system. Thus for ideological reasons, Romano-canon terminology and concepts might be adopted and adapted without crediting the source. We have already seen this process at work in the criteria by which justices of the peace were to examine the accused and relevant witnesses. Only in the eighteenth century would more open recognition of the assistance of the civilian tradition be recognized by legal scholars.

As we have frequently noted, the Romano-canonist tradition developed a system of legal proof which emphasized the role of confession and the testimony of witnesses.[1] Medieval Continental scholars developed a highly sophisticated system of evaluating that testimony. Witnesses were required to have direct sensory perception of the events they testified about, that is, they must be eye- or earwitnesses. Hearsay testimony was excluded at an early date. The credibility of witnesses was related to social and economic status as well as to the opportunity to observe firsthand the fact in question. Thus the testimony of nobles counted for more than that of commoners, ecclesiastics for more than that of laypersons, men more than women, and Christians more than Jews. The value system of the medieval era was thus incorporated into the system of proof. If status and condition helped to shape the doctrine of proof, the goal of that system nevertheless was proof "as clear as the light of day." A complicated system was developed to allow testimony to be given a fractional value. Testimony thus might be considered to constitute half, quarter, or even an eighth proof.

In addition, medieval jurists developed an elaborate system of excluding the testimony of witnesses who were considered less than trustworthy. Minors under fourteen were excluded, as were those under the age of twenty in cases involving crime. Slaves or those who were designated as paupers might not testify. Wives and husbands could not testify against one another, and children could not testify in cases involving parents. Wives usually could not testify in cases in which their husbands were involved. Brothers might testify in criminal, but not in civil, cases. The mentally deficient, perjurers, and criminals were excluded, as were familiars, domestics, and enemies. The number and variety of exclusions must often have created substantial barriers to conviction. Testimony was given under oath with heavy penalties for perjury. A procedural literature dating from the twelfth century and a well-developed treatise literature outlined the system and its complexities in loving detail.

If the system of legal proof severely limited judicial discretion, some element of discretion was retained because judges determined the credit and the capacity of the witnesses. That discretion must have been diminished in practice as civilian judges increasingly dealt with written depositions. Judicial decisions in the Romano-canon system came to be based on files rather than on seeing and hearing the witnesses or the accused—the pattern developed in the English common-law courts.

It is not surprising to find that the Romano-canon approach exerted some influence on the earlier phases of the Anglo-American system. The ecclesiastical courts and the common-law courts developed side by side during the Middle Ages. While the English ecclesiastical courts adopted the academic tradition, they did not automatically exclude consideration of anyone's testimony, and English ecclesiastical judges appear to have engaged in far more evaluation of testimony than the treatises permitted.[2] If ecclesiastical courts deviated from the procedure prescribed, we should not be surprised to find that whatever traces are to be found in the common-law courts should be even more partial and incomplete. As is well known, rather late developing courts, such as Chancery, Star Chamber, and the prerogative courts, employed elements of Continental procedure but did not fully adopt it. Indeed it is possible that the procedural and treatise literature were not rigorously followed in practice in many late medieval Continental jurisdictions where they were overlaid on earlier Germanic and feudal systems.

The first influence of the Romano-canonist principles on the English common-law system not surprisingly was felt in the selection of jurors rather than of witnesses, as the importance of witnesses was recognized by the legal system relatively late. The criteria for challenging jurors, which can be found as early as Glanvill (c. 1187), have long been recognized as originating in the Romano-canon exclusions.[3]

The Romano-canon approach can also be found, albeit in a much-simplified form, in the English testimonial exclusions. These obviously would not be systematically developed until witnesses became a routine part of English trial proceedings. This influence too has been long recognized, and there has been little reluctance to recognize the Romano-canon tradition as the source of common-law jury challenges or the exclusion of various categories of wit-nesses. Dalton's *Country Justice* includes a discussion of who might or might not testify. It was clear that wives might not testify, but the question of children remained open. Children were permitted to testify in a 1612 witchcraft case but it is likely that this was an exception made for an exceptional crime.[4] John Langbein, how-ever, has suggested that Dalton conflated the law of examination with the law of evidence.[5] That conflation, I would suggest, should not be considered an error on Dalton's part but rather an example of how evidentiary criteria designed for one purpose or procedure could migrate to another. If Dalton's criteria for examination were in large part borrowed from the Romano-canon *indicia*, they might be borrowed again as criteria for assessment of witness credibility. They would be no less useful to jurors considering the credibility of those who appeared before them. A suggestion of how such transfers might take place is seen in the migration of the Romano-canon maxim:

> Conditio, sexus, aetas, discretio, fama,
> Et fortuna, fides: in testibus esta requires.

Dalton cites the maxim in connection with examination by the jus-tice of the peace. His successors sometimes used the same verses and similar materials in a section labeled "witnesses."[6] The criteria to be considered by the justices in preliminary examination of wit-nesses were almost identical to those which came to be used to test the credibility of witnesses who appeared before juries in criminal cases. Both dealt with witnesses, albeit in a different procedural context. Indeed, they involved the same persons. The same criteria no doubt also were used by the justices of the peace in deciding lesser criminal causes by themselves. And these are greatly in-debted to the Romano-canon *indicia*, which in turn are indebted to the rhetorical tradition.

In order to assess the borrowing of evidentiary criteria concern-ing witnesses, we will have to know more about one of the big mysteries of English legal history—the process by which English juries were transformed from largely self-informing knowers of the facts into fact evaluators who reached verdicts on the basis of in-formation and testimony introduced in the court. This process is

still relatively little understood, although recent research on medieval juries suggests that they lost their self-informing abilities
considerably earlier than has been thought, if, indeed, they had
ever been fully self-informing.[7]

Recent work on medieval juries suggests that late medieval and
early modern juries were not exclusively composed of men from
the community. If they were not from the vicinity, it is extremely
unlikely that they would have an opportunity to become familiar
with the facts prior to hearing them in court. Sir Thomas Smith,
writing in the mid-sixteenth century, indicated that juries were
unacquainted with the accused despite the vicinage requirement.[8]
Had the testimony of witnesses not become a regular feature of
the jury trial in criminal cases, the criminal justice system would
have become inoperative as the population increased and fewer
face-to-face social contacts became the norm. Without the introduction of witnesses, the jury could not have remained the central
institution it has been for so many centuries.

Recent studies not only indicate that witnesses appeared in English criminal trials earlier than previously thought, but also suggest something of the process by which they may have been introduced. Some information may have been provided by private
prosecutors and administrative and legal officers such as coroners
and justices of the peace. Witnesses, as we have seen, were not
legally necessary for the trial to take place, but it is difficult to
understand how most criminal trials could have been conducted
without them. Fortescue himself describes witnesses, albeit not in
criminal trial, being examined on oath.[9] And Sir Thomas Smith
describes the cross-examination of witnesses. The legislation of
Philip and Mary that revised the bail and committal statutes included a mechanism to bind over witnesses to insure their appearance at trial. Legislation of 1563 compelled witnesses to appear and
made perjury a crime. Defendants might call witnesses, but they
were not permitted to testify under oath. A recent study of Tudor
treason trials concludes that early common-law trials did not permit
parties, relatives, or convicted felons to testify, but that treason
trials of the sixteenth century already exhibited efforts to discredit
witnesses by attacking their reputations and characters and by
pointing to inconsistent statements. In the early sixteenth century
jurors still spoke with witnesses outside of court; by mid-century

they appear to have been testifying in court with some regularity. In 1533, Sir Thomas More was arguing that witnesses should not be permitted to give evidence to jurors except in court. By 1613 the courts were allowing witnesses to testify, but the parties and spouses were not permitted to testify, at least in certain kinds of cases.[10] The courts in the sixteenth and early seventeenth centuries thus exhibit considerable uncertainty over how to treat the testimony of the witnesses who were increasingly becoming a more central feature of jury trials.

Commentators such as Fortescue and Coke emphasized that, unlike the Romano-canon system, English courts were not required to have a set number of witnesses. The Romano-canon two-witness rule that derived from both Roman law and Scripture was not, however, entirely absent from English law. In one form or another most legislative enactments dealing with treason contained the two-witness requirement. The law of 1547 required "two sufficient and lawful witness," that of 1552 "two lawful accusers,"[11] and that of 1661 "two lawful and credible witnesses."[12] It appears, however, that the two-witness requirement for treason lapsed temporarily. Thus when Sir Walter Raleigh, who was tried for treason in 1603, appealed to the two-witness requirement, Lord Chief Justice Popham ruled that the treason statute had been repealed.[13] The appropriateness of two witnesses in treason cases, however, had become part of the mental furniture of many Englishmen and was required by the treason legislation of 1696.[14] The treason exception to the normal absence of a two-witness rule was thus introduced by legislative enactment and not by the judiciary. The two-witness requirement was to be found in some nontreason statutes as well, for instance the Blasphemy Act of 1697.[15]

Although there seems to have been little doubt among legal writers that juries might convict on the basis of a single witness or even without any witnesses, it is not clear how well known this fact was. Robert Boyle, a sophisticated intellectual of the late seventeenth century and friend of Sir Matthew Hale, used language reminiscent of the two-witness rule. He noted that:

For though the testimony of a single witness shall not suffice to prove the accused party guilty of murder; yet the testimony of two witnesses though but of equal credit, that is, a second testimony added to the first though of itself never a whit more credible than the former, shall ordinarily suffice to prove a man guilty.[16]

It is not surprising to find Boyle familiar with the two-witness rule. It was employed after all in the ecclesiastical courts and in Chancery and had been employed by Star Chamber before its abolition in 1640. That he quite wrongly suggests that the two-witness rule applies to murder trials in common-law courts indicates how powerfully the Romano-canon position played on English minds even when the common-law courts rejected it. Hale, himself, while rejecting the two-witness rule in his public writings, reveals his attraction to it for capital cases in a diarylike fragment.[17]

During the mid-seventeenth century, when Puritan sentiments were most likely to have had an impact on law or at least discussion about law, we also find traces of the biblically sanctioned two-witness rule. Several of the more radical Puritan reformers, for instance Gerrard Winstanley, were anxious to introduce a two- or three-witness rule for serious crimes. Leveller John Lilburne also favored the two-witness rule for capital crimes.[18] While there was a great deal of harsh criticism of the prerogative courts, Star Chamber and Chancery, little criticism, with the exception of the *ex officio* oath, focused on the civilian characteristics of these institutions.[19]

There are also traces of the two-witness requirement to be found in the more Puritan of the American colonies. The 1641 Massachusetts Body of Liberties required two or three witnesses, or "that which is equivalent," in capital cases.[20] The same standard also characterized the criminal law of the New Haven Colony, perhaps the most biblically oriented colony. It was the scriptural sanction, of course, which had initially provided the foundation for the Romano-canon rule. Puritan impulses—both English and American—thus appear to have slightly modified English antipathy to the notion of a specified number of witnesses.[21] The law of the American colonies, however, soon became more like that of the mother country.[22]

The credibility, rather than the number, of witnesses was of central concern to the English. Here they relied more directly on their own, rather than on Continental, traditions. I noted earlier the significant role played by religious and epistemological writings in the development of the satisfied conscience, moral certainty, and beyond reasonable doubt concepts. Religious and philosophical argument also played a part in English efforts to formulate legal doctrines for dealing with the testimony of witnesses.

Protestants engaged in repudiating Roman Catholic doctrines of authority of the papacy, and the authority of tradition focused on the authority of the Scripture. For Protestants, Scripture alone was the basis of religious truth. One of the crucial arguments for the truth of Scripture focused on the validity of testimony of the witnesses to the events and miracles of the New Testament. The tracts and sermons, particularly of Restoration Anglicans, abound in references to credible and incredible witnesses and the reasonableness of believing witness testimony.[23] An example from John Tillotson, a leading Anglican divine who later became Archbishop of Canterbury, suggests the nature of this tradition. While sense perception and personal experience provide the highest degrees of evidence, the testimony of witnesses was of crucial importance. Witnesses must possess the intelligence and mental capacities that permit them to gain "competent knowledge" of the facts or events to which they testify. They must also be devoid of malicious intent or design to deceive. Indeed, for Tillotson the testimony of a witness with these capacities could be considered as morally certain. Edward Stillingfleet, another Anglican divine, offered a comparable discussion of the means of evaluating the credit of testimony. Seth Ward, like many Anglican defenders of the reasonableness of belief in Scripture and of belief in the existence and attributes of the deity, felt it necessary to discuss the nature of testimony, the credibility of witnesses, the problems of conflicting and concurrent testimony, and the qualities most desirable in witnesses.[24]

Sir Matthew Hale's *Primitive Origination of Mankind*, another work in this genre, also focused on the nature of testimony and the necessity of weighing the veracity of witnesses. He emphasized the importance of the number of eyewitnesses to an event and notes that the testimony of "credible and authentic witnesses" was to be preferred to that of those who were "light and inconsiderable." He indicates that firsthand testimony is preferable to hearsay, and that the testimony of disinterested witnesses is to be preferred to that of interested parties.[25] As we have seen, Hale was well read in Roman law. Both his religious and legal writings are replete with the legal terminology of that tradition. His work is symptomatic of the way in which Continental legal doctrine, Protestant theology, and English epistemology were commingled in the creation of credibility doctrines.

Hale simultaneously emphasizes the superiority of the common law to the civil law and borrows concepts from the latter tradition. He praises the public character of the jury trial, the absence of a two-witness rule, and the superiority of oral over written testimony. He indicates that "the very Manner of a Witness's delivering his Testimony will give a probable Indication whether he speaks truly or falsely." Echoing the Romano-canon law maxims that were ultimately derived from classical rhetorical sources, Hale suggests that "The very Quality, Carriage, Age, Condition, Education and Place of Commorance of a Witness" is best appreciated when the jurors can see and hear the witnesses and thus give "the more or less Credit to their Testimony."[26] Hale, of course, emphasizes that jurors were not bound to give verdicts according to the testimony and were free to credit one witness over several who disagreed. Like Justice Vaughan in Bushel's case, he insists that the jury "upon their own Knowledge may know a Thing to be false that a Witness swore to be true, or may know a Witness to be incompetent or incredible, . . . and may give their Verdict accordingly."[27] This passage suggests that the knowledge that jurors might possess and that the judge might not, was not so much personal knowledge of the facts but knowledge that there was something defective about the witness and his testimony. But the assumption is that evidence presented would be that of witnesses. The self-informing jury may have disappeared in fact, but it was retained in theory as a means of justifying and reinforcing its institutional independence.

The jury trial is also justified by Hale as a truth-seeking instrument. Indeed its ability to determine the credibility and the "force and efficacy of their testimonies" and its requirement of unanimity meant that it was in a better position to "discover the Truth of a Fact, than any other Trial whatsoever."[28] Its use of witnesses thus had become a mark of its superiority.

We have seen how Locke's *Essay Concerning Human Understanding* both summarized and systematized the conceptions of Anglican divines and naturalists. He writes that probable knowledge depends on observation, experience, and "the testimony of others vouching their observations and experience. In the testimony of others is to be considered: (1) The number. (2) The integrity. (3) The skill of the witnesses. (4) The design of the author, where it is a testimony out of a book cited. (5) The consistency of the parts, and circumstances of the relation. (6) Contrary testimonies."[29]

A proposition was to be judged more or less probable depending on "certainty of observation, as the frequency and constancy of experience, and the number and credibility of testimonies do more or less agree or disagree with it."[30] For Locke, then, probability relied on testimony, "as the relators are more in number, and of more credit, and have no interest to speak contrary to the truth, so that matter of fact is like to find more or less belief."[31] Locke's *Essay* unquestionably builds on the English probabilistic tradition of Glanvill, Wilkins, and Boyle. But Locke also spent considerable time in the Netherlands, where the civil law prevailed, and dealt with testimonial issues in a parallel way.

Locke's focus on the importance of testimony was continued and developed in the growing tradition of empirical epistemology; it also found its way into the legal treatise tradition from the time of Gilbert onward. We must recall that Gilbert relied heavily on Locke, and that he had published an abstract of Locke's *Essay*. *The Law of Evidence* was thus placed on a Lockean foundation. Gilbert devoted lengthy sections to witnesses, which included discussions of those excluded from testifying for want of integrity, interest, age, mental capacity, and so on.[32] Locke's statements on testimony are also reproduced. The first and lowest form of proof was the oath of a single witness, who "naturally obtains Credit unless there be some Appearance of Probability to the contrary." His credit, however, may be overthrown by the "Incredibility of the Fact, and the Repugnancy of his Evidence" to experience and observation. His testimony was to be doubted if he failed to provide "the Reasons and Causes" of his knowledge. Interestingly, two witnesses were considered "one Step higher" than one.[33]

The evidence treatise was an expanding genre and produced specialized treatises as well as general ones. We will note only one which focuses heavily on testimony, William M. Best's *Principles of the Law of Evidence with Elementary Rules for Conducting the Examination and Cross-Examination of Witnesses*. Best's discussion of the credit due human testimony is a compound of Locke and his successors, the Romano-canon writers, modern and not so modern, and earlier English evidentiary works. Thus, for Best, the credit due testimony is "the compound ratio of the witness's means of acquaintanceship with what he narrates, and of his intention to narrate it truly." With respect to the latter, it was necessary to consider "Whether he labours under any interest or bias, which may sway him to pervert the truth. . . . His veracity on former occasions . . . [and] [h]is manner and deportment in delivering his testimony." Best quotes the canonist, Lancellottus, at length on the last item. Best also insists that the manner of giving evidence is often no less material than the testimony itself. "An over-forward and hasty zeal on the part of the witness, giving testimony . . . his exaggeration of circumstances, his reluctance in giving adverse evidence, his slowness in answering, his evasive replies, his affection of not hearing or not understanding the question, . . . precipitancy in answering, . . . his inability to detail any circumstances wherein, if his testimony were untrue, he would be open to contradiction, . . . are all to a greater or less extent obvious marks of insincerity." Best, however, also notes that demeanor consisting of "confusion, embarrassment, hesitation . . . and even vacillating or contradictory answers" were not themselves proof of dishonesty. The capacity of a witness to give a "faithful account" depended on opportunities for observing the matter narrated, and the witness's "powers, either natural or acquired, of perception and observation." Here it was important to ascertain whether he is a "discreet, sober-minded person, or imaginative and imbued with a love of the marvelous, and also whether he lies under any bias likely to distort his judgment." Also to be considered is "The probative force arising from concurrent testimonies," which is the "compound result of the probabilities of the testimonies taken singly. . . . But when testimonies conflict or clash with each other, we must form the best conclusion we can as to their *relative* values." In weighing testimony it was necessary to consider the consistency of the narration and the possibility and probability of the matter related, probability in this context meaning the "likelihood of anything to be true, deduced from its conformity, to our knowledge, observation and experience."[34]

Best, however, insisted that it would be absurd to attempt to lay down rules for estimating the credit due to witnesses. Courts ought to be confined to making rules about admissibility of evidence, and leaving "its weight to the application of the tribunal."[35] The jury's verdict thus "does not proceed solely on the story told by the witness, but on the moral conviction of its truth, based on its intrinsic probability and his manner of giving his evidence."[36] Best's work represents about as far as the Anglo-American law had come by the mid-nineteenth century. Its mixture of Romano-canon and English Protestant thinking, combined with the ideas of probability developed by seventeenth-century English epistemologists, all then subordinated to the independence of the jury, is the essence of the Anglo-American tradition on witness credibility.

Hearsay

Although we know that hearsay testimony was excluded from both canon and civil law proceedings from a very early date, we still do not know a great deal about the evolution of the hearsay exclusion in Anglo-American law. It is difficult to determine whether the exclusion of secondhand testimony, which probably occurred sometime in the late seventeenth century, was an independently evolved, direct, practical response to the increasingly frequent use of witnesses, to the silent adoption of the Romano-canon rule, or was the result of the growing epistemological concern and sophistication of the period.[37] Perhaps it was a combination of all three. Certainly one could not expect such a rule to develop much earlier, that is, before it was widely recognized that witnesses played a central role in jury trials. Such a rule would have been difficult to conceptualize and institute as long as jurors were still both allowed and expected to know things on their own. As long as it was acceptable for jurors to possess knowledge derived from common fame, or from members of their community, it would be difficult to formally institute a rule forbidding hearsay. I have already noted that this vision of the jury was prolonged well after it had become a fiction because it protected juries from judicial dominance. Only as the fiction waned could a hearsay rule for witnesses appear. At about the same time that the hearsay rule was developing, jurors were being told that if they had information to offer to fellow jurors, they should testify under oath as did other witnesses.[38]

Hostility to hearsay testimony, however, was common in nonlegal settings before it became part of English law. Quintilian's much-read *Institutes of the Orator* had discussed how hearsay might be used both positively and negatively by the orator. Early modern historians, both English and Continental, frequently made reference to the Polybian critique of hearsay. Naturalists of the seventeenth century, anxious to eliminate fable and imaginary flora and fauna from natural history, also emphasized the necessity of firsthand and corroborating testimony. Anglican theologians seeking to demonstrate the validity of Scripture emphasized the superiority of firsthand over hearsay testimony.[39] In a nonlegal religious publication in 1677, Sir Matthew Hale insisted that hearsay was less valuable than evidence presented by a credible, firsthand witness.[40]

Locke, too, concerned himself with the problem of hearsay. Interestingly he made reference to an English legal rule which provided that even though an attested copy of a record was good proof, the copy of a copy attested even by credible witnesses could not be admitted as proof. He takes this rule as a specific application of the more general principle:

that any testimony, the further off it is from the original truth, the less force and proof it has. . . . The being and existence of the thing itself is what I call the original truth. A credible man vouching his knowledge of it is a good proof; but if another equally credible do witness it from his report, the Testimony is weaker; and the third that attests the hearsay of a hearsay is yet less considerable.[41]

If there was a hearsay rule in law by 1690, Locke was apparently unaware of it.

The notion that hearsay evidence was inferior to firsthand testimony was thus well known to the civil law and to the English intellectual community before it governed English legal practice. Its history in English law begins in the sixteenth century and is fully developed only in the early eighteenth century. Until the middle of the seventeenth century, hearsay was considered questionable but was not often excluded. For several decades there was a great deal of hostility to hearsay, but more was said of its reliability than of its admissibility.[42] Although no date or ruling marks the exclusion of hearsay testimony, it is already noted in Edward Waterhouse's *Fortescue Illustratus* of 1663.[43] Most scholars, however, believe the change occurred somewhere between 1675 and 1690, the same era in which theologians and naturalists were so vociferously expressing similar views.[44] It is noteworthy that Best's mid-nineteenth-century rationale of the hearsay exclusion echoes Locke: "The farther evidence is removed from its primary source, the weaker it becomes."[45]

All of this leaves us with no real evidence of borrowing from the Romano-canon law. Yet it is difficult to believe that a well-established legal rule of courts just across the Channel, and indeed of civil-law influenced courts operating in England, was totally ignored by common lawyers once their attention came to focus on witness testimony. Is it plausible that they totally ignored what they knew of another law while deriving a new, very similar common-law rule solely from their literary, religious, philosophical, and scientific interests? Perhaps, but those interests themselves were somewhat indebted to the canon and the civil law, which in turn were indebted to the ancient rhetorical tradition. Romano-canon influence, whether remote or more direct, seems likely.[46]

Circumstantial Evidence and Presumption

The direct testimony of witnesses, however, was not the only evidence presented to jurors. They also considered circumstantial evidence and drew inferences from that evidence. The story is long and complicated and still has many pieces missing. In telling it, I must begin with the Romano-canon tradition. Once we have become aware of the ambivalent and sometimes contradictory patterns within Continental practice and theory, we will be in a better position to see how circumstantial evidence came to be used by early modern English courts and to understand the initial English ambivalence toward it. Our survey will also require investigation of a subplot dealing with the special category of secret crimes, which, following civilian notions, permitted conviction on the basis of circumstantial evidence. This leads to another brief discussion of witchcraft, the secret crime which received most attention in England. I then return to our examination of seventeenth- and eighteenth-century attitudes toward circumstantial evidence and presumption, looking at the accumulated data of trials, justices' handbooks, and other legal writings. In addition I will trace the eighteenth-century argument over the relative merits of circumstantial and testimonial evidence, as well as the process by which civil law conceptions of circumstantial evidence and presumption became more openly recognized by English lawyers both as significant doctrines and as borrowings from the Continent. I conclude the discussion of presumption and circumstantial evidence with a brief treatment of the treatise literature, arguing that this systematic literature exhibited two features—the selective appropriation of civilian doctrine and the epistemological tradition of the eighteenth and early nineteenth centuries. These were combined in such a way that presumption based on circumstantial evidence, once considered inferior to testimonial evidence, came to serve as the basis for moral certainty and conviction beyond reasonable doubt.

As noted earlier, circumstantial evidence and presumption were considered to be a species of probability in the rhetorical traditions of the ancient world. In that world the indirect, or artificial, proofs in orations and law courts were associated with probability, as indeed were all rhetoric and knowledge of everyday affairs.

Quintilian's conception of artificial proofs, developed in the context of the judicial oration, played an important role in the development of the concept of circumstantial evidence. For Quintilian, signs, or tokens, indications, and vestiges which "consist of some certain thing to mean and point out another," constituted a variety of argument. Bloodstains thus might be a sign that murder had been committed. They might, however, he reminds the fledgling orator, be the result of a bloody nose. The presence of blood-soaked clothing did not necessarily mean a murder had occurred. Supported by other circumstances, however, it might serve as powerful testimony against the accused. Other supporting circumstances might include threats by the accused or discovery at the murder scene. Such signs, or *indicia* as they would later be called, could be used by both accuser and defendant. They were only decisive "as far as otherwise well supported."[47] Quintilian not only suggests that signs may be more or less certain or doubtful but also indicates, in a passage that would be echoed both in Continental and English law, that some signs might be very powerful in conjunction with other proofs.

"Arguments," like "signs," were important to the judicial oration. Some arguments, he noted, may be drawn from "persons," and the judicial orator might emphasize birth because children were likely to be like their parents. Parentage thus could be considered a cause of their honest or scandalous lives. Gender, too, might be employed because women were more likely to have committed certain crimes more than other ones. Age, education, bodily habits, fortune, social and economic status, occupation, personal traits, and inclination were all grist for the judicial oration.[48] These categories, as we have noted earlier, were employed by canonists and civilians and became the basis of the *indicia* of the Romano-canon system and the causes of suspicion employed in the Anglo-American system of arrest procedure and pretrial examination. The distinction between inartificial and artificial proofs in somewhat modified form provided the conceptual basis of the familiar Roman and Anglo-American categories of direct and indirect proof. The former consisted of two categories, testimony and documentary proof; the latter consisted of indirect, or circumstantial, evidence and the presumptions which were drawn from them. Our concern now is with circumstantial evidence and presumption, although it is necessary to refer back to direct proofs, which were preferred officially in the Romano-canon tradition.[49]

During the medieval era canonists and civilians developed a system of legal full proofs and fractional proofs designed to contain elements of both certainty and probability. If in one sense the founders and practitioners of the Romano-canon legal tradition recognized that legal proofs were probabilistic in character and could not easily be assimilated into the notion of demonstrative proof, they nevertheless assigned the designation of "full proof" to certain varieties and quantities of probabilistic evidence. In the area of criminal law, either confession or the testimony of two good witnesses constituted full proof. Only these would yield proof "clear as the light of day." There were also categories of "half" and "quarter" proof, constructed for instance from the testimony of women, or those who were not credible, or from the testimony of one witness as opposed to two. Such fractional proofs, however, could not sustain a conviction.

Indirect proof consisted of such things as rumor, fame, suspicion, signs, conjecture, the *indicia*, presumptions, and circumstantial evidence, which were categorized in loving detail by medieval canonists and civilians. An elaborate treatise literature was developed between the twelfth and sixteenth centuries that articulated the various categories and the distinctions among them in the greatest detail.[50] While there was a good deal of originality among the canonists and civilians, much of what they wrote was derived from the rhetorical tradition exemplified by Aristotle, Cicero, and Quintilian.

According to the Romano-canon theorists, indirect or circumstantial proof, no matter how good, did not constitute legal proof. Such a high standard of proof had a number of consequences, but in two important developments indirect or circumstantial evidence would play a major role. Indirect proofs, those items which made up the *indicia*, as we have seen earlier, were employed in the Romano-canon tradition as a means of evaluating those charged with a crime. If there were sufficient *indicia*, or circumstantial evidence, it was possible for the judge to put the individual in question to torture, which might elicit a confession, which would then constitute legal proof.

The standard of legal proof proved to be so high that it often could not be achieved without resort to torture. Given the categories of witnesses that were excluded entirely from testifying and the size of many medieval villages, it must have been often impossible to convict those for whom reasonably good evidence of guilt existed. The first efforts to circumvent the standard of legal proof and to substitute other evidentiary criteria appear to have begun among canonists. They developed the notion of notorious crime, a crime so well known that it was known to all. Notoriety required public outcry, good circumstantial evidence, and public notice to most of the populace. A more important development for our purposes occurred in several Italian communal jurisdictions in the twelfth or thirteenth century. Richard Fraher and Giorgia Alessi Palozzola have traced the development of an alternate tradition which allowed inquisitorial judges sufficient discretion to convict the obviously guilty on circumstantial evidence without meeting the requirements of full legal proof.[51] As early as in the thirteenth-century work of William Durantis, it was held possible to convict in special circumstances on the basis of presumption derived from circumstantial evidence. Civilian Thomas de Piperata's *Tractatus de fama* would have permitted urban magistrates to convict on the basis of "undoubted indicia" or circumstantial evidence. Although de Piperata's views were not widely followed, Italian magistrates often exercised the power to punish without the full proof required by the civil law. There was considerable discussion in the thirteenth century concerning *fama*, *indicia*, arguments, and presumptions. Another thirteenth-century civilian treatise writer, Albertus Gandinus, indicated that it was possible to convict for capital crimes on the basis of *indicia indubitata*, a condition which was met when the *indicia* were so strong that they compelled the conscience of the judge to believe them. If only "undoubted indicia" were available, however, penalties could only be monetary and corporal, rather than capital.[52]

Fourteenth-century Italian judges convicted on conclusive *indicia* using the authority of Bartolus and Baldus de Ubaldis. Bartolus thought that presumptions and *indicia* could yield proof as clear as the light of day. Although not so sympathetic to the notion of "notorious" crime, Bartolus had a notion of "manifest" crime; for example, a manifest homicide may be said to occur when one sees a man fleeing from a house with a bloody sword, and someone has been killed.[53]

Conviction on the basis of *indicia indubitata* and violent presumption continued in the late medieval and early modern periods on the Continent. Thus Angelus Aretinus indicated that when circumstantial evidence provided a clear explanation of the facts through "sufficient signs" so that the intellect was satisfied, conviction was appropriate. Like Bartolus, he employed the famous bloody sword example that the English typically attributed to Coke. Other examples of the doctrine, or very similar variants, of condemnation on *indicia indubitata* can be found in Julius Clarus, Antonius Matthaeus, and Mascardus.[54]

In some situations, then, good circumstantial evidence could result in conviction. The judge evaluated this evidence freely, unbound by a specific set of guidelines. His intellect and conscience were to be satisfied that the individual had committed the crime in question. Judicial discretion, which had been curtailed very sharply in the system of legal proofs, was thus allowed a free evaluation of the facts in some cases. The judge, however fully convinced, could not under this exception impose the death penalty. The milder punishments, which might include fines, corporal punishment, or banishment, and which were characteristic of the *poena extraordinaria* based on circumstantial evidence, would have a lengthy history from the thirteenth century onward.

Although it is unclear how often this alternative mode of conviction and punishment was administered in France, Germany, Italy, and elsewhere, it seems likely that it was becoming a regular part of the legal system. Recent research indicates that the *poena extraordinaria*, or suspicion punishment as it was sometimes called, became a common feature of the early modern French legal system.[55]

Medieval canonists and civilians also recognized that certain types of crime were unlikely ever to produce the required quality and quantity of witness testimony. They therefore permitted the use of circumstantial evidence for exceptional crimes where the normal standards of evidence could not be expected. We have already had occasion to refer to the *crimen exceptum*. In these crimes, circumstantial evidence could be used to exact the full penalties of the law. The Romano-canon system thus came to have a dual system of proof. The preeminent one was that of legal proof, which required two witnesses or confession. The secondary tradition of the *poena extraordinaria* and *crimen exceptum* not only depended on proofs that did not constitute full proof but also relied very heavily on circumstantial evidence. The treatises on circumstantial evidence and presumptions continued to be produced in the early modern period, and older works were reissued. Indeed, the development of printing must have made scholastic and civilian treatises better known than they had been.

Notions of *indicia* and circumstantial evidence were linked to the well-developed Romano-canon doctrines of presumption, which were already being categorized in Tancred and William Durantis. The latter distinguished presumptions as *temeraria*, or light, *probabilis*, derived from suspicion and fame, and *violenta*.[56] Violent presumption attained a grade of probability that authorized the judge to condemn. These categories were to be found in Sir Edward Coke's *Institutes* several centuries later. Subsequent English commentators attributed them to Coke and avoided mention of their Romano-canon origin. There was by then a well-developed scholarly treatise tradition dealing with presumption. One of the most influential treatises in this tradition was that of Jacobus Meno-

chius, whose *Tractatus de praesumptionibus*, based on the ancient
rhetorical distinctions between artificial and inartificial proofs, includes discussions of presumption, *indicia*, conjecture, and signs,
all discussed in terms of probability.[57]

We must not think of Continental evidentiary theory as frozen.
By the eighteenth century the French legal system had come under
a good deal of criticism by Enlightenment commentators. Some
critics advocated adoption of the English jury system. Others were
dissatisfied with the notion that those accused of difficult to prove
crimes should be convicted on the basis of less evidence, and that
equivocal evidence and even conjecture were sufficient for some of
the most atrocious and improbable crimes. Cesare Beccaria noted
that crimes such as adultery, sodomy, and infanticide could be
proved by presumption and half proofs, and he ridiculed legal systems which implied that the individual might be half guilty and half
innocent.[58]

Civil law writers of a philosophical bent also attempted to place
the law in a more universal, natural law context.[59] It was in this
form that the civil law had its greatest impact on British thinkers
and writers. If the civil law could be viewed not so much as an alien
and rival system but as one of several legal systems based on a
broad set of universal principles shared by the English legal system, it would be far easier to view favorably the principles and
practices of the civilians. The natural law approach of Domat and
Pothier had a considerable impact on English thinking about problems of evidence. Once a natural law framework made assimilation
possible, earlier treatises of Menochius, Farinaccius, and Mascardus too became intellectually available.

England

With this background we now return to the English scene, noting
similarities to and possible influences of the Continental tradition.
Like the canonists and civilians, for many generations the English
viewed circumstantial evidence as inferior to that of witnesses and
sometimes claimed to employ it only in exceptional or secret
crimes. Over time and very gradually the English came to doubt
the superiority of direct testimony over circumstantial evidence
and debated the relative values of each in providing the higher

degree of certainty, or rather of probability. In time, circumstantial evidence came to have virtually the same status as direct proof in reaching decisions beyond reasonable doubt.

Between the period in which juries made their decisions based largely on personal knowledge and the enunciation of the satisfied conscience language of the late seventeenth century, judges or jurors were not entirely clear on what basis they should reach their decisions. As we have seen, the uncertainty concerning how to treat the testimony of witnesses constituted one area of difficulty. How to treat circumstantial evidence proved to be even more difficult. There was, of course, commonsense, which suggested commonsense inferences. For example, a theft had been committed and the suspected person had been caught with the stolen goods. It seems likely that in such instances convictions often took place without reference to, or discussion of, the nature of circumstantial evidence, how that evidence could be established with sufficient certainty to make a judgment, or the quality of the inferences to be drawn from such evidence. We must surmise that convictions frequently occurred without the assistance of legal doctrine. We should note, however, that Sir Walter Raleigh protested the use of circumstantial evidence and insisted on the necessity of two witnesses.[60]

By the time Bracton was writing, concepts of presumption had already been developed by the canonists. Bracton's, and later Coke's, comments on presumption, which did not appear in connection with crime, owed a good deal to the Romano-canon doctrine. Both Bracton, whose work was printed for the first time in 1569, and Coke were thus extremely important for the entry and popularization of the Romano-canon concepts that became the basis for the English doctrines of circumstantial evidence and presumptions of fact. Presumptions of fact are the inferences that followed from circumstantial evidence. Neither Bracton nor Coke indicated his indebtedness to non-English sources, and subsequent English commentators, either deliberately or out of ignorance, would cite only them. As noted earlier, the English of the late medieval and the early modern eras were particularly reluctant to draw attention to foreign elements in their law.

Bracton refers to presumption in several contexts. If full and sufficient proof of age could not be determined by witnesses and kinsmen, other things, for instance bodily appearance, were "strong presumption" of age.[61] He also refers to presumption in connection with rumor and suspicion, areas more directly connected with the evidence for crime. Rumor and suspicion could lead to "a strong presumption." Such presumptions arise when someone is apprehended over the body of a dead man with his knife dripping with blood or when he has fled from the body. In such instances of "overwhelming presumption," no other proof was necessary, and such presumptions did not admit of proof to the contrary.[62]

Already in Bracton, then, is the notion that some presumptions were rebuttable and some were not. Some presumptions were strong enough to constitute proof. Others were not. Bracton's bloody sword example will be encountered again in Coke and in the countless citers of Coke's *Institutes*. As we have seen, this bloody sword example was employed by Bartolus and his many successors as an example of conclusive proof for murder.[63]

It was Sir Edward Coke's brief categorization of presumptions, however, which made an enormous impact on the English legal tradition. His treatment was quoted and cited as authoritative for well over a century after it was enunciated.

Coke cited Bracton for the proposition that there were two kinds of proof:

probatio duplex, viz, as by witnesses *viva voce;* as by deeds, writings, and instruments. And many times juries, together with other matter are much induced by presumptions; whereof there be three sorts, *viz,* violent, probable, and light or temerary. *Violenta praesumptio* is manie times *plena probatio;* as if one be runne thorow the bodie with a sword in a house, whereof he instantly dieth and a man is seene to come out of that house with a bloody sword, and no other man was at the time in the house. *Praesumptio probables* moveth little; but *praesumptio levis seu temeraria* moveth not at all.[64]

This passage, although written in connection with fee-simple tenure, was destined for a long and important history in the Anglo-American criminal law. As we have seen, Coke's formulations of these concepts were widely cited by English and American writers in the context of pretrial examination, but they also played an important role in treatments of trial proceedings. Juries could convict on the basis of "violent presumption," while presumptions of a lesser variety—"probable presumptions"—served as a basis for decision in the various pretrial procedures. Coke's famous brief passage outlining the three varieties of presumption and the bloody sword passage constituted, for many generations, the most authoritative statements of presumption and circumstantial evidence in English law texts.

Coke, however, did recognize that presumptions must be employed carefully in the criminal law. If presumptions were sometimes the proper basis for conviction, they also were sometimes erroneous. He referred to a case in which a man had been wrongfully executed upon presumptions. He reported that case "for a double caveat, first the judge, that they in cases of life judge not too hastily upon bare presumptions."[65] Although Coke did not discuss the differences between presumptions of law and presumptions of fact, he assumes the categories, another long-standing Romano-canon convention.[66]

Witchcraft

Coke's discussion of circumstantial evidence and presumption was not the only one. Perhaps just as important were those portions of the justice of the peace handbooks that dealt with the crime of witchcraft and other secret crimes. The crime of witchcraft may have had a far greater role in the development of English criminal law than we have hitherto suspected, not because so many individuals were caught in its net, but because doctrinal writings on witchcraft provide the most extensive early public discussion of circumstantial evidence.

On the Continent the crime of witchcraft was a *crimen exceptum*, which, because of its secret commission, was to be handled differently from ordinary crimes. The *crimen exceptum* that provoked the most discussion in England was witchcraft. In most Continental jurisdictions it was recognized that in such crimes the normal standards of proof, two good witnesses or confession, would rarely be met. They therefore permitted conviction on the basis of *indicia*, that is, circumstantial evidence.[67] The witchcraft literature, both English and Continental, is full of the language of signs, or *indicia*, and half proofs.

English law, however, never adopted the Continental system of

full and half proof, *indicia* as a preliminary to torture, or the requirement of two witnesses or confession for conviction. How,
then, can we explain the intrusion of many elements of this system
into the English law of evidence? A major element in any explanation may be the English preoccupation with witchcraft. Witchcraft statutes were enacted in England in 1542, 1543, and 1604.[68]

English discussion of this *crimen exceptum* exhibits a curious
mixture of common-law and civil law terminology. Like their Continental counterparts, English jurists accepted that circumstantial
evidence and presumptions must replace eyewitness testimony in
secret crimes, such as witchcraft, where eyewitnesses were unlikely to be found. The English thus used the Continental notion
of crimes unlikely to be witnessed, but they placed such crimes in
an institutional context where proof by a specified number of witnesses had never been required. Yet the Continental system of full
proof and half proof left traces. Coke, as we have seen, related
presumption to *plena probatio*, or full proof. The handbook material on witchcraft employs the language of full proof and half
proof, notes the superiority of proof by two witnesses, and au-
thorizes the admission of circumstantial evidence. These Continental incursions are all the more notable because in English law
the jury consulted its conscience, or understanding, and was never
required to use specified criteria of proof in shaping its judgment.

The language of full and half proofs and of "light and weighty
presumptions" is common in the English witchcraft literature. The
role of presumption and circumstantial evidence, however, was ambiguous in the English witchcraft literature. George Gifford and
Thomas Cooper differentiated between the standards for examination and indictment, where presumption, suspicion, and circumstantial evidence were permissible, and the standards for conviction, which required "proof." Proof for them meant confession or
the testimony of two sufficient witnesses—the Continental standard of proof.[69] John Cotta expressed uncertainty whether "circumstances and presumption" alone were sufficient to convict, and
Reginald Scot denounced the Continental practice of relying on
"presumptions and conjectures as sufficient proofs."[70] The concepts
of presumption and circumstantial evidence were thus familiar to
the English public, although it was divided or unclear as to whether
circumstantial evidence and presumption in witchcraft cases were

limited to bringing the accused to trial or whether they might support conviction. Far from exhibiting the normal English antipathy to Continental legal language, the witchcraft writers advert to it repeatedly.

The evidentiary language connected with the crime of witchcraft found its way into the handbooks for the justices and remained there until the mid-eighteenth-century repeal of the witchcraft statutes. Dalton's popular *Country Justice*, first published in 1618, included materials on the "signs" of witchcraft. Witchcraft was one of the felonies where one could not expect direct evidence, and so he offers a series of observations or signs to assist in its "better discovery." The list was expanded in later editions and was transmitted to other English and American justicing handbooks. While the signs appear in the context of examination, printed marginal notations indicate that they were also to be used for conviction.[71] From Dalton onward the justices' manuals emphasize that in secret murders, poisoning, and witchcraft "where open and evident proofs are seldom to be had, there, it seemeth half proofs are to be allowed and good cause of suspicion."[72] Suspicion, however, was rarely equated with proof, and there was hesitancy over the full acceptability of circumstantial evidence.

Sir Robert Filmer, writing in 1653, after the last outburst of witchhunting in England, attempted to discredit and refute the still popular work of the Puritan theologian William Perkins. Filmer argued that Perkins himself had recognized that each of his signs might be wrong or misleading. Presumption and signs might be employed by the examining magistrate but proofs were necessary for conviction. Filmer reminded his readers that torture, which was acceptable to Perkins when "Strong and great presumptions" existed, was not used in England, that foreign standards were irrelevant, and that England was "tyed to a stricter Rule." English juries were not to condemn on the basis of "bare presumptions, without sound and sufficient proofs."[73] The nature of these proofs was not specified. The role of presumption and circumstantial evidence was obviously rather puzzling to the English of the seventeenth century, yet courts clearly were using it to convict in a variety of offenses.

For our purposes, however, what is important is that there was uncertainty as to how and under what circumstances circumstantial evidence might play a role. The category of *crimen exceptum* suggests that what were considered lesser proofs were sometimes admissible. Presumption and circumstantial evidence, as on the Continent, appear to have been considered a lower species of proof. Some authorities clearly believed that the kinds of signs, or circumstantial evidence, that were appropriate to pretrial examination or grand jury indictment were inappropriate for trial. Others felt differently at least for *crimen exceptum* and other cases in which the presence of witnesses was not expected.

Sixteenth- and Seventeenth-Century England

The scarcity of fully documented cases makes generalization impossible, but by the mid-sixteenth century references to circumstantial evidence and presumption occur in the published *State Trials*. In the *Trial of Sir Nicholas Throckmorton* (1554), the accused expressed concern about the sergeant seducing "the minds of the simple and unlearned Jury." "For . . . I know how by persuasions, enforcements, presumptions, applying, implying, inferring, conjecturing . . . the circumstances, the depositions . . . that unlearned men be enchanted to think and judge [things to be treason which are not]." Circumstantial evidence and the inferences derived from it might easily be distorted by the "powers Orators have." While we cannot make too much of these brief comments, they do suggest that Throckmorton felt presumptions drawn from circumstantial evidence were weaker than the testimony of witnesses and were easily manipulated.

In 1581, Edmund Campion, accused of treason, objected to trial "by shifts of probabilities and conjectural surmises, without proof of the crime by sufficient evidence and substantial witnesses." Without "witnesses *viva voce*" testifying to the circumstances, one might be convicted simply "upon the persuasion of any orator or vehement pleader." He went on to object to convictions for theft or any other crime based on the circumstances that the parents or companions of the accused were thieves and the accused was an evil liver. Such were "odious circumstances to bring a man in hatred with the jury and no necessary matter to conclude him guilty." Campion thus insisted that the case against him must be "proved and not urged, declared by evidence and not surmised by fancy." Only bare circumstances had been laid against him and not evidence. There was only "a naked presumption . . . and nothing vehement nor of force against me." Because presumptions were only "bare and naked Probabilities," he asked that the jury "set circumstances aside, set presumptions apart," and "set that reason for your rule which is warranted by certainty." That rule was "sufficient and manifest Evidence."[74] The trial of Campion certainly suggests that the concepts of circumstantial evidence and presumption were sufficiently well known for a defendant to voice them. His argument also suggests that circumstantial evidence and the presumptions drawn from them were considered inferior to the evidence of direct witnesses.

The 1603 treason trial of Sir Walter Raleigh raised the question of the validity of circumstantial or presumptive evidence. When Raleigh complained that only one witness had testified against him, the judge expressed surprise, stating that horse thieves were often condemned without any witnesses at all. The judge in Raleigh's trial used an example of someone rushing into the king's chamber while the king was alone, killing the king and rushing out with a bloody sword. Shall "he not be condemned to death?" the judge asked, suggesting that such circumstantial evidence was often sufficient for conviction.[75] Many crimes would not, of course, have been committed in front of witnesses or jurors. Circumstantial evidence filled the gap.

In seventeenth-century England we have confusion. From one point of view, any accused person might be convicted on the basis of circumstantial evidence, given that the jury was permitted to make its decision on whatever evidence was presented to it. We also have Coke's view that violent presumption was often sufficient for conviction. From another, we have a rather well-developed special category of secret crimes for which circumstantial evidence was thought to be permissible, though perhaps less than desirable. This contradiction does not seem to have been noticed or have been of interest to seventeenth-century lawyers or critics of the law. In 1650, however, adultery was made a capital offense under the impact of Puritan radicalism. The comments of several contemporaries indicate that presumptive evidence was considered sufficient for conviction precisely because adultery was now among the secret crimes for which eyewitnesses would not be available. In 1651, one

commentator indicated the courts should base conviction on reasonable presumption and cease to insist on certain proofs that were
almost impossible to gain without confession or a good deal of
spying. William Sheppard, a respected Puritan law reformer,
agreed on the appropriateness of circumstantial evidence for this
crime, because "the way of conviction being so difficult that it is
hard to prove."[76]

The English were not, of course, uninformed about the civil law,
since the classic treatises were available in Latin, and the ecclesiastical courts in England employed an almost identical procedure.
They must also have known through reading and travel of the development of the practice of milder punishments based on circumstantial evidence.[77]

The seventeenth-century ambivalence concerning circumstantial evidence was expressed by both Sir Edward Coke and Sir Matthew Hale. Both recognized that circumstantial evidence must
often be employed by courts, but they expressed considerable caution as to its use. Coke, as we noted earlier, cautioned judges, especially in capital cases, to "judge not too hastily upon bare presumption." Hale recognized that if there were exceptional crimes
where presumptions and circumstantial evidence were necessary,
there were also attendant dangers. Accusations were easily made
but difficult to prove, and no matter how innocent the accused
might be, such accusations were difficult for the accused to defend
against. Hale was thus willing to allow the lesser form of evidence
in crimes such as rape and forgery, which were unlikely to be
witnessed.[78]

The arena in which circumstantial evidence might be appropriate was capable of expansion and could be extended beyond cases
of hidden murder to rape and forgery. In a 1681 case it was noted
that "dark cases" must be proved by circumstances. In a case which
involved attempted assassination, the judge stated that proofs
ought "to be very great, but the jury should not expect them to be
as clear, as a matter of Right, . . . and things that are done in the
Face of the Sun." The deed in question, which was "done in the
dark," thus required consideration of circumstantial evidence.[79] By
this time circumstantial evidence clearly played a substantial role
in criminal law, but there continued to be some discomfort in employing it. Circumstantial evidence, if sometimes necessary, was

still viewed as a less desirable form of evidence. And jurors, who were sometimes given instructions to evaluate the credibility of witnesses, were given no advice as to how to evaluate "circumstances" or how to deal with testimony which did not mesh with circumstantial evidence.

Although most of our evidence comes from the treason trials of the 1670s and 1690s, there is a brief mention of circumstantial evidence in a 1663 burglary case tried at Old Bailey. In this instance, Lord Chief Justice Hide told the jury to consider "the whole," that is, evidence and the circumstances in addition to the testimony of witnesses. Here the "whole," which seems to have referred to a combination of witness testimony and circumstantial evidence, was for the jury's deliberation. In another 1663 trial the same judge told the jury, "I leave the evidence to you . . . pregnant, strong, undeniable circumstances are good evidence."[80] In an Old Bailey trial for manslaughter two decades later, jurors were told that there was no grudge or malice "appearing by the Evidence, and Circumstances of the Fact."[81] In a case of theft the accused was acquitted because there was "no positive evidence, and the Circumstances not being sufficient."[82] The distinction between evidence, which in a criminal case meant eyewitness testimony or documents, and the circumstances, or circumstantial evidence, had become conventional. Indeed, it is likely that the distinction was adopted at the time witnesses became an important element in criminal trials. Evidence, which was not the result of witness testimony, was obviously of some other kind.

The published *State Trials* indicate that notions of circumstantial evidence had become commonplace by the time of the Popish Plot trials. In the *Trial of Andrew Bromich* (1679), the jury was asked to consider the testimony of "a real positive witness, and the circumstantial evidence" of a second witness.[83] In this instance, and in the case of *Fitzharris*, the concept was again used in connection with testimony. Thus one of the witnesses "gave a large and full account" of the reasonable design with "very considerable Circumstances, to demonstrate the Reality of his Testimony."[84] In the *Trial of Carr*, the defense told the judge and jury that there was no "positive evidence" in the case, and they only had "very conjectural Evidence" that was very "uncertain." They only had "remote and conjectural Evidence," which they argued was not sufficient for conviction.[85] Defendants, thus, were also quite familiar with the distinction. The judge disagreed, however, saying in this particular kind of case they could not expect witnesses. He echoed the language of the *crimen exceptum* and other secret crimes in noting that:

In things of this nature, we are fain to retreat to such probable and conjectural Evidence as the matter will bear. I believe some of you have been of Juries at the Old Bayley, and that even for Men's Lives, you have very often, not a direct Proof of the Fact, of the Act, or of the actual killing: but yet, you have such Evidence by Presumption, and seems reasonable to Conscience.[86]

Circumstantial evidence was clearly sufficient to convict.

The greater receptivity to circumstantial evidence found toward the end of the seventeenth century occurs at the same time the English were becoming somewhat more sympathetic to Continental legal concepts and practices. Hale was well read in the civil law and often stated that he wished that the English had a better knowledge of that legal tradition.[87] Giles Dunscombe's *Trials Per Pais* not only refers very favorably to the works of Farinaccius and Mascardus but also complains of the "want of such Books in our Law." The lack of English treatises on evidence was beginning to be felt. Yet however valuable such systematic treatments might be, Dunscombe nevertheless still felt it necessary to declare that he had no wish to see trial by jury replaced by the Continental mode of trial.[88] Dunscombe is a harbinger of the later view that the knowledge provided by civilian treatise writers could be usefully employed and need not be accompanied by the destruction or diminution of English law and legal institutions. But he is still a little nervous.[89]

Eighteenth-Century England

By the eighteenth century there was certainly no question that both circumstantial and testimonial evidence were regularly employed to reach convictions.[90] In the 1721 trial of Josh Hill, it was reported that in some previous case there was some "strong presumptive Evidence, . . . yet not being sufficient to convict him" he was acquitted.[91] Presumptive evidence thus might be either strong enough or too weak to convict. The jury's conscience and understanding must be satisfied of guilt whether based on direct testimony or circumstantial evidence or some combination thereof. Although there were gradations, these would not, or could not, be specified. Thus in the trial of Sir John Freind for treason, the solicitor general noted that "such a concurrence of evidence and other circumstances" has greatly increased the weight of the proof against the prisoner.[92] The categories of positive, that is, direct testimonial, and indirect presumptive, or circumstantial, evidence were commonplace throughout the eighteenth century.[93]

The eighteenth century, however, witnessed two important developments. The first was the debate over the relative values of direct testimonial and circumstantial evidence. The second was the beginning of the open Anglo-American assimilation of the civilian tradition of writing on presumption and circumstantial evidence.

It is not clear what triggered the debate concerning the value of circumstantial evidence. For many generations the English, who often convicted criminal defendants on the basis of "circumstances," seemed to have felt somewhat reluctant to do so except in those special crimes where testimonial evidence was almost certain to be lacking. Presumptive evidence thus appeared to be a less valid, or less certain, mode of proof. The traditional preference for direct testimonial over circumstantial evidence seems to have been reversed during the course of the eighteenth century. Circumstantial evidence was elevated above testimonial evidence on the grounds that witnesses might lie. The maxims "circumstances cannot lie" and "facts cannot lie" appear to have become commonplace.

The 1752 trial of Mary Blandy for murder by poisoning used both the traditional notion that proof of secret crimes necessarily depended on circumstantial evidence and presumption and the newer doctrine that circumstantial evidence was more convincing because facts cannot lie. Circumstantial evidence was said to amount to violent presumption, which constituted complete proof. Mr. Baron Legge told the jury "where a violent presumption necessarily arises from circumstances, they are more convincing and satisfactory than any other kind of evidence because facts cannot lie." "To suppose the contrary" to violent presumption "where circumstances speak so strongly would be absurd."[94]

Discussion of the relative merits of direct testimony and circumstantial evidence played a central role in the *Trial of John Barbot*, which took place shortly after that of Mary Blandy. In this case the defendant, himself an attorney, insisted on the necessity of positive evidence. The solicitor general, however, asserted that the doctrine was false and "plainly contradicts all our reason and experience." Indeed hardly any criminal could be convicted without it. Circumstantial evidence "is the best and surest of all kinds [of evidence] and the least likely to deceive and mislead." Men may lie but facts did not. Facts collected from several individuals "point to the same center of Truth, these can never mislead the judgement or impose upon the belief; but justify and confirm the other, and are the surest and most unerring guides to conduct the truth." He insisted that judicial charges that instructed jurors to evaluate "the whole matter" meant that they must consider more than "positive, ocular, point blank evidence." If only the positive evidence of witnesses were required, juries would be unnecessary. And if direct evidence alone were required, it would be impossible to convict in secret crimes. He suggested that circumstantial evidence "may be, and frequently is, sufficient in itself to convict." When circumstances speak so strongly, "to believe the contrary would be absurd." The number of witnesses was not crucial. "No, 'tis the joint result of the whole evidence taken and considered together; and what upon examining and weighing that, shall appear to you, or (as the well-known term is) you shall find to be the Truth." "Every fact is to stand on its own circumstances; and that, and that only, is taken to be proved, of which the consciences and belief of the jury are convinced." Evidence that does not convince the conscience and belief of the jury, "though it consists of a thousand particulars, is not enough."[95]

The judge clearly agreed. In murder and the "like atrocious crimes . . . the law has relaxed much of its severity and scrupulousness in the proofs" and did not "absolutely require positive proofs." He agreed with Crown counsel "where the circumstances are so closely connected, and linked together, as in this case, and amount as fully to what is called a *violenta praesumptio*, admits this as full proof, and in my opinion, more so than any one positive evidence, whose memory may be deceitful, or who may possibly be suborned; but in facts made apparent from circumstances, which are dumb, we cannot be deceived." And in this case the circumstances "carry too glaring a proof to admit of much doubt."[96]

Similar views were expressed by Justice Buller in 1781. He charged a jury

that a presumption which necessarily arises from circumstances is very often more convincing and more satisfactory than any other kind of evidence, because it is not within the reach and compass of human abilities to invent a train of circumstances which shall be so connected together as to amount to a proof of guilt, without affording opportunities of contradicting a great part if not all of these circumstances.[97]

Juries, however, may have resisted. William Paley was convinced that juries had become overly scrupulous about convicting those accused of secret crimes on the basis of indirect, that is, circumstantial, evidence. Paley complained that juries in these cases refused to condemn "whilst there exists the minutest possibility of his innocence."[98] Paley was especially critical of juries reluctant to convict "where positive proof is wanting." While he did not recommend that jurors should "indulge conjectures, should magnify suspicion into proofs, or even to weigh probabilities in gold scales," he felt that they should convict where the "preponderation of evidence is so manifest as to persuade every private understanding of the prisoner's guilt." He denounced a popular maxim suggesting that circumstantial evidence fell short of positive proof. "A concurrence of well authenticated circumstances" is "stronger ground of assurance than positive testimony, unconfirmed by circumstances." And he, too, favored the maxim "circumstances cannot lie." Though Paley admitted that conclusions deduced from circumstantial evidence were "probable inference" (civilians would have used the term "presumption" here), he found them superior to positive proof in law, that is, to the sworn testimony of a single witness who might be lying.[99] A rather similar position was taken by Edmund Burke. "When circumstantial proof is in its greatest perfection, that is, when it is most abundant in circumstances, it is much superior to positive proof."[100]

These new and more explicitly expressed attitudes may have been the product of the more general concern for the probative value of various kinds of proof found in eighteenth- and early nineteenth-century English thought. Perhaps some of that interest, particularly that of Paley, can also be attributed to the widespread feeling that crime was a growing problem and was not being sufficiently vigorously prosecuted. The English adaption of the maxim "facts cannot lie" remains mysterious.

Conditions relating to the operation of the criminal justice system may have played a role. I noted earlier that heightened concern for crime had led to voluntary prosecution associations which offered financial rewards for apprehending and convicting thieves. Private individuals, or "thief takers" who were rewarded for seeking and obtaining convictions, thus had a considerable incentive to obtain convictions. Perjured testimony was thus not infrequently used to obtain conviction of innocent victims. As a result, juries, at least in certain cases, were becoming suspicious of testimony unsupported by strong circumstantial evidence.[101]

The Treatises

The treatise literature dealing with circumstantial evidence and presumption is quite different from the legal literature of the pre-treatise genres. Unlike the justice's handbook or the scholarly works of Hale and Hawkins on pleas of the Crown, the treatises attempt systematization and completeness. They are built on a triple foundation—the existing English tradition as embodied in older authorities and case materials, the systematization and sometimes the substance of the civilians filtered through the natural law school, and the epistemological and logical formulations of the Lockean and the Scottish Common Sense school of philosophers.

At this point we must look at the civilian tradition as filtered through the philosophically oriented natural-law writers Jean Domat and Robert Pothier. Domat's *Civil Law in Its Natural Order* outlines several types of truth, much as would Gilbert's Lockean-based treatise on evidence. Domat distinguishes the truths of demonstration from those of matters of fact. Truth in matters of fact may be known with a certainty comparable to that of the sciences and "is a certainty which persuades fully."[102] While Domat did not employ a Lockean notion of degrees of probability, his treatment is roughly consistent with the Lockean approach.

Domat also provided a brief generalized treatment of presumption. Presumption was defined as the "consequences drawn from a fact that is known, to serve for the discovery of the truth of a fact that is uncertain, and which one seeks to prove.[103] There were two varieties,

some of which are drawn by a necessary consequence from a principle that is certain; and when these sorts of presumptions are so strong that one may gather from them the certainty of the fact that is to be proved, without leaving any room for doubt, we give them the name of proofs, because they have the same effect, and do establish the truth of the fact which was in dispute. The other presumptions, are all those which form only conjectures, without certainty, whether it be that are drawn only from an uncertain foundation, or that the consequence which is drawn from a certain truth is not very sure.[104]

Some presumptions were "so strong, that they amount to a certainty, and held as proofs even in criminal matters; and others are only conjectures which leave some doubt." The category into which a particular presumption fell depended on the

certainty or uncertainty of the facts from which the presumptions were gathered, and on the justness of the consequences which are drawn from those facts, to prove the facts in dispute. And this depends on the connection that may be between the known facts and those which are to be proved. Thus one draws consequences from causes to their effects, and from effects to their causes. . . . And it is out of these different principles that signs, conjectures and presumptions are formed.[105]

Presumptions were also treated as being "concluding" or "uncertain." The former pass for truth without the necessity of further corroboration if the contrary was not proved. The latter alone form a "bare conjecture" and do not make "that which is presumed pass for truth." The difference between presumptions having "the effect of proof, and those which leave some doubt" formed the basis for another distinction. Some presumptions are authorized by law to be held as proofs. The law leaves the effect of others to the prudence of the judge.

Judges were given no discretion as to "strong" presumptions or "proofs." The evidence of two good witnesses, and other such proofs, are "taken for a full conviction." For Domat, then, legal proof itself was a species of presumption. Despite the fact that witnesses might err, two unimpeachable witnesses yielded a certainty that persuades. There was then a certain arbitrariness. Law determined the difference between proof and the weaker categories of presumption. When there is no "proof" or no "strong" or "concluding" presumption but only weak presumptions, signs, conjectures, imperfect evidence, or other sorts of proofs that the law has not directed to be considered certain, the judges may discern what may be received as proof and what ought not to have that effect.[106]

Pothier's influential *Treatise on the Law of Obligations or Contracts*, translated by William Davis Evans, testifies to the desire to draw on other legal systems and to develop the neglected "science of jurisprudence." Evans's translation is accompanied by an almost treatise-length appendix which illustrates English law on the topics discussed. Evans praised the evidence treatises of Mascardus, Menochius, and Everhardus to his English readers. Mascardus's four-volume folios are described as a "full and well digested view of the nature of evidence in general and of the different proofs applied in various contexts." He recommended Everhardus's "extensive and perspicuous view" of the application of the "general principles of evidence," noting that his discussion might "materially facilitate the exposition" of important issues of daily occurrence amongst ourselves. Evans, whose notes and lengthy appendix suggested that his own discussion on the law of evidence had been written prior to that of Thomas Peake, wrote with a dual purpose. The first was that of "immediate practical reference"; the second was to assist in the investigation of others "desirous of taking a scientific view of the subject."[107] The practical and the theoretical would thus both be served.

Only a small portion of Pothier's treatise dealt with presumption and proof, but his brief discussion proved to be highly influential. Pothier divides presumptions into the traditional civil law categories of presumptions *juris et de jure*, which admit of no contradictions, presumptions *juris*, which are established by legal authority but are open to contradiction, and common presumptions, which Evans describes as "mere inferences." Pothier's approach is more oriented to definition, invoked more authorities, and is less philosophically grounded than Domat's. Presumptions are again distinguished from proof, in that the latter "attests a thing directly and of itself," while presumption "attests it by a consequence deduced from another thing." These consequences are founded upon what commonly and generally takes place. Presumptions *juris et de jure* excluded all evidence to the contrary and were superior to documentary proof, parole proof, and confessions because they might not be overturned by proof to the contrary.[108] Presumptions of law are established by law or by argument from law or legal authority, and have the "same credit as proof." Other presumptions, often called "simple," standing alone do not form any proof. They only serve to "confirm and complete the proof which is otherwise given." Sometimes, however, the "concurrence of several presumptions united is equivalent to a proof."[109]

From the early eighteenth century onward there was a considerable effort by treatise writers to place the English law of evidence, including the treatment of presumption and circumstantial evidence, on a more sound epistemological foundation. While not all legal processes and rules fit perfectly on that foundation, treatise writers nevertheless strove to put them there. As we have seen, the epistemology they built upon was an empirical philosophy initiated by Locke and developed by the Common Sense school. While the treatise writers did not agree in philosophical detail, the fundamental premise of all was that the law dealt with matters of fact, and knowledge about matters of fact necessarily fell into the realm of probability. Although juridical findings could never reach the demonstrative certainty of geometry, they could, under optimal conditions, reach the pinnacle of probability, which was a moral certainty that no reasonable person would have reason to doubt. (I have outlined this in Chapter 1.) In the early formulations it did not appear as if circumstantial evidence and the presumptions drawn from that evidence were deemed as probabilistically strong as those drawn from testimony. Only gradually did circumstantial evidence and the conclusions drawn from it come to have the same status with respect to certainty. By the early nineteenth century, circumstantial evidence also was considered to be capable of establishing moral certainty or certainty beyond reasonable doubt. Although circumstantial evidence came of age only in the nineteenth century, it had been employed long before that time, indeed probably as early as the jury trial itself, as the basis for conviction.

As noted elsewhere, the fact that the English tradition of natural philosophy was empirical in nature and was based on notions of probability and degrees of certainty meant that the languages of religion, epistemology, natural philosophy, and law could, at least for a time, each use concepts drawn from the others. In the late nineteenth century, scientific philosophy tended again to draw away from its probabilistic orientation, and legal thinkers felt less comfortable associating legal knowledge with natural knowledge. But from the time of Locke and through the building of the treatise tradition, degrees of probability in matters of fact played a central role. Indeed, discussions of probability in the eighteenth and nineteenth centuries also incorporated the doctrine of mathematical probability, and treatise writers as well as others explored the possibility that the doctrine of chances, that is, of mathematical probability, might be applied to the law. (See Appendix 1.)

It is noteworthy that several of the most influential post-Lockean British empiricists and associationists were Scottish, and the Scots, unlike the English, had incorporated much of the civil law tradition into their own. In Scotland, one would not expect to find hostility to civilian legal conceptions and practice. The assimilating role of the Scottish Enlightenment must therefore be recognized in tracing the interaction and transmission of civil law concepts to Anglo-American treatise tradition.

Most English, as well as Continental, treatise writers assume or state a categorization of evidence which can be traced to rhetoricians such as Cicero and Quintilian. The categorization, well developed and elaborated in the civil law tradition, divided evidence into the direct and the indirect—direct typically being written evidence, things, and the testimony of witnesses. Indirect evidence, sometimes called circumstantial evidence, was of two types: conclusive, that is, where the connection between the principal fact (*factum probandum*) and evidentiary facts (*factum probans*) is a necessary consequence of nature, and presumptive, where the connection is one of greater or lesser probability. English materials suggest that by the time of the development of the treatise tradition these categories were well established but not entirely clear. The category of indirect evidence was a difficult one. The notion of circumstantial evidence was often still entangled with the concept of presumption. If presumptions were often distinguished from proofs, they also might constitute sufficient proof.

Most of the English treatise writers, like the canonists and civilians, divide presumptions into presumptions of fact and presumptions of law. While these categories are important, particularly in demonstrating continuity with the civilian tradition, we are interested primarily with presumptions of fact. Although I have already discussed the uses of concepts of presumption and the related concepts of circumstantial evidence, circumstances and suspicion in connection with arrest, pretrial examination, and indictment, here we are concerned with evidence presented at trial. The English treatise literature on evidence does not deal with evidentiary issues and concepts related to pretrial phases of criminal procedure.

Consideration of the English treatise tradition necessarily begins with Geoffrey Gilbert's *Law of Evidence*, written sometime prior to 1726 and published in a variety of editions during the second half of the eighteenth century. A brief examination of Gilbert helps to chart both the direction of conceptual change and the growing receptiveness to the civilians. Early editions speak briefly on the subject of presumptions, noting Coke's violent, probable, and light varieties. Presumption is defined "as it is defined by the Civilians," "a Conjecture arising from a certainty, which supported by another certainty, it is esteemed Truth." When a fact itself could not be proved, that "which comes nearest to the Proof, is the Proof of Circumstances that necessarily and usually attend such Facts, and are therefore called Presumptions not Proofs for they stand instead of the Proofs of the Fact until the contrary be proved."[110]

Later editions also emphasize the civilian distinction between presumptions of law and presumptions of fact. Thus the 1795 edition distinguishes along civilian lines between presumptions of law, which were "necessary and absolutely conclusive," and those of fact, which were either violent or "merely" probable.[111] Capel Lofft, the editor, not only indicates indebtedness to the civilians, but also explicitly organizes the subject matter according to the scheme of the Roman jurists.[112]

The early editions employ Coke's familiar categories of violent, probable, and light presumptions but accept only the first two, indicating that light presumptions "weigh nothing and are not to be considered." The designation "violent presumptions" was appropriate "when Circumstances are proved that do necessarily attend the Fact." But every presumption is more or less violent, according as "the circumstances do more or less usually accompany the Fact to be proved."[113] Coke's famous bloody sword example of violent presumption continued in all editions.

Circumstantial evidence is discussed in the 1791, Capel Lofft edition, where it is described as of varying force. In its highest degree it might amount to a full proof independent of the integrity of the witnesses, because circumstances, unlike witnesses, did not have the "power to falsify." Later editions of Gilbert thus provide further evidence of the eighteenth-century concern with the relative value of testimonial and circumstantial evidence. Violent presumption was required for conviction in capital cases.[114] Circumstances might also be "very weak, suspicious or positively unworthy of credit."[115] It is noteworthy that, although this treatment of circumstantial evidence is included in Lofft's abstract of Locke's *Essay Concerning Human Understanding*, Locke himself did not discuss circumstantial evidence and presumption.

As noted in Chapter 1, Gilbert viewed the law of evidence as grounded in intellectual processes and employed Locke's *Essay Concerning Human Understanding* (1690) as the foundation of his work. Because Locke does not explicitly discuss presumptive knowledge, Gilbert's materials on presumption were not put in an epistemological framework. Lofft's revision retains the Lockean foundation, and he states that Locke's *Essay* was especially important "in the weighing of Evidence and the Investigation of the Principles of Proof." He also referred to Hartley, Price, Watt, Priestly, and Wilkins.[116] Lofft's revision was thus to be up-to-date epistemologically as well as legally. Like so many later evidentiary writers, Lofft insisted the law of evidence "is more connected with the sublime Principles of moral and political Science, and the knowledge of human Nature, none more interesting to the Gentlemen and the Scholar."[117] Logic and the art of reasoning were of "more importance" to the law "than perhaps to any other practical Study."[118]

Our discussion of the concepts of moral certainty and reasonable doubt suggests the interaction between philosophical and legal discourse. It is therefore not surprising to find what we usually think of as philosophical texts discussing presumption and circumstantial evidence, as well as legal texts referring to more philosophical treatments of inference and the degree of probability or certainty which can be inferred both from testimony and from nontestimonial sources. Thus Kirwan's *Logick*, much-cited by legal writers, contained references to legal works such as Capel Lofft's edition of Gilbert. Kirwan's discussion of presumption, both violent and probable, was presented precisely as it appeared in the legal texts and with the same citations.[119] Gambier's *Guide to the Study of Moral Evidence* blended the epistemological and the legal to an even greater extent. His discussion of probable inference drawn from facts or premises too was replete with references to the legal treatise writers.[120]

Such cross-references in Lofft, Kirwan, and Gambier are easily explained. Philosophers and logicians were concerned with the nature of knowledge. They were concerned not only with knowledge derived from direct sense experience and from experience transmitted by others, that is, by testimony, but also with the probability or certainty of inferences about nondirectly observed facts drawn from observed facts. Philosophers seeking practical applications were inclined to examine that part of the European legal tradition which dealt with testimonial and circumstantial evidence and the conclusions or presumptions which might be drawn from them. Practical legal scholars, particularly from the time of Locke onward, were inclined to look at how more abstract and systematic thinkers approached similar problems.

Such interaction had occurred earlier as well. Ancient philosophers, rhetoricians, and legal thinkers, too, had exhibited mutual borrowing. And development of the medieval canon and civil law owed much to scholastic modes of reasoning. In an era such as the late eighteenth and early nineteenth centuries, when neither philosophy nor the general outlines of the law of evidence appeared too arcane, these traditions could fruitfully draw on one another. Indeed a late eighteenth-century text insisted that a barrister's essential professional knowledge had its foundation both in natural law and in the rules which reason dictates concerning the credit of witnesses and concerning the weight due to different degrees of probability, to analogy, and to circumstantial evidence. The legal profession was advised not to confine itself narrowly to study of parliamentary statutes and the practice of British courts, but to obtain a knowledge of the laws of other nations, both ancient and modern.[121] The insularity of earlier generations was thus being abandoned at the same time a new openness to epistemological and logical developments was occurring.

It seems likely too that the philosophical context played a role in breaking down the distinction between secret and other crimes. The category of secret crimes was required as long as a sharp distinction was drawn between findings of fact based on eyewitness testimony and findings based on inference from reported circumstances. Eighteenth-century thinkers had then engaged in a dispute over the relative certainty of conclusions drawn from direct and indirect evidence. Nineteenth-century legal thinkers, relying on philosophic discussions of logic and epistemology, increasingly came to view presumption as something that ran through the inferences and conclusions drawn from all factual reports. They preserved the term "presumption" for inferences drawn from circumstantial evidence, but by the time Thomas Starkie wrote, both testimonial evidence and circumstantial evidence were capable of reaching the height of moral certainty, that is, the status of beyond reasonable doubt. The need for a distinction between secret and other crimes thus disappears.

Natural philosophers too continued to be interested in these kinds of issues. Empirical scientists, like lawyers, needed to consider the character and status of the inferences they drew from the observed facts of nature and experimental evidence. Daniel McKinnon, in his *Philosophy of Evidence*, insisted that the law of evidence was "founded in correct logic," and that the judicial investigation of truth rested on a "comprehensive view of human nature." Epistemology, psychology, and logic were all essential to the analysis of legal evidence. Indeed McKinnon's purpose was to "facilitate the acquisition of this species of knowledge by placing the principles on which it is founded as much as possible within the reach of every intelligent mind, . . . by showing their connection with general science."[122]

McKinnon employed the conventional division between positive and presumptive proof, defining the latter as inference from a set of facts. Such inferences established a probability "more or less strong, according to the circumstances from which it is deduced." Rules were established "to define the limits of reasonable and improbable presumptions, and to point to the proper objects of deliberation in a court of justice." While some presumptions were determined by the law, others were the result of the proper functioning of the human mind. Although McKinnon does not refer directly to the civilians, he employs the familiar distinction between violent and probable presumptions. The former "afford competent legal evidence," and it was sometimes expedient to act on these as on a certainty. Courts after all must adopt their proceedings to the "general practices and understandings of mankind." To demand a higher degree of certainty would be both inconvenient and impractical. Probable presumptions, on the other hand, "are proper subjects of deliberation for a jury." McKinnon explains the nature of probability to show why in some instances presumptive evidence is acceptable and in other instances it must be rejected. He uses the language of weighing and balancing. Thus violent presumption exists "where the circumstances appear, the balance is not at all equivocal," while in probable presumption there is "room for deliberation and suspense." In civil cases jurors might strike a "fair balance" and decide according to the preponderance of the evidence and presumptions. In criminal cases, however, they must acquit if the facts were at all doubtful. McKinnon also explores the "limits of reasonable presumption," or probability, and the "comparative degrees of presumption," only some of which afford the proper subject for jury deliberation.[123]

Thomas Starkie's *Practical Treatise of the Law of Evidence* is the dominant English treatise of the period and provides an excellent illustration of the developments I have been describing.[124] Not only is Starkie the most philosophically oriented of early nineteenth-century law treatise writers, but he also exhibited little of the traditional reluctance to openly utilize the Roman law tradition. Starkie thus recognized that if much of the thinking on presumption and circumstantial evidence was indebted to the civilian tradition, the concept of circumstantial evidence and the *indicia* could be traced even further back to Quintilian and the ancients. Starkie specifically recognizes, as few English writers before him were willing to, that circumstantial evidence corresponded to the *indicia* of the Romano-canon tradition.

Juries, especially in criminal cases, relied on presumption, that is, they were often called upon to presume and infer motive. Starkie notes the variety of conduct or circumstantial evidence that typically afforded such inferences, for instance, seeking opportunity and means to commit the act, attempts to avoid suspicion or inquiry by flight, and concealing evidence. These *indicia* also played a prominent role in the "causes of Suspicion" relevant to arrest and to pretrial evidentiary evaluations. Confession too was viewed as presumptive evidence. That presumption might disappear, however, if there was further evidence of promises or threats. Presumptions, Starkie insisted, quoting Hale's caution, did not themselves conclusively establish guilt, and extreme caution had to be exercised in convicting on the basis of them. Nevertheless it was often proper to do so. After all, humanity operated with "almost as much regularity and uniformity as mechanical laws of nature," and many inferences about the natural world were extremely sound. Newton's theories and the theories of other natural scientists that explained the connection between natural phenomena and their causes were not very different from the inferences drawn from circumstantial evidence.[125] Starkie's references to Newton and natural science suggest the need for detailed investigation of the mutual indebtedness and interaction between the scientific philosophy of the eighteenth and nineteenth centuries and the English and Romano-canon law of evidence.

While Starkie retains the distinction between the evidence likely to be available for secret crimes and other types of crimes, he makes it clear that direct and indirect evidence may be of equal evidentiary value. Circumstantial evidence was becoming independent from the set of offenses with which it had been associated for so many generations. Circumstantial evidence and the presumptions which followed from it were capable of moral certainty, the highest kind of certainty available in matters of fact. Juries could thus confidently and without apology reach decisions beyond reasonable doubt on the basis of inferences from circumstantial evidence.[126]

Simon Greenleaf's *Treatise on the Law of Evidence* is the American equivalent of Starkie. As seen in Chapter 1, he founds the law of evidence on the familiar probabilistic theory of knowledge. In addition, however, he borrows freely from the civilian evidentiary treatises of Alciatus, Carpzov, Farinaccius, Mascardus, Menochius, and Pothier.[127] He employs the traditional division of direct and indirect proof, both of which rested on "our faith in human veracity, sanctioned by experience." Indirect, or inferential, proof, however, added "the experienced connection between collateral facts, [already] proved, and the fact, which is in controversy."[128] Presumptions, following the civilian and increasingly the Anglo-American traditions, are divided into those of law and those of fact, the former of which were either conclusive or disputable.[129] The portions of Greenleaf's text which deal with these categories are full of citations to civilian authorities. Greenleaf argues that presumptions of fact do not belong exclusively to the law.

[T]hey belong equally to any and every subject matter and are to be judged by the common and received tests of the truth of propositions, and the validity of arguments. They depend upon their own natural force and efficacy in generating belief or conviction in the mind, as derived from those connections, which are shown by experience, irrespective of any legal relations.[130]

Unlike the presumptions of law, which might be reduced to fixed rules and which constituted a branch of jurisprudence, presumptions of fact were employed "by means of the common experience of mankind without the aid or control of any rules of law whatever."[131] Such presumptions, which were the same everywhere, "embrace all the connections and relations between the facts proved and defended, whether they are mechanical or physical, or of a purely moral nature."[132] Here again is evidence of the early nineteenth-century assumption that the facts of the physical and social worlds are to be understood in the same way, that is, according to our best understanding of the way the human mind deals with factual and experiential data. Precisely because the process of ascertaining one fact "from the existence of another" was done without the aid of rules of law, it was therefore "within the exclusive province of the jury," who were unlimited "by any boundaries but those of truth; to be decided by themselves, according to the convictions of their own understanding."[133] In Greenleaf's discussion of presumption, then, we see an assimilation of scientific and legal evidence, both of which are treated in terms of the same probabilistic epistemological foundation, and also an assimilation of the civilian and the English evidentiary traditions.

The Anglo-American treatise tradition was an expansive one. The general treatises on evidence were followed by more specialized ones. Two of the most well known were William Wills's *Essay on the Principles of Circumstantial Evidence*[134] and William Best's *Treatise on Presumptions of Law and Fact with the Theory and Rules of Presumptive or Circumstantial Proof in Criminal Cases.*[135] Wills's text was designed to demonstrate that circumstantial evidence was "a means of arriving at moral certainty."[136] He relies on Locke, Butler, Kirwan, Whately, Stewart, Gambier, Abercrombie, and Bentham, among others. Wills believed that the English cases could, like every other part of the "great system of jurisprudence," be reduced to "consistent and immutable principles of reason and natural justice." Like treatise writers from Gilbert to Starkie, he began with a general treatment of the various kinds of evidence and the nature of assurance produced by different kinds of evidence. He was anxious to make the principles of legal evidence conform to the principles of evidence in philosophy; that is, he wished them to conform to the way one arrives at and draws conclusions from human knowledge. Judicial evidence was thus seen as a part of logic.[137] Most truths were "probable," and we have "no other guide than our own consciousness or the testimony of our fellow men."[138] Wills discussed both testimony, the "most comprehensive and important" basis of moral evidence, and circumstantial evidence, concentrating on the latter. His discussion of presumption was deeply and openly indebted to the civilians. Yet if Wills was in many respects indebted to civilian conceptual formulations, he had no doubt that the beyond reasonable doubt standard was superior to the Continental system of legal proof which prescribed precisely the kind and amount of evidence required.[139] Here again the use of civilian conceptualization did not require a repudiation of the national legal tradition.

For Wills, crime, insofar as it fell within the cognizance of courts, was "an act proceeding from a wicked motive."[140] Every such act required a voluntary agent and must have occurred in some particular place and time. There must also have been some indication of guilt. Evidence of preparations for the crime, disguises, flight, concealment, the possession of fruits of the crime, and numerous other particulars might assist in determining the judgment. We have met some of these signs, or indications of guilt, in our discussion of the arrest and preliminary hearing, noting their ancient and medieval origins.[141]

Wills provided some rules of induction that were particularly applicable to circumstantial evidence, though he insisted that the process of reasoning and inference was not different from the process of scientific inquiry. The rules for estimating the force of arguments and the truth of propositions belong to "the province of logic," and the maxims of evidence consist of a "selection of logical rules applied to a particular subject matter."[142] Wills thus shares the assumption of most late eighteenth- and early nineteenth-century writers on legal evidence that there was nothing peculiar about the logic of the law or legal reasoning about facts.

Presumption was defined as "a probable consequence, drawn from facts, either certain, or proved by direct testimony as to the truth of a fact alleged, but of which there is not direct proof."[143] Wills carefully distinguishes presumption, an act of judgment, from the circumstantial evidence on which it is based. He also attempted to clarify the differences between direct and indirect, or circumstantial, evidence, indicating that traditional labels were often indiscriminately applied and confused with "lamentable results." Wills discussed the relative value of direct and indirect evidence in the context of ancient and Continental sources. Even if the best writers, both ancient and modern, concurred in treating the cogency and effect of circumstantial evidence as inferior, he felt that direct and circumstantial evidence should not be so sharply contrasted because both were equally fallible. Thus he sharply criticized the maxim that circumstances cannot lie and noted, "It is astonishing that sophisms like these should have passed current without animadversion."[144]

Wills also provided a discussion of presumptions. These, which were classified as legal or natural, were derived from the civilians. He thus cites Mascardus and Menochius in particular. Natural presumptions to be just "must be dictated by nature and reason," though it was impossible, "without a dereliction of every rational principle, to lay down positive rules of presumption." Because arbitrary presumptions could not be reduced to fixed principles, Wills desired that they be employed only rarely by courts in criminal jurisprudence.[145]

While Wills admired and borrowed from the civilians, he was also critical. He insisted that English law did not recognize the *semi plena probatio* based on circumstances and suspicion that might lead to torture. He also found the traditional civilian subdivisions of *indicia*, signs, *adminicula*, *coniecturae*, *dubia*, and *suspiciones* to be arbitrary and useless. Arbitrary technical rules for estimating the force and efficacy of particular facts leading to presumption were foolish for they were a "matter purely of reason and logic." He attributed these rules to an effort to escape a "still greater absurdity," the view that a single witness was worthless. Because presumptions were not thought to have the same force as testimony, the civilians had required the concurrence of several presumptions as an "imaginary equivalent" for two eyewitnesses. But it seemed obvious to Wills that "a single presumption might be conclusive, and that an accusation of many presumptions may be of but little weight." Presumptions must not be counted but weighed according to the same principles used to estimate the effect of testimonial evidence. Wills also criticized as unreasonable the Continental device of giving lesser punishments on the basis of circumstantial evidence.[146]

The classification of presumption found in Coke was also unsatisfactory. Wills found Coke's categories of violent or necessary, probable or grave, and slight to be "specious," "fanciful," and inaccurate. Presumptions might be violent but not necessary. He preferred Best's categorizations of violent or strong and slight— but none of the classifications was very useful because it was impossible to lay down rules for distinguishing the various classes from one another.[147]

Thus Wills insists that there are scarcely any rules of judgment, perhaps none, that relate exclusively to judicial inquiries founded on circumstantial evidence. He nevertheless produced five rules. The first was, "The facts alleged as the basis of any legal inference must be strictly and indubitably connected with the *factum probandum*." The second required that the burden of proof be on the party "who asserts that existence of any fact which infers legal accountability."[148] The third was the best evidence rule. The next perhaps derived from Starkie: "In order to justify the inference of legal guilt from circumstantial evidence, the existence of the inculpatory facts must be absolutely incompatible with the innocence of the accused, and incapable of explanation upon any other reasonable hypothesis than that of his guilt."[149] The penalties of the penal law were justifiable "only when the strength of our convictions is equivalent to moral certainty."[150] His last rule required that

"If there be any reasonable doubt, as to the reality of the connection of the circumstances of evidence with the *factum probandum*, or as to the completeness of the proof of the *corpus delicti*, or as to the proper conclusions to be drawn from the evidence, it is safer to err in acquitting than in conviction."[151]

By the nineteenth century, the beyond reasonable doubt standard had come to cover both testimonial *and* circumstantial evidence. Whatever differences of opinion had existed in earlier decades as to the treatment of these two types of evidence, at least with respect to their capacities to elicit conviction, seem to have disappeared.

William Best wrote two extremely important treatises on evidence. Both amply illustrate my argument concerning the three traditions that came to constitute the mid-nineteenth-century approach to presumptive evidence. There was the long tradition embodied in the legal literature and case materials that stretched back into England's medieval past, the newer effort to ground the Anglo-American principles of evidence on a sound theory of knowledge, and the even newer effort to openly and critically employ elements of the evidentiary traditions of the civil law.

Best's *Principles of the Law of Evidence* begins with the familiar treatment of human understanding—the sources of ideas, the objects about which the mind is conversant, the intensity of persuasion, and the notation of probabilistic judgment.[152] While by far the greater part of this work is devoted to witnesses, portions of it also deal with presumption. Using Bonnier's *Traité de preuves*, Best argued that the law may establish artificial weight to natural principles in order to reach decisions. While it was often impossible to arrive at a perfect knowledge of truth in particular cases, social necessity did not allow the suspension of judgment that might be possible in other spheres of life. Presumption, therefore, was established by law.

Taking his cue from the civilians, Best notes that presumptions are of two kinds, presumptions of law and presumptions of fact, categories better known in England as "irrebuttable presumptions" and "inclusive, or rebuttable, presumptions." His analysis of presumptions of law relied on Alciatus, Menochius, and Pothier, and his discussion is studded with citations to Domat, Grotius, Mascardus, Matthaeus, and Bonnier. He was, nevertheless, like Wills, often critical of the civilians. He notes some of the "mischievous presumptions" which continued to plague the laws of modern France, as well as the continuing Continental tendency to count presumptions rather than to reach a holistic judgment based on the overall weight of evidence. The civilians had forgotten that proof "means persuasion wrought in the mind and consequently must depend not on the number of instruments of evidence employed, but on their force, credibility and concurrence."[153]

Best's views on presumption and circumstantial evidence, however, were explored in far greater detail in his *A Treatise on Presumptions of Law and Fact with the Theory and Rules of Presumptive or Circumstantial Proof in Criminal Cases*, which featured a quotation from Alciatus's *Tractatus de Praesumptionibus* on the title page, a sure sign to his readers that he would draw on the learning of the civilians.[154] Although he acknowledged the earlier work of Wills and Phillipps, Best felt that a systematic treatise on presumption and circumstantial evidence was still lacking. His would provide not only an analysis of the general principles on which they were based, but also a discussion of presumptive proof in criminal cases. Best acknowledged his general indebtedness to the civilians and his special indebtedness to Menochius and Alciatus on presumptive proof.[155]

Best begins in what is now a thoroughly predictable way, with a Lockean, or rather post-Lockean, discussion of the probabilistic nature of human knowledge: "The foundation of judgement is probability, or the likelihood of a proposition or fact being true or false, deduced from its conformity or repugnancy to our general knowledge, observation, and experience."[156] In all cases of probable reasoning, the proof was presumptive and "the inference to which it gives rise a presumption." In its comprehensive sense, presumption could be defined to be "where, in the absence or until actual certainty of the truth or falsehood of any proposition or fact can be obtained, an inference affirmative or disaffirmative of that truth or falsehood is drawn by a process of probable reasoning."[157] Proofs of fact, the concern of his treatise, were "evidenced to the mind," either directly by the senses or indirectly "by reasoning from other truths which have been evidenced directly." Evidence was "any matter of fact, the effect, tendency, or design of which, when presented to the mind is to produce a persuasion therein affirmative or disaffirmative of the existence of other matter of fact, and the former, the evidentiary fact."[158]

Employing a combination of philosophical reasoning and civilian example, Best discusses the modes of reasoning and the connection between various kinds of facts. In some instances the connection is a necessary consequence of the law of nature. In others a finding of fact may be "where the existence of the evidentiary facts is sufficiently strong to produce in the mind a persuasion, belief, or conviction of the existence of the principal fact" without excluding its nonexistence from the limits of physical impossibility. To this class "belong those cases where the existence of the principal fact is only inferred by a process of presumptive or probable reasoning from that of the evidentiary facts."[159]

Best insisted that no field of investigation, including the judicial, was justified in departing from the general principles which govern the investigation of all truth with the exception that the "municipal law" from "motives of policy" occasionally found it necessary to take into consideration the "peculiar habits of society" or to prevent particular "mischiefs." Such exceptions occasionally resulted in "technical rules," which limited the operation of the general principles of investigation.

In one sense, Best argued, all judicial knowledge was presumptive. Direct evidence presumed the veracity of witnesses and the genuineness of documents. Indirect evidence simply involved a different form of presumption. Where the fact in dispute "has either fallen under the cognizance of the senses . . . so that its truth or falsehood can only be deduced by a special inference from facts proved directly, the evidence of that fact is said to be circumstantial." When the conclusion does not follow necessarily from the facts proved, "but is deduced by probable inference, the evidence is said to be presumptive and the inference drawn a presumption."[160] In this connection, Best not only cites the natural law oriented civilians Domat and Pothier, but also refers to Aristotle, Quintilian, and Cicero for the distinction between direct and indirect evidence. He notes that the French "*indice*" was equivalent to circumstantial evidence, but not to presumption. That is, it designated the facts giving rise to the inference, rather than the inference itself.[161] Best evidently felt that there was still some confusion in the Anglo-American tradition over the distinction between circumstantial evidence and the presumptions inferred from it.

Having established the nature of presumption, he followed the civilians in categorizing these as the presumptions of man, that is, natural presumptions, and the presumptions of law, which are of a more technical nature. He also added a category of *praesumptiones mixtae*, or mixtures of presumptions of law and fact. Each is discussed in great detail, taking pains to show the similarity between English and civilian concepts. He notes too that presumptions of law were subject to change and that some of these, which at one time were absolute and irrebuttable in English law, were no longer so. The English courts were moving in the direction of restricting rather than expanding irrebuttable presumptions.[162]

The range of presumptive reasoning was so great that attempts to "reduce" presumptions into definite classes "according to their degrees of probative force" were bound to be ineffectual. Some classifications, like those outlined by Mascardus and Coke, had become common. Best notes Coke's categories of violent, probable, and light presumption as well as his bloody sword example of violent presumption. He rejects the example on the grounds that there were a number of hypotheses which would reconcile the bloody sword facts with innocence.[163] He, like Wills, found the Cokean and civilian classifications of presumptions into violent, probable and slight to be of questionable value.

Best's own preference was for a classification of presumptions of fact based on consideration of their effect on the burden of proof. Presumptions of man could be divided into slight or strong as they affected the burden of proof. "Slight presumptions" sufficient to "excite suspicion" do not, taken singly, amount to proof or shift the burden of proof. He cites Huberus and Matthaeus on this particular point, and frequently his treatment and examples are drawn from the civil law treatise writers. But even "slight presumptions," when they form a link in a chain of evidence, may render complete a body of proof otherwise imperfect. The concurrence of a large number of slight presumptions may both shift the burden of proof and amount to proof of the most convincing kind—even in a capital case.[164] "Strong presumptions" shifted the burden of proof and were entitled "to great weight, and where there is no other evidence are generally decisive in civil cases. In criminal, and more especially in capital ones, a greater degree of caution is, of course, requisite."[165]

Presumptions of law and "strong" presumptions of fact were often difficult to distinguish. In legal systems where both are intrusted to a single judge, the distinction was "almost imperceptible in practice." In common law, however, these must be kept quite distinct, for jurors were not permitted to disregard presumptions of law.[166]

The third part of Best's treatise centered on the theory and rules of presumptive proof in criminal cases and on the "probative force and informative circumstances of the most usual species of it." He is thus concerned with circumstantial evidence and the inferences which may be drawn from it. The elements in a chain of presumptive proofs are

moral and physical coincidences which individually indicate delinquency in the accused; and the probative force of the whole depends on the *number, independence, weight* and *consistency* of those elementary circumstances. A *number* of circumstances, each individually very slight, may so tally and confirm each other, as to leave no room for doubt . . . but if they are not *independent* of each other and all arise from one source, an increase in the number . . . does not increase the probability of the hypothesis.[167]

Best's language echoes Locke's analysis of testimonial evidence. Although the rules of admissibility are the same in both civil and criminal proceedings, presumptive evidence was often needed in proof of crime. Best echoes Dalton in arguing that visible proofs "must not be expected in works of darkness." Interestingly, he cites a judicial opinion of 1781, though the phraseology and the concept can be found in the English justice of the peace manuals from the sixteenth century and was probably already well established by that time. The notion, of course, had provided the rationale for the *crimen exceptum.*

Best insists that a chain of presumptive evidence may afford as convincing a proof as one based on direct testimony. Reliance on circumstantial evidence did not mean a decision had been made on the basis of inferior or less conclusive proof. Whether founded on direct or presumptive evidence, condemnation must "flow from an unbiased moral conviction of . . . guilt." Best noted, however, that the "true principles on which presumptive proof rests have not always been understood by those who administer justice." Histories of many nations provided examples of individuals who have been "sacrificed to the ignorance, haste, or misdirected zeal of judges and jurymen dealing with this peculiar mode of proof."[168]

The consequence in England of these miscarriages of justice was a prejudice, sometimes even "an outcry," against convictions based on presumptive evidence. For Best, however, no "species of judicial evidence" was infallible. Both the positive testimony of witnesses and the jury verdict itself rested on the probability or presumption that the "witnesses are neither deceived themselves nor wilfully deceiving them."[169] Confessions created the same problem. Even the "freest and fullest" may turn out to be untrue. It would be absurd to demand only evidence which "cannot lie" because it would be a demand for evidence without the intervention of human testimony, that is, evidence which presented itself directly to the senses of the judge. Anything less must only be "an indefinitely high degree of probability," and this was "as attainable by a well conducted process of reasoning from circumstances as from evidence either of a direct or confessional nature." Citing Locke's *Essay Concerning Human Understanding*, Best notes that in all important transactions of life and in all the "moral, and most of the physical sciences," we must rely almost exclusively "on probable presumptive reasoning."[170]

Best also thought it necessary to refute an even more mischievous position—that presumptive evidence was superior to all other modes of proof. Juries, Best suggests, had sometimes been informed by the bench, even in capital cases, that circumstantial evidence is more convincing than other varieties because facts cannot lie. He spends considerable time and effort in refuting this position, indicating that direct and presumptive evidence each had peculiar advantages and "characteristic dangers."[171] The doctrines of moral certainty and proof beyond reasonable doubt are firmly joined to both direct and circumstantial evidence.[172]

The treatise writers of the late eighteenth and nineteenth centuries make formal and explicit the interplay of ideas and practices that had begun in the seventeenth century, if not earlier. The fundamental practice is that a lay jury arrives at a general criminal verdict by whatever mental processes it possesses, on the basis of whatever it hears in the courtroom, and on whatever knowledge it brings into that courtroom. Even with the twentieth-century paraphernalia of the social sciences, it has proven impossible to know how juries really decide. We will never know whether juries were much affected by the learned lore of circumstances, inferences, and presumptions. What we do know is that law as a learned profession and the more general learned culture of England and America came to express what the jury did as a systematic empirical inquiry—an inquiry whose system was of classical origins, in accord with natural law, shared by the civil law, and consonant with the central epistemological teachings of the English traditions of religion, science, and philosophy.

Conclusion

What we have been observing in this chapter is a crisis, albeit a crisis that was so low-key and took so long to resolve itself that it was barely evident even to those who played central roles in its resolution. The English jury had replaced a perfect fact finder, God. Of course it was not a perfect replacement. Initially, however, it was thought to come fairly close because it brought to the courtroom precisely what a Westminster judge could not: personal knowledge of the facts surrounding the alleged crime. Precisely because that knowledge provided the jury with its special, near divine, spark, the English clung to the belief that local juries possessed and used that spark long after the changing conditions of English life had undermined that belief. Gradually and eventually, however, the English were forced to acknowledge that juries found facts and reached verdicts on the basis of what they heard in the courtroom. Proof then became the sticking point. Not every legal system has survived that sticking point. The extremely demanding standard of proof in orthodox Muslim law, eyewitness testimony of two adult male believers, led to the migration of nearly the whole of criminal prosecution from the courts of the kadis to the courts of the police who did not employ the orthodox law. We have seen how the Romano-canon system was led to torture to obtain confession and to categorization which allowed lesser proofs to elicit lesser penalties.

In the course of the development of the jury, the English grappled with the problem of witnesses. The shift in the balance between personal knowledge of jurors and witness testimony, or perhaps from jurors as witnesses to jurors as hearers of witnesses, was so gradual that no great difficulty was experienced in eventually learning to base verdicts solely on witness testimony and in evaluating the credibility of the witnesses. Under biblical and civil law influences, the English did flirt with and then quickly reject the two-witness rule. When juries knew personally, much of what they knew was hearsay, although individuals hardly doubt the hearsay they know themselves. When juries rely on witnesses, however, hearsay becomes perceived as a salient problem. That problem was solved largely by reference to contemporary developments in English religion, science, and philosophy and probably by some covert attention to Continental practice, which had addressed the issues much earlier.

If the jury was to retain its special legitimacy as fact finder, the central problem was clearly that of circumstantial evidence presented in testimony by persons who were not themselves eyewitnesses to the crime. A small part of this problem was resolved by transferring a little of the jury's fact-finding to the judge through the creation of presumptions of law. The vast bulk of circumstantial evidence nevertheless remained, and that evidence did not automatically resolve itself into verdicts. Conviction could only occur on the basis of inferences drawn from the circumstances presented. Through doctrines of presumption of fact, the English learned community persuaded the larger community that the jury, now bereft of personal knowledge, still maintained the divine fact-finding spark. The classical heritage and their own great epistemological traditions assisted the English in their understanding that jury inference was but a sub-species of the soundest method that humans could construct for knowing facts. Another source of persuasion was also employed, at first covertly and then openly. Just across the Channel, and indeed in several places in the heart of England, another great legal system had developed an elaborate body of doctrines about circumstantial evidence and inference, which it employed successfully even while clinging to the rule of perfect proof for conviction. Never having encumbered themselves with that rule, or rather having finessed it by placing their faith in the jury, the English were all the more able to borrow portions of the law of circumstantial evidence and inference that the Romano-canon lawyers had developed. These Continental comparisons and their natural law accompaniments further reassured the English that what their juries were doing was a universal practice of civilized people and was the best method of fact finding. Whatever actually went on in the jury room, what could be seen was a systematic application of a well thought out and widely shared technique of factual inquiry, controlled inference, and rigorous findings. By the nineteenth century the jury had passed triumphantly through the crisis of its transition from knower to evaluator and could be seen as being in possession of a technique justified by both the oldest and the newest in scientific and philosophic thought and legal practice.

Chapter Five

Conclusion

We have examined a number of English institutions, the most important being the trial jury, which developed from a largely self-informing body, with few if any doctrinal formulations to guide it, to an institution bound by elaborate rules of evidence and procedure. The trial jury has had a continuous role from the twelfth century to the present, but the justification for its role in criminal law has changed enormously. First conceived of as a body of knowers of facts, it consisted of important local men who presumably would possess the requisite local knowledge to reach decisions as sure as those of the ordeal which had brought to bear the knowledge and justice of God. Gradually and imperceptibly jurors began to hear witnesses testify as to direct and circumstantial evidence. Juries thus gradually became fact evaluators. Emphasis on the vicinage requirement and on the jury's ability to know and evaluate facts independent of the judge continued into the late seventeenth century, thus obscuring the fact that jurors by that time could make little claim to independent knowledge, that is, knowledge brought to, rather than gained in, the courtroom. Yet the insistence on the old ways was not mere anachronism. It provided a legitimating screen that protected the jury's old claim to truth-telling while a new one was sought.

In the new system jurors sit as fact evaluators who assess both the direct testimony of eyewitnesses and indirect circumstantial evidence. The beyond reasonable doubt doctrine evolved as judges came to inform jurors that they must evaluate the testimony of witnesses. The language of satisfied conscience conceivably might have been used even when jurors thought of themselves as self-informing, but the beyond reasonable doubt language suggests a standard to be attained after a rational consideration of evidence. Somewhat more slowly there developed the position that inferences made by jurors from circumstantial evidence might yield proof beyond reasonable doubt. The medieval trial jury thus survived into the modern world with a new, intellectually satisfying justification for its decision-making role in the criminal justice system. Armed with the formula "beyond a reasonable doubt and to a moral certainty" and a circumstantial evidence doctrine to replace the self-knowledge that had itself replaced God's knowledge, the criminal trial jury thus could maintain its role as the central actor and legitimator of the Anglo-American justice system. Indeed, the jury has provided so much satisfaction that pretrial procedures have frequently tended to gravitate toward the same formulas and doctrines that justify the jury trial. We have seen this tendency at work particularly in connection with American preliminary hearings and with the whole history of grand juries.

Both in England and the United States the jury's guilt-finding capacity, guided first by collective personal knowledge and then by a beyond a reasonable doubt evidentiary standard, has been so powerful that it has created an insoluble dilemma for pretrial proceedings. On the one hand, if the jury is so good a truth finder, all those accused should be tried. On the other, the cost both to the accused and to society of trying all accusations is unreasonably high given the potential for bad faith among accusers. So some standard must be devised to choose which accused persons shall be tried. We only know of one really good standard, that used by the jury itself. Yet to use that standard at preliminary stages is self-defeating. It is to hold a trial in order to decide whether to hold a trial. In the absence of any agreed upon, distinct, and quantifiable levels of probability of guilt below the jury standard, that dilemma is insoluble. And so magistrates are instructed by law to pass forward all felony accusations, but in fact do not do so. Controversialists endlessly debate the standard for grand jury indictments. A hiatus occurs in the debate only when, for a magic moment, *prima facie* case seems to provide a distinct probability of guilt one level below the beyond a reasonable doubt jury standard. "Probable cause" becomes the banner under which parades the failure to resolve the dilemma and the need to pretend that it has been resolved.

From its inception, the jury has been characterized by an insistence that only those proven guilty be convicted. Both the grand jury and the trial jury were to screen out cases not adequately based. What we have traced is the development of two legal doctrines designed to guide jurors in the achievement of this goal. The beyond reasonable doubt standard was shaped from an amalgam of religious epistemology and methodology and Lockean empirical philosophy. This doctrine has remained in place from the time of its formulation in the eighteenth century and has been accepted with little criticism.[1] There has been no movement to increase or decrease the degree of certitude that jurors are to experience.[2]

We have seen a somewhat different development in connection with circumstantial evidence, although here, too, the practice of convicting on circumstantial evidence was in place long before intellectually acceptable doctrines concerning it emerged. These doctrines show traces of Romano-canon borrowings from their earliest use in English common law relating to crime despite the reluctance on the part of early modern English lawyers to recognize such indebtedness. The relative valuation of testimonial and circumstantial evidence in the early modern period tends to parallel that of the Continent. That indebtedness was only openly recognized with the beginning of the treatise tradition when treatise writers were anxious to place their work in the context of universal principles and a sound theory of knowledge. Thus the formulas that emerged to rationalize and legitimate English jury practice are derived from English religious and philosophical learning and from Continental practices dressed in the language of universal principles of natural law that had itself become part of English learning.

In tracing this and other stories of institutionalization and legitimation, I have been particularly concerned with the migration of legal concepts, which we have followed and investigated in three, sometimes intertwined, ways. The first has been to investigate the relationship between legal concepts of evidence and proof and similar concepts found in other varieties of discourse—religious, rhetorical, historical, and epistemological. We have seen that casuistry, moral philosophy, natural philosophy, and epistemology were important to the shaping of the beyond reasonable doubt doctrine and that the rhetorical tradition played an important role in shaping the Romano-canon and then the Anglo-American legal traditions. I have repeatedly suggested that evidentiary doctrine owes a good deal to other intellectual traditions and enterprises. It appears as if susceptibility to outside influences is greatest on those occasions when legal professionals lack their own doctrinal formulas or when their inherited formulas are inadequate to a new problem.

The second way was to trace the migration or borrowing of doctrinal concepts from one part of the Anglo-American legal system to another. We have focused primarily on probable cause, noting its successive use in several pretrial procedures, most recently its transfer from American preliminary hearings to grand jury proceedings.

The third and most difficult task has been to trace the migration or borrowing of concepts from the Romano-canon to the Anglo-American system of criminal jurisprudence. I have not argued for a general reception. Borrowed concepts were grafted onto a working indigenous legal system. Borrowing thus did not result in a fundamental change in the procedural or institutional setting of the borrower. As the English legal system added new institutions and procedures (for example, pretrial examination), it drew on the intellectual and legal traditions most readily available. National pride and fear of the Continental inquisition process made early modern Englishmen reluctant to openly recognize those debts.

If this study suggests that several of the doctrinal elements of the English criminal laws of evidence were derived from canon and civil law sources, I am simply saying that English law developed within the context of a family of Western legal traditions. Given the work of Harold Berman and others on the contribution of the canonists, the overlap between English and Romano-canon legal thought should not be surprising.[3] More generally it would be impossible to explain English cultural and constitutional history without reference to European-wide religious, intellectual, and sociopolitical developments. Not all the borrowing took place in one direction. The French adopted the jury for criminal cases, grafting it onto an already working judicial system and developing the concept of "intime conviction," a reasonably close facsimile of proof beyond a reasonable doubt.

The story of borrowing and developing doctrine is, of course, in part a political story. Political motivations and controversies surrounded grand jury indictment standards—both during their clearest emergence in the 1670s and 1680s and in later centuries. The conflict is often between central authority and local participation. Indeed we have noted a continuing thread of perceived tension between the judicial agents of central authority and the interests of the local citizenry. Often these tensions became incorporated into party politics, and for long periods there are Whig and Tory theories of the grand jury. The Whigs and their successors have focused on the rights of individual citizens. Tories are much concerned with the need to prosecute and punish criminals. Both the crime control model and the civil and individual rights model have been important in the development of evidentiary standards for arrest, pretrial examination, and grand jury indictment. There appears to be a persistent, long-term tension between the two models in Anglo-American thinking about pretrial procedure. When that tension temporarily is resolved in one segment of those proceedings, it tends to pop up in another.

The array of politics, institutions, and ideas that we have been analyzing is complex. Because the ideas we examined in this book tended to migrate both from one institution to another and from one legal system to another, a sequential, institutional organization from arrest through trial (which would have been most comforting to lawyers) would have hopelessly compromised the orderly presentation of ideas. To have followed an exclusively intellectual organization would have kept us hopping constantly between institutions. As a result, what I have presented is a kind of musical composition in which such themes as moral certainty, beyond reasonable doubt, common fame, presumption, the causes of suspicion, and probable cause are developed and then appear and reappear as various institutional movements are played out. In the real world of legal development, one idea from one source is rarely neatly and forever matched with one institution.

Our basic concerns have been doctrinal change, continuity, and migration. I have attempted to present doctrine in the context of institutional needs, the intellectual and cultural environment, the culturally available materials from neighboring legal traditions, po-

litical ideology, and, where possible, the immediate social and political context.

Although this study has focused on doctrine, it has made use of
more socially and politically oriented historical studies whenever
possible. It nevertheless is perhaps best described as a member of
the species intellectual history of which the history of legal doctrine is a subspecies. The development of legal ideas, some of them
very long-lived, has played an important role in shaping the ways
in which legal systems work, or at least in shaping contemporary
and subsequent perceptions of how they work. Some concepts have
been found useful over very long periods of time in quite different
social and economic contexts, while other concepts seem to have
been generated from, and be suitable to, only one set of immediate
socio-political conditions. Furthermore, even those historians who
are primarily interested in the ways in which doctrine is shaped by
economic and social conditions and interests cannot investigate
such matters until there is a fairly clear notion of the substance of
that doctrine. Tracing the evolution of evidentiary concepts thus
should be useful not only to those who are interested in the developments themselves but also to those who wish to explore the relationship between legal concepts and the political and economic
environments.

Law is a particularly challenging branch of intellectual history
because, at least in the common-law world, the actors being observed have a particular interest in disguising what the historian
seeks to discover. The participants value continuity, and particularly value an appearance of domestic and familiar provenance for
all their wares. Innovation in legal doctrine is more difficult to trace
than innovation in the natural sciences because its creators and
elucidators prefer to obscure rather than to highlight the new or
the newly borrowed. Even major new legal doctrines are pro-
claimed to be old or are dressed in traditional language and garb.
The more successful the creators or modifiers of legal doctrine have
been, the more difficult it is for either their contemporaries or later
historians to detect their innovations.

Doctrinal history may be criticized as a species of what has derisively been labeled "tunnel history," which traces a single topic
through time, presumably with insufficient attention to its environment or context at any given moment. Those concerned with the

history of legal doctrine and concepts are required to make difficult choices. One choice is to focus on relatively brief periods of time, examining the particular legal concept or concepts in the complex web of intellectual, social, political, and economic conditions of that period. Another involves taking a longer view—perhaps several centuries—in which the intellectual, sociological, and political contexts undergo substantial, and perhaps even revolutionary, changes. Such long-term approaches cannot provide the same detailed attention to context, but they do provide access to the evolution of doctrinal traditions. On the whole, I have taken the long view, with its attendant advantages and disadvantages, but I have occasionally attempted to present a denser, richer environmental context, drawing on the research of others and the availability of appropriate source material. The longer perspective is, however, essential for tracing the central intellectual dynamic of the history of the law of evidence, for that dynamic is one in which ideas or doctrines created in one era and context are adapted and recycled in another. And as the recycling takes place, the operational meaning or the words of the doctrine, or both, may change, a little or a lot. The development of "probable cause" out of "suspicions," "half proofs," and "presumptions" and its migration from one pretrial institution to another is the most dramatic of many examples.

If I have attempted to combine what historians of science have come to call "internalist" and "externalist" approaches, greater attention has been given to the former. My approach nevertheless falls into the contextualist mode because legal ideas are placed whenever possible in a religious, philosophical, and political, as well as legal, context.

The studies presented here are preliminary and necessarily somewhat fragmentary. A good deal is known about some of the institutions, procedures, and doctrines of the criminal law for some periods and little is known about others. For instance, the political controversy surrounding the grand jury in the late seventeenth century briefly illuminates its development, but little is known about its actual operations in the sixteenth and eighteenth centuries. Similar high points and hiatuses exist for the trial jury and preliminary hearings.

Source materials are fragmentary and no doubt often misleading. One principal source, the published *State Trials*, presents a picture of criminal proceedings that can hardly reflect what occurred in ordinary criminal prosecutions. The state trials were highly visible, political cases in which Crown prosecutors were anxious to convict, judges were usually under royal pressure, and public attention was manifest. In the average criminal prosecution, there was no state prosecutor and little public attention. Justice of the peace manuals and legal treatises no doubt were highly influential as guides to practice for many magistrates and judges, but they were not quite the law. They were often such catalogues of contradictions that following them could lead to several different behavior patterns.

No one could fail to notice the influence of both civil and canon law on English evidentiary law. Romano-canon law had developed preliminary procedures and directly confronted the problem of witness testimony before the English. Some of the borrowing is obvious. Some is hidden by the reluctance of common lawyers to admit to it. In some instances, parallel practice probably developed independently, for the problems of dealing with an English and a French thief are about the same. My own knowledge of Continental law is too limited to allow more than a rudimentary examination of these cross-Channel connections. Further comparative criminal law studies should prove illuminating.

About the same thing can be said of the ties between the English and the American law of evidence. For the most part I have treated American practices as an extension of English. Such an approach seems particularly justified for the seventeenth century where the major concentration of this book lies. I have traced some of the divergence that exists, particularly for the later centuries and particularly where they provide special illumination of underlying problems and tensions. If the United States has been treated as a second fiddle, then Ireland and the Dominions have hardly been heard from at all. Further comparative study here, too, might yield important results.

This study is not only short on nations but also on institutions. The development of the police and of public prosecution have obviously had a major impact on evidentiary practices and doctrines. So has the enormous overloads placed on these institutions and the courts by the growth of urban populations. As yet, little can be said about particular doctrinal responses to these phenomena.

This last point reminds us that this has been a study largely of doctrine, rather than practice. Even now, after a considerable vogue in empirical studies of the contemporary criminal process, we know little of the actual evidentiary standards in routine cases employed by police, warrant-granting magistrates, prosecutors, grand juries, and trial judges and juries. Phrases like "probable cause" and "beyond reasonable doubt" are notorious black boxes for students of behavior. This book has been about the way legal professionals and relatively educated persons sought for a criminal-evidence epistemology that would satisfy them that justice was being done. It is about the construction of doctrines that would legitimate a fact-finding regime that was obviously full of human error and on which the lives and liberties of many citizens depended. It may be argued that what people actually do to and for one another in the course of criminal proceedings is far more important than what they say about what they do, and how they justify what they do. Yet we have passed beyond the pseudo-sophistication of alleging that doctrine is merely a smoke screen for practice. What lawyers and judges say to one another and to witnesses, jurors, the accused, the accusers, and police has a great deal to do with how they all behave. How they justify what they do has a great deal to do with the survival of the institutions and practices being justified. Here I have sought to trace various developments in doctrines of proof, that is, of knowing in the context of law, that have been crucial to the fates of the accused and the institutions that process the accused in England and America.

Appendix

The frequent reference to the concept of probability no doubt reminds the reader of mathematical notions of probability and of contemporary discussion of the role of mathematical probability and the law. Early modern thinkers, both Continental and English, considered the utility and applicability of mathematical concepts in the legal sphere. Indeed it has recently been suggested that the origins of mathematical probability are deeply indebted to Romano-canon legal concepts, which in turn were indebted to classical rhetorical concepts of the probable. They also appear to be related to what we traditionally label circumstantial evidence and presumptive proof.[1]

The beginnings of mathematical probability are usually dated to the mid-seventeenth century, with the 1654 correspondence between Blaise Pascal and Pierre Fermat and the 1657 calculations of expectations of games of chance by Christiaan Huygens. Most seventeenth- and eighteenth-century developments were concentrated in France. Laplace elaborated and systemized this work in 1819. Lorraine Daston and James Franklin not only suggest that concepts of mathematical probability owed much to legal doctrine but also note that attempts at legal application occurred very early. Mathematical probability was linked first to contracts where risk was involved and then to assessments of testimonial evidence. Daston views the latter as part of a wider effort to apply probability theory to the moral sciences and dates the period of greatest interest in applying mathematical probability to the legal sphere from 1699 to c. 1837. Interest appears to have declined in France as the French abandoned the system of legal proofs,[2] and as natural law theorists emphasized that legal notions of proof should be made more consistent with those of natural reason.[3]

Some English thinkers became interested in applications of probability theory, but perhaps, because their approach to evidence had never involved notions of half, quarter, and eighth proofs, they were less innovative both in creating theories of mathematical probability and in applying those theories. Nevertheless the *Philosophical Transactions* of the Royal Society in 1699 included an anonymous article on estimation of concordant testimony. It reported an effort to mathematize "moral certainty absolute" in which "the mind of man entirely acquiesces." The author attempts to measure the credibility of the reporter according to his integrity, fidelity, and his double ability of "apprehending what is delivered" and of "retaining it" so it can be transmitted.[4]

Most Anglo-American writers who considered the possibility of applying probability calculations to the legal arena in the eighteenth and early nineteenth centuries, however, rejected such attempts, largely on the ground that positive proof was necessary for conviction in criminal cases. If several of the philosophical works of Hartley, Kirwan, Whately, and Gambier discussed applications of mathematical probability to the law, most concluded that the calculations did not reach the beyond reasonable doubt standard.[5] John Stuart Mill was adamantly opposed to the attempt to apply the calculus of probability to the credit of witnesses and to legal judgments, and he criticized the attempts of Laplace and other French mathematicians who had attempted to apply probability theory in law.[6] Thomas Starkie, relying on Wood's *Algebra* and Laplace's *Theorie analitique des probabilités*, discussed the mathematical calculations of probabilities in connection with the concurrence of a number of independent probabilities in circumstantial evidence which increased in a compounded and multiplied proportion. While Starkie thought that one might reach a high probability by such calculations, he concluded they were nevertheless insufficient for conviction.[7] Wills referred derisively to the efforts of mathematicians who proposed numerical fractions for expressing moral certainty. He dismissed the logical explorations of Kirwan and Whately, feeling that their efforts to provide mathematical form to moral reasoning were unworkable in practice. Wills also denied Bentham's assertion that justice could be as precise as chemistry, and he indicated that the Benthamite scale that David Hoffman described in his *Course of Legal Study* was futile. Bentham had proposed a thermometerlike scale to measure belief, with positive and negative sides divided into degrees. Witnesses presumably would be asked to measure the strength of their beliefs.[8]

Best's treatise on presumptive evidence contains an appendix that deals with the application of probabilities to judicial evidence. Relying on Laplace's efforts to deal with testimonial and circumstantial evidence, Best concluded that circumstantial evidence can yield a higher probability than testimony. Best's more general treatise on evidence also takes up the topic. He, like Wills, rejects the Benthamite scale for measuring the certainty of witnesses. He also discusses the value of Laplace's (1819), Lacroix's (1833), and Poisson's (1837) efforts to calculate probabilities in connection with legal testimony. He discussed the *Encyclopaedia Britannica* article on probability, which had insisted on an analogy between life-insurance calculations and legal testimony.[9]

Notes

Preface

1. John Beattie, *Crime and the Courts in England, 1600–1800* (Princeton, 1986); John Langbein, *Prosecuting Crime in the Renaissance: England, Germany, France* (Cambridge, 1974); Thomas A. Green, *Verdict According to Conscience: Perspectives on the English Criminal Trial Jury, 1200–1800* (Chicago, 1985).

2. See James Thayer, *A Preliminary Treatise on Evidence at the Common Law* (Boston, 1898); John Wigmore, *The Principles of Judicial Proof as Given by Legal, Psychological and General Experience* (2d ed., Boston, 1931).

Chapter One

1. See Chapter 2 for a discussion of the presentment, or accusing, jury. See also Paul R. Hyams, "Trial by Ordeal: The Key to Proof in the Early Common Law," in *On the Laws and Customs of England*, ed. M. S. Arnold, Thomas A. Green, Sally A. Scully, and Stephen D. White (Chapel Hill, 1981), 90–126.

2. Roger D. Groot, "The Early Thirteenth-Century Criminal Jury," in *Twelve Good Men and True: The Criminal Trial Jury in England, 1200–1800*, ed. J. S. Cockburn and Thomas A. Green (Princeton, 1988), 18. Groot suggests presentment juries were used primarily to report those who had been suspected of crimes. This collection focuses on the jury composition and the tension between judges and juries.

3. Thomas A. Green, "A Retrospective on the Criminal Trial Jury, 1200–1800," in *Twelve Good Men*, ed. Cockburn and Green, 365. See also Green, *Verdict According to Conscience: Perspectives on the English Criminal Trial Jury, 1200–1800* (Chicago, 1985).

4. Edward Powell, "Jury Trial at Gaol Delivery in the Late Middle Ages: The Midland Circuit, 1400–1429," in *Twelve Good Men*, ed. Cockburn and Green, 78. See also Thomas A. Green, "The Jury and the English Law of Homicide, 1200–1600," *Michigan Law Review* 74 (1976): 423–499, at 424. See also, in *Twelve Good Men*, J. B. Post, "Jury Lists and Juries in the Late Fourteenth Century," 73, 74, 75; Bernard W. McLane, "Juror Attitudes toward Local Disorders: The Evidence of the 1328 Trailbaston Proceedings," 56–67.

5. Sir John Fortescue, *De Laudibus Legum Anglie*, ed. and trans. S. B. Chrimes (Cambridge, Mass., 1942), chap. 26. Witnesses were "neighbors able to live of their own repute and fair-minded." They were not brought into court by either party, but were chosen by a respectable and impartial officer and compelled to come before the judge.

6. Post, "Jury Lists," 75.

7. Edward Powell, "Jury Trial," 96. Powell estimates that criminal trials took an hour or less. Acquittals in cases of larceny, the staple of the gaol delivery business, were frequent. Cases brought by indictment resulted in a higher level of acquittals than for those initiated by appeal (89, 98, 105). It was not until the late seventeenth century that juries, at least on the home circuit, began to deliberate on each case as it was concluded. John Beattie, "London Juries in the 1690s," *Twelve Good Men*, ed. Cockburn and Green, 220.

8. Powell, "Jury Trial," 108, 110.

9. See John Langbein, *Prosecuting Crime in the Renaissance: England, Germany, France* (Cambridge, Mass., 1974). Powell suggests the change had occurred earlier. "Jury Trial," 79.

10. K. M. Teeven, "Seventeenth-Century Evidentiary Concerns and the Statute of Frauds," *Adelaide Law Review* 9 (1983): 225.

11. P. G. Lawson, "Lawless Juries? The Composition and Behavior of Hertfordshire Juries, 1573–1624," in *Twelve Good Men*, ed. Cockburn and Green, 123–124. Jurors were from the county but not usually from the parish where the offense occurred. Sir Matthew Hale's late seventeenth-century emphasis on the vicinage requirement thus did not conform to practice. Jurors were required to be of the vicinity until 1705.

12. See John M. Mitnick, "From Neighbor Witness to Judge of Proofs: The Transformation of the English Civil Juror," *American Journal of Legal History* 32 (1988): 203, 204. Mitnick describes the development of the English practice of granting new trials for verdicts given by juries against the evidence. For discussion of the criminal jury trial see Green, *Verdict According to Conscience*.

13. Quoted in Mitnick, "From Neighbor Witness," 219, citing J. Spedding, *An Account of the Life and Times of Francis Bacon* (London, 1880),

1:513. Almost identical language is contained in "The Royal Proclamation for Jurors: October 5, 1607," in *Stuart Royal Proclamations*, ed. J. F. Larkin and P. L. Hughes (Oxford, 1973), 1:168.

14. Matthew Hale, *History and Analysis of the Common Law of England* (London, 1820), xxviii, xxix, 346–347; *The History of the Pleas of the Crown*, 2 vols. (London, 1736), 2:277; see also Hale, *The Primitive Origination of Mankind* (London, 1677), 128; Barbara Shapiro, "Law and Science in Seventeenth-Century England," *Stanford Law Review* 21 (1969): 757–760.

15. See Richard H. Popkin, *The History of Scepticism from Erasmus to Spinoza* (Berkeley, 1979).

16. For efforts to link Bacon's scientific and legal views see Paul Kocher, "Francis Bacon and the Science of Jurisprudence," *Journal of the History of Ideas* 8 (1957): 3–26; Harvey Wheeler, "The Invention of Modern Empiricism: The Juridical Foundations of Francis Bacon's Philosophy of Science," *Law Library Journal* 76 (1983): 78–120; Kenneth Cardwell, "Francis Bacon and the Inquisition of Nature" (Paper delivered at the Pacific Coast Conference of British Studies, April 1986); Mark Neustadt, "The Relationship between Francis Bacon's Scientific and Legal Reform Programs" (Paper delivered at the International Congress of the History of Science, 1985).

17. See Barbara Shapiro, *Probability and Certainty in Seventeenth-Century England: A Study of the Relationships between Natural Science, Religion, History, Law and Literature* (Princeton, 1983); Henry Van Leeuwen, *The Problem of Certainty in English Thought, 1630–1690* (The Hague, 1963); R. M. Burns, *The Great Debate on Miracles* (London, 1981), 19–40; R. S. Westfall, *Religion and Science in Seventeenth-Century England* (New Haven, 1958).

18. John Wilkins, *Of the Principles and Duties of Natural Religion* (London, 1675), 7–8. Emphasis mine. See also 10–11.

19. Ibid., 7–8.

20. Walter Charleton, *Immortality of the Human Soul* (London, 1657), 186–188. Descartes also used the term "moral certainty" in connection with things about which "it seem[s] impossible to doubt . . . without extravagance" (e.g., that one has a body and that there are stars and the earth). René Descartes, *Discourse on Method*, trans. Arthur Wollaston (London, 1960), 1960.

21. See Shapiro, "Law and Science," 727–766, and *Probability and Certainty*, 163–193; Theodore Waldman, "Origins of the Legal Doctrine of Reasonable Doubt," *Journal of Historical Ideas* 20 (1959): 299–316; D. L. Patey, *Probability and Literary Form* (Cambridge, 1983); R. M. Sargent, "Scientific Experiment and Legal Expertise: The Way of Experi-

ence in Seventeenth-Century England," *Studies in the History and Philosophy of Science* 20 (1989): 9–46; Stephen A. Siegel, "The Aristotelian Basis of English Law, 1450–1800," *New York University Law Review* 56 (1981): 18–59.

22. John Locke, *An Essay Concerning Human Understanding*, ed. Alexander Fraser, 2 vols. (New York, 1959), bk. 4, chap. 16, secs. 6, 7, and 8. Locke frequently employs the language of witnesses.

23. Ibid., bk. 4, chap. 16, secs. 6–7.

24. Ibid., bk. 4, chap. 16, sec. 8.

25. Ibid., bk. 4, chap. 16, sec. 9. Section 10 contains a discussion on attesting documents and copies of documents and on hearsay evidence. Locke emphasized "that any testimony, the further off it is from being the actual truth, the less force and proof it has."

26. See Shapiro, *Probability and Certainty*, 15–73.

27. Ibid., 140–149, 155–159. See also Sargent, "Scientific Experiment," 19–45; Steven Shapin and Simon Schaeffer, *Leviathan and the Air Pump* (Princeton, 1985).

28. Seth Ward, *A Philosophical Essay toward an Eviction of God*, 1667 ed. (London, 1654), 84–88, 90, 99–101, 102, 107ff., 117.

29. Edward Stillingfleet, *Origines Sacrae* (London, 1662), passim. See also R. T. Carroll, *The Common Sense Philosophy of Bishop Edward Stillingfleet, 1635–1699* (The Hague, 1975); Richard Popkin, "The Philosophy of Bishop Stillingfleet," *Journal of the History of Philosophy* 9 (1971): 303–319. See also Samuel Parker, *A Demonstration of the Law of Nature and of the Christian Religion* (London, 1681), Preface, xxvii, xxix, 176, 179; Gerard Reedy, *The Bible and Reason: Anglicans and Scripture in Late Seventeenth-Century England* (Philadelphia, 1985); John Henry, "Roman Catholicism and the 'Motive Forces of the New Science'" (Paper delivered at International Workshop, Fifty Years of the Merton Thesis, May 1988, Tel Aviv University).

30. Joseph Addison, *The Works of the Right Honorable Joseph Addison* (London, 1721), 420.

31. Locke, *Essay*, bk. 4, chap. 15, sec. 5. His criteria may owe something to canon and civil law—suggesting the mutual influence of philosophy and law. Locke's residence in the Netherlands would undoubtedly have familiarized him with the civil law. See also Burns, *The Great Debate*, 59–61.

32. T. B. Howell, ed. *Complete Collection of State Trials*, 34 vols. (London, 1809–1826), 1: 392, 402, 521, 880, 881, 886, 901, 1013, 1054, 1320. (Hereafter referred to as *State Trials*.) "On your conscience . . . would you believe them?" 1 *State Trials*, 1071. See also 1 *State Trials*, 1049, 1051, 1061. In the Trial of Sir Thomas More (1535) jurors were told that

the decision about witness credibility rested on the "conscience and discretion" of the jury. 1 *State Trials*, 401. More was informed by the judge that the jury had found him "Guilty in their Conscience." 1 *State Trials*, 402. See also 1 *State Trials*, 1151. For Bacon's draft, see William Holdsworth, *A History of English Law*, 16 vols. (London, 1926–1964), 1: 333. For the proclamation, which was corrected and revised by Robert Cecil, see *Stuart Royal Proclamations*, 1: 167–171.

33. Matthew Hale, *History of the Common Law of England*, ed. Charles M. Gray (Chicago, 1971), 164, 165. Civil law judges in contrast were "precisely bound by rules."

34. Ibid., 164. Hale's *History of the Pleas of the Crown* also distinguishes between legal and credible witnesses (2: 277). Hale's legal writings do not indicate that he rejected the introduction of hearsay evidence from the courtroom. For a discussion of the hearsay rule see Chapter 4.

35. Hale, *Primitive Origination*, 129.

36. Ibid., 52, 128.

37. See Holdsworth, *History of English Law*, 9: 196, 204–209; J. H. Wigmore, "The Required Number of Witnesses," *Harvard Law Review* 15 (1901): 83, 88–90. Several sixteenth-century trials also indicate jurors were concerned with the credibility of witness testimony. See 1 *State Trials*, 392, 880, 881.

38. Before 1661 the law of treason seems to have required only the testimony of "legal," not "credible," witnesses. Older views, however, did not immediately disappear. Evidently few of the peers who had condemned the Earl of Stafford had "believed the witnesses." The witnesses had "sworn the facts," and therefore the peers claimed they had no choice but to accept them. Sometime after the trial Judge North angrily informed the peers who had expressed this view that their behavior was "contrary to the very institution of trials." They must not try "the grammatical construction of words . . . but the credibility of persons and things . . . which required collation of circumstances and a right judgement . . . if you believe the witnesses find, else not." Roger North, *The Lives of the Norths*, ed. A. Jessopp, 3 vols. (London, 1890), 1: 303–314.

Confusion concerning the treatment of witnesses by the jury was not the only type of difficulty. While it is clear that jurors had become judges of the facts, they were nevertheless still entitled to know things on their own. If by 1650 one judge had ruled that a juror who wished to present evidence must be heard on oath in court like any other witness; another judge in 1670 insisted they might still act on their knowledge. See R. W. Baker, *The Hearsay Rule* (London, 1950), citing *Benett v. Hartford* (1650); Sir John Vaughan, *The Reports and Arguments* (London, 1677), 135, 149. In 1698 Judge Holt ruled still somewhat tentatively: "In Case a

Jury give a Verdict upon their own knowledge, they ought to tell the Court so, but the fairest way would be for such of the Jurors as had knowledge of the matter before they are sworn, to inform the court of the thing, and be sworn as witnesses." Sir John Holt, *A Report of Diverse Cases* (London, 1708), 404. See also Mitnick, "From Neighbor Witness," 201–235.

39. See Green, *Verdict According to Conscience*, passim.

40. Most of the cases cited are from state trials because so few other reports include the charge to the jury. While we must rely heavily on state trials, which are unevenly distributed over time and frequently involve emotional political trials rather than more typical ones, we must use them because there is virtually no other evidence available. While the outcome of many of these cases was often predetermined, there is no reason to believe that the bench employed atypical legal concepts and terminology. But see Green, *Verdict According to Conscience*, 251–252. *The Proceedings at Old Bailey* are too brief to be helpful. Most report little more than verdicts. The High Court of Justice, the revolutionary tribunal that tried Charles I in 1649, ruled that the court was fully satisfied in its judgments and consciences "that the king was guilty."

41. 6 *State Trials*, 67, 82; 6 *State Trials*, 530, 559; 6 *State Trials*, 566, 614, 615; 6 *State Trials*, 879, 891.

42. Edward Waterhouse, *Fortescue Illustratus* (London, 1663), 259.

43. 6 *State Trials*, 999, 1005, 1006, 1008, 1110. If judges could direct verdicts, there would be no need for a jury. Justice Vaughan also noted that a jury might have personal knowledge of the case that the judge might not have. For discussion of the Penn-Mead trial and Bushel's case, see Green, *Verdict According to Conscience*, 200–249; John A. Phillips and Thomas C. Thompson, "Jurors v. Judges in Later Stuart England: The Penn-Mead Trial and 'Bushell's Case,'" *Law and Inequality: A Journal of Theory and Practice* 4 (1986): 189–229.

44. 8 *State Trials*, 13, 1386; 9 *State Trials*, 653, 666.

45. 7 *State Trials*, 250, 255; 7 *State Trials*, 715, 726; 7 *State Trials*, 959, 1054; 8 *State Trials*, 527, 550; 8 *State Trials*, 243, 338; 8 *State Trials*, 447, 489; 9 *State Trials*, 127, 178, 183; 9 *State Trials*, 299, 350; 9 *State Trials*, 637, 654.

46. 7 *State Trials*, 159, 220; 7 *State Trials*, 591, 681, 686; 7 *State Trials*, 1162, 1179; 8 *State Trials*, 243, 338; 8 *State Trials*, 747, 810.

47. 7 *State Trials*, 311, 414; 7 *State Trials*, 79, 135, 751; 7 *State Trials*, 1183, 1207; 7 *State Trials*, 1111, 1130. See also 7 *State Trials*, 715, 726; 8 *State Trials*, 747, 757. In other instances juries were required not only to weigh the credibility of witnesses but also to weigh and consider circumstantial evidence. 7 *State Trials*, 715, 726; 7 *State Trials*, 1162, 1179, 1180.

48. John Hawles, *The Englishman's Right: A Dialogue between a Barrister at Law and a Juryman* (London, 1680), 11.

49. Ibid., 35, 38, 47.

50. Henry Care, *English Liberties, or the Free-Born Subject's Inheritance* (London, n.d.), 214. See also Thomas Williams, *The Excellency and Praeheminence of the Laws of England* (London, 1680), 18. Many Whig writers of this era also used the language of the "satisfied" or "fully persuaded conscience" as appropriate for grand jury "verdicts." See Chapter 2.

51. See Thomas Wood, *English Casuistical Divinity in the Seventeenth Century* (London, 1952); H. R. McAdoo, *The Structure of Caroline Moral Theology* (London, 1949), 66; see also 79–80; Edmund Leites, ed., *Conscience and Casuistry in Early Modern Europe* (Cambridge, 1988), 123–124; Albert R. Jonsen and Stephen Toulmin, *The Abuse of Casuistry: A History of Moral Reasoning* (Berkeley, 1988). Green's *Verdict According to Conscience*, the most thorough study of the English criminal trial jury to date, does not explore the concept of conscience.

52. This had also been the position of most scholastic casuists, including St. Thomas Aquinas. Most held that conscience was an art of the practical intellect, not a moral feeling or movement of the will. T. F. Merill, *William Perkins: His Pioneer Works on Casuistry* (The Hague, 1966), x.

53. Ibid., 3, 5.

54. Ibid., 9, 32.

55. The position of William Ames, a casuist writing a decade or two after Perkins, also emphasized that the exercise of conscience involved an act of practical judgment and "proceeded from the Understanding." Ibid., 38; McAdoo, *Caroline Moral Theology*, 79.

56. Jeremy Taylor, *Ductor Dubitantum, or The Rule of Conscience in all her General Measures, Serving as a Great Instrument for the Determination of Cases of Conscience* (London, 1660), 3, 4. It is possible that the legal analogies of the casuists were drawn in part from the ecclesiastical courts, which employed Romano-canon procedure.

57. Ibid., 3, 30, 55. Taylor also discussed the "confident or erroneous conscience," "the probable or thinking conscience," and the "doubting conscience." The first is described in much the same way as latitudinarian theologians and natural philosophers described dogmatism and superstition. The "probable or thinking conscience," which lay between the "sure" and the "doubting" conscience, could, at least on certain occasions, be "made certain by accumulation of many probabilities operating the same persuasion" (90). Such an accumulation of probabilities might be

called "a moral demonstration." It required that both sides of a question be examined by an unbiased will. Christianity might be proved by "moral demonstration" (93–107). The "doubting conscience" was considered by Taylor to be a "disease" rather than a guide to human action (157).

58. McAdoo, *Caroline Moral Theology*, 77, quoting Robert South, *Works* (Oxford, 1828), sermon 23, no page cited.

59. John Locke, *Two Tracts on Government*, ed. Philip Abrams (Cambridge, 1967), 225.

60. John Locke, *Essays on the Law of Nature*, ed. W. von Leyden (Oxford, 1954), 165.

61. Samuel Pufendorf, *Of the Law of Nature and Nations*, 1st English ed. (London, 1703), 11, 17–18. Six editions were printed in England between 1691 and 1739.

62. Ibid., 17, 21. It seems likely that concepts relevant to the law and philosophy of evidence may be traced by considering the evolution of moral theology, moral evidence, and discussions of evidence in the human and natural sciences. Samuel Clarke's *Discourse Concerning Natural Religion*, 3d ed., 1711 (London, 1706) explicitly uses the language of "satisfaction," "evidence of matter of fact," "reasonable and sufficient proof" in connection with legal dispute and proofs of Christianity, 14, 331–334, 336–337. For a discussion of Thomas Reid on moral judgments, see S. A. Grove, *The Scottish Philosophy of Common Sense* (Oxford, 1960), 239–240, 245, 246. Like the casuists, Reid insists that moral judgments were rational judgments and were based on feeling or sentiment. Such judgments were not "demonstrative" but "highly probable" because they depended on particular matters of fact.

63. See John Langbein, "The Criminal Trial before the Lawyers," *University of Chicago Law Review* 45 (1978): 263–316; John Langbein, "Shaping the Eighteenth-Century Trial: A View from the Ryder Sources," *University of Chicago Law Review* 50 (1983): 1–136.

64. 10 *State Trials*, 147, 242; 11 *State Trials*, 297, 370; 12 *State Trials*, 645, 810; 12 *State Trials*, 833, 870; 12 *State Trials*, 949, 1042; 12 *State Trials*, 1377, 1455; 13 *State Trials*, 63, 133; 13 *State Trials*, 139, 265; 13 *State Trials*, 313, 393. In a perjury trial the jury was directed to "weigh and consider what is sworn now, and from thence to make a conclusion whether you are not satisfied that innocent blood has been spilt by means of this fellow." 10 *State Trials*, 1079, 1212. "Take care to examine strictly and impartially . . . and weigh the evidence which has been given on all sides . . . it is incumbent upon you to inquire whether you have not sufficient reason to be satisfied that the truth is now" (1212). "If you think that the witnesses swear true, as I cannot see any colour of objection,

there does not remain the least doubt . . . that the accused" was guilty
(1211). The accused in this case was Titus Oates. See J. P. Kenyan, "The
Acquittal of Sir George Wakemann, 18 July 1679," *Historical Journal* 14
(1971): 693–708.

65. In the *Trial of Stafford* (1680), however, the prosecution indicated
that "the evidence is so strong, that I think admits of no doubt." The
proofs are "so clear and evident, as will leave no room to your lordships
to believe" Stafford's protestations. 7 *State Trials*, 1293, 1305, 1515, 1517.
In the *Trial of Langhorn* the recorder indicated there was not the "least
reason for the most scrupulous men to doubt the credibility of the witnesses." *Trial of Langhorn* (London, 1679), 67. See also 10 *State Trials*,
1211.

66. "If you are satisfied with the whole matter" was not an atypical
formulation. 14 *State Trials*, 377, 445; 16 *State Trials*, 93, 299. The phrase
"the whole matter" refers to a combination of witness testimony and circumstantial evidence. See also Chapter 3.

67. 14 *State Trials*, 517, 535; 15 *State Trials*, 521, 611; 15 *State Trials*,
613, 651; 16 *State Trials*, 93, 299; 17 *State Trials*, 461, 522; 17 *State Trials*,
1063, 1078–1089; 17 *State Trials*, 1079, 1090.

68. 16 *State Trials*, 93, 299; 17 *State Trials*, 161, 208–209.

69. Occasionally different terminology was employed. Thus one judge
used, "if you are sensible and convinced." 17 *State Trials*, 1625, 1675.
Another indicated a guilty verdict was appropriate if the jury had no doubt
upon the evidence, (17 *State Trials*, 211, 226). Doubt in the jury's mind
was still not often raised.

70. For the increased importance of legal counsel in criminal trials see
Langbein, "The Criminal Trial," 263–316. See also Felix Rackow, "The
Right to Counsel: American and English Precedents," *William and Mary
Quarterly* 11 (1954): 4–27.

71. 21 *State Trials*, 687, 713, 813, 814; 25 *State Trials*, 226, 288; 25
State Trials, 783, 876; 26 *State Trials*, 387, 414; 26 *State Trials*, 595, 652;
26 *State Trials*, 721, 811; 26 *State Trials*, 839, 872. Another common formula asked the "opinion" of the jury. 19 *State Trials*, 1177, 1233; 25 *State
Trials*, 876, 877; 25 *State Trials*, 1003, 1154; 26 *State Trials*, 910, 1008; 27
State Trials, 1, 138. "Opinion" had a far lower status than "satisfied belief"
in common terminology and would have been viewed as far below "moral
certainty."

72. 19 *State Trials*, 485, 647; 21 *State Trials*, 687, 814; 21 *State Trials*,
847, 949–950; 22 *State Trials*, 175, 208; 26 *State Trials*, 225, 280–281.

73. 9 *State Trials*, 745, 845; 21 *State Trials*, 485, 647; 22 *State Trials*,
753, 822; 25 *State Trials*, 1003, 1154; 27 *State Trials*, 1, 138.

74. 24 *State Trials*, 199, 1383. See also 25 *State Trials*, 1003, 1154. The "judgment" would consider whether the weight of the evidence was sufficient or not. 26 *State Trials*, 1, 222.

75. 26 *State Trials*, 225, 286. A guilty verdict was appropriate "if your understandings are absolutely coerced to believe." Coerced assent for Locke and others was associated with the highest degree of probability, or "moral certainty."

76. 26 *State Trials*, 437, 457. In another case the jury was advised to judge "by the result of the evidence and the clear impressions that the result shall make upon your minds." It was not to judge on mere probabilities. 25 *State Trials*, 743, 731. In another they were to find the truth "according to your conscience and the best of your judgments." 26 *State Trials*, 295, 350. In still another, the evidence was to carry "conviction brought home to your minds." 26 *State Trials*, 295, 351. See also 26 *State Trials*, 353, 386; 26 *State Trials*, 387, 437; 23 *State Trials*, 1167, 1386.

77. 15 *State Trials*, 783, 876, 877. In another case jurors were told, "If the scale should hang doubtful," and they were not "fully satisfied," they should acquit. 21 *State Trials*, 485, 647; see also 22 *State Trials*, 471, 519. In another case jurors were told to acquit if "there remains any doubt upon the case." 25 *State Trials*, 1, 739. Judges who raised the possibility of doubt were also more likely to suggest the possibility of acquittal. Jurors were thus more likely to be reminded that the benignity of English law was in favor of life and of the legal maxim that it is preferable for ten or even one hundred guilty men to go free than for one innocent man to die. The maxim, which may have a Romano-canon origin, appears in Hale's unpublished diary. See Maija Jansson, "Matthew Hale on Judges and Judging," *Journal of Legal History* 9 (1989): 208.

78. *The Genuine Trial of Swann* (London, 1752), 4.

79. Anthony A. Morano, "A Reexamination of the Reasonable Doubt Rule," *Boston University Law Review* 55 (1975): 507–528.

80. William Paley's lectures written in the 1760s and 1770s, however, complained of the

overstrained scrupulousness, or weak timidity of juries, which demands often such proof of a prisoner's guilt, as the nature and secrecy of his crime scarce permit of; and which holds it is the part of a *safe* conscience not to condemn any man, whilst there exists the minutest possibility of his innocence. . . . I do not mean that juries should indulge conjectures, should magnify suspicions into proofs, or even that they should weigh probabilities in *gold scales*; but when the preponderation of evidence is so manifest as to persuade every private understanding of the prisoner's guilt; when it furnishes the degree of credibility, upon which men decide and act in all other doubts, and which experience hath shown that they may decide and act upon with sufficient safety; to reject such proof, from an insinuation of uncertainty that belongs to all human affairs, and from a general dread lest the charge of innocent blood should lie at their doors, is a conduct which . . . is authorized by no considerations of rectitude or utility.

William Paley, *Principles of Moral and Political Philosophy*, 9th ed., Boston, 1818 (London, 1785), 354–355. Paley rejected the validity of the maxim that it is better that ten guilty persons escape than a single innocent man should suffer (356).

81. See Morano, "A Reexamination," 516–519.

82. *The Legal Papers of John Adams*, ed. L. Wroth and H. Zobel, 3 vols. (Cambridge, Mass., 1965), 3:270, 271, 273, 292, 299, 300, 309. John Adams, on another occasion, argued that juries had the right and duty "to find the Verdict of the Case according to his own best Understanding, Judgment and Conscience," even though it might be in direct opposition to the direction of the court (1: 230).

83. Geoffrey Gilbert, *The Law of Evidence* (Dublin, 1754). It would not, therefore, be unreasonable to expect beyond reasonable doubt language any time after 1754, the year Gilbert's treatise first appeared. Yet it does not appear in the published *State Trials* until 1795, and it is not to be found in Coke, Hale, or Blackstone.

84. *Whole Proceedings of Old Bailey* (London, 1777), 110–111.

85. 26 *State Trials*, 721, 811. They were also instructed to convict if they believed the evidence.

86. 26 *State Trials*, 222, 280–281, 286, 289.

87. 26 *State Trials*, 295, 351. Jurors in the same case were also told that they should decide "according to your conscience, and the best of your judgments" (349, 350); 26 *State Trials*, 353, 385–387. In another 1796 case, the judge informed the jury, "if you believe that from any rational consideration," a particular witness was not entitled to credit, they must acquit. If they were "in suspense" or "suspended in doubt," they should also acquit. 26 *State Trials*, 387, 414, 419.

In the *Trial of Sheares* (1797), the judge indicated that if the jury "entertain any rational doubt, not merely a capricious doubt, but the doubt of sensible men," then they should acquit. 27 *State Trials*, 355, 391. In a 1798 case they were advised that if they "entertain a fair and conscientious doubt" as to the credit of the witnesses or as to "the sufficiency of the evidence," they should acquit. *Trial of MacCann* (1798), 27 *State Trials*, 399, 453–454.

In still another 1798 Irish case, defense counsel indicated that if the jury's conscience was satisfied on the evidence then they should convict, but if they had a rational doubt then they should acquit. The judge noted that if they were "not satisfied with the weight of the evidence, or entertain[ed] such doubts upon the cases, as rational and conscientious minds may well indulge in," they should acquit. If "satisfied" in their "consciences" that the evidence were true, they must find the accused guilty. *Trial of Byrne* (1798), 27 *State Trials*, 455, 494, 523. See also the *Trial of Bond* (1798), 27 *State Trials*, 523, 611; *Trial of Tuite* (1799), 27 *State Trials*, 1121, 1135. In 1803, Lord Nocking explained they were to acquit if they had a "rational and well grounded doubt." *Trial of Donnelly* (1803), 28 *State Trials*, 1069, 1097.

88. *Trial of Kennedy* (1796), 26 *State Trials*, 353, 386–387.

89. *Trial of Glennan* (1796), 26 *State Trials*, 437, 457. See also *Trial of the Bishop of Bangor* (1796), 26 *State Trials*, 463, 527. The beyond reasonable doubt standard also appeared in the *Trial of Dun* (1796), 26 *State Trials*, 872, 877, 878, and the *Trial of Finerty* (1797), 26 *State Trials*, 901, 1008. In the *Trial of Finney* (1798) the judge indicated that the evidence must be "full and complete in your minds, and such as ought to satisfy your conscience." They were to be "satisfied beyond all possibility of doubt, that the testimony which you have heard is true." 26 *State Trials*, 1019, 1132.

90. *Trial of Lyon* (1799) for seditious libel, reprinted in Francis Wharton, *State Trials of the United States during the Adminstrations of Washington and Adams* (Philadelphia, 1849), 333, 336.

91. Wharton, *State Trials*, 458, 548. Many American colonies permitted defense counsel earlier than the English, despite the fact there initially were few trained lawyers in the colonies. The right to counsel was embodied in the Sixth Amendment. The absence of defense counsel had been justified by Coke on the grounds that guilt should be so obvious that no defense was possible and that the judge would act as counsel for the defense. Edward Coke, *Institutes of the Lawes of England* (London, 1628–1644), 3: 137. See also William Hawkins, *A Treatise of the Pleas of the Crown* (London, 1717), chap. 39, sec. 2. Blackstone, however, complained that it was not reasonable to deny counsel in cases of felony and yet to allow them for misdemeanor. William Blackstone, *Commentaries on the Laws of England*, 4 vols. (London, 1765–1769), 4: 355. In 1696 legislation permitted counsel in cases of treason. In 1836 a right to counsel was provided. See Rackow, "The Right to Counsel," 4–27.

92. Wharton, *State Trials*, 553, 554, 578, 586. In the *Trials of Richard Smith*, defense counsel reminded the jury "if there remain a single doubt, it is your duty to have that doubt completely removed, before you convict." *Trials of Richard Smith* (1816), 206.

93. Commonwealth v. Webster, 59 Mass. (5 Cush.), 320 (1850). This definition was widely adopted. Morano, "A Reexamination," 523 n. 23.

94. Although the beyond reasonable doubt doctrine became a feature of both English and American law, it must have operated somewhat dif-

ferently insofar as judges were differentially regulated in assisting jurors in making their determination. Although I often refer to the Anglo-American legal tradition, one should not assume that English and American practice developed in identical ways. An important example is found in divergent approaches to judicial comment on the facts and expressions of opinion as to the credibility of witnesses. Although these practices were accepted in the eighteenth century by both English and colonial judges, they began to be abandoned and prohibited in American jurisdictions beginning in 1795 and were eliminated in most American jurisdictions between 1835 and 1860. By 1913, forty-one states prohibited judicial comment, largely on the grounds that the prohibition would produce a more impartial trial. Critics insisted jurors were better fact finders than judges and that to allow judicial comment would, in effect, turn the fact-finding process over to the judiciary. American suspicion of the judiciary appears to have increased as that of the English waned. If differences in democratic sentiment were significant, so too were the differences between English and American judges. The former were fewer in number and were selected from among the most respected members of the legal profession. The far more numerous American judges were recruited from a much broader spectrum of the population and were frequently elected. English judges became more powerful in relation to jurors from c. 1725 as they increasingly relied on the directed verdict, which reduced jury participation in decision making. See Kenneth Krasity, "The Role of the Judge in Jury Trials: The Elimination of Judicial Evaluation of Fact in American State Courts from 1795–1913," *University of Detroit Law Review* 62 (1985): 595, 596, 608, 610, 616, 619. For a somewhat parallel development in which English judges gained control over juries in civil cases see Mitnick, "From Neighbor Witness," 201–235. In 1854 English legislation introduced the possibility of trial of facts by a judge without a jury. The result was the near disappearance of the civil jury (234).

95. For the treatise tradition see A. W. B. Simpson, "The Rise and Fall of the Legal Treatise: Legal Principles and the Forms of Legal Literature," *University of Chicago Law Review* 48 (1981): 632–680; William Twining, "The Rationalist Tradition of Evidence Scholarship," in *Well and Truly Tried: Essays on Evidence in Honour of Sir Richard Eggleston*, ed. Enid Campbell and Louis Waller (Sydney, Australia, 1982), 211–249.

96. Gilbert, *Law of Evidence*, 1–2. Editions appeared in 1756, 1760, 1761, 1764, 1769, 1777, 1788, 1790, 1791–1794, 1795–1797, 1801. His treatise was composed before 1726, the year of his death.

97. Ibid., 3. Gilbert discusses both certainty and probability. Certainty was obtained by a "clear and distinct perception" of the senses and

a "way of knowledge by necessary Inferences" (1–2). See also Geoffrey Gilbert, *Abstract of Mr. Locke's Essay on Human Understanding* (Dublin, 1752), 42, 45–47.

As we judge by our Experience, so also we judge by the Sight, Observation, and Experience of others; and this is called Testimony. And in this light things are considerable: (1) The Number. (2) The Integrity. (3) The Skill of the Witnesses. (4) Their True Design and Interests. (5) The Consistency of the Parts and Circumstances of the Relation. (6) Contrary Testimonies. (7) The Consistence of what is attested with our own Observation and Experience. And (8) The Distance of such relators from the Sight and View of the Thing which they attest; which is so far weakened as they themselves take it from others, and the Thing related doth not fall under their own View or Experience. These are the Criterions of Probability, touching Facts depending on mere human Agents. (48–49)

For an important treatment of the history of legal evidence, see William Twining, *Theories of Evidence: Bentham and Wigmore* (London, 1985). Twining views the Anglo-American evidence scholarship of Gilbert to be rooted in English empiricism, that is, in Locke, Bentham, J. S. Mill, Sidgwick, and modern analytical philosophers such as A. J. Ayers (see 1–18).

98. Twining, *Theories of Evidence*, 4.

99. See Shapiro, *Probability and Certainty*, chaps. 1 and 2, and Shapiro, *John Wilkins, 1614–1672: An Intellectual Biography* (Berkeley, 1969); Theodore Waldman, "Origins," 312–313.

100. John Morgan, *Essays upon the Law of Evidence*, 2 vols. (London, 1789), 1: 1, 2–3, 4–5. Morgan also refers to Paley on evidence. Witness credibility and circumstantial evidence governed judgment in legal trials (1: 39, 48–49). The credibility of a witness was to be judged from his "state and dignity in the world," his religiosity, moral condition, interest in the cause, intelligence, and memory (1: 46). The quality, education, behavior, and understanding of a witness must also be taken into account (1: 12–13). See also 1: 47, 146–255.

Morgan also discussed concurrent testimony, circumstantial evidence, the doctrine of presumptions, and how to evaluate the credibility of witnesses. Morgan, like most later writers on evidence, devotes a good deal of time and space to a proper understanding of presumptions and circumstantial evidence. See Chapter 4.

101. James Wilson, *The Works*, ed. James DeWitt Andrews, 2 vols. (Chicago, 1896), 1: 486, 505.

102. For a discussion of the Scottish school, see S. A. Grove, *The Scottish Philosophy of Common Sense* (Oxford, 1960), 3–6, 27, 87–92, 96, 138. Reid thus disagreed with Locke's distinction between knowledge and judgment. Thomas Reid, *Essays on the Intellectual Powers of Man* (Cam-

bridge, 1850), 328–329. See also 313–317. For Reid on probable reasoning see 411ff. Reid was also concerned with doubt. "Belief is mixed with doubt more or less, until we come to the highest degree of evidence, when all doubt vanishes and the belief is firm and immovable . . . this is called certainty" (413–415).

103. Wilson, *Works*, 1: 518, 519.

104. Ibid., 1: 508, 510.

105. Ibid., 1: 503–504; 2: 232. Wilson raised the issue of the jurors' doubt while considering the problem of unanimous verdicts. If a "single doubt" remains in the mind of any juror, it must produce the dissent of that particular juror. If that dissent is believed, all other jurors should agree to an acquittal (235). Wilson may have been the first to discuss the problem of producing unanimous verdicts in the context of evidentiary concerns.

106. Leonard McNally, *The Rules of Evidence on Pleas of the Crown* (London and Dublin, 1802), 3.

107. Daniel McKinnon, *The Philosophy of Evidence* (London, 1812), 20, 24, 25, 27, 64. Common sense "must be the only guide" for determining the jury's belief (53).

108. Samuel Phillipps, *Theory of Presumptive Proof* (London, 1814), 58. Quoted in anonymous article in *American Law Review* 10 (1876): 642–664, 658. Zephaniah Swift's *Digest of the Law of Evidence in Civil and Criminal Cases* (Hartford, 1810) indicates evidence "must be sufficient to convince and satisfy the mind," and if the jury entertains a reasonable doubt, then it was bound to acquit (151). The 1806 Kentucky revision of the criminal law not only begins with a Lockean treatment of evidence in criminal prosecutions, but also discusses the several degrees of evidence and certainty in history, natural history, astronomy, and law. It also contains the beyond reasonable doubt language. Harry Toulmin and James Blair, *A Revision of the Criminal Law of the Commonwealth of Kentucky*, 2 vols. (Frankfurt, Kentucky, 1806), 2: 317–318.

109. David Hartley, *Observations on Man* (London, 1749), 204–230, 362.

110. Isaac Watts, *Logick, or The Right Use of Reason in the Inquiry after Truth*, 1st ed., 1724 (London, 1775), 175, 177, 247, 266–271.

111. George Campbell, *The Philosophy of Rhetoric*, ed. L. Bitzer (Carbondale, Ill., 1963), 44, 55. See also 43ff. *The Philosophy of Rhetoric* was composed about 1750 and published in 1776.

112. Richard Kirwan, *Logick, or An Essay on the Elements, Principles and Different Modes of Reasoning*, 2 vols. (London, 1807), 1:x.

113. Ibid., 1:146, 151. See also 224.

114. See, e.g., ibid., 2: 354, 555. Among others, he refers to Gilbert,

Capel Lofft, and Thomas Peake, authors or editors of evidence treatises. He particularly praises McNally.

115. James Gambier, *A Guide to the Study of Moral Evidence, or of that Species of Reasoning which Relates to Matters of Fact and Practice* (Boston, 1834), 49.

116. Ibid., 49, 50.

117. Ibid., 55.

118. Ibid., 17.

119. Ibid., 57–58, 59.

120. Ibid., 66.

121. Ibid., 17. The book treated the different kinds of moral evidence, e.g., observation, testimony, and mixed. Testimony is direct or incidental, spoken or written. The credibility of testimony is also discussed. Report, tradition, analogy, and the differences between presumption and proof are analyzed.

122. John Abercrombie, *Inquiries Concerning the Intellectual Powers and the Investigation of Truth* (Edinburgh, 1820), 17–19, 79, 82–84, 89–93.

123. James Glassford, *An Essay on the Principles of Evidence and Their Applications to the Subject of Judicial Inquiry* (Edinburgh and London, 1820), ii, iii.

124. Ibid., vii–viii, 8.

125. Thomas Starkie, *Practical Treatise on the Law of Evidence*, 2 vols., 1833 ed. (London, 1824), 15.

126. Ibid., 478.

127. Ibid., 514.

128. David Hoffman, *A Lecture on Law* (Baltimore, 1826), 17–18, 17n–18n.

129. Ibid., 19. Hoffman's *Course of Legal Study* (Baltimore, 1817) recommended Locke's *Essay*, Paley's *Principles of Moral and Political Philosophy*, Reid's *Essays on the Intellectual Powers of Man*, Pufendorf's *Law of Nature and Nations*, and McNally's *Rules of Evidence* (219). Bentham's early writings are also discussed. Hoffman also recommended that American law students study the civil law. He particularly recommended Domat on proofs and presumptions and the evidentiary works of Everhardus, Mascardus, Menochius, and Farinaccius (235, 251–269).

130. Jeremy Bentham, *Rationale of Judicial Evidence*, 5 vols. (London, 1827). See Twining, *Theories of Evidence*, 26, 29. For the Benthamite approach to evidence, see 19–108. For Bentham's use of degrees of persuasion and moral certainty see 55–56. See also Gerald J. Postema, "Fact, Fictions, and Law: Bentham on the Foundations of Evidence," in *Facts in Law*, ed. William Twining (Wiesbaden, 1983), vol. 16, 37–64;

William Twining, "Rule Scepticism in Bentham's Theory of Evidence," in *Facts in Law*, 65–81.

131. See Simpson, "The Rise and Fall of the Legal Treatise," 632–679. William Wills, *An Essay on the Principles of Circumstantial Evidence* (London, 1838) shares many features of the more general treatise.

132. Simon Greenleaf, *Treatise on the Law of Evidence*, 2d. ed. (Boston, 1844), 4–5. Greenleaf also noted that our "faith in human testimony, as sanctioned by experience; that is upon the generally experienced truth of the statements of men of integrity, having capacity and opportunity for observation, and truth. This belief is strengthened by our previous knowledge of the narrator's reputation for veracity; by the absence of conflicting testimony; and by the presence of that, which is corroborating and cumulative." (P. 14)

133. Ibid., 14, 15, 18. See also 50–51, 54–55.

134. James Thayer, *A Preliminary Treatise on Evidence at the Common Law* (Boston, 1898), 268–269, 271–272, 273–275, 284. For Thayer's differentiation of the rules of evidence and the precepts of logic, see Twining, *Theories of Evidence*, 6–8.

Sir James Fitzjames Stephen indicated that his work was founded on Mill's *Logic* as Gilbert's was founded on Locke's. Sir James Fitzjames Stephen, *Digest of the Law of Evidence* (New York, 1885), xii. William Best indicated judicial evidence was "for the most part, nothing else than natural evidence, restrained or modified by rules of positive law." Best claimed he was seeking the principles behind the cases. William Best, *The Principles of the Law of Evidence*, 6th ed. (London, 1875), 2. For a discussion of the "human understanding," the nature of truth, and witness credibility see 4–29. See also 56–62.

135. John Wigmore, *The Principles of Judicial Proof as Given by Legal, Psychological and General Experience*, 2d ed. (Boston, 1931), 3–5. For an important recent discussion of Wigmore see Twining, *Theories of Evidence*, 109–166.

136. Wigmore, *Principles*, 5–6.

137. Twining, *Theories of Evidence*, 125. See also 114–116, 119–122.

138. Although the to a moral certainty and beyond reasonable doubt formulations have been in place in most Anglo-American jurisdictions for many decades, there still has been an ongoing discussion of these formulations. While this is not the place to carry on a thorough investigation of the modern jurisprudential discussion of jury instructions, it is appropriate to suggest something about the nature of twentieth-century discussion.

In a good many United States jurisdictions the phrase "to a moral certainty" has been coupled with belief "beyond reasonable doubt." This coupling has caused confusion and ambiguity as the term "moral certitude" disappeared from common usage. Justice Stanley Mosk's concurrence in the California case of *People v. Brigham* [25 Cal. 3d 283, 292–316, 599 P.2d 100, 107–121, 157 Cal. Rptr. 905, 913–27 (1979) (Justice Mosk concurring)] suggests something of the growing concern. His view, which was recently incorporated into a bill before the California legislature, would strip everything except the phrase "reasonable doubt" from the judicial instruction. In the activity surrounding this discussion and in the proposals for change, the phrase "moral certainty" has been singled out as causing the most difficulty. Indeed Justice Mosk himself recently issued a challenge: "I'd like to hear someone attempt to tell . . . [us] what moral certainty is." *San Francisco Chronicle*, 6 May 1986, p. 9, col. 1. This chapter has suggested that moral certainty and beyond reasonable doubt were originally viewed as synonymous. In this context, elimination of a term which no longer carries any commonly understood meaning probably makes sense. After all, the term "satisfied conscience," which also carried much the same meaning, has for the most part been dropped as belief in the rational and judicial characteristics of "conscience" has waned. There is thus reason and judicial precedent for attempting to make the language of judicial instruction consistent with common usage. Although archaic legal terminology constitutes little problem for legal professionals familiar with legal languages and terms of art, it can be problematic for the layperson who only occasionally serves on criminal juries.

Perhaps because English and Australian jury instructions have not contained the language of moral certainty, discussion in those countries has centered on whether or not judges may, or should attempt to, explain the meaning of "reasonable doubt" to juries—or whether the term should be used at all. Thus, in a much-cited English case of 1952 Lord Goddard C. J. states:

I have never yet heard any Court give a real definition of what is a 'reasonable doubt' and it would be very much better if that expression were not used. Whenever a court attempts to explain . . . the explanation tends to result in confusion rather than clarity. It is far better instead of using the words 'reasonable doubt' and then attempting to say what is a reasonable doubt, to say to a jury: 'You must not convict unless you are satisfied by the evidence given by the prosecution that the offense has been committed.'

R v. Summers, (1952) 1 T.L.R. 1164. English courts still attempt to improve on the traditional formulation.

Australian courts have retained the beyond reasonable doubt formulation, and it is thought undesirable for judges to attempt to enlarge or explain it. See *R v. Deathe*, (1962) V.R. 650 (Vic. Sup. Ct. F.C.); *Harold v. the King*, (1941) Q.S.R. 190 (Q. Ct. of Cr. App.). In *Dawson v. the*

Queen, currently the leading Australian case, C. Dixon C. J. indicated it is a

mistake to depart from time-honored formula [beyond reasonable doubt]. It is, I think, used by ordinary people and is understood well enough by the average man in the community. The attempts to substitute other expressions, of which there have been many examples not only here but in England, have never prospered. It is wise as well as proper to avoid such expressions.

Dawson v. the Queen, 106 *Commonwealth Law Reports,* 18; *A.L.J.R.* 360 (1962). See also *Brown v. the King,* (1913) 17 RR 570; 20 *A.L.R.* 197; *R v. Murray,* (1924) V.L.R. 374; 46 *A.L.T.* 35 (Vic. Sup. Ct. F.C.); *Thomas v. the Queen,* (1) (1960) *C.L.R.* 584. See also C. E. W. "Reasonable Doubt in Criminal Cases," *Australian Law Journal* 1 (1928): 291–292, 372–373. For a review of English and Australian developments, see Sir Richard Eggleston, "Sixth Wilfred Fullegar Memorial Lecture: 'Beyond Reasonable Doubt,'" *Monash Law Review* 4 (1977): 1–19.

Chapter Two

1. Naomi Hurnard not only attempted to trace a tradition of communal accusation throughout the later Saxon and Norman periods, but also suggested that compurgation, rather than the ordeal, was the rule when communal accusation was based solely on circumstantial evidence. Naomi Hurnard, "The Jury of Presentment and the Assizes of Clarendon," *English Historical Review* 61 (1941): 371–410.

2. It has recently been suggested that early presentment juries were even more concerned with evidentiary matters than Hurnard thought. Roger Groot finds that early presentment juries did more than merely submit those suspected to the ordeal. He believes that they gave their opinion of the accuracy of the accusation and only those they thought truly accused were sent to the ordeal. Roger D. Groot, "The Jury of Presentment before 1215," *American Journal of Legal History* 26 (1982): 1–24.

3. For parallels between canon law and early grand jury procedures see R. H. Helmholz, "The Early History of the Grand Jury and the Canon Law," *University of Chicago Law Review* 50 (1983): 613–627.

4. Groot, "Jury of Presentment," 21.

5. Raoul C. Van Caenegem, rejecting Hurnard's contention of a continued existence from Anglo-Saxon times, emphasizes the example of the ecclesiastical courts and Norman institutions as central in the institution of public prosecution of crime as well as in the role of the Crown. "Public Prosecution of Crime in Twelfth-Century England," in *Church and Government in the Middle Ages,* ed. C. N. L. Brooke et al. (Cambridge, 1976),

41–76. See also J. W. Baldwin, "The Intellectual Preparation for the Canon of 1215 against Ordeals," *Speculum* 36 (1961): 613–663.

6. Groot, "Jury of Presentment," 4, citing Glanvill, *The Treatise on the Laws and Customs of the Realm of England Commonly called Glanvill*, ed. D. D. G. Hall (1965), 174, 175.

7. In practice this meant reporting community suspicion and rumor. But they also appeared to have evaluated the accusation. Before the accused underwent the ordeal, the jurors personally had to suspect the accused. Thus a good man suspected by the community rarely faced the ordeal. In most cases analyzed by Groot, the jurors' opinion of the guilt of the accused can be distinguished textually from the accusation. Groot calls this "an adjudicatory act," and suggests that the verdict of suspected or not suspected was in many respects equivalent to guilty or not guilty, even though the decision was at this stage self-informing—not weighing testimony. He has called this a "medial," rather than "final," decision in that those suspected would still be required to make their proof by ordeal. Groot, "Jury of Presentment," 6, 11, 23, 23n, 24.

8. Roger Groot, "The Early Thirteenth-Century Criminal Jury," in *Twelve Good Men and True: The Criminal Trial Jury in England, 1200–1800*, ed. J. S. Cockburn and Thomas A. Green (Princeton, 1988), 8, 22.

9. Richard Helmholz suggests that the prosecution of offenders on the basis of "public fame" was borrowed by the Assize of Clarendon from the ecclesiastical courts. Helmholz, "The Early History of the Grand Jury and the Canon Law," 620, 624. See also Richard Wunderli's discussion of ill fame as a basis for prosecution in fifteenth-century ecclesiastical courts. "London Church Courts and Society on the Eve of the Reformation," *Speculum*, Anniversary Monographs, no. 7 (Cambridge, Mass., 1981): 31–32, 40.

10. Thomas A. Green, *Verdict According to Conscience: Perspectives on the English Criminal Trial Jury, 1200–1800* (Chicago, 1985), 22, 25–26; R. B. Pugh, "Some Reflections of a Medieval Criminologist," *Proceedings of the British Academy* 59 (1973): 83–104.

11. John Langbein has suggested that as local magistrates undertook a more active prosecutorial role, they "sealed the fate of the jury of accusation." The task of gathering and assessing information and suspicion, crucial to deciding whether or not a trial would take place, had passed to the justices of the peace by the later sixteenth century and had insured the passivity of both grand and petty juries. Grand juries were, he argues, thus reduced to largely ceremonial functions. John Langbein, *Prosecuting Crime in the Renaissance: England, Germany, France* (Cambridge, Mass., 1974), 119, 120, 127, 127n.

If Langbein is correct, there would be little reason to concern oneself with the evidentiary standard of the grand jury. Why would one bother to investigate an institution of so little importance? First, its ideological status alone suggests that its study cannot be ignored. In addition, Thomas Green's investigation of trial jury discretion suggests that grand juries were unlikely to have become entirely passive instruments. Petty juries carefully exercised discretionary and nullification powers to insure results that seemed reasonable, particularly in cases involving life and death. Early modern trial juries frequently undervalued stolen goods to avoid inflicting the death penalty and distinguished between intentional homicide and manslaughter. Green, *Verdict According to Conscience*, 13, 144.

J. S. Cockburn, too, believes that grand juries had become largely ceremonial and rarely returned *ignoramus* verdicts. He, however, found that committing magistrates were often not present at the assizes, and thus could not have played an active prosecutorial role. J. S. Cockburn, *A History of English Assizes, 1558–1714* (Cambridge, 1972), 73–75, 77–79.

If petty jurors, usually of lower social status than grand jurors, exercised discretion in the presence of judges of considerably higher social standing and status, it seems unlikely that grand jurors, typically chosen from the more respected and powerful members of the community, would adopt a passive stance toward justices of the peace who were typically their social equals. For the social composition of sixteenth- and seventeenth-century grand and petty juries, see P.G. Lawson, "Lawless Juries? The Composition and Behavior of Hertfordshire Juries, 1573–1624," in *Twelve Good Men*, ed. Cockburn and Green, 122, 123, 124, 127, 130. Lawson rejects the notion that grand juries were passive (139, 140). See also Stephen Roberts, "Jurors and the Middling Sort: Recruitment and Performance at Devon Quarter Sessions, 1649–1670," in *Twelve Good Men*, 185, 188–189, 190.

Recent research suggests that the grand jury continued to be an important part both of the system of criminal justice and of local regulation. Cynthia Herrup's study of seventeenth-century Sussex indictments reveals that 25 percent of suspicions brought to the grand juries were rejected. She concludes that the comment in the early eighteenth-century *A Guide to Grand Juries* (prominently cited by Langbein) that states that the endorsement of private accusations were "a matter of course, a ceremony of matter of form," did not apply to grand juries she studied. See Cynthia Herrup, "The Common Peace: Legal Structure and Legal Substance in East Sussex, 1594–1640" (Diss., Northwestern University, 1982), 3. See also Herrup, *The Common Peace: Participation and the Criminal Law in Seventeenth-Century England* (Cambridge, 1987). The

Guide was a polemical work, and, thus, should not be taken as clear evidence of contemporary practice. Herrup's study indicates that grand jurors continued to play a significant role in the criminal process.

Aggressive investigation is also suggested by J. S. Morrill's study of mid-seventeenth-century Cheshire grand juries. Morrill, like Herrup, rejects the view that seventeenth-century grand juries were subservient, ignorant, and conservative. See *The Cheshire Grand Jury, 1630–1660: Government and Society during the English Revolution* (Oxford, 1974), 21, 45. S. K. Roberts's study, which like Morrill's was concerned primarily with presentments and local administration, also suggests an active, inquiring body. Bills of indictment were quite likely to be rejected by the grand jury. See S. K. Roberts, "Initiative and Control: The Devon Quarter Sessions Grand Jury, 1649–1670," *Bulletin of the Institute for Historical Research* 57 (November, 1984): 167. See also Stephen Roberts, "Jurors and the Middling Sort," 189–190, 193. J. A. Sharpe's study of the Essex assize and quarter session records of 1620–1680 also indicates that grand juries often refused to indict on a wide range of criminal charges. See "Enforcing the Law in the Seventeenth-Century Village," in *Crime and the Law: The Social History of Crime in Western Europe Since 1500*, ed. V. Gatrell et al. (London, 1980), 94–97, 108, 117, 118. Somerset grand juries found many bills *ignoramus*. Thomas Barnes, *Somerset Assize Orders, 1629–1640*, Somerset Record Society 65 (London, 1959): xix. See also Alan Macfarlane and Sarah Harrison, *The Justice and the Mare's Ale: Law and Disorder in Seventeenth-Century England* (Cambridge, 1981), 99–100; J. S. Cockburn, "Trial by the Book? Fact and Theory in Criminal Process, 1558–1625," in *Legal Records and the Historian*, ed. J. H. Baker (London, 1978), 71. Francis Snyder, who has studied eighteenth-century criminal prosecution, rejects the view that justices of the peace had become public prosecutors. See "Using the Criminal Law, 1750–1850," in *Policing and Prosecution in Britain, 1750–1850*, ed. Douglas Hay and Francis Snyder (Oxford, 1989), 24–25.

12. *William Lambarde and Local Government: His "Ephemeris" and Twenty-Nine Charges to Juries and Commissions*, ed. Conyers Read (Ithaca, 1962), 59, 120.

13. H. Bracton, *On the Laws and Customs of England*, trans. and ed. S. E. Thorne, 4 vols. (Cambridge, Mass., 1968), 2: 403. Suspicion was thus distinct from rumor. It was "not a vague notion but arose when rumour originates among good and responsible men. As also from a precedent act, which must stand until the contrary is proved."

14. Herrup, "The Common Peace," 5. See also Herrup, "New Shoes and Mutton Pies: Investigative Responses to Theft in Seventeenth-Century East Sussex," *The Historical Journal* 27 (1984): 811–830.

15. Ibid., 6, 10–12. They were wary about accusations which might have been motivated by revenge. Although technically they were only to hear evidence for the prosecution, they might hear evidence for the defense if countercharges had been presented by the accused.

16. The grounds for suspicion in cases of felonies and murder are laid out in Richard Crompton's 1606 enlargement of Anthony Fitzherbert's *L'office et auctoritie de justices de peace* (London, 1606), 98–101. Fitzherbert was published originally in law French in 1538. There were many English editions. Crompton's enlarged editions were frequently printed. Stanford, citing legislation of Henry VIII, uses the language of "vehement suspicion" (London, 1560), 89.

The widely distributed handbooks prepared for the justice of the peace yield remarkably little information. Though they typically contain sections on indictment, they offer little guidance on how grand jurors' decisions should be formed. William Lambarde's *Eirenarcha, or Of the Office of the Justice of the Peace* (London, 1581) suggests little more than that the indictment consists of finding a bill of accusation to be true. Crompton's *L'office*, which contains considerable material on grand jury charges and exhortations, does not deal with evidentiary matters.

John Cowell's *Interpreter* (London, 1607) merely notes that an *ignoramus* was appropriate when grand jurors "mislike their evidence, as defective or too weak to make good the presentment" (7). William Fulbecke, comparing legal words in the common and the civil law, indicates the term *accusatio* was equivalent to a presentment. William Fulbecke, *A Direction or Preparative to the Study of the Law*, 1600 ed. (London, 1620), 72.

17. Conrad Russell, *Parliaments and English Politics, 1621–1629* (Oxford, 1979) 177, 177n, 302.

18. Fulbecke, *Direction or Preparative*, 75–76. These statements also appear in the 1600 ed.

19. Michael Dalton, *The Country Justice* (London, 1635), chap. 186.

20. Sir Edward Coke, *Institutes of the Lawes of England* (London, 1628–1644), 3:25. William Sheppard, the leading producer of legal materials in the Civil War and interregnum era, noted, like Cowell, that an *ignoramus* was appropriate when the grand jury "mislike their evidence as defective or too weak to make good the point." *An Epitome of all the Common and Statute Laws* (n.p., 1656), 384. No standard is suggested for the *billa vera*. This volume, which contains a law dictionary, was published at the command of Lord Protector Oliver Cromwell.

21. John Cotta, *The Trial of Witchcraft* (London, 1616), 80–81. The volume was dedicated to Sir Edward Coke and to the judiciary more generally.

22. Ibid., 85.

23. Richard Bernard, *Guide to Grand Jurors in Cases of Witchcraft* (London, 1627), 25. This book was also dedicated to the legal profession.

24. Ibid.

25. Ibid., 25, 42, 46, 53, 233. See also "A Dialogue Concerning Witches," in *The Witchcraft Papers*, ed. Peter Haining (London, 1974), 92–107.

26. See Donald Veall, *The Popular Movement for Law Reform, 1640–1660* (Oxford, 1970); Stuart Prall, *The Agitation for Law Reform during the Puritan Revolution* (The Hague, 1966); Mary Cotterell, "Interregnum Law Reform: The Hale Commission of 1652," *English History Review* 83 (1968): 1689–1704; Barbara Shapiro, "Law Reform in Seventeenth-Century England," *American Journal of Legal History* 19 (1975): 280–312.

27. See Barbara Shapiro, *Probability and Certainty in Seventeenth-Century England: A Study of the Relationships between Natural Science, Religion, History, Law and Literature* (Princeton, 1983), passim.

28. Institutional changes, too, may have been at work. Before the early modern era, grand juries often relied on presentments from hundred juries in finding indictments. Hundred juries reported the "common fame," or voice of the community's suspicion, and grand juries, therefore, were often determining only whether these were the community's suspicions. As hundred jurors declined, and there does not seem to be clear evidence of when or how this decline occurred, grand jurors were increasingly engaged in evaluating charges by persons they did not know, against persons they did not know, and about events they did not know. They were no longer in a position to know if the charges were validated by common fame. The decline of the hundred jury may thus have played some role in provoking discussion of grand jury standards. I owe this information and insight to Norma Landau.

29. [Sir John Somers], *The Security of English-Men's Lives* (London, 1681), 17–18.

30. *The Diary of John Milward*, ed. Caroline Robbins (Cambridge, 1935), 167–168, 170. See also *The Peoples Ancient and Just Liberties Asserted* (London, 1670), 60; Somers, *Security of English-Men's Lives*, 18. Kelyng insisted grand jurors limit themselves to matters of fact and not concern themselves with matters of law. This issue was raised because grand jurors changed charges of murder to manslaughter. *Diary of John Milward*, 169.

31. *Diary of John Milward*, 169. Thomas Green suggests that Kelyng's treatment of petty juries was an exaggeration of current practice but not an exception to it. Juries and grand juries were attempting to undermine the effect of the Conventicle Act, especially in Quaker cases, and were

continuing to reduce murder charges to manslaughter. Green, *Verdict According to Conscience*, 209, 209n, 248–249.

32. Matthew Hale, *The History of the Pleas of the Crown*, 1800 ed., 2 vols. (London, 1736), 2: 312.

33. *Peoples Ancient and Just Liberties Asserted*, 60.

34. *Diary of John Milward*, xcii, 185, 190–191.

35. For a discussion of Vaughan and of Bushel's case, see Green, *Verdict According to Conscience*, 200–264; John A. Phillips and Thomas C. Thompson, "Jurors v. Judges in Later Stuart England: The Penn-Mead Trial and 'Bushell's Case'," *Law and Inequality: A Journal of Theory and Practice* 4 (1986): 189–229; *Diary of John Milward*, 88–89, 159–160, 162–163, 167–170.

36. Zachary Babington, *Advice to Grand Jurors in Cases of Blood* (London, 1677).

37. Ibid., Author to the Reader, 4, 79. Grand jurors ought to be permitted to "voice and advance" the charges "to the highest pitch (that by any reasonable presumption) it will bear" (116).

38. Ibid., 115, 118, 119, 130. See also 124. He cites Bracton and Stamford on public fame and "several badges and marks of Suspicion," and noted Bracton's chapter is "well worth the reading" (121). These "marks of suspicion" were included in the justicing handbooks in connection with arrest and pretrial examination.

39. Ibid., 123–124.

40. Ibid., 125–126. See also 63, 106.

41. Ibid., 183. See also 116.

42. Hale, *History of the Pleas of the Crown*, 2: 157, 158. While there are a number of extant printed grand jury charges, these, as earlier charges, omit almost any reference to the criteria for *billa vera* and *ignoramus* endorsements. Charges continue to focus on jury qualifications and attitudes, provide an outline and brief description of indictable crimes, and direct the grand jurors' attention to particularly pressing problems.

43. See *Office of the Clerk of the Assize* (London, 1676, 1672, and 1682) and *The Office of the Clerk of the Peace* (London, 1676). Although neither one provides guidance on evidentiary standards, they do suggest that something close to the probability standards of Babington and Hale were widely used. The assize guide notes "if upon the Evidence the grand jury have good cause to find the Bill," then they endorse it *billa vera*, and "if they have no colour to find the same," then they write *ignoramus*. *Clerk of the Assize*, 1682 ed., 34. "Good Cause" and "no colour" language reappear in *Clerk of the Peace*, 1681 ed., 144. Another manual, however, indicated that an *ignoramus* was appropriate if the grand jury

were "not satisfied by the Evidence." J. W., *Officium Clerici Pacis* (London, 1686), 52.

In one of the Popish Plot trials, grand jurors were advised that they required only "probable evidence" because their verdict was only an "accusation." *Trial of Reading* (London, 1679), 2. In the 1678 murder indictment of the Earl of Pembroke, the lord high steward insisted that Pembroke was *not* being charged "by common voice and fame." He indicated that indictment was "no more than a bare accusation," vehemently declaring "God Forbid, they who neither did not hear the evidence on both sides, should no way prejudice your trial by their partial examination." T. B. Howell, ed., *Complete Collection of State Trials*, 34 vols. (London, 1809–1826), 9: 1309, 1317.

We can gain insight from impeachment proceedings, which sometimes were likened to grand jury indictments. In the debate on Clarendon's impeachment (1667), the comparison between impeachment accusation and indictment was both made and rejected. *Diary of John Milward*, 34. Sir John Holland argued against the view that "an accusation without examination or proof" was enough for indictment and insisted that the charges must "be true." Some insisted that witnesses be examined and that proof was required, while others felt that an accusation based on common fame was sufficient. Still others complained about inadequate secrecy, another issue which became important in the grand jury debates of 1680–1682. *Diary of John Milward*, 34, 101, 102, 111, 143, 144, 232, 234. Though common fame implied something stronger than rumor for Serjeant Maynard, it fell short of provable fact. "Common fame was no ground to accuse a man when the matter of Fact is not clear. To say an Evil is done, therefore this man did it, is strange in Morality, more in Logick." Howard Nenner, *By Colour of Law: Legal Culture and Constitutional Politics in England, 1660–1689* (Chicago, 1977), 12, citing *Proceedings . . . Touching the Impeachment . . . of Clarendon*.

The grand jury analogy was also made in impeachment proceedings against Sir Edward Seymour. Sir Leonine Jenkins insisted that there must be "moral assurance" of the truth of the charge. 8 *State Trials*, 127, 149. Here, again, the House of Commons was unclear as to what standard was to guide them.

The House of Lords had debated several decades earlier whether or not common fame provided a sufficient basis to accuse the duke of Buckingham. Conrad Russell, *Parliaments and English Politics, 1621–1629* (Oxford, 1979), 302. For Sir Francis Bacon's impeachment see 2 *State Trials*, 1091, 1093.

44. [Francis Smith], *An Impartial Account of the Tryal of Francis Smith* (London, 1680), preface, 5.

45. *The Grand Jury-man's Oath and Office Explained and the Rights of English-men Asserted* (London, 1680), 5, 6. This tract is usually attributed to John Hawles, a prominent Whig lawyer. If Hawles is the author, he changed his views after the Shaftesbury trial. See John Hawles, *The Englishman's Right* (London, 1680).

46. Ibid., 8.

47. Ibid., 8–9.

48. Ibid., 9–10. The author, like Babington, uses the term "supposition."

49. Ibid., 11, 19–21. An *ignoramus* was appropriate if the facts were proved but the jury did not believe the matter charged was a crime. Grand jurors were necessarily involved in matters of law as well as fact. The juryman noted that indictments often included terms like *vi et armis*, which were seldom proved. The barrister admitted the problem of legal fictions, noting that terms of this sort were matters of form, but that they sometimes raised the color of crime where there had been none (13–17). Secrecy was essential precisely because indictment was only "an Accusation or Charge." Revelation of the "Force of the Evidence" might lead to flight or to tampering with or "Sweeten[ing] the Evidence" when the case came to trial (5–6).

50. *A Modest Vindication of the Proceedings of the late Jury at the Old Baily, who returned the Bill against Stephen Colledge Ignoramus* (London, 1681), 1.

51. *The Letter of the Grand Jury of Oxford to the Grand Jury of London* (London, 1681), 1.

52. *The Tryals of Several Notorious Malefactors . . . at Old Bailey, October 17–19, 1681* (London, 1682), 3. W. J.'s *Letter from Ignoramus* (London, 1682) expressed great distress that those who swore against Rouse had been examined and cross-examined in open court, "a thing not known in our days." Although the author thought there might be "a few precedents of like nature in former Ages," he thought that the practice was not in keeping with present practice. In the Colledge case the witnesses were heard in court but examined privately (3).

53. *Tryals of Several Notorious Malefactors*, 3.

54. "Proceedings at the Old Bailey upon a Bill of Indictment against Anthony, Earl of Shaftesbury," 8 *State Trials*, 759, 762, 770.

55. Ibid.

56. Ibid., 772, 802–803. The grand jury had asked if any of the prosecution witnesses had been indicted. It wished to discredit the witnesses to avoid a repetition of the Colledge situation. The jury foreman probed the witnesses. J. R. Jones, *The First Whigs: The Politics and the Exclusion Crisis, 1678–1683* (London, 1970), 192–192n. Hale's still unpublished

History of the Pleas of the Crown endorsed grand jury evaluation of witness credibility.

57. 8 *State Trials*, 802–803.

58. 4 *State Trials*, 1311.

59. *Ignoramus Vindicated in a Dialogue between Prejudice and Indifference* (London, 1681), 1, 2.

60. Ibid., 4–5.

61. Ibid., 9.

62. Ibid., 11.

63. Ibid. In addition, "juries may have evidence from personal knowledge . . . that what is deposed in Court is absolutely false." The judge knows only what has been learned in court, while the jury may know that the witnesses may be "stigmatized and Infamous" (12).

64. Ibid., 12. The tract also expressed the fear that standing juries might be instituted, thus becoming only "the Court's Echos."

65. Somers, *The Security of English-Men's Lives*, 17–18, 20–21, 23. See also 53. Somers became a leading Whig lawyer after the Revolution of 1688.

Jurors would do well to be suspicious of prosecution lawyers who "have Evidence dressed up with all that Lawyer wits can give it" (81). Somers was particularly critical of judges who "by degrees" were turning grand juries into "a mere matter of form," rather than "openly and advowedly" destroying them. Changes in the administration of justice were to be accomplished by legislators, not judges. Somers implies not that grand jury indictments were not yet a "matter of form" but that they were in danger of becoming so (53, 108–109, 116–117, 121). On the secrecy issue see 44ff.

66. Ibid., 21, 53, 82, 126, 127, 128, 129. "For this Reason the Council of Areopagites, and some others of the best Judicatures that have been in the world utterly rejected the use of Rhetoric looking upon the art of persuading by incertain probabilities, as little differing from that of deceiving, and directly contrary to their ends, who by the knowledge of truth desire to be led into the doing of Justice" (127).

67. Ibid., 128, 129.

68. Ibid., 124, 130–131.

69. Ibid., 27–29, 31, 142.

70. Ibid., 29, 122, 124.

71. Ibid., 82, 119, 122, 145, 147–148, 151. Somers also argued that the "doctrine of indicting upon slight grounds" was against the law, reason, and the practice of "former times." Citing Coke, he insisted that indictments formerly had been made upon "plain and direct proofs and not upon Probabilities and inferences." The high acquittal rates of the

past were attributed to the diligence and integrity of grand jurors. He thus advocated a return to "the good old way" (146, 151). Coke, however, had referred to cases where the accused was not present.

72. Henry Care, *English Liberties, or The Free-Born Subjects Inheritance* (London, n.d.). The Wing catalog indicates a 1680 date, but references to the Shaftesbury proceedings and to an Old Bailey trial suggest a 1681 or 1682 first printing. Other editions appeared in 1682, 1691, and 1700. Enlarged editions were printed in 1703, 1719, and 1721.

Care emphasizes diligent inquiry, the search for truth, the evaluation of witness credibility, the importance of the vicinage requirement, the problem of malice, the rejection of Pemberton's probability standard, and independence from the judiciary. He, like Somers, insists that if grand jurors were not Judges of Evidence, "they were nothing" (216). He explicitly adopts the satisfied conscience standard. "People may tell you that you ought to find a Bill upon any probable Evidence," or "tis a matter of Course, of ceremony, a Business of forms, only an Accusation. . . . But if this were all, to what purpose have we Grand Juries at all?" Why, he queried, would the "wisest and best men be chosen, why would they be so strictly sworn?" A *billa vera* meant, "It is True," "we are fully satisfied" (219–220). He, like most Whig pamphleteers, insisted that grand and petty juries were judges of law as well as fact and was hostile to the judiciary (207–208).

For another Whig discussion of grand juries see the anonymous *Earl of Shaftesbury's Grand Jury Vindicated from the Aspersions Cast upon them in the late Address from Some of the Middle Temple* (London, 1682). Edmond Saunders, who was thought to be the author, was soon appointed to the bench. The tract, which assembled the usual collection of Whig arguments, rejected the probability standard and relied heavily on Vaughan's opinion in Bushel's case.

73. *Guide to English Juries, Setting forth Their Power and Antiquity by a Person of Quality* (London, 1682). The *Guide* was reprinted in 1689, 1699, 1702 and 1725.

74. The author claimed the clerks' interest in fees led them to multiply the number of indictments. They were thus motivated "to say" that "colour of Evidence" or "probability of a thing being" true was sufficient. They also insisted that what they did "is but a matter of course, a Ceremony, a matter of form, barely an Accusation." Ibid., 53, 73. See also 77, 79–82; cf., *Office of the Clerk of the Assize*, 32; *The Office of the Clerk of the Peace*, 144.

75. To endorse a *billa vera* they must be "satisfied" that the evidence is true or know it themselves. *Guide to English Juries*, 82. See also 52. Indeed, they "must know beyond all doubt" before they provide such

endorsement (68). "Mature and settled judgments" by "good and great deliberation, considerateness, Reasoning, and Satisfaction according to one's own Conscience" were required for a *billa vera* (46). To reach that state they must inquire diligently as their oath required. They must "True Presentment make," not a "Probable" one. They must weigh the evidence and not reach a decision according to "Presumption." The author also rejects the suggestions that all the grand jury does is "present in form" and that its presentment is "only suppositious, . . . and nothing positive or certain." (54–56).

76. Ibid., 7–8, 56–57. See also 63–64, 132.

77. Ibid., 71, 73, 76.

78. Roger North, *Examen*, 1740 ed. (London, 1685), 113, 114.

79. *Billa Vera: or the Arraignment of Ignoramus* (London, 1682), 7–8.

80. Ibid., 8–9, 13–14, 26.

81. Ibid., 10.

82. Ibid., 11, 28.

83. Ibid., 11, 15, 16.

84. Joseph Keble's *Assistance to Justices of the Peace* (London, 1683) indicated that grand jurors were to evaluate witness credibility. They were not, however, to try an issue but to "offer an Information, the truth or falsehood whereof" would be tried by the petty jury (264).

85. Gilbert Burnet, *History of My Own Times*, ed. Osmond Airy, 2 vols. (Oxford, 1900), 2: 302–303.

86. *Poems on Affairs of State: Augustan Satirical Verse, 1660–1714*, ed. H. S. Schless, 7 vols. (New Haven, 1968), 3: 76–95. See also *Poems on Affairs of State*, vols. 3 and 4, passim; *Ignoramus-justice* (1682); *The Ignoramus Ballad* (1681); *Ignoramus: an Excellent New Song* (1681); *A New Ignoramus* (1681). The prologue and epilogue of Dryden's *Duke of Guise* (1683) also refers to *ignoramus* juries. Another series of 1682 political poems focused on the London and Middlesex shrieval election. See *Poems on Affairs of State*, 3: 207ff.

87. *Poems on Affairs of State*, 3: 80.

88. See W. J. Jones, *Politics and the Bench: The Judges and the Origins of the English Civil War* (London, 1971).

89. See A. F. Havinghurst, "The Judiciary and Politics in the Reign of Charles II," *Law Quarterly Review* 66 (1950): 62–78, 229–252.

90. See for example *The Triumph of Justice over Unjust Judges* (London, 1681).

91. See Norma Landau, *The Justices of the Peace, 1679–1760* (Berkeley, 1984).

92. But see *The Compleat Statesman* (London, 1683). About thirty pages are devoted to grand juries and the Shaftesbury proceedings.

93. Sir James Astry, *A General Charge to all Grand Juries* (London, 1703; reprint, 1725), 14. Astry emphasized that Babington's volume had been licensed by the Lord Keeper and "has been since approv'd of by all the learned Judges" and was "often given in Charges by them in their Circuits."

94. Ibid., 11, 13. A later handbook, *The Complete Juryman, or a Compendium of the Laws Related to Jurors*, issued in 1744 and 1752, does not discuss the evidentiary requirements of grand juries.

95. John Hawles, *Remarks upon the Trial of Fitzharris* (London, 1689). Hawles discusses a number of treason trials and the Shaftesbury grand jury proceedings.

96. Ibid., 46, 47.

97. Ibid., 48. He denied Chief Justice Pemberton's contention that grand juries could not consider the credibility of witnesses and opposed the practice of allowing King's Counsel to be present and give advice during grand jury proceedings.

98. *A Display of Tyranny* (1689), aimed primarily at the Tory judiciary, again referred to the Shaftesbury case. The author, like Hawles, was outraged at judicial denial that grand jurors could consider the credit of witnesses, and insisted on using Vaughan's language in Bushel's case that grand jurors "were within the compass of their own Understandings and consciences to have their Judgements" (79).

99. Thomas Wood, *Institute of the Laws of England*, 2d ed. (The Savoy, 1722), 823.

100. Matthew Hale, *History of the Pleas of the Crown*, 2: 157–158.

101. Ibid. William Hawkins, another authoritative treatise writer, indicates only that an indictment is an "Accusation, . . . which is found to be true." *A Treatise of the Pleas of the Crown*, 1771 ed. (London, 1717), 209.

102. Henry Fielding, *Charge Delivered the Grand Jury* (London, 1749), 25–26, citing Hale, *History of the Pleas of the Crown*, 2: 157.

103. Ibid., 27. London grand jurors, however, often served frequently. Veteran grand jurors might be familiar with criminous thief takers who were given monetary rewards for apprehending thieves. The latter frequently encouraged criminal activity so that they might report it.

104. Herbert Packer, "Two Models for the Criminal Process," *University of Pennsylvania Law Review* 113 (1964): 1–68.

105. William Blackstone, *Commentaries on the Laws of England*, 1st American ed., 1771–1772, 4 vols. (London, 1765), 2: 301, 303.

106. Richard Woodeson, *A Systematic View of the Laws of England*, 3 vols. (London, 1792), 2: 559.

107. Ibid., 2: 558, 559.

108. John Shore, *A Charge Delivered at the Quarter Sessions of the Peace . . . April 5, 1714* (London, 1714), 21–28. See also 8. The charge was published at the request of the judges.

109. *The Charge of William Cowper to the Grand Jury of Westminster* (London, 1719), 33–35.

110. *The Charge of Daniel Dolbins to the Grand Jury* (London, 1725), 5.

111. *The Charge of Daniel Dolbins* (London, 1725), 4. (Not the same charge as previous note.)

112. Sir John Gonson, *Five Charges to Several Grand Juries*, (London, 1740), 10–11. Many early eighteenth-century charges, especially those given to Middlesex and Westminster grand juries, were highly politicized. Many were presented with bills of indictment against those publishing Tory or Jacobite propaganda. I owe this information to Norma Landau.

113. *The Charge of T. Morley* (1749), 5. Chief Justice Morley of the King's Bench in Ireland, gave this charge in the course of a highly emotional libel case. Morley indicated that grand juries must "think the accusation probable." See also *A Critical Review of the Liberties of the Subject*, 2nd ed. (Dublin, 1750). Dismissals on the basis of evidence favoring the defendant were reported to be frequent. Richard Cox, *A Charge Delivered to the Grand Jury* (Dublin, 1758), 27–28.

James Wilson indicated that the probability standard was very common. It is also suggested by one of the few reports at the Old Bailey sessions that mentions grand jury standards. The "probable guilt of a prisoner is sufficient to find a bill." *Whole Proceedings at Old Bailey February, 1777* (London, 1777), 97. See also *Charges to Grand Juries* (Worcester, 1780), 8, 11.

114. *Whole Proceedings at Old Bailey February, 1777*, 97.

115. Richard Burke, *Charge Delivered to the Grand Jury* (Bristol, 1793), 6–7.

116. John Beattie, *Crime and the Courts in England, 1660–1800* (Princeton, 1986), 83. See also 401. The figures are from the Surrey assizes.

117. For the composition of grand juries see Ibid., 320–331. See also P. J. R. King, "'Illiterate Plebians, Easily Misled': Jury Composition, Experience and Behavior in Essex, 1735–1815," in *Twelve Good Men and True: The Criminal Trial Jury in England, 1200–1800*, ed. J. S. Cockburn and Thomas Green (Princeton, 1988), 278–279, 283, 294; Douglas Hay, "The Class Composition of the Palladium of Liberty: Trial Jurors in the

Eighteenth Century," in *Twelve Good Men*, 311, 344; John Beattie, "London Juries in the 1690s," in *Twelve Good Men*, 234, 235, 244.

118. Beattie, *Crime and the Courts*, 321–327. Blackstone described grand jurors as "gentlemen of the best figures in the county." *Commentaries*, 4: 299.

119. Landau, *Justices of the Peace*, 54–56. By the second decade of the eighteenth century, one-third to one-half of grand jurors were justices of the peace. They still dominated grand jury panels in the 1750s. Landau suggests they were probably less deferent to judges than they had been in the past (60). See also Cockburn, *History of the English Assizes*, 114–115, 123, 240.

120. Leroy Clark, *The Grand Jury: The Use and Abuse of Political Power* (New York, 1975), 13. Maryland and Connecticut documents mentioned grand juries in 1637 and 1641 respectively. There is no evidence of the jury in New York before 1681. The report of a 1666 Maryland grand jury indicated that grand juries met privately and considered the depositions of sworn witnesses which had been taken by the justices of the peace. Raphael Semmes, *Crime and Punishment in Early Maryland* (Baltimore, 1938), 21–22; Richard Younger, *The People's Panel: The Grand Jury in the United States, 1634–1941* (Providence, 1963), 4–20. See also Morris Ploscowe, "Development of Present Day Criminal Procedures in Europe and America," *Harvard Law Review* 48 (1935): 433–473.

121. In 1686 the governor of Virginia wrote several letters to England requesting information on the proper form of grand jury instructions. Ploscowe, "Development of Present Day Criminal Proceedings," 468, 468n.

122. Richard Burn, *The Justice of the Peace and Parish Officer*, 1772 ed. (London, 1754), 2: 453–454.

123. Richard Starke, *Office and Authority of the Justice of the Peace* (Williamsburg, 1774), 214; William Hening, *The New Virginia Justice* (Richmond, 1795), 250; *An Abridgement of Burn's, Justice of the Peace and Parish Officer* (Boston, 1773), 124.

124. Younger, *People's Panel*, 26–28. John Peter Zenger was eventually brought to trial by a prosecutor's information after grand juries twice refused to indict.

125. John Hawles's *Englishman's Right: A Dialogue Between a Barrister at Law and a Juryman* was the first American reprint of any English law book. It was published in Boston in 1693 and reprinted again in America in 1772, 1788, and 1806. Care's *English Liberties* was printed in Boston in 1686. Five thousand copies were seized. It was printed again in the colonies in 1721 and 1774. Morris Cohen, "Legal Literature in Colonial Massachusetts" (Unpublished manuscript), 16–18.

126. *Excerpts from the most approved Authorities . . . with respect to the Office and Duty of Grand Juries* (n.p., n.d.), 22–23, 25, 32–33. See also 34–35. See also *British Liberties, or the Freeborn Subject's Inheritance* (Boston, 1776), 369–370, 377–381, 384–391.

127. We should be reminded, however, that institutions might function differently in different political contexts. Thus grand juries and juries in the American colonies did not behave like those in Ireland. Different selection processes in the two imperial jurisdictions meant that Irish grand and petty juries were more compliant and yielded more proimperial indictments and convictions than did their American counterparts. See John Reid, *In a Defiant Stance: The Condition of Law in Massachusetts Bay, the Irish Comparison, and the Coming of the American Revolution* (Philadelphia, 1977). The tension between the Whig and Tory standards is to be seen in the New York trial of Nicholas Bayard (1702). In this case the solicitor general insisted that the grand jury was to inquire only for the king and "to receive or send for no other evidence than what are brought for the King." Counsel for the defense then queried, "And how shall the truth be known, if the grand jury are permitted to have no other evidence but what are brought 'ex parte Regis?'" and suggested that such a procedure was contrary to the grand juror's oath to find the truth. The Crown response was precisely what might be anticipated. "All the books speak of the king's evidence only, and agree, that the grand jury may and ought to find upon probable evidence, as appears in Babbington [sic]." 14 *State Trials*, 471–481.

128. Younger, *People's Panel*, 44–55.

129. Francis Hopkinson, *The Miscellaneous Essays*, 2 vols. (Philadelphia, 1792), 2: 194.

130. Ibid., 1: 194, 195, 196, 202, 217.

131. Ibid., 1: 222. See also 1: 219, 223, 224, 227, 229, 232, 234, 235.

132. Ibid., 2: 210.

133. Ibid., 2: 211–212, 213.

134. Respublica v. Schaeffer, 1 Dallas, 237.

135. Respublica v. Schaeffer, at 237.

136. See Marvin E. Frankel and Gary P. Naftalis, *The Grand Jury: An Institution of Trial* (New York, 1977), 12–13.

137. *The Works of James Wilson*, ed. Robert McCloskey, 2 vols. (Cambridge, Mass., 1967), 2: 210, 212.

138. Ibid., 2: 212–213.

139. Ibid., 2: 213.

140. Ibid., 2: 215–222.

141. Charles Cottu used the Continental language of "presumption" to describe English grand jury standard. These must be *assez fortes* to

find a true bill. *The Administration of Criminal Justice in England* (London, 1822), 49, 54, 67.

142. Joseph Chitty, *A Practical Treatise on the Criminal Law*, Philadelphia, 1819 ed., 3 vols. (London, 1816), 1: 261.

143. Thomas Starkie, *Practical Treatise on the Law of Evidence*, 1853 ed., 2 vols. (London, 1824), 1: 544. The judge in *Rex v. Burdett* (1820) did not use the term *"prima facie* case," but a similar formulation. He did not, however, refer to the grand jury. ". . . no person is to be required to explain or contradict until enough has been proved to warrant a just conclusion against him, in the absense of explanation or contradiction." *English Reports* (Full reprint) vol. 106 (London): 873, 898.

144. Starkie, *Practical Treatise*, 1853 ed., 1: 544.

145. *American Jurist* 8 (1832), 218–219. Shaw recognized that "party spirit" and "sectarian zeal" might affect grand jurors in periods of "peculiar states of excitement." He also insisted the evidence must be "legal evidence" (217).

146. *Charge to the Grand Jury*, 30 Fed. Cas. 998, 999.

147. Francis Wharton, *A Treatise of the Criminal Law of the United States*, 3d ed. (Philadelphia, 1855), 125.

148. *Charge to the Grand Jury*, 30 Fed. Cas. 1036, 1038, 1039.

149. *Charge to the Grand Jury*, 30 Fed. Cas. 976.

150. *Charge to the Grand Jury*, 30 Fed. Cas. 992, 993.

151. Ibid., 993, 994.

152. George Edwards, *The Grand Jury: Considered from an Historical, Political and Legal Standpoint* (1906; reprint, New York, 1973), 105.

153. Sir James Fitzjames Stephen, *Digest of the Law of Criminal Procedure in Indictable Offenses* (London, 1883), 121.

154. Edwards, *Grand Jury*, 105.

155. Ibid., 142–143. See also 108.

156. The term *"prima facie* case" does not appear in Blount, *Law Dictionary* (1717), Cowell, *The Interpreter* (1684, 1727); Jacob, *The New Law Dictionary* (1729, 1809), Cunningham, *A New and Complete Law Dictionary* (1765), or Tomlins, *Law Dictionary* (1836). The concept begins to appear in some mid-nineteenth-century law dictionaries, although initially not in connection with grand juries. Bouvier's *Law Dictionary*, 2d ed., 1856 (Philadelphia, 1843), provided numerous citations to support the statement "Prima facie evidence of a fact is in the law itself sufficient to establish the fact unless rebutted" (363). Neither Burrill's *New Law Dictionary* (1851), a reworking of Spelman's *Glossary* (1851), adapted to American jurisprudence, nor *Anderson's Dictionary of Law* (1893) link *prima facie* evidence with the grand jury. Burrill cites Bracton and Starkie. In 1873, however, Benjamin Abbott's *Dictionary of Terms and*

Phrases in American or English Jurisprudence (Boston, 1879) indicates
the phrase *prima facie* was in "common use, and of very wide application." It is explicitly associated with the grand jury, citing Starkie and
Mozley and Whitley. The 1890 edition of *The Century Dictionary* (not a
law dictionary) also associates the *prima facie* case with the grand jury, as
does the 1891 edition of *A Dictionary of Law*, p. 935, citing Mozley and
Whitley. Mozley and Whitley define a *prima facie* case:

A litigating party is said to have a *prima facie* case when the evidence in his favor
is sufficiently strong for his opponent to be called upon to answer it. A *prima facie*
case, then, is one which is established by sufficient evidence, and can be overthrown only by rebutting evidence adduced to on the other side. In some cases,
the only question to be considered is whether there is a *prima facie* case against
the accused: and for this purpose therefore, it is not necessary for them to hear
the evidence for the defense.

This appears in Herbert Mozley and George Whitley, *Law Dictionary*,
3d ed., 1908 (London, 1879).

The sequence of American cases in the 1830s that linked the *prima
facie* case with the grand jury and the belated introduction of *prima facie*
case into the law dictionaries may suggest the Americans were persuaded
of Starkie's formulation earlier than the English.

Joel Bishop's *Commentaries on the Law of Criminal Procedure* (Boston, 1866) suggests that various judges and law writers had tried to explain
a "middle kind of certainty . . . as a guide to those who would determine
whether a particular indictment is sufficient or not." Bk. 2, chap. 4, sec.
48, p. 736. See also bk. 6, chap. 43, sec. 736.

157.   Chitty, *Criminal Law*, 2: 162.

158.   See Younger, *People's Panel*, 56ff. See also Edwards, *Grand Jury*.

159.   Younger, *People's Panel*, 56, citing *The Works of Jeremy Bentham*, ed. John Bowring (Edinburgh, 1843), 2: 139–141, 171. The mount-
ing criticism is described in Younger, *People's Panel*. In the early nineteenth century, population increases meant that grand juries were being
asked to review 300 to 400 cases a week. Legislative efforts to introduce
a system of public prosecution along U.S., Irish, or Scottish lines, which
would screen out clearly inappropriate bills, all failed. Francis Snyder,
"Using the Criminal Law, 1750–1850," in *Policing and Prosecution in
Britain, 1750–1850*, ed. Douglas Hay and Francis Snyder (Oxford,
1989), 36.

160.   William Forsyth, *History of Trial by Jury* (London, 1852), 216–
217, 221–223. F. W. Maitland, *Police and Justice* (London, 1885), 139.

161.   Younger, *People's Panel*, 185.

162.   See Ibid., 60–75, 138–139, 226–230. See also S. D. Thompson

and E. G. Merriam, *A Treatise on the Organization, Custody and Conduct of Juries, Including Grand Juries* (St. Louis, 1882). See also David Bodenheimer, "Criminal Justice and Democratic Theory in Antibellum America: The Grand Jury Debates in Indiana," *Journal of the Early Republic* 5 (1985): 481–501. See also Helene Schwartz, "Demythologizing the Historic Role of the Grand Jury," *American Criminal Law Review* 10 (1972): 755–757.

163. Hurtado v. Calif., 110 U.S. 516, 535 (1984).

164. Long after *Hurtado*, the Supreme Court began the "selective incorporation" of the Bill of Rights into the Fourteenth Amendment. It has incorporated nearly everything except the grand jury provision. Indeed the "selective" part of the selective incorporation doctrine appears to be kept alive almost solely for the purpose of avoiding the imposition of the grand jury requirement in the states.

165. Jerold H. Israel, "Grand Jury," in *Encyclopedia of Crime and Justice*, ed. Sanford Kadish (New York, 1983), 2: 814–815. Even in those jurisdictions many prosecutions proceeded by information because defendants may waive the indictment. This is a common practice for those making guilty pleas. See also Frankel and Naftalis, *Grand Jury*, 26–31. The development of public prosecutors in the United States and their role in grand jury proceedings meant that the grand jury functioned somewhat differently in England than in the United States. See Joan E. Jacoby, *The American Public Prosecutor: A Search for Identity* (Lexington, Mass., 1980), 19, 29. In some colonies, public prosecutors appear to have been introduced with grand juries. Prosecuting attorneys had the discretion to initiate and terminate criminal cases. See also 32, 111, 113, 138, 145–146.

166. See Chapter 3.

167. See, for example, Samuel Dash, "The Indicting Jury: A Critical Stage?" *American Criminal Law Review* 10 (1972): 807–828.

168. Alaska Crim. R. 6 (q) (1981).

169. Rideout v. Superior Court, 67 *Cal. Reports*, 2d Series, 471, 1967. See also U.S. v. Heap, 345 F.2d 170 (2d Cir. 1965); Lester Orfield, "The Federal Grand Jury," *Federal Rules Decisions* 22 (1959): 343–463.

170. Alan C. Wright, *Federal Practice and Procedure: Criminal*, 4 vols. (St. Paul, 1969 and 1982), chapt. 4m, rule 6, sec. 110.

171. Yale Kamisar, Wayne LaFave, and Jerold H. Israel, *Modern Criminal Procedure* (St. Paul, 1980), 990.

172. See Note, "The Rules of Evidence as a Factor in Probable Cause in Grand Jury Proceedings and Preliminary Examinations," *Washington University Law Quarterly* (1963): 102–124.

173. Quoted in Orfield, "Federal Grand Jury," 343, 435.

174. Quoted in Peter Aranella, "Reforming the Federal Grand Jury and the State Preliminary Hearing to Prevent Conviction without Adjudication," *Michigan Law Review* 78 (1980): 485.

175. Quoted in Ibid.

176. Ibid., 486.

177. United States v. O'Shea, 447 F. Supp. 330, 331 (1978).

178. Lloyd Moore, *Moore's Federal Practice* (New York, 1979), 6–60.

179. *American Jurist* 8 (1832): 218.

180. United States v. Reed, 27 Fed. Cas. 727, 735, cited in Aranella, "Reforming the Federal Grand Jury," 488.

181. *Charge to the Grand Jury*, 30 Fed. Cas. 1036, 1039 (1861).

182. *Charge to the Grand Jury*, 30 Fed. Cas. 992, 993, 994 (1872). Edwards's 1904 study indicated that the grand jury employed the same rules of evidence as the petty jury, and that it was the duty of the district attorney to prevent the grand jury from hearing incompetent evidence. Receiving hearsay or irrelevant testimony, however, was not sufficient grounds for quashing the indictment. Edwards, *The Grand Jury*, 142, 143.

183. Aranella, "Reforming the Federal Grand Jury," 464–586.

184. Holt v. United States, 218 U.S. 245 (1910).

185. Note, *Washington University Law Quarterly* (1963): 101, 105–106.

186. See Frankel and Naftalis, *Grand Jury*, 26–30, 69–116.

187. United States v. Costello, 321 F. 2d 668, 677 (2d Cir. 1955).

188. 321 F.2d at 679.

189. United States v. Costello, 350 U.S. 362, 363 (1956). Justice Burton's concurrence reiterated the view that indictments were invalid only if there were "no substantial or rationally pervasive evidence" (364). The probable cause standard for arrest satisfied Justice Burton's standard. See Aranella, "Reforming the Federal Grand Jury," 493n.

190. *Costello* must also be seen in the context of the twentieth-century tendency to reduce the scope of hearsay exclusions.

191. Lawn v. United States, 355 U.S. 339 (1958); United States v. Blue, 384 U.S. 251 (1966).

192. United States v. Calandra, 414 U.S. 338, 344–345 (1974).

193. 414 U.S. 349.

194. Aranella, "Reforming the Federal Grand Jury," 496. The prosecution presumably screens out cases with little likelihood of conviction. The grand jury protects the "factually" innocent.

195. Ibid., 500–501.

196. Quoted in Ibid., 502, citing *Justice Department Standards*, 3002.

197. Ibid., 503. Only about 20 percent of the federal prosecutions

involve preliminary examinations because most defendants are indicted before the hearing is held, and the indictment then obviates the need for the hearing (535–536).

198. The two-trial issue becomes even more salient in the context of plea bargaining. For most accused persons in the United States, the preliminary hearing is not a preliminary to trial but about the only trial they will have. For this reason counterpressures inevitably arise to the tendency to lower both *prima facie* case and probability standards. For the same reason pressures also arise to allow greater and greater defense participation in preliminary hearings. These latter pressures then threaten the paradox that preliminary hearings may become more adversarial, and thus more cumbersome and redundant, than grand jury proceedings. At the moment, the preliminary hearing is in the same state of instability and cyclical debate that characterized the grand jury until the *prima facie* case synthesis, and the grand jury itself is back in that same state.

199. See Herbert Packer, "Two Models of the Criminal Process," *University of Pennsylvania Law Review* 113 (1964): 1–68. See also Abraham Goldstein, "The State and the Accused: Balance of the Advantage in Criminal Procedure," *Yale Law Review* 69 (1960): 1149–1199.

Chapter Three

1. See J. W. Baldwin, "The Intellectual Preparation for the Canon of 1215 against Ordeals," *Speculum* 36 (1961): 613–636; R. C. Van Caenegem, "The Law of Evidence in the Twelfth Century: European Perspectives and Intellectual Background," *Proceedings of the Second International Congress of Medieval Canon Law* (Vatican City, 1965).

2. Aristotle *Rhetoric* 1.2. Cicero provided a list of signs, e.g., blood, pallor, or lust, which may have occurred before, during, or after the crime. Cicero *De inventione*, Loeb Classical Library, vol. 2 (Cambridge, Mass., 1949), 1.48.

3. Quintilian, *Institutes of the Orator*, trans. J. Patsaill (London, 1777), bk. 1: 1–5.

4. See Alessandro Giuliani, "The Influence of Rhetoric on the Law of Evidence and Pleading," *Juridical Review* 62 (1969): 216–251.

5. Quintilian, *Institutes*, bk. 4, chap. 9. See also Cicero *De inventione*. These rhetorical categories also would have an enormous impact on fiction writers from the late sixteenth century to the eighteenth century who were hoping to create a different kind of probability. They employed circumstances, persons, times, places, and events, connecting them in such a way as to produce an intelligible or conjectural structure of verisimilitude. Thus verisimilitude was "probable" but not "true." The "probable

fictions" were praised by Sidney and his neoclassical successors as superior to the truths of history. The signs or circumstances of Cicero and Quintilian were thus put to a wide variety of uses.

6. Quintilian, *Institutes*, bk. 4, chap. 10.

7. C. A. Morrison, "Some Features of the Roman and English Law of Evidence," *Tulane Law Review* 33 (1959): 582.

8. See Richard M. Fraher, "Conviction According to Conscience: The Medieval Jurists' Debate Concerning Judicial Discretion and the Law of Proof," *Law and History Review* 7 (1989): 32–40.

9. These yielded proof "as clear as the light of day." The two-witness rule had a basis in Scripture. It was recognized that confessions might be forced and that demented persons sometimes confessed to crimes they had not committed. Misdemeanors did not require "legal proof" and were decided by magistrates on the basis of "free proof." See Adhemar Esmein, *A History of European Criminal Procedure with Specific Reference to France*, trans. J. Simpson, in Continental Legal History Series, vol. 5 (Boston, 1913); C. L. von Bar et al., *A History of Continental Criminal Law*, Continental Legal History Series, vol. 6 (Boston, 1916).

10. See Fraher, "Conviction According to Conscience," 23–88; Giorgia Alessi Palazzola, *Prova legale e pena: La crisi del sistema tra evo medio e moderno* (Naples, 1979); John Langbein, *Torture and the Law of Proof* (Chicago, 1977); Alfred Soman, "Deviance and Criminal Justice in Western Europe, 1300–1800: An Essay in Structure," *Crim. Justice History* 1 (1980): 1–28; C. A. Morrison, "Roman and English Law of Evidence," 577–594. Because crimes proved by this method resulted in monetary penalties, exile, corporal punishment, or the galley sentence in France, expansion of this mode of proof must have resulted in a substantial reduction in capital punishment.

11. See Alfred Soman, "Criminal Jurisprudence in Ancient Regime France," in *Crime and Criminal Justice in Europe and Canada*, ed. Louis A. Knafla (Waterloo, Ontario, 1981), 43–75, and "La justice criminelle aux XVIe–XVIIe siècles: Le Parlement de Paris et les sièges subalternes," in *La faute, la repression et le pardon: Philologie et histoire jusque à 1610*, vol. 1 (Brest, 1982), 15–52.

12. See Walter Ullmann, "Some Medieval Principles of Criminal Procedure," *Juridical Review* 59 (1947): 1–28; Richard Wunderli, "London Church Courts and Society on the Eve of the Reformation," *Speculum*, Anniversary Monographs no. 7 (Cambridge, Mass., 1981); Charles Donahue, "Proof by Witnesses in the Church Courts of Medieval England: An Imperfect Reception of the Learned Law," in *On the Law and Customs of England: Essays in Honor of Samuel E. Thorne*, ed. Morris Arnold et al. (Chapel Hill, 1981), 127–158; Harold Berman, *Law and Revolution:*

The Formation of the Western Legal Tradition (Cambridge, Mass., 1983), 151–155; Jean P. Levy, *La hiérarchie des preuves dans le droit savant du moyen âge despuis la renaissance du droit romain jusqu'à la fin du XIV siècle* (Paris, 1939); R. C. Van Caenegem, "La Preuve dans le droit du moyen âge occidental," in *Recueils de la Société Jean Bodin, pour l'histoire comparative des institutions* (Brussels, 1965), 17: 691–740.

13. Sir John Fortescue, *De Laudibus Legum Anglie*, ed. and trans. S. B. Chrimes (Cambridge, Mass., 1942). It appeared in print for the first time in 1545. There were ten English editions between 1567 and the end of the seventeenth century.

14. For a discussion of the English civilians, see Brian Levack, *The Civil Lawyers in England, 1603–1641: A Political Study* (Oxford, 1973); Daniel R. Coquillette, "Legal Ideology and Incorporation I: The English Civilian Writers, 1523–1607," 1–89, and "Legal Ideology and Incorporation II: Thomas Ridley, Charles Malloy, and the Literary Battle for the Law Merchant," *Boston University Law Review* 61 (1981): 315–376, and "Legal Ideology and Incorporation III: Reason Regulated—The Post-Restoration English Civilians, 1653–1735," *Boston University Law Review* 67 (1987): 289–361. Coquillette discusses the efforts of civilians to incorporate civil law doctrines into the common law. The first stage (1523–1607) is characterized by a civilian effort to synthesize with the common law and by an effort at comparative law. The second is characterized by a reaction led by Coke and the common lawyers against these efforts. The third period (1629–1688) left the English civilians with a narrow, specialized role.

15. Coquillette, "Legal Ideology and Incorporation I," 85. See also S. B. Chrimes, "The Constitutional Ideas of Dr. John Cowell," *English History Review* 44 (1949): 461–480.

16. If "reduced to one method," he thought the similarities would become visible. Quoted in Coquillette, "Legal Ideology and Incorporation I," 73.

17. Ibid., 85, quoting Coke and Cowell. Coquillette suggests that Cowell's *Institutes of the Laws of England* was viewed by Coke as a rival to his own *Institutes* which he was preparing. Cowell's *Institutes* were in part designed to facilitate combining Scotland's civilian-oriented and England's common-law legal systems, a project of great interest to King James.

The romanization of the law of Scotland began in the second half of the fifteenth century. The systematic introduction of Roman law occurred in the sixteenth and seventeenth centuries. As early as 1605, Sir Thomas Craig indicated that both England and Scotland were borrowing from the Roman law but that the influence was not being acknowledged in England. Peter Stein, "The Influence of Roman Law on the Law of Scotland," in *The Character and Influence of Roman Law: Historical Essays* (London, 1988), 339.

18. *The Works of Francis Bacon*, ed. J. Spedding et al., vol. 13 (London, 1872), cited in Coquillette, "Legal Ideology and Incorporation I," 17n.

19. Quoted in Coquillette, "Legal Ideology and Incorporation III," 306. Edward Waterhouse's *Fortescue Illustratus* (London, 1663), which had the impramatur of the judges (including Hale), spoke favorably of the civil law. He indicated that Fortescue, for rhetorical purposes, had exaggerated the differences between the common and the civil law. The latter was "a very noble and learned law and conforms in the greatest part of it, to natural equity" (259). English civilians are praised for their "great learning" and "usefulness" (213, 214, 224, 228, 256). Coke's and François Hotman's hostility to the civil law and their negative comparisons were "as odious to revive" as comparisons between Oxford and Cambridge. Waterhouse insisted that in the cases of laws and universities "I do equal honour to both" (236). The civil law was "very fit for Empire," but the English common law was "fit for British Empire" (119); see also 223, 260.

20. Gilbert Burnet, *The Life and Death of Sir Matthew Hale* (London, 1682), 38.

21. William M. Best, *A Treatise on Presumptions of Law and Fact with the Theory and Rules of Presumptive or Circumstantial Proof in Criminal Cases* (Philadelphia, 1845). See also Coquillette, "Legal Ideology and Incorporation IV: The Nature of Civilian Influence on Modern Anglo-American Commercial Law," *Boston University Law Review* 67 (1987): 929–934; Peter Stein, "Roman Law and English Jurisprudence: Yesterday and Today," in *The Character and Influence of Roman Law: Historical Essays* (London, 1988), 152–165.

22. Thomas Wood, *A New Institute of the Imperial or Civil Law*, 4th ed. (London, 1715), 86. Fleta, Bracton, and the "most ancient" of them would look "very Naked if every Roman lawyer should pluck away his Feathers," and Coke used terms and maxims of both the civil and common law (86). Wood notes, too, a recent epitomization and translation of Vulteius on obligations and contracts by a Mr. West who "passed it off for the pure common law of England" (86). The civil and common laws might not be of the same "Root or Stock," but "inoculating and grafting" have made their body and branches grow very much alike. The civil law was thus interwoven with the common law, and its study should be much encouraged to better understand the common law. Wood conceived of his own work as a part of that project (87–89).

23. See A. W. B. Simpson, "The Rise and Fall of the Legal Treatise:

Legal Principles and the Forms of Legal Literature," *University of Chicago Law Review* 48 (1981): 632–679. See also Chapter 4, pp. 186–243.

24. Jean Domat, *Civil Law in Its Natural Order*, trans. William Strahan, 2 vols. (Boston, 1853), 1:789ff. Strahan's 1722 translation was a favorite of both American and English jurists.

25. William Evans's translation contains a long appendix on applications to English law. Pothier, *A Treatise on the Law of Obligation or Contract*, trans. William Evans, 2 vols. (Philadelphia, 1826), 98. Evans the barrister/translator suggests the new attitude. He praises the "science of jurisprudence" which has been so neglected. Jurisprudence is viewed as "a moral science," as a rational science "founded upon the universal principles of moral rectitude . . . modified by habit and authority" (49).

26. Peter Stein, "The Attraction of the Civil Law in Post-Revolutionary America," *Virginia Law Review* 52 (1966): 403–434; Francis R. Aumann, "The Influence of English and Civil Law Principles upon the American Legal System during the Critical Post-Revolutionary Period," *University of Cincinnati Law Review* 12 (1938): 289–317; William Howe, *Studies of the Civil Law and Its Relation to the Laws of England and America* (Boston, 1896). Despite the obvious and immense importance of English law, several states enacted laws forbidding the citation of post–1776 English decisions. Kentucky briefly prohibited citations to *any* English decisions. English precedents were labeled the "rags of despotism" by some radicals. Anti-Federalists were often suspicious of aristocratic judges and lawyers and English institutions. Aumann, "Influence of English," 293, 294, 296, 298n, 305. See also Richard Cosgrove, *Our Lady the Common Law: An Anglo-American Legal Community, 1870–1930* (New York, 1987).

27. Stein, "The Attraction of the Civil Law," 406, 413.

28. James Kent, *Commentaries on American Law*, ed. W. Browne (St. Paul, 1894), 206. For Kent, the civil law was the source of these "comprehensive views and solid principles which have been applied to elevate the jurisprudence of modern nations" (202).

29. In 1825 it was reported: "In our courts of justice the writings of the civilians are referred to freely and fearlessly. The *Institutes* of Justinian and the commercial treatises of Pothier, Emerigon, and Roccus, are naturalized among us; and in many libraries, Bynkershoek, Heineccius, and Valin, have taken their place by the side of Blackstone and Coke. Our printed reports show the fruits of this liberal study." Aumann, "Influence of English," 310, quoting *North American Review* (October, 1825).

30. For a brief period there was also considerable openness to French law, in both its revolutionary and Napoleonic garbs. Ibid., 306–307; David Hoffman, *A Course of Legal Study* (Baltimore, 1817), 229–230.

31. David Hoffman, *A Course of Legal Study*, 2d ed., 1836 (Baltimore, 1817). The author of Fleta, Britton "as well as modern writers and judges, like Holt and Mansfield" have been indebted to the civil law and "their pages and judicial decisions are often illuminated by the pure and lustrus wisdom of Roman Jurisprudence" (258). Holt is quoted as having said that "the laws of all nations are doubtless raised out of the civil law, as all governments are sprung out of the ruins of the Roman Empire." "No nation has been more copiously supplied from the purest strains of the civil law, and at the same time given it so little credit for which it had received, as Great Britain" (259).

32. Students should study Mascardus, Menochius, and Farinaccius, as well as the more natural law oriented evidentiary writings of Domat and Everhardus, the "most distinguished authors on the civil law of evidence." Ibid., 269. See also Hoffman, *A Lecture on Law* (Baltimore, 1826), 17.

33. Hoffman, *A Lecture*, 17. See also 1–19. A review of the second edition (1836) of *A Course of Study* in the *North American Review* noted that Hoffman was equally at home among the voluminous treatises of both the Roman and the Continental law. Hoffman emphasized the importance of the "philosophical and scientific treatises of the distinguished legal writers of France and Germany as a corrective to the narrow spirit which an exclusive devotion to the common law is liable to produce." Most English treatises were "merely formularies for practice, written without reference to general principles and without any pretention that scientific arrangement which is deemed so indispensable on the Continent" (74).

34. Stein, "The Attraction of Civil Law," 432; Aumann, "The Influence of English," 315, 315n.

35. F. Pollock and W. Maitland, *History of English Law*, 2 vols. (London, 1959), 2: 582–583.

36. Jack K. Weber, "The Birth of Probable Cause," *Anglo-American Law Review*, 11 (1982): 156–158. Evidently the traditional hue and cry had already fallen into disuse as the most common way of apprehending serious offenders. Hue and cry warrants were a later development.

37. 34 Edw. 3, c. 1.

38. Lloyd E. Moore, *The Jury: Tool of Kings: Palladium of Liberty* (Cincinnati, 1973), 54.

39. Henry Bracton, *On the Laws and Customs of England*, trans. and ed. Samuel Thorne, 4 vols. (Cambridge, Mass., 1968), 4: 404, 408. Bracton, still in connection with indictment, noted that it required repeated complaint and ill repute. He admitted, however, that the "uproar and public outcry are at times made of many things which in truth have no

foundation," and thus the idle talk of the people is not to be heeded. He often cited Tancred.

40. Pollock and Maitland, *History of English Law*, 2: 582–583.

41. J. G. Bellamy, *Crime and Public Order in England in the Later Middle Ages* (London, 1973), 102–103.

42. Included in John H. Langbein, *Prosecuting Crime in the Renaissance: England, Germany, France* (Cambridge, Mass., 1974), 274. Several suspicions found together were a legally sufficient basis for torture (275).

43. William Lambarde, *Eirenarcha, or Of the Office of the Justice of the Peace*, 1614 ed. (London, 1581), 93. The list of what may engender suspicion is also included in the 1588 edition; see 220–221.

44. Ibid., 93, 119. The action for false imprisonment long preceded the development of the handbook tradition. Crompton, in 1606, notes the availability of such an action if arrest occurred "sans cause reasonable suspiciousment." Crompton, *L'office et auctoritie de justices de peace* (London, 1606), 100r–100v. "Reasonable" suspicions were necessary and presumably an estimate of whether the "causes of suspicion" were involved here.

45. Michael Dalton, *The Country Justice*, (London, 1635), 336, 337, 338.

46. Ibid.; see also 303–304. The statement concerning the constable's authority to arrest without a warrant (Cap. 118) was added after the first edition.

47. Ibid., 330.

48. See Barbara Shapiro, "Law Reform in Seventeenth-Century England," *American Journal of Legal History* 19 (1975): 280–312; Donald Veall, *The Popular Movement for Law Reform, 1640–1660* (Oxford, 1970); Mary Cotterell, "Interregnum Law Reform: The Hale Commission of 1652," *English History Review* 83 (1968): 689–704; Stuart Prall, *The Agitation for Law Reform during the Puritan Revolution, 1640–1660* (The Hague, 1966).

49. William Sheppard, *An Epitome of All the Common and Statute Law* (London, 1659), 649–650.

50. Ibid., 563, citing Chief Justice Bridgman and cur. Marb c. 23.

51. William Sheppard, *A New Survey of the Justice of the Peace, His Office* (London, 1659), 38. See also *A Manual or Analecta* (London, 1641), 21. Dalton and Lambarde are cited for "Circumstances observable in the behavior of felons."

52. For a discussion of the transformation of the medieval hue and cry into its seventeenth-century written, rather than word-of-mouth, form

and its eighteenth-century replacement by newspaper advertising see John Styles, "Print and Policy: Crime Advertising in Eighteenth-Century England," in *Policing and Prosecution in Britain*, ed. Douglas Hay and Francis Snyder (Oxford, 1989), 55–95.

53. Sir James Fitzjames Stephen, *A History of the Criminal Law of England* (London, 1883), 190.

54. Sheppard, *Epitome*, 650.

55. William Sheppard, *The Whole Office of the County Justice of Peace* (London, 1652), 34, citing Dalton, *Country Justice*, 374, 375, 376, 404, 408.

56. Sir Edward Coke, *Institutes of the Lawes of England*, 4 parts (London, 1628–1644), 4: 177. Julius Goebel and J. R. Naughton suggest Coke himself was confused. In the Twelfth Report he says the justice of the peace can issue a warrant. The Fourth Report indicates a warrant on suspicion is not lawful. *Law Enforcement in Colonial New York* (New York, 1944), 419.

57. A private person may arrest anyone who actually committed a felony or whom he suspects on reasonable grounds of having committed a felony. The constable could arrest anyone he personally suspected if he had reasonable grounds to believe that they had committed a felony, whether or not a felony had actually been committed. Matthew Hale, *History of the Pleas of the Crown*, 2 vols. (London, 1736), chap. 50, 1: 579, citing Dalton, *Country Justice*, cap. 117b. See Jack K. Weber, "The Rise of Probable Cause," 156–167; J. L. Lambert, "Reasonable Cause to Arrest," *Public Law* (1973): 285–294; Jerome Hall, "Legal and Social Aspects of Arrest without a Warrant," *Harvard Law Review* 49 (1936): 567–592.

58. Hale, *History of the Pleas of the Crown*, 1: 579, citing Dalton, *Country Justice*, cap. 117b.

59. Ibid., 580. Hale insisted that general warrants to apprehend all suspected persons were void.

60. Ibid., 109–110; see also 107–108.

61. Ibid., 588, citing 2 Edw. 4, 8b.

62. Ibid., citing Dalton, *Country Justice*, cap. 118.

63. Ibid., 92.

64. Hale also made it clear, on the bases of statutory authority of 14 Henry 7.8 and 34 Edw. 3., c. 1 that if the justice "hath either from himself or by credible information from others of a felony done, and just cause of suspicion of any person," he may himself arrest and commit "the suspected party."

65. *The Complete Justice*, largely a compilation of Lambarde, Crompton, and Dalton, was published frequently with minor changes at least

ten times from 1632 to 1681, when it was enlarged by Richard Chamberlain. Some editions were called *A Manual or Analecta*. Larry M. Boyer, "The Justice of the Peace in England and America 1506–1776," *Quarterly Journal of the Library of Congress* 34 (1977): 318.

66. Alan Macfarlane and Sarah Harrison, *The Justice and the Mare's Ale: Law and Disorder in Seventeenth-Century England* (Cambridge, 1981), 86. See also 90.

67. Richard Chamberlain, *The Complete Justice* (London, 1681), 399.

68. Richard Bolton, *Justice of the Peace in Ireland* (Dublin, 1683). See also Richard Kilburn, *Choice Presedents . . . Relating to the Office and Duty of a Justice of the Peace*, 8th ed., 1715 (London, 1680).

69. William Nelson, *The Office and Authority of a Justice of the Peace* (London, 1707), 469.

70. Hale, *History of the Pleas of the Crown*, 89n, citing Ms. Rep.

71. Henry Fielding, *An Inquiry into the Causes of the Rate Increase of Robbers* (London, 1751), 74, citing Hale, *History of the Pleas of the Crown*, 2: 103.

72. William Hawkins, *A Treatise of the Pleas of the Crown*, 2 vols., Savoy, 1724 ed. (London, 1717), 2: 76.

73. Ibid.

74. Richard Burn, *The Justice of the Peace and Parish Officer* (London, 1754). In 1780, Burn's handbook was in its fourteenth edition. This list is an elaboration of the earlier treatment of common fame and circumstances and materials drawn from Lambarde, Dalton, and others for pretrial examination.

75. Hawkins, *Pleas of the Crown*, 2: 76–77.

76. Ibid., 2: 84, 85.

77. Ibid., 2: 85.

78. William Hening, *The New Virginia Justice* (Richmond, 1795), 450. He specifically cites Hale and Hawkins and rejects the authority of Coke.

79. William Blackstone, *Commentaries on the Laws of England*, 4 vols. (London, 1765), 4: 252, 287. Blackstone, citing Hale and Hawkins, still makes the point of acknowledging that this view was contrary to Coke's.

80. Joel Bishop, *Commentaries on the Criminal Law*, 3d ed., 1866, 2 vols. (London, 1856, 1859), bk. 6, chap. 39, p. 625.

81. Ibid., 639.

82. Ibid., 653, citing East, *Pleas of the Crown*, 332. This seems to refer to private individuals again, not the justice of the peace.

83. Joseph Chitty's early nineteenth-century *Practical Treatise on the Criminal Law* echoes Hale, indicating the magistrate's competence to evaluate the suspicion of others for a warrant and anyone may apprehend

without a warrant if the crime had been committed and if there is a reasonable ground to suspect the individual to be guilty. Individuals might arrest upon probable suspicion and might direct a police officer to arrest if there were "a reasonable and probable ground for suspicion." Joseph Chitty, *A Practical Treatise on the Criminal Law*, 3 vols., Philadelphia, 1819 ed. (London, 1816), 1: 12–13, 14.

84. A. H. Manchester, *Sources of English Legal History: Law, History and Society in England and Wales, 1750–1950* (London, 1984), 248. See also Wilbur Miller, *Cops and Bobbies: Police and Authority in New York and London, 1830–1870* (Chicago, 1973), 56–58, 60.

85. Sir James Fitzjames Stephen, *A Digest of the Law of Criminal Procedure in Indictable Offenses* (London, 1883), 61.

86. W. C. Anderson, *Dictionary of Law* (New York 1893), 1000, citing Blackstone, *Commentaries*, 4: 252.

87. See J. L. Lambert, "Reasonable Cause to Arrest," 285–295.

88. Ibid., 287, citing Stacey v. Emery, 97 U.S. 624 (1878).

89. Ibid., 287.

90. Wayne LaFave, *Arrest: The Decision to Take a Suspect Into Custody* (Boston, 1965), 11, citing Draper v. United States, 358 U.S. 307, 315–316 (1959).

91. Ibid., 15, 16, 17.

92. Ibid., 241, citing a 1939 case.

93. Ibid., 244–245.

94. Quoted in Ibid., 245.

95. Ibid., citing Goldsmith v. United States, 177 F.2d 335, 345 (D.C. Cir. 1960).

96. Ibid., 249, citing Brinegar v. United States, 338 U.S. 160, 176 (1949).

97. Dalton, *Country Justice*, quoted in Burn, *Justice of the Peace*, 1722 ed., 3: 105.

98. Coke, *Institutes*, 4: 177.

99. Sheppard, *Epitome*, 38.

100. Hale, *History of the Pleas of the Crown*, 7.

101. The warrant required the constable to make a diligent daytime search and to bring the goods and person accused of the theft to be examined by the justice. Joseph Shaw, *Parish Law* (Savoy, 1734), ix. Giles Jacob, *The Modern Justice*, 3d ed. (London, 1720) provided a search warrant form which allowed searches of houses and persons "whom you shall justly suspect to have taken" specified goods (1: 195).

102. *An Abridgement of Burn's, Justice of the Peace and Parish Officer* (Boston, 1773), 7.

103. The constable was authorized to enter the house in the daytime

and there "diligently to search." Burn, *Justice of the Peace*, 1772 ed., 3: 107–108. See also Hening, *New Virginia Justice*, 450.

104. See Nelson Lasson, *The History and Development of the Fourth Amendment to the Constitution* (Baltimore, 1937), 42, 44. The status of evidence obtained in the course of an illegal search and seizure did not come before the federal courts until 1822 (52–53). See also Bradford P. Wilson, *Enforcing the Fourth Amendment* (New York, 1986), 45–47.

105. Illinois v. Galic, 462 U.S. 213, 231–232 (1983).

106. United States v. Leon, 468 U.S. 897 (1984).

107. Silas Wasserstrom and L. M. Seidman, "The Fourth Amendment as Constitutional Theory," *Georgetown Law Journal* 77 (1988): 33.

108. Brinegar v. United States, 338 U.S. 160, 173–176 (1949).

109. Quoted in "Fifteenth Annual Review of Criminal Procedure: United States Supreme Court and Courts of Appeal, 1984–1985," *Georgetown Law Journal* 74 (1986): 499, 517.

110. Ibid. Information need not be admissible at trial (518). They have, however, insisted that the finding be made by a neutral detached magistrate (rather than a police officer), who weighs the information in a "nontechnical sense and realistic manner" (520–521).

111. See Wasserstrom and Seidman, "Fourth Amendment as Constitutional Theory," 19–112. See also Ronald J. Bacigal, "The Fourth Amendment in Flux: The Rise and Fall of Probable Cause," *University of Illinois Law Forum* (1979): 763–808.

112. See Langbein, *Prosecuting Crime in the Renaissance*.

113. For the use of torture in England, see David Jardine, *A Reading on the Use of Torture in the Criminal Law of England* (London, 1837); John Langbein, *Torture and the Law of Proof* (Chicago, 1977); James Heath, *Torture and English Law: An Administrative and Legal History of the Plantagenets to the Stuarts* (London, 1982).

114. For a discussion of the legal education of sixteenth- and seventeenth-century justices, see John Gleason, *The Justices of the Peace in England, 1558–1640* (Oxford, 1969), 83–84, 94–95. The change in the literacy level of the justices was part of the transformation of the gentry and the aristocracy. For a discussion of the extent to which criminal investigation remained private and communal despite the introduction of formal state enforcement structure, see Cynthia Herrup, "New Shoes and Mutton Pies: Investigative Responses to Theft in Seventeenth-Century East Sussex," *Historical Journal* 27 (1984): 811–830.

115. *Office of the Clerk of the Assize* (London, 1682), however, suggests that the documents certified by the justice of the peace could be read to the jury if the evidence was for the king and if the witness "falter in his testimony, to refresh his memory" (48). The same advice was given

to clerks for quarter sessions. After 1700, however, the practice appears to have ended.

116. Lambarde, *Eirenarcha*, 1614 ed., 229.

117. Richard Crompton, *L'office et auctoritie de justices de peace*, (London, 1606), 34; Dalton, *Country Justice*, 1618 ed., 296; Bolton, *Justice of the Peace*, 524–525; George Webb, *The Office and Authority of a Justice of the Peace* (Williamsburg, 1736), 140. Burn, the author of the most popular of the eighteenth-century manuals, based his comments on Fitzherbert, Crompton, Lambarde, and especially Dalton. Burn, *Justice of the Peace*, 12th ed., 1: xiii. Burn notes that too many of his predecessors had removed Dalton's qualifying language "by delivering in the absolute, which Mr. Dalton published under the several degrees of assent or doubtfulness." Burn promised to restore the more tentative language. He also added materials from Stanford, Coke, Hale, and Hawkins, again being careful to leave in such language as "it seemeth" and "it hath been said by some," "it seemeth the better opinion," or "it seemeth to be agreed" (xi).

118. See Langbein, *Prosecuting Crime in the Renaissance*.

119. Jacob, *Modern Justice*, 190. Jacob sounds doubtful but says no more.

120. Dalton, *Country Justice*, 1635 ed., cap. 165. This statement appeared in most handbooks.

121. Thomas G. Barnes, *The Clerk of the Peace in Caroline Somerset* (Leicester, 1961), 20.

122. Langbein, *Prosecuting Crime in the Renaissance*, 275, 310, 312.

123. Dalton, *Country Justice*, 1618 ed., 40.

124. Ibid.

125. Bolton, *Justice of the Peace*, 33.

126. See Gleason, *Justices of the Peace*, passim. See also J. H. Hexter, "The Education of the Aristocracy," in *Reappraisals in History* (New York, 1962), 71–116.

127. Lambarde, *Eirenarcha*, 1614 ed., 217.

128. Ibid., 219.

129. Cicero *De inventione* 1.34–43, 48; *Rhetorica ad herennium*, Loeb Classical Library, vol. 2 (Cambridge, Mass., 1954), 2.8.

130. Lambarde, *Eirenarcha*, 1614 ed., 218.

131. Ibid., 219.

132. Ibid.

133. Crompton, *L'office*. See also Thomas Wilson, *The Art of Rhetorique* (London, 1585), 91–92, 112–113.

134. Crompton, *L'office*, 100r.

135. Ibid., 98r, 99v, 100r. Bracton is nearly always cited in discussions of common fame.

136. Ibid., 110v.

137. Dalton, *Country Justice*, 1635 ed.

138. Ibid., title page.

139. Ibid., 40.

140. Ibid., 297, citing Crompton, *L'office*, 100.

141. Ibid., 297.

142. Ibid., 296, 297, 300. "Persons" required consideration of whether the accused fell into certain legal categories which might require different treatment, e.g., principal or accessory, children, insane, or if the injured party were king, commonwealth, magistrate, or master (303).

143. J. A. Sharpe, *Crime in Seventeenth-Century England: A County Study* (Cambridge, 1983), 166–167.

144. Quoted in Dalton, *Country Justice*, 1635 ed., 303. Coke's discussion of presumption did not occur in a passage dealing with pretrial examination. Coke, in another context, insists that only the grand jury might dismiss charges on the basis of "insufficient evidence."

145. *Trat's Murder* (1624), quoted in Langbein, *Prosecuting Crime in the Renaissance*, 53.

146. English handbooks note that torture was permitted *after* conviction in order to obtain information from accessories. This also is found in the civil law.

147. Joseph Keble, *An Assistance to Justices of the Peace* (London, 1683), 202, 604–605. This volume bore the imprimatur of twelve judges.

148. Ibid.

149. Hale, *History of the Pleas of the Crown*, 1: 583, 588. In another publication, Hale indicated that the justice could not discharge the accused simply because he did not believe him to be guilty. Sir Matthew Hale, *Pleas of the Crown, or a Methodical Summary* (London, 1678), 98.

150. Hawkins, *Pleas of the Crown*, 2: 99. Hawkins retains the language of violent presumption.

151. Sir Thomas Smith, *De Republica Anglorum* (Cambridge, 1906).

152. Langbein, *Prosecuting Crime in the Renaissance*, 96–97.

153. *William Lambarde and Local Government: His "Ephemeris" and Twenty-Nine Charges to Juries and Commissions*, ed. Conyers Read (Ithaca, N.Y., 1962).

154. Granville Leveson-Gower, "Notebook of a Surrey Justice," *Surrey Archeological Collections* 9 (1888): 183, 192, 196.

155. Macfarlane and Harrison, *Justice and the Mare's Ale*, 84, citing Fleming, *Letters*, 2629.

156. Joel Samaha, *Law and Order in Historical Perspective: The Case of Elizabethan Essex* (New York, 1974), xiii, 80–81, 84.

157. See Robert Shoemaker, "Crime and Community: Prosecution of Misdemeanor in Middlesex County, 1663–1725," Ph.D. diss., Stanford University, 1985), 47, 48, 73; J. A. Sharpe, "Enforcing the Law in the Seventeenth-Century Village," in *Crime and the Law: The Social History of Crime in Western Europe Since 1500*, ed. V. Gatrell et al. (London, 1980), 97–119.

158. *The Justicing Notebook of William Hunt*, ed. Elizabeth Crittal, Wiltshire Record Society, 37 (1982), 13, 14, 42, 46. See also Herrup, "New Shoes and Mutton Pies," passim.

159. Sharpe, "Enforcing the Law," 109–110, 112. See also Sharpe, *Crime in Seventeenth-Century England*.

160. See Martin Shapiro, *Courts: A Comparative and Political Analysis* (Chicago, 1981), 157–193.

161. See Langbein, *Prosecuting Crime in the Renaissance*, 262.

162. Thomas Cooper, *The Mysterie of Witchcraft* (London, 1617), 274–276, 277–278. Cooper would also have permitted torture. Sixteenth- and seventeenth-century chapbooks also reveal that in witchcraft cases the magistrate in both investigation and examination went well beyond the behavior prescribed by the Marian statutes. Langbein, *Prosecuting Crime in the Renaissance*, 52.

163. Similar langauge appears in Bolton, *Justice of the Peace*, 95.

164. Dalton, *Country Justice*, 1635 ed., 209. Robert Filmer, writing in 1653, indicated that "while 'presumptions' and 'signs' could and should be used during the magistrate's examination, each of these might be wrong or misleading."*Advertisement to the Grand Jurymen of England*, 1680 ed. (London, 1653), 308.

165. Bail would not have been possible in cases of witchcraft.

166. See Keith Thomas, *Religion and the Decline of Magic* (New York, 1979); Christina Larner, "Crimen Exceptum? The Crime of Witchcraft in Europe," in *Crime and the Law*, ed. Gatrell et al., 49–75. An American magistrate's handbook of 1736 recognized the exercise of judicial discretion in cases of witchcraft. The justice was advised to refuse information "without strong and apparent Cause provided by sufficient witnesses." George Webb, *The Office and Authority of a Justice of the Peace*, (Williamsburg, 1736), 361. See also Barbara Shapiro, *Probability and Certainty in Seventeenth-Century England* (Princeton, 1983), 194–226; Brian Levack, *The Witch-hunt in Early Modern Europe* (London, 1987).

167. In the 1715 edition of *Country Justice*, long after witchcraft had ceased to be prosecuted, a note was added on the role of "natural causes in diverse strange diseases." Unless the diabolic compact could be proved

by "evident marks or tokens," it was not sufficient to suppose that the devil was the agent. Dalton, *Country Justice*, 1715 ed., 386.

168. Bolton, *Justice of the Peace*, 95.

169. 3 Edw. 1, c. 15. For an excellent summary of the history of bail, see Hermine Herla Meyer, "Constitutionality of Pretrial Detention," *Georgetown Law Journal* 50 (1972): 1139–1186. By 1275 the concept of varying degrees of suspicion was in common use.

170. Hawkins, *Pleas of the Crown*, 2: 98, 99. Hawkins seems to have been doubtful about whether "former scandalous behavior" plus slight evidence of the current offense were sufficient to create such a presumption.

171. T. F. T. Plucknett, "A Commentary on the Indictments," in *Proceedings before Justices of the Peace*, ed. B. H. Putnam (London, 1938), 433. See Meyer, "Constitutionality of Pretrial Detention," 1157–1158; for post-1952 developments, see 1160ff.

172. See Bertram Osborne, *Justices of the Peace, 1361–1848* (Shaftesbury, Dorset, 1960), 35–71; Norma Landau, *The Justices of the Peace, 1679–1760* (Berkeley, 1984).

173. Sheppard, *The Whole Office*. Edmund Bohun, *Justice of the Peace, His Calling: A Moral Essay* (London, 1684), 11, 35, 36, 41, 57. He also discussed the problems of malicious suits and bias, both favorable and hostile, (114–116). For a late eighteenth-century work emphasizing the justice's role as truth seeker, see Thomas Gisborne, *An Enquiry into the Duties of Men in the Higher and Middle Classes of Society* (London, 1794), 278, 280–282. For the importance of the changing religious and philosophical views on the image of justice on the criminal law, see Randall McGowen, "The Image of Justice and Reform of the Criminal Law in Early Nineteenth-Century England," *Buffalo Law Review* 32 (1983): 89–125, and McGowen, "The Changing Face of God's Justice: The Debates over Divine and Human Punishment in Eighteenth-Century England," *Criminal Justice History* (1986): 63–97.

174. Lambarde, *Eirenarcha*, 1619 ed., 116–121. Such sureties provided a kind of "preventative justice." Blackstone, *Commentaries*, 4: 251. The justices were obliged to demand sureties of those whom "there is probable grounds to suspect of *future* misbehavior" (emphasis mine). The judgment of the magistrates thus also was to be exercised so as to prevent future offenses.

175. Dalton's *Country Justice* was purchased by the General Courts of Virginia and Massachusetts. See Hugh Ranken, *Criminal Trial Proceedings in the General Court of Colonial Virginia* (Williamsburg, 1965), 44–75; *Conductor Generalis, or the Office and Duty of the Justice of the Peace* (Philadelphia, 1722). This volume was largely taken from Nelson's *Office*

and Authority of a Justice of the Peace. Enlarged editions were published
in Philadelphia and New York in 1749. The 1764 edition was largely based
on Burn. See also Webb, *Office and Authority of a Justice of the Peace;*
Richard Starke, *Office and Authority of the Justice of the Peace* (Williamsburg, 1774); Hening, *New Virginia Justice.* The Webb handbook was almost identical to that of Burn. See Boyer, "Justice of the Peace in England
and America," 315–326.

176. Joseph H. Smith, *Colonial Justice in Western Massachusetts,
1639–1672,* 145. See also William Nelson, *Americanization of the Common Law* (Cambridge, Mass., 1975), 106–107.

177. Gail Marcus, "'Due Execution of the Generall Rules of Righteousnesse': Criminal Proceedings in New Haven Town and Colony,
1638–1658," in *Saints and Revolutionaries: Essays in American History,*
ed. David Hall (New York, 1984), 103, 108. The New Haven Colony
adopted neither grand jury indictment nor jury trial.

178. Kathryn Preyer, "Penal Measures in the American Colonies: An
Overview," *American Journal of Legal History* 28 (1982): 330; Rankin,
Criminal Trial Proceedings, 78–79. Starke, *Office and Authority of the
Justice of the Peace,* 114–115. The examining court is unmentioned by
Hening (1793), although it was printed in Virginia and designed for the
Virginia market. This is further evidence that handbooks did not always
reflect practice!

179. Webb, *Office and Authority of a Justice of the Peace,* 32, citing
Dalton, *Country Justice,* 432.

180. Ibid., 361.

181. *The Works of James Wilson,* ed. Robert McCloskey, 2 vols. (Cambridge, Mass., 1967), 2: 675, citing Hawkins, *Pleas of the Crown,* 87.

182. David Freestone and J. C. Richardson, "The Making of English
Criminal Law (7): Sir John Jervis and His Acts," *Criminal Law Review*
(1980): 6. See also W. W. Pue, "The Criminal Twilight Zone: Pretrial Procedures in the 1840s," *Alberta Law Review* 21 (1983): 335–363; John Beattie, *Crime and the Courts in England, 1660–1800* (Princeton, 1986), 268–
281.

183. Beattie, *Crime and the Courts,* 268–281.

184. Ibid., 359–361. See also John Langbein, "Shaping the
Eighteenth-Century Criminal Trial: A View from the Ryder Sources,"
University of Chicago Law Review 50 (1983): 1–136, and Langbein, "The
Criminal Trial before the Lawyers," *University of Chicago Law Review*
45 (1978): 263–306.

185. See Landau, *Justices of the Peace,* 184–187, 189–190, 200, 203.

186. Beattie, *Crime and the Courts,* 274, citing *Covent Garden Journal,* 25 February 1752. See also John Styles, "Sir John Fielding and the

Problem of Criminal Investigation in Eighteenth-Century England," *Transactions of The Royal Historical Society*, 5th ser., vol. 33 (1983): 127–150.

187. Quoted in Beattie, *Crime and the Courts*, 275.

188. Blackstone, *Commentaries*, 4: 293. Burn's 1772 edition of *Justice of the Peace* retains Dalton's traditional language forbidding discretion (1: 524–525). Costs were transferred from the accuser to the public in the 1750s to increase prosecution.

189. See Jennifer Davis, "A Poor Man's System of Justice: The London Police Courts in the Second Half of the Nineteenth Century," *Historical Journal* 171 (1984): 309–335. The London police courts were established in 1792 and took their final form in 1838, replacing the metropolitan "trading justices." Like their rural counterparts, they conducted a great deal of nonjudicial business, acted as mediators and arbitrators, and by summary authority convicted and punished a large variety of small offenses.

190. Leon Radzinowicz, *A History of English Criminal Law and Its Administration from 1750*, 4 vols. (London, 1948–1968), 1: 715.

191. Charles Cottu, *The Administration of Criminal Justice in England* (London, 1822), 113. He reported that the disappointed complainant might still take his case directly to the grand jury. Cottu felt, however, that compared to their Continental counterparts, the justices were not anxious to discover the motivation for crimes and made no effort to search for proofs (33, 38). They thus did not appear to have performed a prosecutorial role.

192. Patrick Devlin, *Criminal Prosecution in England* (New Haven, 1958), 12.

193. Beattie, *Crime and the Courts*, 341. See also C. K. Allen, "The Presumption of Innocence," in *Legal Duties and Other Essays in Jurisprudence* (Oxford, 1931), 253–294.

194. Beattie, *Crime and the Courts*, 276, citing Chitty, *Criminal Law*, 2d ed., 4 vols. (1826), 1: 89.

195. 11 and 12 Vict., c. 42. See Freestone and Richardson, "The Making of English Criminal Law." The 1848 act also codified summary procedure. For a discussion of the Jervis Act and pretrial procedure of the 1840s, see Pue, "The Criminal Twilight Zone," 335–363. Legislation in 1867 permitted the defense to call witnesses as well.

196. 30 and 31 Vict., c. 35, s. 2. See F. W. Maitland, *Justice and Police* (London, 1985), 129. Interestingly, by 1883 Stephen felt that the preliminary hearing had become too judicialized and was becoming a separate trial. *History of the Criminal Law of England*, 1: 229.

197. Rex v. Governor of Brixton Prison, *Ex parte* Bidwell, 118, 305. In 1967 the procedure was considerably simplified.

198. See Phillip B. Kurland and D. W. M. Waters, "Public Prosecutions in England, 1854–1879: An Essay on English Legislative History," *Duke Law Journal* (1959): 493–562.

199. For the role of advertising in England c. 1700 and 1730 see Styles, "Print and Policy," 55–95. See also David Philips, "Good Men to Associate and Bad Men to Conspire: Associations for the Prosecution of Felons in England, 1760–1860," in *Policing and Prosecution in Britain, 1650–1850*, ed. Douglas Hay and Francis Snyder (Oxford, 1989), 114–170, and P. J. R. King, "Prosecuting Associations and Their Impact on Eighteenth-Century Essex," also in *Policing and Prosecution*, 171–209. King's study indicates that the associations failed to make a significant impact on jury verdicts.

200. There is still no satisfactory explanation for the origins of the American public prosecutor. Dutch, Scottish, and French antecedents have been suggested. See Joan E. Jacoby, *The American Public Prosecutor: A Search for Identity* (Lexington, Mass., 1980), 3–4, 19–20. Congress established the office of the attorney general and created U.S. attorneys in 1789. The Canadians also developed a form of public prosecution. Jacoby traces the transformation from a weak, minor court official to a central law-enforcement officer. See also Joseph Kress, "Progress and Prosecution," in *Crime and Justice in America, 1776–1976*, ed. Graeme R. Newman (Philadelphia, 1976).

201. Jacoby, *American Public Prosecutor*, 29–30, 138–142, 146–159.

202. Ibid., 29–30, 32. For the relationship between grand jury and prosecutor see 138–142.

203. Munn v. Dupont, 3 Wash. 37 (1811).

204. Bacon v. Towne, 4 Cush. (Mass.), 238 (1849).

205. Ibid.; Bacon v. Towne, 4 Cush. (Mass.), 233.

206. Humphries v. Parker, 52 (Maine), 505 (1864).

207. Greer v. Whilfield, 4 Lea (Tenn.), 90 (1879).

208. Graham Greene, *Our Man in Havana* (London, 1970), 164.

Chapter Four

1. See Adhemar Esmein, *A History of Continental Criminal Procedure in Specific Reference to France* (Boston, 1913); Harold Berman, *Law and Revolution: The Formation of the Western Legal Tradition* (Cambridge, Mass., 1983); Mirjan R. Damaska, *The Faces of Justice and State Authority: A Comparative Approach to the Legal Process* (New Haven, 1986); Walter Ullmann, "Medieval Principles of Evidence," *Law Quarterly Review* 62 (1946): 77–87; Andre Laingue and Arlette Lebigry, *Histoire du droit penale, 2: La procedure criminelle* (Paris, 1986); Raoul Van

Caenegem, "History of European Civil Procedure," *International Encyclopedia of Comparative Law*, vol. 16 (Tübingen, 1973), 2, 3–79.

2. The Romano-canon system of proof was already in place in the northern province by the late thirteenth century, and by the early fourteenth century it was fully implemented in the two English archdioceses. See Charles Donahue, "Proof by Witnesses in the Church Courts of Medieval England: An Imperfect Reception of the Learned Law," in *On the Laws and Customs of England*, ed. Morris Arnold et al. (Chapel Hill, 1981), 141. While the English ecclesiastical courts took over the system of proof outlined in the academic treatises, some variation existed in practice. Thus some testimony was accepted from those who were not eyewitnesses, and some who testified should technically have been disqualified (127–158).

3. Theodore Plucknett, *A Concise History of the Common Law*, 5th ed. (Boston, 1956), 298, 433. Bracton's rules also echo canonist witness disqualifications. Bracton was first printed in 1569. See also Plucknett, "The Relations between Roman Law and English Common Law," *University of Toronto Law Journal* 2 (1939): 24.

4. Michael Dalton, *The Country Justice* (London, 1618), 261–262.

5. John Langbein, *Prosecuting Crime in the Renaissance: England, Germany, France* (Cambridge, 1974), 124.

6. See Richard Chamberlain, *The Complete Justice* (London, 1681), 449.

7. See J. S. Cockburn and Thomas A. Green, eds., *Twelve Good Men and True: The Criminal Trial Jury in England, 1200–1800* (Princeton, 1988).

8. Sir Thomas Smith, *De Republica Anglorum* (Cambridge, 1906), 98.

9. Sir John Fortescue, *De Laudibus Legum Anglie*, ed. and trans. S. B. Chrimes (Cambridge, Mass., 1942), chaps. 25–26.

10. Smith, *De Republica Anglorum*, 99–101. See also 67, 79, 80. For discussions of witnesses who are jurors and infamous and interested witnesses see Anon., *The Law of Evidence*, 2 vols. (Savoy, 1717), 8, 20–66. Richard L. Marcus, "The Tudor Treason Trials: Some Observations on the Emergence of Forensic Themes," *University of Illinois Law Review* (1984): 698, 699–701, citing *Trial of Udall* (1590), 1 *State Trials*, 1281; Kevin Teeven, "Problems of Proof and Early English Contract Law," *Cambrian Law Review* (1984): 54, 55.

11. Geoffrey Elton, *The Tudor Constitution* (London, 1960), 67–68, 72–76.

12. Treason Act, 13 Car. 3, c. 1. For discussion of the evolution of the 1696 treason legislation, see Samuel Reznick, "The Statute of 1696: A Pioneer Measure in the Reform of Judicial Procedure in England," *Jour-*

nal of Modern History 2 (1930): 5–26; Walter Simon, "The Evolution of Treason," *Tulane Law Review* 35 (1961): 669–698; Lamar Hill, "The Two-Witness Rule in English Treason Trials: Some Comments on the Emergence of Procedural Law," *American Journal of Legal History* 12 (1968): 95–111.

13. T. B. Howell, *Complete Collection of State Trials*, 34 vols. (London, 1809–1826), 2: 15–18. The issue of a single witness was also raised in the *Trial of John Fisher, Bishop of Rochester* (1535), 1 *State Trials*, 401, 402, and the *Trial of Sir Nicholas Throckmorton* (1554), 1 *State Trials*, 880, 886. When Bacon, during his impeachment trial of 1620, objected to a single witness as insufficient, Coke replied that one witness was sufficient especially to prove "a work of darkness." 2 *State Trials*, 1093.

14. See John H. Wigmore, "The Required Number of Witnesses: A Brief History of the Numerical System in England." *Harvard Law Review* 15 (1901): 82–108.

15. Chamberlain's *Complete Justice* (London, 1681) lists offenses that required either one or two witnesses. His rather lengthy list of offenses requiring two witnesses were all established by statute, perhaps suggesting the Crown and Parliament were more willing to invoke the two-witness rule. Laymen may have been less suspicious of Romano-canon features than was the legal profession. The statutes cited include those passed during the reigns of Henry VIII, Edward VI, Elizabeth, James I, and Charles II (450). Two witnesses were required to convict a woman for concealing the death of her child. 21 Jac., c. 27 (1623). Perjury, too, required two witnesses. Legal commentators such as Hale who contrast the benefits of the English legal system with that of the Continent, however, continue to emphasize that English juries were not required to have a specified number of witnesses. Sir Matthew Hale, *History and Analysis of the Common Law of England* (London, 1820), 346–347. Wigmore suggests that most perjury cases prior to 1640 had been tried by Star Chamber, which, like Chancery and the ecclesiastical courts, regularly employed the two-witness rule, and that the two-witness requirement continued after such cases were transferred to the common-law courts. Adultery, which was made a felony in 1650 and required two witnesses, also had been previously tried by the ecclesiastical courts.

16. Robert Boyle, "Some Considerations about the Reasonableness of Reason and Religion," in *The Works of Robert Boyle* (London, 1772), 4: 182.

17. Maija Jansson, "Matthew Hale on Judges and Judging," *Journal of Legal History* 9 (1989): 208. Jewish law "expected a full evidence to convict such a malefactor and would not pass that sentence only upon con-

nections and implorations of circumstances that contained not in themselves a full evidence."

18. Donald Veall, *The Popular Movement for Law Reform, 1640–1660* (Oxford, 1970), 128, 154; Stuart E. Prall, *The Agitation for Law Reform during the Puritan Revolution, 1640–1660* (The Hague, 1966), 71. See also Lilburne, "Large Petition of the Levellers" (1647), in *Puritanism and Liberty*, ed. A. S. P. Woodhouse (Chicago, 1938), 322–323; Jansson, "Matthew Hale on Judges," 208.

19. Prall, *Agitation for Law Reform*, 22. Admiralty, which employed civilian procedure, was left alone during the Commonwealth and Protectorate (34).

20. Edwin Powers, *Crime and Punishment in Early Massachusetts, 1620–1692* (Boston, 1966), 91. The phrase "that which is equivalent" was interpreted to mean one clear witness and "concurrent and concluding circumstances." See also Gail Marcus, " 'Due Execution of the Generall Rules of Righteousnesse': Criminal Proceedings in New Haven Town and Colony, 1638–1658," in *Saints and Revolutionaries: Essays in American History*, ed. David Hall (New York, 1984).

21. It has been suggested that New Englanders were less fearful of the civil law than were the English because it was practiced by fellow Calvinists in Scotland and the Netherlands.

22. See William Nelson, *Americanization of the Common Law: The Impact of Legal Change on Massachusetts Society, 1760–1830* (Cambridge, Mass., 1975).

23. See Gerard Reedy, *The Bible and Reason: Anglicans and Scripture in Late Seventeenth-Century England* (Philadelphia, 1985); Henry Van Leeuwen, *The Problem of Certainty in English Thought, 1630–1690* (The Hague, 1963).

24. For Lilburne see Van Leeuwen, *Problem of Certainty*, 40; see also Edward Stillingfleet, *Origines Sacrae* (London, 1662), 237–240; Seth Ward, *A Philosophical Essay toward an Eviction of the Being and Attributes of God*, 5th ed., 1677 (London, 1654), 90, 99–100, 102, 117.

25. Sir Matthew Hale, *The Primitive Origination of Mankind* (London, 1677), 129. Hale occasionally employs civil law language. He notes "That evidence at Law which taken singly or apart makes but an imperfect proof, *semiplena probatio*, yet in conjunction with others, like *Silurus* his twigs, that were easily broken apart, but in conjunction or union were not to be broken" (130). Hale's *Analysis of the Laws of England* (London, 1713) appears to have been influenced by the structure of Justinian's *Institutes*.

26. Sir Matthew Hale, *The History of the Common Law of England*,

ed. Charles M. Gray (Chicago, 1971), 163–164. For a similar statement
emphasizing jurors' knowledge of the accused, the nature of the offense,
and the credit of the accused and his witnesses, see Zachary Babington,
Advice to Grand Jurors in Cases of Blood (London, 1677), 4.

27. Hale, *History of the Common Law*, 165. Jurors were of the vicinage and "oftentimes know the Witnesses and the Parties" (167).

28. Ibid., 164, 165, 167.

29. John Locke, *An Essay Concerning Human Understanding*, ed.
Alexander Fraser, 2 vols. (New York, 1959), bk. 4, chap. 4, sec. 4.

30. Ibid., bk. 4, chap. 4, sec. 6.

31. Ibid., bk. 4, chap. 4, sec. 5.

32. Geoffrey Gilbert, *The Law of Evidence* (London, 1756), 121–161.
The 1769 and 1788 editions are almost identical. The 1791 edition by
Capel Lofft was much enlarged. For a discussion of the treatise tradition,
see A. W. Simpson, "The Rise and Fall of the Legal Treatise: Legal Prin-
ciples and the Forms of Legal Literature," *University of Chicago Law
Review* 48 (1981): 632–680.

33. Gilbert, *Law of Evidence*, 1756 ed., 150–151; see also 154–155.
See also Capel Lofft, 1791 ed., 1: 403–409. John Morgan's *Essays Upon
the Law of Evidence*, 2 vols. (London, 1789) is very similar to Gilbert.
He notes one witness is sufficient to prove any single fact, although the
concurrence of two or more corroborate the proof. He emphasizes the
importance of observing the quality, age, education, understanding, behavior, and inclination of the witnesses. The credit of witnesses was to be
judged from their state and dignity in the world. Their skill, knowledge,
memory, and moral condition were also important. The lowest proof was
the oath of one witness. Two witnesses were "one step higher" than one
witness and were sometimes required by law. 1: 9, 12, 46–47, 293–294,
296. For a discussion of witness credibility in connection with the grand
jury see Sir John Somers, *The Security of English-Men's Lives* (London,
1681), 38, 142. See also Joseph Keble, *An Assistance to Justices of the
Peace* (London, 1683), 264; George Stanhope, *The Duty of Witnesses. A
Sermon* (London, 1701). Stanhope, a chaplain to the king, employs the
concept of moral certainty and suggests that two witnesses are usually
required (26). The sermon was preached at the Maidstone Assizes before
L. C. J. Holt and was published at the request of the high sheriff of Kent.

34. William M. Best, *The Principles of the Law of Evidence*, 6th ed.
(London, 1875), 18–19, 20, 21, 22. See also 24.

35. Ibid., 102.

36. Ibid., 749.

37. John H. Wigmore, "History of the Hearsay Rule," *Harvard Law
Review* 17 (1904): 436–458; R. W. Baker, *The Hearsay Rule* (London,

1950); Edward M. Morgan, *Some Problems of Proof under the Anglo-American System of Litigation* (New York, 1956), 106–140.

38. In 1650, jurors in *Bennett v. Hartford* were told that if they give evidence, it should be done in open court. Baker, *Hearsay Rule*, 10, citing (1650) Style 233. We do not yet know about the evolution of the concept that jurors were *not* to know facts on personal knowledge and "should be in a state of legal ignorance." Best, *Principles of the Law of Evidence*, 117. Hearsay evidence was rejected by Somers, in connection with grand jury "verdicts." Somers, *Security of English-Men's Lives*, 141.

39. See Barbara Shapiro, *Probability and Certainty in Seventeenth-Century England* (Princeton, 1983), 21, 274.

40. Hale, *Primitive Origination of Mankind*, 128.

41. Locke, *Essay Concerning Human Understanding*, bk. 4, chap. 14, sec. 10.

42. Wigmore, "History of the Hearsay Rule," 435, 445, 454. Edward M. Morgan, "Hearsay Dangers and the Application of the Hearsay Concept," *Harvard Law Review* 62 (1948): 180–181; Baker, *Hearsay Rule*, 7–9.

43. Edward Waterhouse, *Fortescue Illustratus* (London, 1663), 350.

44. Even after the hearsay exclusion was established, hearsay was considered acceptable if used to confirm or corroborate other testimony. This principle was employed in Raleigh's trial of 1603. It is to be found in Gilbert's *Law of Evidence* and was accepted until the end of the eighteenth century. Wigmore, "History of the Hearsay Rule," 443, 447. Several eighteenth-century texts connected the hearsay rule with the best evidence rule. Baker, *Hearsay Rule*, 15.

45. Best, *Principles of the Law of Evidence*, 377.

46. See Alessandro Giuliani, "The Influence of Rhetoric on the Law of Evidence and Pleading," *Juridical Review* 62 (1969): 216–251. For a more general discussion of rhetoric and English law, see D. S. Bland, "Rhetoric and the Law Student in Sixteenth-Century England," *Studies in Philology* 53 (1957): 498–508; R. J. Schoeck, "Rhetoric and Law in Sixteenth-Century England," *Studies in Philology* 50 (1953): 110–127; Wilfred Prest, "Dialectical Origins of Finch's Law," *Cambridge Law Journal* 36 (1977): 326–352. See also V. P. Mortari, "Dialectica e giurisprudenza: Studio sui trattati di dialettica legale del sec. XVI," *Annali di Storia del Diritto* 1 (1957): 293–401.

47. Quintilian, *Institutes of the Orator* (London, 1777), bk. 4, chap. 9.

48. Ibid.

49. For a similar treatment in Cicero, see *De partitione oratoria*, Loeb Classical Library, vol. 4. Cicero considers the qualities of persons, e.g.

health, appearance, age, sex, intellectual abilities, moral character, emotional dispositions, social condition, education, occupation, associates, power, and wealth. The place and time (day, night, season) of the event are to be considered, as are the traces (weapon, blood, crying out). Also to be considered were trembling and changing color. Consideration of these circumstances of an action could lead to the discovery of probability. For a somewhat more elaborate treatment, see Cicero, *De inventione*, Loeb Classical Library, vol. 2.

50. For examples of this tradition see Tancred, *Ordo iudiciarius*; William Durantis, *Speculum iudiciale*; Albertus Gandinus, *Tractatus de maleficiis*; Thomas de Piperata, *Tractatus de fama*; Julius Clarus, *Practica criminalis*; Joannes Menochius, *De praesumptionibus, conjecturis, signis et indiciis, commentoris* (1608); Antonius Matthaeus, *De criminibus*; Prosper Farinaccius, *Praxis et theorica criminales*; Josephus Mascardus, *Les conclusiones probationum*.

51. See Richard Fraher, "Conviction According to Conscience: The Medieval Jurist's Debate Concerning Judicial Discretion and the Law of Proof," *Law and History Review* 7 (1989): 23–88; Giorgia Alessi Palazzola, *Prova legale e pena: La crisi del sistema tra evo medio e moderno* (Naples, 1979). See also James Franklin, "The Ancient Legal Sources of Seventeenth-Century Probability," in *The Uses of Antiquity in the Scientific Revolution*, ed. S. Gaukroger, pub. forthcoming.

52. See Fraher, "Conviction According to Conscience," passim; Palazzola, *Prova legale e pena*, 61–66, 79–81; John Langbein, *Torture and the Law of Proof* (Chicago, 1977); Mirjan Damaska, "The Death of Legal Torture," *Yale Law Journal* 87 (1978): 866. The concept of half proof appears c. 1200 in the writing of Glossator Azo. Franklin, "Ancient Sources," citing Azo, *Lectura super Codicem*, bk. 4, tit. 1 (reprint, Turin, 1966), 254.

53. Bartolus pointed out that transient facts cannot be notorious. Fraher, "Conviction According to Conscience," 51–54. See also Damaska, "Death of Legal Torture," 867.

54. Fraher, "Conviction According to Conscience," 55–56. See also Palazzola, *Prova legale e pena*, passim.

55. The efforts of judges of the Parlement of Paris to gain control over and limit the use of torture by provincial judges not only reduced the use of judicial torture but also increased reliance on circumstantial evidence—evidence which constituted less than "legal proof." See Alfred Soman, "Criminal Jurisprudence in Ancien-Regime France: The Parlement of Paris in the Sixteenth and Seventeenth Centuries," in *Crime and Criminal Justice in Europe and Canada*, ed. Louis A. Knafla (Waterloo, Canada, 1981), 43–75, and "La justice criminelle aux XVIe–XVIIe siècles:

Le Parlement de Paris et les sièges subalternes," in *La faute, la repression et le pardon: Philologie et histoire jusque à 1610*, vol. 1 (Brest, 1982), 16–52. Soman's research complements that of John Langbein. See Langbein, *Torture and the Law of Proof.* See also Damaska, "Death of Legal Torture," 860–883. The *Carolina* appears to insist on the necessity of full legal proof, but sixteenth-century Germany as well as France used the *poena extraordinaria* (867).

56. Palazzola, *Prova legale e pena*, 46–47. The same categories are to be found in *Summa de ordine judiciario* of Damoso, cited in Palazzola (47–48). James Franklin suggests that canonists and civilians developed gradations of proof from the *Digest* and that the violent-probable-light grading of presumptions can be found by the 1150s. In the mid-thirteenth century, Aquinas identified three varieties of suspicion. "One is violent, to the contrary of which proof is not admitted, as when someone is found alone with a woman, naked on a bed, in a secret place, at a time apt for intercourse. The second is the probable (*probabilis*). . . . Third is the rash, which arises from a light conjecture . . . although the first kind does not have the certainty of something actually sensed, or the certainty of demonstration, it does have certainty sufficient for proof in law. For the same kind of certainty is not required in all things, as is said in Aristotle's *Ethics*." Quoted in Franklin, "Ancient Sources," 12. Aquinas also mentioned the half proofs of the lawyers.

57. Ibid., 115–117. Menochius also indicates that judges might condemn on the basis of presumption in the absence of full proof if penalties were diminished. Similar treatments are to be found in the treatises of Alciatus, Carpzov, and Matthaeus.

58. Cesare Beccaria, *An Essay on Crimes and Punishment*, 1983 ed., Brookline, Mass. (1764), 54–55.

59. See Paul Foriers, "La conception de la preuve dans l'école le droit natural," in *La Preuve: Deuxième partie: Moyen âge et temps modernes*. Recueils de la Société Jean Bodin pour l'histoire comparative des institutions (Brussels, 1965), 169–192.

60. Marcus, "Tudor Treason Trials," 702, citing 2 *State Trials*, 15.

61. Henry Bracton, *On the Laws and Customs of England*, ed. and trans. Samuel E. Thorne, 4 vols. (Cambridge, Mass., 1968), 4: 330. An edition appeared in 1640.

62. Ibid., 2: 386; see also 2: 404.

63. The bloody sword example of violent presumption was a standard of medieval jurists. Some Romano-canonist medieval lawyers, however, suggested the possibility of self-defense or other explanations. Ullmann, "Medieval Principles of Evidence," 86.

64. Sir Edward Coke, *The First Part of the Institutes of the Lawes of*

England: or, A Commentary upon Littleton (1628), sec. 1, 6b. Coke indicated in connection with charter, or feoffments, that where the witnesses were dead, violent presumption of continual and quiet possession
"stands for a proofe." The bloody sword example of presumption also
appears in William Staunford, *Les plees del coron* (London, 1557), 11b.3,
c. 14. This volume is based primarily on Bracton and the yearbooks. There
were 6 editions before 1600.

65. See Sir Edward Coke, *Third Part of the Institutes of the Lawes of
England* (Philadelphia, 1853), chap. 104, 232.

66. Thus Coke noted that no presumptions were to be admitted against
presumptions of law (ibid.). Wrongs shall never be presumed (ibid., 373).
The Anglo-American presumption of innocence may be derived from this
maxim.

67. An alternative approach was to reduce the standard further and
allow half proofs for conviction. Jean Bodin advocated this approach to
proof in witchcraft cases.

68. For several decades after the statutes both the common people and
the governing classes believed in the possibility of witchcraft. Without
the willing participation of accusers, justices of the peace, grand juries,
judges, and juries, the processes of arrest, examination, indictment, trial,
and punishment could not have occurred. For discussion of witchcraft in
England, see Alan Macfarlane, *Witchcraft in Tudor and Stuart England*
(London, 1979); Keith Thomas, *Religion and the Decline of Magic* (New
York, 1979); C. L'Estrange Ewen, *Witch Hunters and Witch Trials* (London, 1929); Shapiro, *Probability and Certainty*, 194–226. See also Christina Larner, "Crimen Exceptum? The Crime of Witchcraft in Europe,"
in *Crime and the Law: The Social History of Crime in Western Europe
Since 1500*, ed. V. A. C. Gatrell, et al. (London 1980), 49–75; Brian Levack, *The Witch-hunt in Early Modern Europe* (London, 1987).

69. Gifford thus invoked civil law standards for conviction. George Gif-
ford, "Dialogue Concerning Witches and Witchcraft," in *The Witchcraft
Papers*, ed. Peter Haining (1593; reprint, London, 1974); Thomas Cooper,
The Mysterie of Witchcraft (London, 1617), 276–278.

70. John Cotta, *The Trial of Witchcraft* (London, 1616), 85. Cotta's
work was dedicated to Sir Edward Coke and the legal profession. Reginald
Scot, *Discoverie of Witchcraft* (1584; reprint, London, 1964), 42; see also
40–43. Scot, who considered most confessions to be "idle, false, incon-
stant and of no weight," came close to denying that witchcraft existed (61).

71. Dalton, *Country Justice*, 1618 ed., 273, 1 cap. 107. Convictions for
witchcraft, however, had fallen off sharply by 1620 except for a brief flurry
in the 1640s.

72. E.g., Richard Bolton, *A Justice of the Peace in Ireland* (Dublin,
1683), 95.

73. Robert Filmer, *An Advertisement to the Grand Jurymen of England Touching Witchcraft*, 1680 ed. (London, 1653), preface, 308. Perkins's categorizations of proofs into "less sufficient" and "more sufficient" were, according to Filmer, used erroneously because his less sufficient really "meaneth insufficient." Indeed his "unsufficient sufficient proofs" were weaker and worse than his presumptions, which he confesses are "no proofs at all." Perkins's "less sufficient proofs" included proofs of red hot irons, scratching the suspected, and burning items belonging to the suspected. Perkins's "more sufficient proofs" were confession and the testimony of two witnesses (306, 309, 312).

The language of vehement suspicion and presumption also appear in the literature of colonial American witchcraft. Late seventeenth-century New Englanders appear to have been familiar with and perhaps puzzled by these concepts. In one case there was "just ground of vehement suspicion," but this was not deemed "Legally guilty according to Inditement." When the same party was brought to trial again a few years later (1680), the court decided the evidence was insufficient for indictment but was sufficient for punishment. There was "not full proof" that the individual was a witch, but "The Court vehemently suspects her so to be." The accused was imprisoned. In another case in which an individual was acquitted, the court indicated that the accused was "suspiciously Guilty of Witchcraft, but not legally guilty, according to lawe and evidence wee have received." When the evidence was strong, but insufficient, the accused might be required to pay court costs and might be punished. Carol F. Karlsen, *The Devil in the Shape of a Woman: Witchcraft in Colonial New England* (New York, 1989), 56, 59, 60.

74. 1 *State Trials*, 1053, 1054, 1065, 1070, 1071. See also *Trial of Udall* (1590), 2 *State Trials*, 1281.

75. 2 *State Trials*, 18. In the 1606 trial of Henry Garnet the judge referred "to many apparent proofs, and evident presumptions" while the defendant, like Campion a few years earlier, asked that the jury not credit things where there was "no direct proof" nor "to condemn him by circumstances or presumptions." 2 *State Trials*, 253, 256.

76. Keith Thomas, "The Puritans and Adultery: The Act of 1650 Reconsidered," in *Puritans and Revolutionaries*, ed. Donald Pennington and Keith Thomas (Oxford, 1978), 279, citing Daniel Taylor, *Certain Queries* (London, 1651), 9–10, and William Sheppard, *England's Balme* (London, 1657), 159–160. Adultery had previously been under the jurisdiction of the ecclesiastical courts. The act of 1650 resulted in very few convictions (280).

77. The English also received some instruction on the principles of the civil law from such English works as Robert Wiseman's *Law of Laws, or the Excellency of the Civil Law* (London, 1657). Wiseman introduced

the standard distinction between direct and indirect proofs. He indicated that the civil law did not require "direct and positive proof" but would admit of "strong and forcible presumptions also, that by arguments of conjecture drawn from one thing to another, brings forth the certainty of the things in issue." Wiseman, *Law of Laws*, 1686 ed., 27, citing Wiesenbach. With appropriate reference to Menochius on presumption, he indicates that presumptions might have the same force as proofs. He explained, however, that no proof, presumptive or direct, was sufficient without the testimony of two witnesses and cited the Romano-canon maxim that the testimony of one witness in serious crimes was the same as that of no witnesses at all (37). See also Waterhouse, *Fortescue Illustratus*, 260.

For further discussion of the civil law and the civilians in England, see Brian Levack, *The Civil Lawyers in England, 1603–1641: A Political Study* (Oxford, 1973); Theodore Plucknett, "Roman Law and English Common Law," 24–50; Peter Stein, "Continental Influences in English Thought, 1600–1900," in *La Formazione Storica del diretto moderno in Europa*, ed. L. S. Olschki (Florence, 1977), 1105–1125; Dafydd Jenkins, "English Law and the Renaissance, Eighty Years On: In Defense of Maitland," *Journal of Legal History* 2 (1981): 107–142; Gino Gorla and Luigi Moccia, "A 'Revisiting' of the Comparison between 'Continental Law' and 'English Law,'" *Journal of Legal History* 2 (1981): 143–156; Luigi Moccia, "English Attitudes to the 'Civil Law,'" *Journal of Legal History* 2 (1981): 157–169; J. H. Baker, "English Law and the Renaissance," *Cambridge Law Journal* 44 (1985): 46–61. See also articles by Daniel R. Coquillette cited in Chapter 3 and bibliography.

78. Coke, *Third Part of the Institutes*, chap. 104; Sir Matthew Hale, *Historia Placitorium Coronae* (London, 1734), 239. The recent effort to interpret Hale's willingness to accept less than normal evidence in cases of witchcraft and rape as the result of his hostility to women fails to take into account that these crimes fell into the traditional category of infrequently witnessed crimes. See Gilbert Geis, "Lord Hale, Witches and Rape," *British Journal of Law and Society* 5 (1978): 26–44. But see David Lanham, "Hate, Misogyny and Rape," *Criminal Law Review* 7 (1983): 148–166.

79. The *Trial of John Giles* (London, 1681), 144, 54.

80. The *Trial of Dover*, in Howell, 6 *State Trials*, 13, 559.

81. *The True Narrative*, Old Bailey Trials, 2.

82. Ibid., 3.

83. 7 *State Trials*, 726.

84. *An Account of . . . The Tryal of Mr. Edward Fitzharris* (London, 1681), 1.

85. *Trial of Carr* (London, 1681), 14.

86. Ibid., 22–23.

87. Gilbert Burnet, *The Life and Death of Sir Matthew Hale* (London, 1682), 192.

88. Giles Dunscombe, *Trials Per Pais: or the Law of England Concerning Juries by Nisi Prius* (London, 1702), preface. Numerous editions appeared between 1665 and 1793.

89. William Hawkins does not discuss circumstantial evidence but refers to violent presumptions of guilt in the context of bail. Those under violent presumption of guilt, e.g., those taken with the thing stolen or those known as notorious thieves, ought not be bailed for a "fresh felony whereof there is probable evidence against them." William Hawkins, *A Treatise of the Pleas of the Crown* (London [in The Savoy], 1724), 2:98.

90. Argument from something like circumstantial evidence was common in the writings of natural theologians attempting to prove the existence of God from his effects or works. For the best-known late seventeenth-century example, see John Ray, *The Wisdom of God Manifested in the Works of the Creation* (London, 1691). This mode of thought, typical of the late seventeenth and early eighteenth centuries, culminates in the work of Bishop Butler. Butler emphasized that the "Weight of circumstantial evidence" was "very often altogether as convincing, as that which is the most express and direct." Joseph Butler, *The Analogy of Religion, Natural and Revealed to the Constitution and Course of Nature* (London, 1736), 272.

91. The *Trial of Josh Hill*, 11 *State Trials*, 172.

92. 13 *State Trials*, 55.

93. Blackstone appears to equate circumstantial evidence with presumption. William Blackstone, *Commentaries on the Laws of England*, 4 vols. (London, 1765–1769), 3: 371.

94. *The Trial of Mary Blandy*, in Howell, 18 *State Trials*, 1186, 1187. See also "The Trial of John Woodburne," *Collection of State Trials* (London, 1741), 378.

95. 18 *State Trials*, 1229, 1292, 1293, 1296, 1297, 1298, 1299, 1300, 1301.

96. Ibid., 1314, 1316.

97. William Wills, *An Essay on the Principles of Circumstantial Evidence*, 1857 ed. (London, 1838), 44, citing Donellan's case; see also 45–46. See also *A Defense and Substance of the Trial of John Donellan* (London, 1781).

98. William Paley, *The Principles of Moral and Political Philosophy*, 9th ed., Boston, 1818 (London, 1795), 354–355. Nine editions had been issued by 1818.

99. Ibid., 355.

100. Quoted in Wills, *Circumstantial Evidence*, 44, from Edmund Burke, *Works*, 2: 623. For a discussion of the relative value of direct and indirect (circumstantial) evidence, see 42–50. For a discussion of the eighteenth-century preference for circumstantial evidence and its impact on the development of the novel, see Alexander Welsh, "Burke and Bentham on the Narrative Potential of Circumstantial Evidence," *New Literary History* 21 (1989–1990): 607–627.

101. Francis Snyder, "Using the Criminal Law," in *Policing and Prosecution in Britain, 1750–1850*, ed. Douglas Hay and Francis Snyder (Oxford, 1989), 47. There were also criminal gangs who staged crimes that they intended to be discovered so that gang members could testify against those whom they had ensnared into participating in the staged felony. See Ruth Paley, "Thief-takers in London in the Age of the McDaniel Gang, c. 1745–1754," in *Policing and Prosecution*, 301–343. See also David Philips, "Good Men to Associate and Bad Men to Conspire: Associations for the Prosecution of Felons in England, 1760–1860," in *Policing and Prosecution*, 113–170.

102. Jean Domat, *Civil Law in Its Natural Order*, trans. W. Strahan, 2 vols. (Boston, 1853), 1: 790, 791.

103. Ibid., 1: 817. See also 1: 795. The *indicia* were facts; conjecture and presumptions were what was reasoned about these facts. See also Foriers, "La conception de la preuve dans l'école le droit natural," 169–192.

104. Domat, *Civil Law*, 1: 792–793.

105. Ibid., 1: 818.

106. Ibid., 1: 791, 795, 818. Domat did not deviate from the two-witness rule.

107. Robert Joseph Pothier, *A Treatise on the Law of Obligations or Contracts*, trans. William Evans, 2 vols. (Philadelphia, 1826), 1: 49, 60, 83, 100. Evans also suggests that the English become more receptive to the learning embodied in American cases and legal analysis. Evans was slightly defensive. While expressing deference to the judiciary, which he obviously thought too conservative and too reliant on precedent, he insisted on the "freedom of rational inquiry" to examine the "correct principles of legal reasoning." While "no friend to wanton innovation," he hoped to modify the law in some areas (1: 100–101).

108. Ibid., 2: 473.

109. Ibid., 2: 474, 477.

110. Geoffrey Gilbert, *The Law of Evidence*, London, 1756 ed., 160–161. In John Morgan's *Essays upon the Law of Evidence*, 2 vols. (London, 1789), treatment is identical to Gilbert's. 1: 9–10, 47.

111. Gilbert, *Law of Evidence*, London, 1795 ed., 304. Only two types

of presumption, "violent" and "probable," are listed because "light" and "rash" presumptions are worth nothing. *Law of Evidence*, 1756 ed., 160–161. The use of the categories in pretrial examination may explain how magistrates came to exercise discretion and drop weak cases. See p. 179.

112. Gilbert, *Law of Evidence*, ed. Capel Lofft, 4 vols. (London, 1791), 1: xxxvi; 1795 ed., 314–315.

113. Gilbert, *Law of Evidence*, 1756 ed., 159–161; 1769 ed., 160, 161.

114. Gilbert, *Law of Evidence*, 1791 ed., 304, 310.

115. Ibid., 1: 37.

116. Ibid., 1: 42, 42n.

117. Ibid., 1: xxxviii.

118. Ibid., 1: 42.

119. Richard Kirwan, *Logick, or an Essay on the Elements, Principles and Different Modes of Reasoning* (London, 1807), 238. *Logick* was dedicated to Lord Norbury, Chief Justice of Common Pleas in Ireland.

120. James Gambier, *A Guide to the Study of Moral Evidence* (Boston, 1834), 105.

121. Thomas Gisborne, *An Enquiry into the Duties of Men in the Higher and Middle Classes of Society* (London, 1794), 227–229.

122. Daniel McKinnon, *The Philosophy of Evidence* (London, 1812), vi, vii, 27.

123. Ibid., 55, 56, 57, 63–64. Hearsay was excluded not only for the practical reason that one could not cross-examine, but also because it did not "import a probability of sufficient strength to command" belief or to be "received as a satisfactory proof of the truth" (65). See also James Glassford, *An Essay on the Principles of Evidence and Their Application to Subjects of Judicial Inquiry* (Edinburgh, 1820), 582–592, 638–680. Glassford's study, intended for the general reader, attempts to incorporate the practice of English and Scottish law.

124. Thomas Starkie, *A Practial Treatise of the Law of Evidence*, 1833 ed., 2 vols. (London, 1824).

125. Ibid., 1: 50–51, 397n.

126. Ibid., 1: 495, 515. Joseph Chitty's *Practical Treatise of the Criminal Law*, 4 vols. (London, 1816) still refers to circumstantial evidence in connection with secret crimes. Because of the "obscurity" of some kinds of crimes, juries are often compelled to "receive evidence which is merely circumstantial and presumptive" (1: 458). Presumptive evidence must arise from the facts and cannot be deduced from the defendant's conduct. Chitty therefore repudiates use of the knowledge that the defendant has previously committed similar offenses (1: 450, citing Samuel M. Phillipps, *Treatise on the Law of Evidence* (London, 1814), 70. He refers to the "curious distinctions" of the older writers on this topic.

127. Simon Greenleaf, *Treatise on the Law of Evidence* (Boston,

1844). The editor of the 1853 edition of *Coke on Littleton* also noted many civilian works on evidence, the "most admired" being those of Mascardus, Menochius, Everhardus, and Farinaccius. Sir Edward Coke, *The First Part of the Institutes of the Laws of England; or a Commentary upon Littleton*, 2 vols. (Philadelphia, 1853), 7a, n. 1.

128. Greenleaf, *Law of Evidence*, 16–17. Greenleaf indicated that circumstantial evidence is sometimes "not with entire accuracy, called "presumptive." "Complex and difficult" operations of the mind caused the evidence "afforded by the circumstances, to be termed presumptive evidence: though, in truth the operation is similar in both cases."

129. Ibid., 18–38.

130. Ibid., 50.

131. Ibid., 51.

132. Ibid., citing Starkie, *Law of Evidence*, 2: 684.

133. Ibid., 55.

134. William Wills, *An Essay on the Principles of Circumstantial Evidence*, 3d ed., 1857 (London, 1838).

135. William Best, *A Treatise on Presumptions of Law and Fact with the Theory and Rules of Presumptive or Circumstantial Proof in Criminal Cases* (Philadelphia, 1845).

136. Wills, *An Essay*, 3d ed., 1857, 274–275.

137. Ibid., 135. Truth was thus either "abstract and necessary" or "probable and contingent," and each required different kinds of evidence (16–17).

138. Ibid.

139. Ibid., 236.

140. Ibid., 51.

141. Wills felt that facts of a circumstantial nature could only be classified into two extremely general classes, those which he calls "moral indications," relating to the relations, language, and conduct of the accused, and those which "are apparently extrinsic" and "independent of the moral conduct and demeanor." Each of these might be subdivided into either inculpatory or exculpatory (ibid., 52).

142. Ibid., 156, 157. He cites Stewart and Mill's *Logic* among others.

143. Ibid., 33.

144. Ibid., 32–43. He cites Menochius, Alciatus, Mascardus, Starkie, Burke, Domat, Bonnier, and Bentham among others. Wills emphasized that circumstances and facts of all kinds must be proved by human testimony. The relative values of circumstantial and direct testimonial evidence were still a matter of considerable dispute, both in and outside the courtroom in the early decades of the nineteenth century. Burke had argued that "when circumstantial proof is in its greatest perfection, that

is when it is most abundant in circumstances, it is much superior to positive proof." P. 42, citing Edmund Burke, *Works*, 1834 ed., 2: 624.

145. Ibid., 36.

146. Ibid., 39–40. He also criticized the civilian approach to confessions which resulted from "arbitrary and unphilosophical rules of evidence, which necessarily have the effect of closing many of the channels of truth."

147. Ibid., 41.

148. Ibid., 157, 166, 167. He cites Starkie and Greenleaf in connection with the second rule.

149. Ibid., 171a. This was "the fundamental rule, the *experimentum crucis* by which the relevancy and effect of circumstantial evidence must be estimated."

150. Ibid. He cited an 1805 case in which Lord Chancellor Baron McDonald said that "the nature of circumstantial evidence was this, that the jury must be satisfied that there is not a rational mode of accounting for the circumstances, but upon the supposition that the prisoner is guilty." Citing *Rex v. Patch*, Surrey Spring Assizes, 1805. He also cites Laplace's *Théorie analytique des probabilités*.

151. Ibid., 175. He cites M. E. Bonnier's *Traité théorique et practique des preuves* in connection with this rule. In discussing the doubt in reasonable doubt, Wills indicated that it must not be a trivial one, e.g., one "as speculative ingenuity may raise, but a conscientious one which may operate on the mind of a rational man acquainted with the affairs of life." (P. 177, citing per Mr. Baron Parke in *Reg. v. Tawell* without full citation.)

152. Best, *Principles of the Law of Evidence*, 6th ed.

153. Ibid., 49–50, 82, 85. The arithmetically calculated subdivisions of half proofs had made matters worse. The Napoleonic Code (1808) was a great improvement because it had abolished the system of legal proofs and instituted "free proof" or "intime conviction" (87). Best was nevertheless critical of "conviction intime" because he thought it implied that French juries were not limited to what was produced in court.

154. William Best, *Treatise on Presumptions of Law and Fact*, (Philadelphia, 1845).

155. Ibid., preface.

156. Ibid., 1–2, 26. He cites Locke's *Essay Concerning Human Understanding*, bk. 4, chap. 14, secs. 3–4.

157. Ibid., 26. He includes a lengthy discussion and citations from Alciatus, Menochius, Matthaeus, Huberus, Vinnius, Struvius, Westenbergius, and Pothier, as well as from Locke, Starkie, and Phillipps on the nature of probable inference (26–27).

158. Ibid., 28. He cites Matthaeus, Mascardus, Huberus, Struvius (28n).

159. Ibid., 29, citing Matthaeus and Quintilian.

160. Ibid., 31.

161. Ibid., 31n.

162. Ibid., 31–32, 35. For the distinction between legal fictions and presumptions, see 33, 36–38.

163. Ibid., 43, 43n.

164. Ibid., 45, 45n, citing Starkie and several civilians.

165. Ibid., 46.

166. Ibid. To do so would result in a new trial.

167. Ibid., 149, 150.

168. Ibid., 151.

169. Ibid., 152. Best cites Domat, Matthaeus, and Pothier, as well as Roscoe's *Circumstantial Evidence* and Paley's *Moral Philosophy*.

170. Ibid., 152–153.

171. Ibid.

172. Best also draws on Bentham as well as civilian and philosophical sources. See ibid., 174ff., 201. Alexander Burrill's *Circumstantial Evidence* (New York, 1856) also combines discussion of the nature of knowledge with Anglo-American legal materials and the evidentiary tradition of the civilians. Bentham, Burrill argued, had been among the first "to perceive its importance and comprehend the range of circumstantial evidence and its application." He also emphasized the importance of Starkie, Phillipps, Wills, and Best. *Circumstantial Evidence*, iii, iv, v. Burrill hoped to reach both a professional and a general audience, the latter especially because of the role of jurors, who could not properly discharge their duties without adequate instruction.

As I noted in Chapter 1, James Thayer, in *A Preliminary Treatise on Evidence at the Common Law* (Boston, 1898), differed from most of his predecessors in that he was less sympathetic to grounding the law of evidence in epistemology and logic, and he sharply differentiated the evidentiary tradition of law from that of the natural sciences. He differed from his predecessors as well in his willingness to employ civilian concepts. Indeed, he viewed the development of the doctrine of presumptions in England primarily as a nineteenth-century one. *Preliminary Treatise*, 343n. Presumptions, for Thayer, operated in advance of argument or evidence "or irrespective of it, taking something for granted; but assuming its existence." Presumptions were neither argument nor evidence but were a means of shortening argument and inquiry. Much of the law was expressed presumptively in the form of *prima facie* rules (314, 315). Thayer thus again marks something of a break with the systematizing philosophical orientation of early nineteenth-century writers and signals a return to a more insular Anglophile point of view.

Conclusion

1. There has been some unhappiness with the fact that contemporary jurors, lawyers, and even judges are no longer familiar with the concept of moral certainty which typically accompanies the verbal formulation of the beyond reasonable doubt doctrine.

2. Also in place, although without doctrinal support, has been the centuries-long practice of jury nullification, in which juries who disapprove of the consequences of overwhelming evidence simply refuse to render a guilty verdict. See Thomas Green, *Verdict According to Conscience: Perspectives on the English Criminal Trial Jury, 1200–1800* (Chicago, 1985).

3. Harold Berman, *Law and Revolution: The Formation of the Western Legal Tradition* (Cambridge, Mass., 1983). Berman gives surprisingly little attention to the law of evidence. See also Mirjan Damaska, *The Faces of Justice and State Authority: A Comparative Approach to the Legal Process* (New Haven, 1986).

Appendix

1. See Lorraine Daston, *Classical Probability in the Enlightenment* (Princeton, 1988); Lorraine Daston, "Mathematics and the Moral Sciences: The Rise and Fall in the Probability of Judgments, 1785–1840," in *Epistemological and Social Problems of the Sciences in the Early Nineteenth Century*, ed. H. N. Jahnke and M. Otte (Dordrect, 1981), 287–309. See also Ian Hacking, *The Emergence of Probability: A Philosophical Study of the Early Ideas About Probability* (Cambridge, 1975); L. Kruger et al., eds., *The Probabilistic Revolution*, vol. 1 of *Ideas in History* (Cambridge, Mass., 1987), 100–125; Daniel Garber and Sandy Zabell, "On the Emergence of Probability," *Archive for History of the Exact Sciences* 21 (1979): 33–53; L. E. Maistrov, *Probability Theory: A Historical Sketch*, trans. K. S. Kotz (New York, 1974), 57, 57n; James Franklin, "The Ancient Legal Sources of Seventeenth-Century Probability," in *The Uses of Antiquity in the Scientific Revolution*, ed. S. Gaukroger (pub. forthcoming).

2. Daston, *Classical Probability*, 6–8, 299–304, 351.

3. Paul Foriers, "La conception de la preuve dans l'école le droit natural," in *La Preuve: Deuxième partie: Moyen âge et temps modernes*. Recueils de la Société Jean Bodin pour l'histoire comparative des institutions (Brussels, 1965), 169–192.

4. "On the Measure of the Force of Testimony in Cases of Legal Evidence," *Philosophical Transactions of the Royal Society* 21 (1699): 361.

5. Daston, *Classical Probability*, 205. Richard Kirwan's *Logick*, 2 vols. (London, 1807), which refers to Capel Lofft's edition of Gilbert's *Law of Evidence*, attempted to do probability calculations of witness testimony. Kirwan concluded that the credibility of witnesses of high credibility could be calculated at nine-tenths and was superior to three witnesses of doubtful credit. *Logick*, 2: 309ff., 316, 324–325, 354. See also Augustus de Morgan, "An Essay on Probabilities," in the *Cabinet Encyclopedia* (London, 1838).

6. Daston, *Classical Probability*, 297, 297n, 372–373.

7. Thomas Starkie, *Practical Treatise on the Law of Evidence*, 2 vols., 1833 ed. (London, 1824), 1: 505, 506n; see also 496n–498n. See also James Glassford, *An Essay on the Principles of Evidence and Their Application to the Subjects of Judicial Inquiry* (Edinburgh, 1820), 42ff., 184–201.

8. William Wills, *An Essay on the Principles of Circumstantial Evidence*, 1857 ed. (London, 1838), 22–24.

9. William Best, *A Treatise on Presumptions of Law and Fact with the Theory and Rules of Presumptive or Circumstantial Proof in Criminal Cases* (Philadelphia, 1845), 205–208; Best, *The Principles of the Law of Evidence* (London, 1875), 87–93, 93n, 94 n. 10.

For twentieth-century attempts to apply probability theory and find mathematical equivalents for "beyond reasonable doubt," see Lawrence Tribe, "Trial by Mathematics: Precision and Ritual in the Legal Process," *Harvard Law Review* 84 (1971): 1329–1393; C. M. A. McCauliff, "Burdens of Proof, Degrees of Belief, Quanta of Evidence, or Constitutional Guarantees?" *Vanderbilt Law Review* 35 (1982): 1293–1335; Kenneth S. Brown and Douglas G. Kelley, "Playing Percentages and the Law of Evidence," *University of Illinois Law Forum* (1970): 23; J. Kaplan, "Decision Theory and the Fact Finding Process," *Stanford Law Review* 20 (1968): 1065. See also Jonathan Cohen, *The Probable and the Provable* (Oxford, 1977); Sir Richard Eggleston, "Sixth Wilfred Fullegar Memorial Lecture 'Beyond Reasonable Doubt,'" *Monash Law Review* 4 (1977): 1–19; Sir Richard Eggleston, "The Probability Debate," *Criminal Law Review* (1980): 678–688; Rita Simon and Linda Mahan, "Quantifying the Burdens of Proof," *Law and Society Review* 5 (1971): 319–342.

Select Bibliography

Primary Sources

Abercrombie, John. *Inquiries Concerning the Intellectual Powers and the Investigation of Truth*. Edinburgh, 1820.

An Abridgement of Burn's, Justice of the Peace and Parish Officer. Boston, 1773.

An Account of . . . The Tryal of Mr. Edward Fitzharris. London, 1681.

Adams, John. *The Legal Papers of John Adams*. 3 vols. Edited by L. Wroth and H. Zobel. Cambridge, Mass., 1965.

Astry, Sir James. *A General Charge to all Grand Juries*. London, 1703, 1725.

Babington, Zachary. *Advice to Grand Jurors in Cases of Blood*. London, 1677.

Bacon, Francis. *The Works of Francis Bacon*. 15 vols. Edited by J. Spedding, R. Ellis, and D. Heath. London, 1872.

Barnes, Thomas G. "A Charge to the Judges of Assize, 1627–1628." *Huntington Library Quarterly* 24 (1961): 251–256.

———. *Somerset Assize Orders, 1629–1640*. Somerset Record Society 65. London, 1959.

Beccaria, Cesare. *An Essay on Crimes and Punishment*. Brookline, Mass., 1983.

Bentham, Jeremy. *Rationale of Judicial Evidence*. 5 vols. London, 1827.

Bernard, Richard. *Guide to Grand Jury Men in Cases of Witchcraft*. London, 1627.

Best, William. *The Principles of the Law of Evidence with Elementary Rules for Conducting the Examination and Cross-Examination of Witnesses*. 6th ed. London, 1875.

———. *A Treatise on Presumptions of Law and Fact with the Theory and Rules of Presumptive or Circumstantial Proof in Criminal Cases*. London, 1844. Philadelphia, 1845.

Billa Vera: or the Arraignment of Ignoramus. London, 1682.

Bishop, Joel. *Commentaries on the Criminal Law.* 2 vols. London, 1856, 1859. Boston, 1866.

Blackstone, William. *Commentaries on the Laws of England.* 4 vols. London, 1765–1769.

Bohun, Edmund. *Justice of the Peace, His Calling: A Moral Essay.* London, 1684.

Bolton, Richard. *A Justice of the Peace in Ireland.* Dublin, 1683.

Bracton, Henry. *On the Laws and Customs of England.* Translated and edited by Samuel E. Thorne. 4 vols. Cambridge, Mass., 1968.

Burke, Richard. *Charge Delivered to the Grand Jury.* Bristol, 1793.

Burn, Richard. *The Justice of the Peace and Parish Officer.* London, 1754, 1772.

Burnet, Gilbert. *History of My Own Times.* Edited by Osmond Airy. 2 vols. Oxford, 1900.

———. *The Life and Death of Sir Matthew Hale.* London, 1682.

Burrill, Alexander. *Circumstantial Evidence.* New York, 1856.

Campbell, George. *The Philosophy of Rhetoric.* Edited by L. Bitzer. Carbondale, Ill., 1963.

Care, Henry. *English Liberties; or the Free-Born Subjects Inheritance.* London, n.d.

Chamberlain, Richard. *The Complete Justice.* London, 1681.

Chitty, Joseph. *A Practical Treatise on the Criminal Law.* 4 vols. London, 1816. Philadelphia, 1819.

Cicero. *De inventione.* Loeb Classical Library. Vol. 2. Cambridge, Mass., 1949.

———. *De partitione oratoria.* Loeb Classical Library. Vol. 4, bk. 3. Cambridge, Mass., 1942.

Clark, Sir George, ed. *The Campden Wonder.* London, 1959.

Cohen, Morris. "Legal Literature in Colonial Massachusetts." Unpublished typescript, n.d.

Coke, Sir Edward. *Institutes of the Lawes of England.* 4 vols. London, 1628–1644. Philadelphia, 1853.

The Compleat Statesman. London, 1683.

The Complete Juryman, or a Compendium of the Laws Related to Jurors. N.p. 1744. Dublin, 1752.

Conductor Generalis, or the Office and Duty of the Justice of the Peace. Philadelphia, 1722.

Cooper, Thomas. *The Mysterie of Witchcraft.* London, 1617.

Cotta, John. *The Trial of Witchcraft.* London, 1616.

Cottu, Charles. *The Administration of Criminal Justice in England.* London, 1822.

Cowell, John. *The Interpreter.* London, 1607.

Cowper, William. *The Charge of William Cowper to the Grand Jury of Westminster*. London, 1719.

Cox, Richard. *A Charge Delivered to the Grand Jury*. Dublin, 1758.

Crompton, Richard. *L'office et auctoritie de justices de peace*. London, 1606.

Dalton, Michael. *The Country Justice*. London, 1618, 1635, 1715.

A Display of Tyranny. London, 1689.

Dolbins, Daniel. *The Charge of Daniel Dolbins to the Grand Jury*. London, 1725.

Domat, Jean. *Civil Law in Its Natural Order*. 2 vols. Translated by William Strahan. Boston, 1853.

Dunscombe, Giles. *Trials Per Pais: or the Law of England Concerning Juries by Nisi Prius*. 4th ed. London, 1702.

Fielding, Henry. *Charge Delivered the Grand Jury*. London, 1749.

———. *An Inquiry into the Causes of the Rate Increase of Robbers*. London, 1751.

Filmer, Robert. *Advertisement to the Grand Jurymen of England Touching Witchcraft*. London, 1653.

Fitzherbert, Anthony. *L'office et auctoritie de justices de Peace*. London, 1583.

Fortescue, Sir John. *De Laudibus Legum Anglie*. Edited and translated by S. B. Chrimes. Cambridge, Mass., 1942.

Fulbecke, William. *A Direction or Preparative to the Study of the Law*. London, 1620.

Gambier, James. *A Guide to the Study of Moral Evidence, or of that Species of Reasoning which Relates to Matters of Fact and Practice*. Boston, 1834.

Gifford, George. *Dialogue Concerning Witches and Witchcraft*. 1593.

Gilbert, Sir Geoffrey. *Abstract of Mr. Locke's Essay on Human Understanding*. Dublin, 1752.

———. *The Law of Evidence*. Dublin, 1754. London, 1756.

———. *The Law of Evidence*. Enlarged by Capel Lofft. 4 vols. London, 1791.

Gisborne, Thomas. *An Enquiry into the Duties of Men in the Higher and Middle Classes of Society*. London, 1794.

Glassford, James. *An Essay on the Principles of Evidence and Their Application to the Subjects of Judicial Inquiry*. Edinburgh, 1820.

Gonson, Sir John. *Five Charges to Several Grand Juries*. 4th ed. London, 1740.

Greenleaf, Simon. *Treatise on the Law of Evidence*. Boston, 1844.

A Guide to English Juries: Setting Forth Their Power and Antiquity. London, 1682.

Haining, Peter, ed. *The Witchcraft Papers*. London, 1974.

Hale, Sir Matthew. *The History of the Common Law of England*. Edited by Charles M. Gray. Chicago, 1971.

————. *The History of the Pleas of the Crown*. 2 vols. London, 1736.

————. *Pleas of the Crown, or a Methodical Summary*. London, 1678.

————. *The Primitive Origination of Mankind*. London, 1677.

Hamilton, A. H. A. *Quarter Sessions from Queen Elizabeth to Queen Anne*. London, 1878.

Hartley, David. *Observations on Man*. London, 1749.

Hawkins, William. *A Treatise of the Pleas of the Crown*. 2 vols. London, 1717. London [in the Savoy], 1724.

[Hawles, Sir John?] *The Grand Jury-man's Oath and Office Explained and the Rights of English-men Asserted*. London, 1680.

Hawles, Sir John. *The Englishman's Right: A Dialogue between a Barrister at Law and a Juryman*. London, 1680.

————. *Remarks upon the Trial of Fitzharris*. London, 1689.

Hening, William. *The New Virginia Justice*. Richmond, 1795.

Hoffman, David. *A Course of Legal Study*. Baltimore, 1817.

————. *A Lecture on Law*. Baltimore, 1826.

Holt, Sir John. *A Report of Divers Cases*. London, 1708.

Hopkinson, Francis. *The Miscellaneous Essays*. 2 vols. Philadelphia, 1792.

Howell, T. B., ed. *Complete Collection of State Trials*. 34 vols. London, 1809–1826.

Hunt, William. *The Justicing Notebook of William Hunt*. Edited by Elizabeth Crittal. Wiltshire Record Society, vol. 37. 1982.

Ignoramus Vindicated in a Dialogue between Prejudice and Indifference. London, 1681.

J. W. *Officium Clerici Pacis*. London, 1686.

Jacob, Giles. *The Modern Justice*. 3d ed. London, 1720.

The Justice of the Peace, His Calling. A Moral Essay. London, 1684.

Keble, Joseph. *An Assistance to Justices of the Peace*. London, 1683.

Kilburn, Richard. *Choice Presedents . . . Relating to the Office and Duty of a Justice of the Peace*. London, 1680.

Kirwan, Richard. *Logick, or An Essay on the Elements, Principles and Different Modes of Reasoning*. 2 vols. London, 1807.

Lambarde, William. *Eirenarcha, or Of the Office of the Justice of the Peace*. London, 1581, 1614.

————. *William Lambarde and Local Government: His "Ephemeris" and Twenty-Nine Charges to Juries and Commissions*. Edited by Conyers Read. Ithaca, N.Y., 1962.

The Law of Evidence. Savoy, 1707.

The Letter of the Grand Jury of Oxford to the Grand Jury of London. London, 1681.

Leveson-Gower, Granville. "Notebook of a Surrey Justice." *Surrey Archeological Collections* 9 (1888): 161–232.

Locke, John. *An Essay Concerning Human Understanding.* Edited by Alexander Fraser. 2 vols. New York, 1959.

———. *Essays on the Law of Nature.* Edited by W. von Leyden. Oxford, 1954.

———. *Two Tracts on Government.* Edited by Philip Abrams. Cambridge, 1967.

McKinnon, Daniel. *The Philosophy of Evidence.* London, 1812.

McNally, Leonard. *The Rules of Evidence on Pleas of the Crown.* London and Dublin, 1802.

A Manual or Analecta. London, 1641.

Milward, John. *The Diary of John Milward.* Edited by Caroline Robbins. Cambridge, 1935.

A Modest Vindication of the Proceedings of the late Jury at the Old Baily, who returned the Bill against Stephen Colledge Ignoramus. London, 1681.

Morgan, John. *Essays upon the Law of Evidence.* 2 vols. London, 1789.

Nelson, William. *The Office and Authority of a Justice of the Peace.* London, 1707.

North, Roger. *Examen.* 1740 ed. London, 1685.

———. *The Lives of the Norths.* Edited by A. Jessopp. 3 vols. London, 1890.

Office of the Clerk of the Assize. London, 1676, 1682.

The Office of the Clerk of the Peace. London, 1676.

"On the Measure of the Force of Testimony in Cases of Legal Evidence." *Philosophical Transactions of the Royal Society* 21 (1699): 359–365.

Paley, William. *The Principles of Moral and Political Philosophy.* London, 1785. Boston, 1818.

The Peoples Ancient and Just Liberties Asserted. London, 1670.

Perkins, William. *Willam Perkins, His Pioneer Works on Casuistry.* Edited by T. F. Merill. The Hague, 1966.

Phillipps, Samuel. *The Theory of Presumptive Proof, or, An Inquiry into the Nature of Circumstantial Evidence.* London, 1815. New York, 1816.

———. *A Treatise on the Law of Evidence.* London, 1814. New York, 1816.

Pothier, Robert J. *A Treatise on the Law of Obligations or Contracts.* Translated by William Evans. 2 vols. Philadelphia, 1826.

Pufendorf, Samuel. *Of the Law of Nature and Nations.* 1st English ed. (London, 1702).

Quintilian. *Institutes of the Orator.* Translated by J. Patsaill. London, 1777.

Reid, Thomas. *Essays on the Intellectual Powers of Man.* Cambridge, 1850.

————. *Inquiry into the Human Mind on the Principles of Common Sense.* London and Edinburgh, 1764.

Rhetorica ad herennium. 2 vols. Loeb Classical Library. Cambridge, Mass., 1954.

Scot, Reginald. *Discoverie of Witchcraft.* 1584. Reprint. London, 1964.

Sheppard, William. *The Court Keepers Guide.* London, 1649.

————. *An Epitome of all the Common and Statute Laws.* London, 1656.

————. *The Justice of the Peace: His Clerk's Cabinet.* London, 1654.

————. *A New Survey of the Justice of the Peace, His Office.* London, 1659.

————. *A Sure Guide for His Majestie's Justice of the Peace.* London, 1669.

————. *The Whole Office of the County Justice of Peace.* London, 1652.

Shore, John. *A Charge Delivered at the Quarter Sessions of the Peace . . . April 5, 1714.* London, 1714.

[Smith, Francis.] *An Impartial Account of the Tryal of Francis Smith.* London, 1680.

Smith, Sir Thomas. *De Republica Anglorum.* Edited by L. Alston. Cambridge, 1906.

[Somers, Sir John.] *The Security of English-Men's Lives, or the Trust, Power, and Duty of the Grand Jurys of England.* London, 1681.

Stanhope, George. *The Duty of Witnesses. A Sermon.* London, 1701.

Starke, Richard. *Office and Authority of the Justice of the Peace.* Williamsburg, 1774.

Starkie, Thomas. *A Practical Treatise of the Law of Evidence.* 2 vols. London, 1824.

Stillingfleet, Edward. *Origines Sacrae.* London, 1662.

Swift, Zephaniah. *Digest of the Law of Evidence in Civil and Criminal Cases.* Hartford, Conn., 1810.

Taylor, Jeremy. *Ductor Dubitantum, or The Rule of Conscience in all her General Measures, Serving as a Great Instrument for the Determination of Cases of Conscience.* London, 1660.

Thayer, James. *A Preliminary Treatise on Evidence at the Common Law.* Boston, 1898.

Toulmin, Harry, and James Blair. *A Revision of the Criminal Law of the Commonwealth of Kentucky.* 2 vols. Frankfort, Ky., 1806.

Trial of Carr. London, 1681.

The Trial of John Giles. London, 1681.

Trial of Langhorn. London, 1679.

Trial of Reading. London, 1679.

The Triumph of Justice over Unjust Lawyers. London, 1681.

The Tryals of Several Notorious Malefactors . . . at Old Bailey, October 17–19, 1681. London, 1682.

Vaughan, Sir John. *The Reports and Arguments of Sir John Vaughan*. London, 1677.

W. J. *A Letter from Ignoramus*. London, 1682.

Ward, Seth. *A Philosophical Essay toward an Eviction of the Being and Attributes of God*. 5th ed., 1677. London, 1654.

Waterhouse, Edward. *Fortescue Illustratus*. London, 1663.

Watts, Isaac. *Logick, or the Right Use of Reason in the Inquiry after Truth*. London, 1724, 1775.

Webb, George. *The Office and Authority of a Justice of the Peace*. Williamsburg, 1736, 1774.

Wharton, Francis. *State Trials of the United States during the Administrations of Washington and Adams*. Philadelphia, 1849.

———. *A Treatise of the Criminal Law of the United States*. 3d ed. Philadelphia, 1855.

Whately, Richard. *Elements of Rhetoric: Comparing an Analysis of the Laws of Moral Evidence and of Persuasion*. 1828. Reprint. London, 1963.

Whole Proceedings of Old Bailey. London, 1777.

Wigmore, John. *The Principles of Judicial Proof as Given by Legal, Psychological and General Experience*. 2d ed. Boston, 1931.

———. *Treatise of the Anglo-American System of Evidence*. Boston, 1940.

Wilkins, John. *Of the Principles and Duties of Natural Religion*. London, 1675.

Williams, Thomas. *The Excellency and Praeheminence of the Laws of England*. London, 1680.

Wills, William. *An Essay on the Principles of Circumstantial Evidence*. London, 1838, 1857.

Wilson, James. *The Works*. Edited by James Dewitt Andrews. 2 vols. Chicago, 1896.

———. *The Works of James Wilson*. Edited by Robert McCloskey. 2 vols. Cambridge, Mass., 1967.

Wilson, Thomas. *The Art of Rhetorique*. London, 1585.

Wiseman, Robert. *The Law of Laws, or the Excellency of the Civil Law*. London, 1657.

Wood, Thomas. *Institute of the Laws of England*. 2d ed. London [in the Savoy], 1722.

———. *A New Institute of the Imperial or Civil Law*. 4th ed. London, 1715.

Woodeson, Richard. *A Systematic View of the Laws of England.* 3 vols. London, 1792.

Secondary Sources

Abrahams, Gerald. *According to the Evidence: An Essay on Legal Proof.* London, 1958.

Adams, J. "Eighteenth-Century Legal Sources." *Durham University Law Review* 78 (1985): 89–93.

Allen, David. *In English Ways: The Movement of Societies and the Transfer of English Local Law to Massachusetts Bay in the Seventeenth Century.* Chapel Hill, 1981.

Anderson, Gary. "The Preliminary Hearing—Better Alternatives or More of the Same?" *Missouri Law Review* 35 (1970): 281–302.

Aranella, Peter. "Reforming the Federal Grand Jury and the State Preliminary Hearing to Prevent Conviction without Adjudication." *Michigan Law Review* 78 (1980): 463–580.

Ashworth, E. J. "The Doctrine of Supposition in the Sixteenth and Seventeenth Centuries." In *Language and Logic in the Post-Medieval Period.* Dordrecht, 1974.

Aumann, Francis R. "The Influence of English and Civil Law Principles upon the American Legal System during the Critical Post-Revolutionary Period." *University of Cincinnati Law Review* 12 (1938): 289–317.

Ayer, A. J. *Probability and Evidence.* New York, 1972.

Babington, Anthony. *A House in Bow Street: Crime and the Magistracy, London 1740–1881.* London, 1969.

Bacigal, Ronald J. "The Fourth Amendment in Flux: The Rise and Fall of Probable Cause." *University of Illinois Law Forum* (1979): 763–808.

Baker, J. H. "Criminal Courts and Procedure at Common Law 1500–1800." In *Crime in England, 1550–1800,* edited by J. S. Cockburn. Princeton, 1977.

———. "Criminal Justice at Newgate, 1616–27." *Irish Jurist,* n.s., 8 (1973): 307–322.

———. "The Dark Age of English Legal History, 1500–1700." In *Legal History Studies,* edited by D. Jenkins. London, 1975.

———. "English Law and the Renaissance." *Cambridge Law Journal* 44 (1985): 46–61.

———. *An Introduction to English Legal History.* 2d ed. London, 1979.

———. "The Refinement of English Criminal Jurisprudence, 1500–

1848." In *Crime and Criminal Justice in Europe and Canada*, edited by L. A. Knafla. Waterloo, Ontario, 1981.

Baker, R. W. *The Hearsay Rule*. London, 1950.

Baldwin, J. W. "The Intellectual Preparation for the Canon of 1215 against Ordeals." *Speculum* 36 (1961): 613–636.

Bar, C. L. von, et al. *A History of Continental Criminal Law*. Boston, 1916.

Barnes, Thomas G. "Examination before a Justice in the Seventeenth Century." *Somerset and Dorset Notes and Queries* 27 (1955): 39–42.

———. "The Making of English Criminal Law (2): Star Chamber and the Sophistication of the Criminal Law." *Criminal Law Review* (1977): 338–347.

Beard, Charles. *The Office of the Justice of the Peace in England*. New York, 1904.

Beattie, John. *Crime and the Courts in England, 1660–1800*. Princeton, 1986.

———. "London Juries in the 1690s." In *Twelve Good Men and True: The Criminal Trial Jury in England, 1200–1800*, edited by J. S. Cockburn and Thomas Green, 214–253. Princeton, 1988.

———. "Toward a Study of Crime in Eighteenth-Century England: A Note on Indictments." In *The Triumph of Culture: Eighteenth-Century Perspectives*, edited by David Williams and Paul Tritz, Toronto, 1972.

Bellamy, J. G. *Crime and Public Order in England in the Later Middle Ages*. London, 1973.

Berman, Harold. *Law and Revolution: The Formation of the Western Legal Tradition*. Cambridge, Mass., 1983.

Bland, D. S. "Rhetoric and the Law Student in Sixteenth-Century England." *Studies in Philology* 53 (1957): 498–508.

Bodenheimer, David. "Criminal Justice and Democratic Theory in Antibellum America: The Grand Jury Debates in Indiana." *Journal of the Early Republic* 5 (1985): 481–501.

Bouwsma, William. "Lawyers in Early Modern Culture." *American Historical Review* 78 (1973): 303–327.

Boyer, Larry M. "The Justice of the Peace in England and America 1506–1776." *Quarterly Journal of the Library of Congress* 34 (1977): 315–326.

Brewer, John, ed. *An Ungovernable People: The English and the Law in the Seventeenth and Eighteenth Centuries*. London, 1978.

Burns, R. M. *The Great Debate on Miracles*. London, 1981.

"The Changing Role of the Jury in the Nineteenth Century." *Yale Law Journal* 74 (1964): 170–192.

Chapin, Bradley. *Criminal Justice in Colonial America, 1606–1660.* Athens, Ga., 1983.

Chrimes, S. B. "The Constitutional Ideas of Dr. John Cowell." *English History Review* 44 (1949): 461–480.

Cockburn, J. S. *A History of English Assizes, 1558–1714.* Cambridge, 1972.

———. "Trial by the Book? Fact and Theory in Criminal Process, 1558–1625." In *Legal Records and the Historian,* edited by J. H. Baker, 60–79. London, 1978.

———, ed. *Crime in England, 1550–1800.* Princeton, 1977.

Cockburn, J. S., and Thomas A. Green, eds. *Twelve Good Men and True: The Criminal Trial Jury in England, 1200–1800.* Princeton, 1988.

Cohen, Jonathan. "The Logic of Proof." *Criminal Law Review* (1980): 77–91.

———. *The Probable and the Provable.* Oxford, 1977.

Cohen, Morris L. "Legal Literature in Colonial Massachusetts." Unpublished typescript, n.d.

Conley, John. "Doing It by the Book: Justice of the Peace Manuals and English Law in the Eighteenth Century." *Journal of Legal History* 5 (1985): 256–297.

Cooper, T. M. "The Scottish Lawyer's Library in the Seventeenth Century." *Juridical Review* 66 (1954): 1–5.

Coquillette, Daniel R. "Legal Ideology and Incorporation I: The English Civilian Writers, 1523–1607." *Boston University Law Review* 61 (1981): 1–89.

———. "Legal Ideology and Incorporation II: Thomas Ridley, Charles Malloy, and the Literary Battle for the Law Merchant." *Boston University Law Review* 61 (1981): 315–376.

———. "Legal Ideology and Incorporation III: Reason Regulated—the Post-Restoration English Civilians, 1653–1735." *Boston University Law Review* 67 (1987): 289–361.

———. "Legal Ideology and Incorporation IV: The Nature of Civilian Influence on Modern Anglo-American Commercial Law." *Boston University Law Review* 67 (1987): 929–934.

Cornish, W. R. "Defects in Prosecuting—Professional Views in 1845." In *Reshaping the Criminal Law,* edited by P. R. Glazebrook, 305–316. London, 1978.

Cosgrove, Richard. *Our Lady the Common Law: An Anglo-American Legal Community, 1870–1930.* New York, 1987.

Cottu, Charles. *The Administration of Criminal Justice in England.* London, 1822.

Damaska, Mirjan R. "The Death of Legal Torture." *Yale Law Journal* 87 (1978): 860–884.

———. "Evidentiary Barriers to Conviction and Two Models of Criminal Procedure." *University of Pennsylvania Law Review* 121 (1973): 507–561.

———. *The Faces of Justice and State Authority: A Comparative Approach to the Legal Process.* New Haven, 1986.

Dash, Samuel. "The Indicting Jury: A Critical Stage?" *American Criminal Law Review* 10 (1972): 807–828.

Daston, Lorraine. *Classical Probability in the Enlightenment.* Princeton, 1988.

———. "Mathematics and the Moral Sciences: The Rise and Fall in the Probability of Judgments, 1785–1840." In *Epistemological and Social Problems of the Sciences in the Early Nineteenth Century*, edited by H. N. Jahnke and M. Otte, 287–309. Dordrecht, 1981.

Davis, Jennifer. "A Poor Man's System of Justice: The London Police Courts in the Second Half of the Nineteenth Century." *The Historical Journal* 171 (1984): 309–335.

Dawson, John. *A History of Lay Judges.* Cambridge, Mass., 1960.

Dession, George. "From Indictment to Information—Implications of the Shift." *Yale Law Journal* 42 (1932): 163–193.

Devlin, Patrick. *Criminal Prosecution in England.* New Haven, 1958.

Donahue, Charles. "The Civil Law in England." *Yale Law Review* 84 (1974): 167–181.

———. "Proof by Witnesses in the Church Courts of Medieval England: An Imperfect Reception of the Learned Law." In *On the Law and Customs of England: Essays in Honor of Samuel E. Thorne*, edited by Morris Arnold et al., 127–158. Chapel Hill, 1981.

Edwards, George. *The Grand Jury: Considered from an Historical, Political and Legal Standpoint.* 1906. Reprint: New York, 1973.

Eggleston, Sir Richard. *Evidence, Proof and Probability.* London, 1978.

———. "The Probability Debate." *Criminal Law Review* (1980): 678–688.

———. "Sixth Wilfred Fullegar Memorial Lecture 'Beyond Reasonable Doubt.'" *Monash Law Review* 4 (1977): 1–19.

Esmein, Adhemar. *A History of Continental Criminal Procedure with Specific Reference to France.* Boston, 1913.

Ewen, C. L'Estrange. *Witch Hunters and Witch Trials.* London, 1929.

"Fifteenth Annual Review of Criminal Procedure: United States Supreme Court and Courts of Appeal, 1984–1985." *Georgetown Law Journal* 74 (1986): 1–996.

Flaherty, David. "Criminal Practice in Provincial Massachusetts." *Colonial Society of Massachusetts* 62 (1984): 191–242.

Ford, T. H. "English Criminal Law Reform from Peterloo to Peel." *Durham University Journal* 76 (1984): 205–216.

Foriers, Paul. "La conception de la preuve dans l'école le droit natural." In *La Preuve: Deuxième partie: Moyen âge et temps modernes*. Recueils de la Société Jean Bodin pour l'histoire comparative des institutions, 169–192. Brussels, 1965.

Forsyth, William. *History of Trial by Jury*. London, 1852.

Fox, R. W. "Expediency and Truth-Finding in the Modern Law of Evidence." In *Well and Truly Tried: Essays on Evidence in Honour of Sir Richard Eggleston*, edited by Enid Campbell and Louis Waller. Sidney, 1982.

Fox, Sanford. *Science and Justice: The Massachusetts Witchcraft Trials*. Baltimore, 1968.

Fraher, Richard. "Conviction According to Conscience: The Medieval Jurists' Debate Concerning Judicial Discretion and the Law of Proof." *Law and History Review* 7 (1989): 23–88.

———. "The Theoretical Justification for the New Criminal Law of the High Middle Ages." *University of Illinois Law Review* (1984): 577–597.

Frankel, Marvin E., and Gary P. Naftalis. *The Grand Jury: An Institution on Trial*. New York, 1977.

Franklin, James. "The Ancient Legal Sources of Seventeenth-Century Probability." In *The Uses of Antiquity in the Scientific Revolution*, edited by S. Gaukroger. Forthcoming.

Freestone, David, and J. C. Richardson. "The Making of English Criminal Law (7): Sir John Jervis and His Acts." *Criminal Law Review* (1980): 5–16.

Geis, Gilbert. "Lord Hale, Witches and Rape." *British Journal of Law and Society* 5 (1978): 26–44.

Gilissen, John. "La Preuve en Europe du XVIie au début du XIXie siècle rapport de synthèse." In *La Preuve: Deuxième partie: Moyen âge et temps modernes*. Recueils de la Société, Jean Bodin pour l'histoire comparative des institutions, 755–833. Brussels, 1965.

Giuliani, Alessandro. "The Influence of Rhetoric on the Law of Evidence and Pleading." *Juridical Review* 62 (1969): 216–251.

Gleason, John. *The Justices of the Peace in England, 1558–1640*. Oxford, 1969.

Goebel, Julius. *Felony and Misdemeanor: A Study in the History of English Criminal Procedure*. New York, 1937.

Goebel, Julius, and J. R. Naughton. *Law Enforcement in Colonial New York*. New York, 1944.

Goldstein, Abraham. "Prosecution: History of the Public Prosecutor." In *Encyclopedia of Crime and Justice*, edited by Sanford Kadish. New York, 1983.

———. "Reflections on Two Models: Inquisitorial Themes in American Criminal Procedure." *Stanford Law Review* 26 (1974): 1009–1025.

———. "The State and the Accused: Balance of the Advantage in Criminal Procedure." *Yale Law Review* 69 (1960): 1149–1199.

Gorla, Gino. "Civilian Judicial Decisions: An Historical Account of The Italian Style." *Tulane Law Review* 44 (1970): 740–749.

Gorla, Gino, and Luigi Moccia. "A Revisiting of the Comparison between Continental Law and English Law." *Journal of Legal History* 2 (1981): 143–156.

Green, Thomas A. "The Jury and the English Law of Homicide, 1200–1600." *Michigan Law Review* 74 (1976): 423–499.

———. "A Retrospective on the Criminal Trial Jury." In *Twelve Good Men and True: The Criminal Trial Jury in England, 1200–1800*, edited by J. S. Cockburn and Thomas A. Green, 358–400. Princeton, 1988.

———. *Verdict According to Conscience: Perspectives on the English Criminal Trial Jury, 1200–1800*. Chicago, 1985.

Greenberg, Douglas. *Crime and Law Enforcement in the Colony of New York, 1691–1776*. Ithaca, 1976.

———. "Crime, Law Enforcement and Social Control in Colonial America." *American Journal of Legal History* 26 (1982): 293–325.

Groot, Roger D. "The Jury of Presentment before 1215." *American Journal of Legal History* 26 (1982): 1–24.

Grove, S. A. *The Scottish Philosophy of Common Sense*. Oxford, 1960.

Hacking, Ian. *The Emergence of Probability: A Philosophical Study of the Early Ideas about Probability*. Cambridge, 1975.

Hall, Jerome. "Legal and Social Aspects of Arrest without a Warrant." *Harvard Law Review* 49 (1936): 567–592.

Hamilton, A. H. A. *Quarter Sessions from Queen Elizabeth to Queen Anne*. London, 1878.

Haskins, George. *Law and Authority in Early Massachusetts*. New York, 1960.

———. "Lay Judges: Magistrates and Justices in Early Massachusetts." In *Law and Colonial Massachusetts*. Boston, 1984.

Havinghurst, A. F. "The Judiciary and Politics in the Reign of Charles II." *Law Quarterly Review* 66 (1950): 62–78, 229–252.

Hay, Douglas. "The Class Composition of the Palladium of Liberty: Trial

Jurors in the Eighteenth Century." In *Twelve Good Men and True: The Criminal Trial Jury in England, 1200–1800*, edited by J. S. Cockburn and Thomas Green, 305–356. Princeton, 1988.

———. "The Criminal Prosecution in England and Its Historians." *The Modern Law Review* 47 (1984): 1–29.

———, ed. *Albion's Fatal Tree: Crime and Society in Eighteenth-Century England*. New York, 1975.

Heath, James. *Torture and English Law: An Administrative and Legal History from the Plantagenets to the Stuarts*. London, 1982.

Helmholz, Richard H. "The Early History of the Grand Jury and the Canon Law." *University of Chicago Law Review* 50 (1983): 613–627.

Henderson, Dwight. *Congress, Courts, and Criminals: The Development of Federal Criminal Law*. Westport, Conn., 1985.

Herrup, Cynthia. *The Common Peace: Participation and the Criminal Law in Seventeenth-Century England*. Cambridge, 1987.

———. "New Shoes and Mutton Pies: Investigative Responses to Theft in Seventeenth-Century East Sussex." *The Historical Journal* 27 (1984): 811–830.

Hill, Lamar. "The Two-Witness Rule in English Treason Trials: Some Comments on the Emergence of Procedural Law." *American Journal of Legal History* 12 (1968): 95–111.

Hindus, Michael. *Prison and Plantation: Crime, Justice and Authority in Massachusetts and South Carolina, 1767–1878*. Chapel Hill, 1980.

Hoeflich, M. H. "John Austin and Joseph Story: Two Nineteenth-Century Perspectives on the Utility of the Civil Law for the Common Lawyer." *American Journal of Legal History* 29 (1985): 37–77.

Holdsworth, William. *A History of English Law*. 16 vols. London, 1926–1964.

———. "The Reception of the Roman Law in the Sixteenth Century." *Law Quarterly Review* 27 (1911): 387–98; 28 (1912): 39–51, 131–47, 236–54.

Horle, Craig. *The Quakers and the English Legal System, 1660–1688*. Philadelphia, 1988.

Houlbrooke, Ralph. *Church Courts and the People during the English Reformation, 1520–1570*. Oxford, 1979.

Hurnard, Naomi. "The Jury of Presentment and the Assizes of Clarendon." *English Historical Review* 61 (1941): 371–410.

Hyams, Paul R. "Trial by Ordeal: The Key to Proof in the Early Common Law." In *On the Laws and Customs of England*, edited by M. S. Arnold, Thomas A. Green, Sally A. Scully, and Stephen D. White, 90–126. Chapel Hill, 1981.

Israel, Jerold H. "Grand Jury." In *Encyclopedia of Crime and Justice*, edited by Sanford Kadish. New York, 1983.

Jacobson, David. "Trial by Jury and Criticism of the Old Regime." *Studies in Voltaire and the Eighteenth Century* 153 (1976): 1099–1111.

Jacoby, Joan E. *The American Public Prosecutor: A Search for Identity.* Lexington, Mass., 1980.

Jansson, Maija. "Matthew Hale on Judges and Judging." *The Journal of Legal History* 9 (1989): 201–213.

Jardine, D. *A Reading on the Use of Torture in the Criminal Law of England.* London, 1837.

Jenkins, Dafydd. "English Law and the Renaissance, Eighty Years On: In Defense of Maitland." *Journal of Legal History* 2 (1981): 107–142.

Jones, J. R. *The First Whigs: The Politics and the Exclusion Crisis, 1678–1683.* London, 1970.

Jonsen, Albert R., and Stephen Toulmin. *The Abuse of Casuistry: A History of Moral Reasoning.* Berkeley, 1988.

Kadish, Sanford H., and Monrad Paulsen. *Criminal Law and Its Process: Cases and Materials.* 3d ed. Boston, 1975.

Kamisar, Yale, Wayne LaFave, and Jerold H. Israel. *Modern Criminal Procedure.* St. Paul, 1980.

Kaplan, J. "Decision Theory and the Fact Finding Process." *Stanford Law Review* 20 (1968): 1065–1092.

Katz, Stanley. "Looking Backward: The Early History of American Law." *University of Chicago Law Review* 33 (1966): 868–873.

Kaye, J. M. "The Making of the English Criminal Law: The Beginnings." *Criminal Law Review* (1977): 4–13.

Kent, Joan. *The English Village Constable, 1580–1642.* Oxford, 1986.

Kenyan, J. P. "The Acquittal of Sir George Wakeman, 18 July 1679." *The Historical Journal* 14 (1971): 693–708.

King, P. J. R. "'Illiterate Plebians, Easily Misled': Jury Composition, Experience and Behavior in Essex, 1735–1815." In *Twelve Good Men and True: The Criminal Trial Jury in England, 1200–1800*, edited by J. S. Cockburn and Thomas Green, 254–304. Princeton, 1988.

———. "Prosecuting Associations and Their Impact on Eighteenth-Century Essex." In *Policing and Prosecution in Britain*, edited by Douglas Hay and Francis Snyder. Oxford, 1989.

Klein, Milton. "Prelude to Revolution in New York: Jury Trials and Judicial Tenure." *William and Mary Quarterly*, n.s. 17 (1960): 339–462.

Krasity, Kenneth. "The Role of the Judge in Jury Trials: The Elimination of Judicial Evaluation of Fact in American State Courts from 1795–1913." *University of Detroit Law Review* 62 (1985): 595–632.

Kress, Joseph. "Progress and Prosecution." In *Crime and Justice in America, 1776–1976*, edited by Graeme R. Newman, 99–117. Philadelphia, 1976.

Kurland, Phillip B., and D. W. M. Waters. "Public Prosecutions in England, 1854–1879: An Essay on English Legislative History." *Duke Law Journal* (1959): 493–562.

LaFave, Wayne. *Arrest: The Decision to Take a Suspect into Custody.* Boston, 1965.

Laingue, Andre, and Arlette Lebigry. *Histoire du droit penale, II: La procedure criminelle.* Paris, 1986.

Lambert, J. L. "Reasonable Cause to Arrest." *Public Law* 29 (1973): 285–294.

Landau, Norma. *The Justices of the Peace, 1679–1760.* Berkeley, 1984.

Langbein, John. "The Criminal Trial before the Lawyers." *University of Chicago Law Review* 45 (1978): 263–306.

———. *Prosecuting Crime in the Renaissance: England, Germany, France.* Cambridge, Mass., 1974.

———. "Shaping the Eighteenth-Century Criminal Trial: A View from the Ryder Sources." *University of Chicago Law Review* 50 (1983): 1–136.

———. *Torture and the Law of Proof.* Chicago, 1977.

Larner, Christina. "Crimen Exceptum? The Crime of Witchcraft in Europe." In *Crime and the Law: The Social History of Crime in Western Europe Since 1500*, edited by V. A. C. Gatrell, Bruce Lenman, and Geoffrey Parker, 49–75. London, 1980.

Lasson, Nelson. *The History and Development of the Fourth Amendment to the Constitution.* Baltimore, 1937.

Lawson, P. G. "Lawless Juries? The Composition and Behavior of Hertfordshire Juries, 1573–1624." In *Twelve Good Men and True: The Criminal Trial Jury in England, 1200–1800*, edited by J. S. Cockburn and Thomas A. Green, 117–157. Princeton, 1988.

Leites, Edmund, ed. *Conscience and Casuistry in Early Modern Europe.* Cambridge, 1988.

Levack, Brian. *The Civil Lawyers in England, 1603–1641: A Political Study.* Oxford, 1973.

———. *The Witch-hunt in Early Modern Europe.* London, 1987.

Levy, Jean P. *La hiérarchie des preuves dans le droit savant du moyen âge despuis la renaissance du droit roman jusqu'à la fin du XIVe siècle.* Paris. 1939.

Lévy-Bruhl, Henri. *La Preuve judiciaire.* Paris, 1964.

McAdoo, H. R. *The Structure of Caroline Moral Theology.* London, 1949.

McCauliff, C. M. A. "Burdens of Proof, Degrees of Belief, Quanta of

Evidence, or Constitutional Guarantees?" *Vanderbilt Law Review* 35 (1982): 1293–1335.

Macfarlane, Alan. *Witchcraft in Tudor and Stuart England.* London, 1979.

Macfarlane, Alan, and Sarah Harrison. *The Justice and the Mare's Ale: Law and Disorder in Seventeenth-Century England.* Cambridge, 1981.

McGowen, Randall. "The Changing Face of God's Justice: The Debates over Divine and Human Punishment in Eighteenth-Century England." *Criminal Justice History* (1986): 63–97.

———. "The Image of Justice and Reform of the Criminal Law in Early Nineteenth-Century England." *Buffalo Law Review* 32 (1983): 89–125.

McLane, Bernard W. "Juror Attitudes toward Local Disorders: The Evidence of the 1328 Trailbaston Proceedings." In *Twelve Good Men and True: The Criminal Trial Jury in England, 1200–1800*, edited by J. S. Cockburn and Thomas A. Green, 36–64. Princeton, 1988.

Maitland, F. W. *English Law and the Renaissance.* Cambridge, 1901.

———. *Justice and Police.* London, 1985.

Marcus, Gail. "'Due Execution of the Generall Rules of Righteousnesse': Criminal Proceedings in New Haven Town and Colony, 1638–1658." In *Saints and Revolutionaries: Essays in American History*, edited by David Hall. New York, 1984.

Marcus, Richard L. "The Tudor Treason Trials: Some Observations on the Emergence of Forensic Themes." *University of Illinois Law Review* (1984): 675–704.

Merriam, E. G., and S. D. Thompson. *A Treatise on the Organization, Custody and Conduct of Juries, Including Grand Juries.* St. Louis, 1882.

Meyer, Hermine Herla. "The Constitutionality of Pretrial Detention." *Georgetown Law Journal* 50 (1972): 1139–1186.

Miller, Wilbur. *Cops and Bobbies: Police and Authority in New York and London, 1830–1870.* Chicago, 1973.

Mitnick, John M. "From Neighbor Witness to Judge of Proofs: The Transformation of the English Civil Juror." *American Journal of Legal History* 32 (1988): 201–235.

Moccia, Luigi. "English Law Attitudes to the 'Civil Law.'" *Journal of Legal History* 2 (1981): 157–168.

Moir, E. *The Justice of the Peace.* London, 1969.

Montrose, J. S. "Basic Concepts of the Law of Evidence." *Law Quarterly Review* 70 (1954): 527–555.

Moore, Lloyd. *The Jury: Tool of Kings, Palladium of Liberty.* Cincinnati, 1973.

———. *Moore's Federal Practice.* New York, 1979.

Morano, Anthony A. "Historical Development of the Interrelationship of Unanimous Verdicts and Reasonable Doubt." *Valparaiso University Law Review* 10 (1976): 223–230.

———. "A Reexamination of the Reasonable Doubt Rule." *Boston University Law Review* 55 (1975): 507–528.

Morgan, Edward M. "Hearsay Dangers and the Application of the Hearsay Concept." *Harvard Law Review* 62 (1948): 180–219.

———. *Some Problems of Proof under the Anglo-American System of Litigation.* New York, 1956.

Morrill, J. S. *The Cheshire Grand Jury, 1630–1660: Government and Society during the English Revolution.* Oxford, 1974.

Morrison, C. A. "Some Features of the Roman and English Law of Evidence." *Tulane Law Review* 35 (1959): 577–594.

Morse, Wayne A. "Survey of the Grand Jury System." *Oregon Law Review* 10 (1972): 101–127.

Murrin, John. "Magistrates, Sinners, and A Precarious Liberty: Trial by Jury in Seventeenth-Century New England." In *Saints and Revolutionaries: Essays in Early American History*, edited by David Hall. New York, 1984.

Murrin, John, and A. G. Roeber. "Trial by Jury." In *The Bill of Rights*, edited by J. Kukla. Richmond, Va., 1987.

Nelson, William. *Americanization of the Common Law: The Impact of Legal Change on Massachusetts Society, 1760–1830.* Cambridge, Mass., 1975.

Nenner, Howard. *By Colour of Law: Legal Culture and Constitutional Politics in England, 1660–1689.* Chicago, 1977.

Nokes, G. D. "The English Jury and the Law of Evidence." *Tulane Law Review* 31 (1956): 153–172.

Orfield, Lester. "The Federal Grand Jury." *Federal Rules Decisions* 22 (1959): 343–463.

Osborne, Bertram. *Justices of the Peace, 1361–1848.* Shaftesbury, Dorset, 1960.

Packer, Herbert. "Two Models of the Criminal Process." *University of Pennsylvania Law Review* 113 (1964): 1–68.

Palazzola, Giorgia Alessi. *Prova legale e pena: La crisi del sistema tra evo medio e moderno.* Naples, 1979.

Paley, Ruth. "Thief-takers in London in the Age of the McDaniel Gang, c. 1745–1754." In *Policing and Prosecution in Britain, 1750–1850*, edited by Douglas Hay and Francis Snyder, 301–343. Oxford, 1989.

Palmer, Robert. *The County Courts of Medieval England, 1150–1350.* Princeton, 1980.

Patey, D. L. *Probability and Literary Form.* Cambridge, 1983.

Philips, David. "Good Men to Associate and Bad Men to Conspire: As-sociations for the Prosecution of Felons in England, 1760–1860." In *Policing and Prosecution in Britain, 1750–1850*, edited by Douglas Hay and Francis Snyder, 113–170. Oxford, 1989.

———. "'A New Engine of Power and Authority': The Institutionalization of Law Enforcement in England, 1780–1830." In *Crime and the Law: The Social History of Crime in Western Europe Since 1500*, edited by V. A. C. Gatrell, Bruce Lenman, and Geoffrey Parker, 155–189. London, 1980.

Phillips, John A., and Thomas C. Thompson. "Jurors v. Judges in Later Stuart England: The Penn-Mead Trial and 'Bushell's Case.'" *Law and Inequality: A Journal of Theory and Practice* 4 (1986): 189–229.

Ploscowe, Morris. "Development of Present Day Criminal Procedures in Europe and America." *Harvard Law Review* 48 (1935): 433–473.

Plucknett, Theodore F. T. *A Concise History of the Common Law*. 5th ed. Boston, 1956.

———. "The Relations between Roman Law and English Common Law." *University of Toronto Law Journal* 2 (1939): 24–50.

Pollock, F., and W. Maitland. *History of English Law*. 2 vols. London, 1959.

Popkin, Richard H. *The History of Scepticism from Erasmus to Spinoza*. Berkeley, 1979.

Post, J. B. "The Admissibility of Defense Counsel in English Criminal Procedure." *Journal of Legal History* 5 (1984): 23–32.

———. "Jury Lists and Juries in the Late Fourteenth Century." In *Twelve Good Men and True: The Criminal Trial Jury in England, 1200–1800*, edited by J. S. Cockburn and Thomas A. Green, 65–77. Princeton, 1988.

Postema, Gerald J. "Fact, Fictions, and Law: Bentham on the Founda-tions of Evidence." In *Facts in Law*, edited by William Twining. Weis-baden, 1983.

Powell, Edward. "Jury Trial at Gaol Delivery in the Late Middle Ages, The Midland Circuit, 1400–1429." In *Twelve Good Men and True: The Criminal Trial Jury in England, 1200–1800*, edited by J. S. Cockburn and Thomas A. Green, 78–116. Princeton, 1988.

Powers, Edwin. *Crime and Punishment in Early Massachusetts, 1620–1692*. Boston, 1966.

Prall, Stuart E. *The Agitation for Law Reform during the Puritan Revo-lution, 1640–1660*. The Hague, 1966.

La Preuve: Deuxième partie: Moyen âge et temps modernes. Recueils de la Société Jean Bodin pour l'histoire comparative des institutions. Brus-sels, 1965.

Preyer, Kathryn. "Jurisdiction to Punish: Federal Authority and the Common Law of Crimes in the Early Republic." *Law and History Review*
4 (1986): 223–267.

———. "Penal Measures in the American Colonies: An Overview." *American Journal of Legal History* 28 (1982): 326–353.

Pue, W. W. "The Criminal Twilight Zone: Pretrial Procedures in the
1840s." *Alberta Law Review* 21 (1983): 335–363.

Pugh, R. B. "Some Reflections of a Medieval Criminologist." *Proceedings
of the British Academy* 59 (1973): 83–104.

Putnam, Bertha. *Early Treatises on the Practice of the Justices of the
Fifteenth and Sixteenth Centuries.* Oxford, 1924.

———. "Sixteenth-Century Treatises for Justices of the Peace." *Toronto
Law Journal* 7 (1947): 137–161.

———, ed. *Proceedings before Justices of the Peace.* London, 1938.

Radzinowicz, Leon. *A History of English Criminal Law and Its Administration from 1750.* 4 vols. London, 1948–1968.

Ram, James. *A Treatise on Facts As Subjects of Inquiry by a Jury.* New
York, 1870.

Rankin, Hugh. *Criminal Trial Proceedings in the General Court of Colonial Virginia.* Williamsburg, 1965.

Reedy, Gerard. *The Bible and Reason: Anglicans and Scripture in Late
Seventeenth-Century England.* Philadelphia, 1985.

Reid, John. *In a Defiant Stance: The Condition of Law in Massachusetts
Bay, the Irish Comparison, and the Coming of the American Revolution.* Philadelphia, 1977.

Reznick, Samuel. "The Statute of 1696: A Pioneer Measure in the Reform
of Judicial Procedure in England." *Journal of Modern History* 2 (1930):
5–26.

Richardson, Mary. "The Improbability of Probable Cause: The Inequity
of the Grand Jury Indictment Versus the Preliminary Hearing in the
Illinois Criminal Process." *Southern Illinois University Law Journal*
(1981): 281–311.

Roberts, S. K. "Initiative and Control: The Devon Quarter Sessions Grand
Jury, 1649–1670." *Bulletin of the Institute for Historical Research* 57
(1984): 165–177.

Roberts, Stephen. "Jurors and the Middling Sort: Recruitment and Performance at Devon Quarter Sessions; 1649–1670." In *Twelve Good Men
and True: The Criminal Trial Jury in England, 1200–1800,* edited by
J. S. Cockburn and Thomas A. Green, 182–213. Princeton, 1988.

Rodgers, C. P. "Legal Humanism and the English Law—The Contribution of the English Civilians." *Irish Jurist* 19 (1984): 115–136.

Roeber, A. G. *Faithful Magistrates and Republican Lawyers: Creators of
Virginia's Legal Culture, 1680–1810.* Chapel Hill, 1981.

Rubini, D. A. "The Precarious Independence of the Judiciary, 1688–1701." *Law Quarterly Review* 83 (1967): 343–365.

"The Rules of Evidence as a Factor in Probable Cause in Grand Jury Proceedings and Preliminary Examinations." *Washington University Law Quarterly* 38 (1976): 102–124.

Rutland, Robert. *The Birth of the Bill of Rights, 1776–1781*. Chapel Hill, 1955.

Samaha, Joel. *Law and Order in Historical Perspective: The Case of Elizabethan Essex*. New York, 1974.

Sargent, R. M. "Scientific Experiment and Legal Expertise: The Way of Experience in Seventeenth-Century England." *Studies in the History and Philosophy of Science* 20 (1989): 9–46.

Schoeck, R. J. "Rhetoric and Law in Sixteenth-Century England." *Studies in Philology* 50 (1953): 110–127.

Schwartz, Helene. "Demythologizing the Historic Role of the Grand Jury." *American Criminal Law Review* 10 (1972): 701–770.

Scott, A. P. *Criminal Law in Colonial Virginia*. Chicago, 1930.

Semmes, Raphael. *Crime and Punishment in Early Maryland*. Baltimore, 1938.

Shapiro, Barbara. *John Wilkins, 1614–1672: An Intellectual Biography*. Berkeley, 1969.

———. "Law and Science in Seventeenth-Century England." *Stanford Law Review* 21 (1969): 727–766.

———. "Law Reform in Seventeenth-Century England." *American Journal of Legal History* 19 (1975): 280–312.

———. *Probability and Certainty in Seventeenth-Century England: A Study of the Relationships between Natural Science, Religion, History, Law and Literature*. Princeton, 1983.

———. "'To a Moral Certainty': Theories of Knowledge and Anglo-American Juries, 1600–1850." *Hastings Law Review* 38 (1986): 153–193.

Shapiro, Martin. *Courts: A Comparative and Political Analysis*. Chicago, 1981.

Sharpe, J. A. *Crime in Early Modern England, 1550–1750*. London, 1984.

———. *Crime in Seventeenth-Century England: A County Study*. Cambridge, 1983.

———. "Enforcing the Law in the Seventeenth-Century Village." In *Crime and the Law: The Social History of Crime in Western Europe Since 1500*, edited by V. A. C. Gatrell, Bruce Lenman, and Geoffrey Parker, 97–119. London, 1980.

Siegel, Stephen. "The Aristotelian Basis of English Law, 1450–1800." *New York University Law Review* 56 (1981): 18–59.

Simpson, A. W. B. "The Rise and Fall of the Legal Treatise: Legal Principles and the Forms of Legal Literature." *University of Chicago Law Review* 48 (1981): 632–680.

Smith, Joseph, and Philip Crowe, eds. *Court Records of Prince George County, Maryland, 1696–1699*. Washington, D.C., 1964.

Snyder, Francis. "Using the Criminal Law." In *Policing and Prosecution in Britain, 1750–1850*, edited by Douglas Hay and Francis Snyder. Oxford, 1989.

Soman, Alfred. "Criminal Jurisprudence in Ancien-Regime France: The Parlement of Paris in the Sixteenth and Seventeenth Centuries." In *Crime and Criminal Justice in Europe and Canada*, edited by Louis A. Knafla, 43–75. Waterloo, Ontario, 1981.

———. "Deviance and Criminal Justice in Western Europe, 1300–1800: An Essay in Structure." *Criminal Justice History* 1 (1980): 1–28.

———. "La justice criminelle aux XVIe–XVIIe siècles: Le Parlement de Paris et les sièges subalternes." *La faute, la repression et le pardon: Philologie et histoire jusque à 1610*. Vol. 1., 15–52. Brest, 1982.

Stein, Peter. "The Attraction of the Civil Law in Post-Revolutionary America." *Virginia Law Review* 52 (1966): 403–434.

———. *The Character and Influence of the Roman Law: Historical Essays*. London, 1988.

———. "Continental Influences in English Thought, 1600–1900." In *La Formazione storica del diretto moderno in Europa*, edited by L. S. Olschki. Florence, 1977.

Stephen, Sir James Fitzjames. *A Digest of the Law of Criminal Procedure in Indictable Offenses*. London, 1883.

———. *Digest of the Law of Evidence*. New York, 1885.

———. *A History of the Criminal Law of England*. London, 1883.

Stevens, Robert. "Basic Concepts and Current Differences in English and American Law." *Journal of Legal History* 6 (1985): 336–346.

Stimson, Shannon. *The American Revolution in the Law*. Princeton, 1990.

Styles, John. "An Eighteenth-Century Magistrate as Detective: Samuel Lister of Little Horton." *The Bradford Antiquary* n.s. 47 (1982): 98–117.

———. "Print and Policy: Crime Advertising in Eighteenth-Century England." In *Policing and Prosecution in Britain*, edited by Douglas Hay and Francis Snyder. Oxford, 1989.

———. "Sir John Fielding and the Problem of Criminal Investigation in Eighteenth-Century England." *Transactions of the Royal Historical Society*, 5th ser., vol. 33 (1983): 127–150.

Teeven, Kevin M. "Problems of Proof and Early English Contract Law." *Cambrian Law Review* (1984): 52–73.

————. "Seventeenth-Century Evidentiary Concerns and the Statute of Frauds." *Adelaide Law Review* 9 (1983): 252–266.

Thomas, Keith. "The Puritans and Adultery: The Act of 1650 Reconsidered." In *Puritans and Revolutionaries*, edited by Donald Pennington and Keith Thomas. Oxford, 1978.

————. *Religion and the Decline of Magic.* New York, 1979.

Thorne, Samuel. "English Law and the Renaissance." In *La Storia del diretto nel guadra delle scienze storiche*, 437–445. Florence, 1966.

Tobias, J. J. *Crime and Police in England, 1700–1900.* London, 1979.

Twining, William. "Evidence and Legal Theory." In *Legal Theory and Common Law*, edited by W. Twining, 62–80. London, 1986.

————. "The Rationalist Tradition of Evidence Scholarship." In *Well and Truly Tried: Essays on Evidence in Honour of Sir Richard Eggleston*, edited by Enid Campbell and Louis Waller, 211–249. Sydney, Australia, 1982.

————. *Theories of Evidence: Bentham and Wigmore.* London, 1985.

————, ed. *Facts in Law.* Association for Legal and Social Philosophy, vol. 16. Wiesbaden, 1983.

Ullmann, Walter. "Medieval Principles of Evidence." *Law Quarterly Review* 62 (1946): 77–87.

————. "Some Medieval Principles of Criminal Procedure." *Juridical Review* 59 (1947): 1–28.

Van Caenegem, Raoul C. "History of European Civil Procedure." *International Encyclopedia of Comparative Law* 16 (Tübingen, 1973): 3–79.

————. "La Preuve dans le droit du moyen âge occidental." In *La Preuve: Deuxième partie moyen âge et temps modernes.* Recueils de la Société Jean Bodin, pour l'histoire comparative des institutions, 691–740. Brussels, 1965.

————. "The Law of Evidence in the Twelfth Century: European Perspectives and Intellectual Background." In *Proceedings of the Second International Congress of Medieval Canon Law.* Vatican City, 1965.

————. "Public Prosecution of Crime in Twelfth-Century England." In *Church and Government in the Middle Ages*, edited by C. N. L. Brooke, et al. Cambridge, 1976.

Van Leeuwen, Henry. *The Problem of Certainty in English Thought, 1630–1690.* The Hague, 1963.

Veall, Donald. *The Popular Movement for Law Reform, 1640–1660.* Oxford, 1970.

Waldman, Theodore. "Origins of the Legal Doctrine of Reasonable Doubt." *Journal of Historical Ideas* 20 (1959): 299–316.

Walker, Samuel. *Popular Justice: A History of American Criminal Justice.* Oxford, 1980.

Wasserstrom, Silas, and L. M. Seidman. "The Fourth Amendment as Constitutional Theory." *Georgetown Law Journal* 77 (1988): 19–112.

Weber, Jack K. "The Birth of Probable Cause." *Anglo-American Law Review* 11 (1980): 155–167.

Weisser, M. *Crime and Punishment in Early Modern Europe.* Hassocks, 1979.

Welsh, Alexander. "Burke and Bentham on the Narrative Potential of Circumstantial Evidence." *New Literary History* 21 (1989–1990): 607–627.

Wigmore, John H. "History of the Hearsay Rule." *Harvard Law Review* 17 (1904): 436–458.

———. "The Required Number of Witnesses: A Brief History of the Numerical System in England." *Harvard Law Review* 15 (1901): 82–108.

Williams, Glanville. *The Proof of Guilt: A Study of the English Criminal Trial.* London, 1955.

Wood, Thomas. *English Casuistical Divinity in the Seventeenth Century.* London, 1952.

Wright, Alan. C. *Federal Practice and Procedure: Criminal.* 4 vols. St. Paul, 1969, 1982.

Wunderli, Richard. "London Church Courts and Society on the Eve of the Reformation." *Speculum,* Anniversary Monographs, no. 7. Medieval Academy of America. Cambridge, Mass., 1981.

Younger, Richard. *The People's Panel: The Grand Jury in the United States, 1634–1941.* Providence, 1963.

Index

355

standards of, 78–86; epistemology of, 94, 112; in Gambier, 34; in Gilbert, 26, 269; in Glassford, 35; in Greenleaf, 38; history of doctrine of, 7–9; in Locke, 9, 23, 69, 196; in McKinnon, 30, 229; role of circumstantial evidence in, 207; in seventeenth century, 54; in Somers, 70; in Taylor, 263

Probability, mathematical, 16, 41, 223, 224, 253–255; and reasonable doubt, 330

Probable cause, xiv, 246, 250, 252; in American grand jury, xiii, 88; in arrest, 139, 141–145, 294; in bail, 169; in Blackstone, 82, 83; in charge to juries, xii; in Fielding, 80; in grand jury indictments, 67–70, 73, 76–77, 85, 111; in nineteenth century, 101; in preliminary hearings, 173–183, 295; in public prosecution, 180–181; and search warrants, 145–148; in Shaftesbury case, 64

Proof: in Bentham, 39; in Best, 236; of Christianity, 264; direct, 322; in Domat, 221–222; evolution of doctrine of, xiv; free, 296, 327; full, 3, 119, 120, 149, 165, 188–189, 202–203, 253, 319; in Gambier, 272; in Greenleaf, 230–231; half, 120, 166, 168, 202, 233, 250, 319, 320, 327; indirect, 30, 32, 201, 322; irrational, 3, 118; in McNally, 30; in Pothier, 222–223; presumptive, 153; in Romano-canon tradition, 51, 115, 118, 121, 296, 313, 319; in Scholasticism, 118; standards for, 42–43; in Wigmore, 39. *See also* Evidence

Prosecution: cost of, 180; by indictment, 293; by information, 293; private, 161, 179–180, 191; role of in grand jury proceedings, 45–46, 92, 94, 96, 107

Prosecution, public, 100–102, 161–162, 251, 275, 278, 292; in Canada, 312; role of police in, 178; in United States, 24, 111, 175, 179, 180–181, 293, 312

Prosecution associations, voluntary, 180, 312

Public prosecutors. *See* Prosecution, public

Pufendorf, Samuel, 14, 17, 18; influence in United States, 125

Puritanism, 193, 213

Quintilian, 116–117, 127, 154, 155, 157, 201–203, 224, 229; evidence in, 237; on hearsay, 198; as source of *indicia*, 152, 201, 296

Raleigh, Sir Walter, 192, 207, 213

Rape, 167, 214

Rationale of Judicial Evidence (Bentham), 36–37

Reid, Thomas, 27–28, 31, 32, 36, 37, 40, 264; doubt in, 271

Religious doctrine: effect on English law, 193; judges' use of, 2, 19–20

Remarks upon the Trial of Fitzharris (Hawles), 77

Restoration era, 16; criminal trials in, 19; evidentiary issues during, 54–55; grand jury during, 58, 85

Rex v. Burdett (1820), 291

Rhetoric, 31, 247; classical tradition of, 116–118, 129, 142, 152, 154, 195, 201, 227, 295; and probability, 68; Renaissance tradition of, 152

Rhetorica ad Herennium, 153

Romano-canon procedure, 115–127, 241, 247, 253; circumstantial evidence in, 200, 203, 229; hostility to, 187–188; influence of in United States, 299, 300; influence of on English law, xiv, xv, 51, 52, 121, 122–124, 189–190, 200–202, 229, 243, 246, 247, 251, 300; influence of on witchcraft cases, 165–166; philosophical components of, 3; presumption in, 205; in Scotland, 297

Rouse, John, 63, 77

Rules of Evidence on Pleas of the Crown (McNally), 29–30

Rumor, 276, 282; in Bracton, 49; as cause for indictment, 97; in medieval era, 48; in Romano-canon tradition, 115; and suspicion, 278

Samaha, Joel, 160–161

Satisfied conscience. *See* Conscience, satisfied

Saunders, Edmond, 285

Scholasticism, 6–7, 16, 118; and civil law, 227

Scot, Reginald, 210, 320

Scotland, 297

Scottish Common Sense school, 26, 27–28, 35, 124, 220, 224, 270; in America, 125

Scripture: credibility of, 10, 12, 194; influence of on laws, 193–194, 242

Search and seizure, xiii, xv, 114, 304–305

Search warrants: in America, 147; discretion of magistrates in, 171; in eighteenth century, 146; and probable cause, 145–148

Compositor: Wilsted & Taylor
Text: 11/13 Caledonia
Display: Caledonia
Printer and Binder: Thomson-Shore, Inc.